Sardinia

Olbia, the
Costa Smeralda
& the Gallura
p144

Alghero
& the
Northwest
p113

Oristano
& the
West
p89

Nuoro
& the
East
p170

Iglesias
& the
Southwest
p56

Cagliari
& the
Sarrabus
p34

THIS EDITION WRITTEN AND RESEARCHED BY

Kerry Christiani, Duncan Garwood

Contents

BOSA P103

CALA GOLORITZÈ P197

Contents

RICOTTA CHEESECAKES
P243

Welcome to Sardinia

This is an island where coastal drives thrill, prehistory puzzles, and sheep (four million of them) rule the roads. Sardinia captivates with its wild interior, dazzling beaches and endearing eccentricities.

Beach Beauties

Believe the hype: Sardinia has some of the dreamiest beaches you'll find without stepping off European shores. Yes, the sand really is *that* white, and the sea the bluest blue. Imagine dropping anchor in Costa Smeralda's scalloped bays, where celebrities and supermodels frolic in emerald waters; playing castaway on the Golfo di Orosei's coves, where sheer cliffs ensure seclusion; or sailing to La Maddalena's cluster of granite islands. Be it walking barefoot across the dunes on the wave-lashed Costa Verde or lounging on the Costa del Sud's silky smooth bays – unroll your beach towel and you'll never want to leave, we swear.

Outdoor Adventure

Whether you go slow or fast, choose coast or country, Sardinia is one of Europe's last great island adventures. Hike through the lush, silent interior to Tiscali's nuraghic ruins. Walk the vertiginous coastal path to the crescent-shaped bay of Cala Luna, where climbers spider up the limestone cliffs. Or ramble through holm oak forests to the mighty boulder-strewn canyon of Gola Su Gorropu. The sea's allure is irresistible to windsurfers on the north coast, while divers wax lyrical about shipwrecks off Cagliari's coast and Nora's submerged Roman ruins.

Island of Idiosyncrasies

As DH Lawrence so succinctly put it: 'Sardinia is different.' Indeed, where else but here can you go from near-alpine forests to snow white beaches, or find wildlife oddities like the blue-eyed albino donkeys on the Isola dell'Asinara and the wild horses that shyly roam Giara di Gesturi. The island is also a culinary one-off, with distinct takes on pasta, bread and *dolci,* its own wines and cheeses – including maggoty *casu marzu pecorino,* stashed away in barns. In every way we can think of Sardinia is different, and all the more loveable for it.

Timeless Tradition

Sardinia has been polished like a pebble by the waves of its history and heritage. The island is scattered with 7000 *nuraghi* (Bronze Age towers and settlements), *tombe dei giganti* ('giant's grave' tombs) and *domus de janas* ('fairy house' tombs). Down every country lane and and in every 10-person, 100-sheep hamlet, these remnants of prehistory are waiting to be pieced together like the most puzzling of jigsaw puzzles. Sardinia is also an island of fabulously eccentric festivals, from Barbagia's carnival parade of ghoulish *mamuthones,* said to banish winter demons, to the death-defying S'Ardia horse race in Sedilo.

ARCHIVOLTO
AURIA

Why I Love Sardinia

By Kerry Christiani, Author

Sardinia was love at first sight for me. No matter how often I return, I find new coastal trails to explore and mountains to climb, hidden bays to kayak to and little-known *agriturismi* tucked away in the silent hinterland. The island is deceptive – it looks small on paper, but unravel it and it is huge. It's like a continent in miniature, shaped by its own language and fierce traditions, its own cuisine and culture, its own history and the mystery that hangs over it like a shroud. Sardinians are proud of their island, and so they should be.

For more about our authors, see page 288

Sardinia

0 ⊕ **N**

0 ————— 50 km
0 ————— 25 miles

Tyrrhenian Sea

Parco Nazionale dell'Asinara
Island wilderness (p131)

Costa Smeralda
Live the sun-kissed high life (p153)

Orgosolo
Ponder political murals in the former bandit capital (p181)

Tiscali
Trek to this ancient enigma (p191)

Gola Su Gorropu
Boulder-hop in Europe's Grand Canyon (p190)

Grotta di Nettuno
Descend 654 steps to this fairytale grotto (p128)

Alghero
Linger in the Spanish-style walled city (p115)

Bosa
Explore this postcard-pretty riverside town (p103)

Isola Maddalena

Parco Nazionale dell'Arcipelago di La Maddalena

Isola Caprera

Baia Sardinia

Porto Rotondo

Porto Pollo

Palau

Romazzino

Santa Teresa di Gallura

Arzachena

Golfo Aranci

Olbia

Siniscola

OroSei

Monti

Orune

Monte Ortobene (955m)

Cala Gonone

Oliena

Nuoro

Dorgali

Tiscali

Tempio Pausania

Orgosolo

Mamoiada

Coghinas

Lago di Coghinas

Ozieri

Tirso

Castelsardo

Golfo dell' Asinara

Marina di Sorso

Torralba

Parco Nazionale dell'Asinara

Stintino

Torre Pelosa

Platamona

Sorso

Sassari

Villanova Monteleone

Macomer

Porto Torres

Porto Ferro

Fertilia

Alghero

Cala Bona

Monte Timidone (361m)

Grotta di Nettuno

Bosa

Torre

Mare di Sardegna

41°N

8°E

9°E

10°E

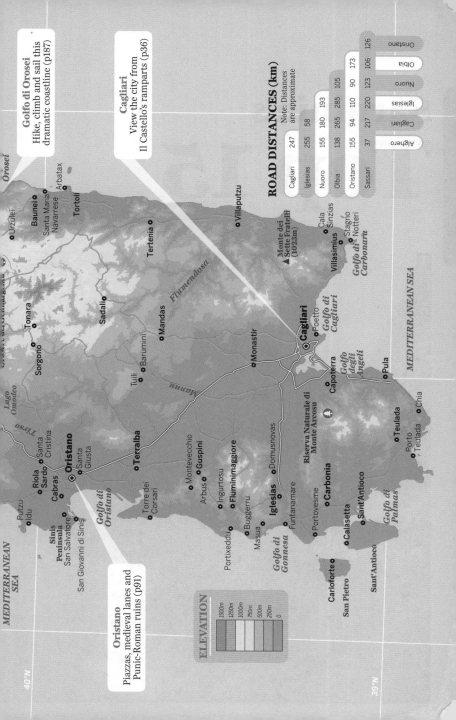

Golfo di Orosei
Hike, climb and sail this dramatic coastline (p187)

Cagliari
View the city from Il Castello's ramparts (p36)

Oristano
Piazzas, medieval lanes and Punic-Roman ruins (p91)

ROAD DISTANCES (km)

Note: Distances are approximate

	Alghero	Cagliari	Iglesias	Nuoro	Olbia	Oristano
Cagliari	247					
Iglesias	255	58				
Nuoro	155	180	193			
Olbia	138	265	285	105		
Oristano	155	94	110	90	173	
Sassari	37	217	220	123	106	126

ELEVATION

- 1500m
- 1250m
- 1000m
- 750m
- 500m
- 250m
- 0

MEDITERRANEAN SEA

MEDITERRANEAN SEA

40°N

39°N

Orosei

Uzzulei
Baunei
Santa Maria Navarrese
Arbatax
Tortolì

Tertenia

Villaputzu

Monte dei Sette Fratelli (1023m)

Cala Sinzias
Villasimius
Stagno di Notteri
Golfo di Carbonara

Sadali
Tonara
Sorgono

Mandas
Barumini
Tuili

Flumendosa

Monastir

Cagliari
Poetto
Golfo di Cagliari

Mannu

Capoterra
Golfo degli Angeli

Pula

Lago Omodeo
Tirso

Santa Cristina
Riola Sardo
Cabras
Oristano
Santa Giusta

Terralba

Montevecchio
Arbus
Ingurtosu
Guspini
Fluminimaggiore

Domusnovas

Riserva Naturale di Monte Arcosu

Putzu Idu
Sinis Peninsula
San Salvatore
San Giovanni di Sinis
Golfo di Oristano

Torre dei Corsari

Portixeddu
Buggerru
Masua

Iglesias
Funtanamare
Portovesme
Golfo di Gonnesa

Carbonia

Sant'Antioco

Teulada
Porto Teulada
Chia

Golfo di Palmas

Calasetta
Carloforte
San Pietro
Sant'Antioco

Sardinia's
Top 15

Golfo di Orosei

1 We can wax lyrical about sparkling aquamarine waters, blindingly white sands and sheer limestone cliffs but, trust us, seeing is believing when it comes to the Golfo di Orosei. Where the mountains collide spectacularly with the sea, this huge, sweeping crescent forms the seaward section of the Parco Nazionale del Golfo di Orosei e del Gennargentu (p187). Set your spirits soaring by hiking its clifftop trails, exploring its sea grottoes in a kayak, or boating along the gulf to hidden coves – each more mind-blowingly beautiful than the last.

Gola Su Gorropu

2 The first glimpse of Gola Su Gorropu (p190) on the scenic hike down from the Genna 'e Silana pass is mesmerising. Dubbed Europe's Grand Canyon, this mighty ravine is for explorers, with 400m-high rock walls and enormous boulders scattered like giant's marbles. At its narrowest point – just 4m wide – the gorge seems to swallow you up, blocking out the sun and silencing the world outside. Were it not for the occasional fellow trekker or climber, the chasm would have the eerie effect of seeming totally lost in time and space.

Costa Smeralda

3 Believe the hype: the Costa Smeralda (p153) is stunning. Here the Gallura's wind-whipped granite mountains tumble down to fjordlike inlets, and an emerald sea fringes a coast that is necklaced with bays like the Aga Khan's favourite, Spiaggia del Principe (p153) – a perfect crescent of frost-white sand smoothed by gin-clear water. Play paparazzi, eyeing up the megayachts in millionaires' playground resorts, or eschew the high life to seek out secluded coves, embedded in fragrant *macchia*, where the views are simply priceless. Top: Spiaggia del Principe

Il Castello, Cagliari

4 Perched on a rocky peak, Cagliari's Il Castello (p37) is never more captivating than at dusk on a warm summer's evening. As the softening light paints the sky purple-pink, the citadel's walls, *palazzi* (mansions) and Pisan towers glow gold. Capture the moment by heading to the laid-back terrace of a bar on the ramparts, where sundowners are served with dress-circle views of the illuminated city.

Nuraghi & Tombe dei Giganti

5 Defensive watchtowers, sacred ritual sites, prehistoric community centres... the exact purpose of Sardinia's 7000 *nuraghi* is unknown. Yet the island's Bronze Age past is still tangible within the semicircular walls of these stone towers and fortified settlements. Most famous and best preserved is the beehive complex of Nuraghe Su Nuraxi (p79), a Unesco World Heritage site. Equally mysterious are the island's *tombe dei giganti* (giants' tombs), megalithic mass graves sealed off by stone stele. Top: *Nuraghi* ruins

Orgosolo

6 Social commentary, politics, end-of-the-world prophecy – all are writ large on the shabby exteriors of houses and cafes in Orgosolo. Once a byword for banditry, today Orgosolo is an enormous canvas for some of the most emotionally charged graffiti you'll ever see. Wandering along the Corso Repubblica (p181), vivid murals recall the big events of the 20th and 21st centuries, from the creation of the atomic bomb to the fall of Baghdad: events that seem a million miles away from this small village in the heart of the tough, mountainous Barbagia. Bottom: Political mural, Orgosolo

Alghero

7 To see Alghero (p115) at its most atmospheric, come in the early evening when crowds fill its maze of dark, medieval lanes and people-watch from the grand cafe terraces on Piazza Civica. Tables are set up along the honey-coloured ramparts, softly lit by lanterns, for alfresco dining with uninterrupted views of the sea and stars. Never mind the expense, you must try Alghero's famous *aragosta alla catalana* (lobster with tomato and onion), a lingering taste of the city's past as a Catalan colony.

Bosa

8 Like many great works of art, Bosa (p103) is best admired from afar. From a distance you can take in the whole picture: the elegant houses in a fresco painter's palette of colours, the fishing boats bobbing on the Fiume Temo, the medieval castle perched on a steep hillside. Linger until evening to see one of Sardinia's prettiest towns without the crowds, walking its narrow alleyways and stopping to sample some of the freshest fish on the west coast at family-run restaurants.

Tiscali

9 Held hostage in the twilight of a collapsed limestone cave, the archaeological site of Tiscali (p191) is an enigma. Though only skeletal ruins remain, with a little imagination you can picture this nuraghic village as it was back in the Bronze Age. Every bit as enchanting as Tiscali itself is the trail through the lush green valley that takes you there – mighty rock faces loom above you, birds of prey wheel overhead and only the sound of your footsteps interrupts the overwhelming sense of calm that blankets this valley. Above: The trail to Tiscali

Oristano

10 One of Sardinia's great medieval cities is Oristano (p91), the capital of the 14th-century province of Arborea. History seeps through the centre's baroque lanes and piazzas, presided over by the graceful domed Duomo. Slow the pace and follow the locals' lead to the Piazza Eleonora d'Arborea to stroll and chat in front of the ornate *palazzi*. Or base yourself here to explore the Punic-Roman ruins of Tharros and the snow-white beaches and bird-filled lagoons of the Sinis Peninsula. Top right: Piazza Eleonora d'Arborea, Oristano

Grotta di Nettuno

11 Whether you glide in by boat from Alghero or take the vertiginous 654-step staircase that zigzags down 110m of sheer cliff, arriving at the Grotta di Nettuno (p128) is unforgettable. Enter the immense, cathedral-like grotto and it really is as though the forces of Neptune, god of the sea, have been at work. All around you are forests of curiously shaped stalactites and stalagmites, reflected in still pools of water. Nothing – not even the midday crowds – can detract from the magic of this underground fairyland.

MICHAL KRAKOWIAK/GETTY IMAGES ©

DEGAS JEAN-PIERRE/HEMIS.FR/ GETTY IMAGES ©

Parco Nazionale dell'Asinara

12 Dangling off the northwest tip of the island in splendid isolation, the rugged green Parco Nazionale dell'Asinara (p131) is one of Sardinia's greatest coastal wildernesses. The unique *asino bianco* (albino donkey) is at home in this outstanding national park, as are peregrine falcons, mouflon, wild boar and loggerhead turtles. For close-up wildlife encounters, hook onto one of the guided walking or cycling tours that take in the island's remote corners. Or go diving in the crystal-clear waters that lap its granite cliffs and dreamy beaches.

Hilltop Villages

13 You're lost on a hairpin-bend-riddled road in the mountains that seemingly leads to nowhere, and no sat nav, map or passing flock of sheep can help you. But then, suddenly, you crest a hill and a quaint village slides into view, surrounded by titanic mountains and sweeping forests. It happens all the time in Sardinia's wild Barbagia and Ogliastra provinces. Up for an offbeat adventure? Get behind the wheel for a head-spinning drive to gloriously remote villages such as Aritzo (p184), pasted high on a mountain slope. Above: Castelsardo (p133)

Foodie Sardinia

14 'Organic' and 'slow food' are modern buzzwords for what Sardinia has been doing for centuries. Trawl the interior for farms selling their own *pecorino*, salami and full-bodied Cannonau red wines; buy artistic-looking loaves and almondy sweets from bakeries and confectioners in Cagliari and Nuoro; and tuck into a smorgasbord of seafood. Or sample the lot at a rustic *agriturismo,* such as Li Mori (p152), where your hosts will ply you with course after course of antipasti, ricotta-filled *culurgiones* (ravioli), slow-roasted suckling pig and honey-drenched *sebadas* (fritters).

Festive Sardinia

15 Be it the death-defying horse races of S'Ardia or *mamuthones* (costumed carnival figures) exorcising winter demons in Mamoiada, Sardinians celebrate in weird and wonderful ways. Time your visit to catch standouts like the medieval tournament Sa Sartiglia (p93) in Oristano in February, Cagliari's Festa di Sant'Efisio (p47) in May or the folkloric parades of Nuoro's Sagra del Redentore (p175) in August. Hungry? Check out our line-up of seasonal food festivals, where you can indulge in everything from chestnuts to sea urchins. Below: Oristano's Sa Sartiglia festival

Need to Know

For more information, see Survival Guide (p250)

Currency
Euro (€)

Language
Sardinian (Sardo) and Italian

Visas
Generally not required for stays of up to 90 days (or at all for EU nationals); some nationalities need a Schengen visa.

Money
ATMs widely available in most resorts and cities. Visa, MasterCard and Cirrus often accepted in major hotels and restaurants; cash only in some smaller establishments.

Mobile Phones
European and Australian mobiles must be set up for international roaming. US cell phones that operate on the 900 MHz and 1800MHz frequencies work in Sardinia.

Time
Central European Time (GMT/UTC plus one hour)

When to Go

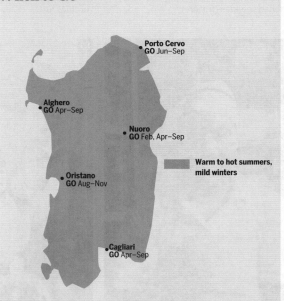

Porto Cervo
GO Jun–Sep

Alghero
GO Apr–Sep

Nuoro
GO Feb, Apr–Sep

Oristano
GO Aug–Nov

Warm to hot summers, mild winters

Cagliari
GO Apr–Sep

High Season
(Jul & Aug)

➡ Crowds flock to coastal resorts and room rates skyrocket.

➡ Prices also rise over Easter and school holidays.

➡ Roads are at their most congested.

➡ Hot days good for the beach.

Shoulder
(Apr–Jun & mid-Sep–Oct)

➡ Room rates are significantly lower.

➡ The weather is changeable and the sea chilly.

➡ Excellent for hiking, cycling and climbing.

➡ Sights and beaches are less crowded.

Low Season
(Nov–Mar)

➡ Days are shorter, weather is colder and wetter.

➡ Many sights, hotels and restaurants are closed.

➡ Prices up to 50% less than high season.

➡ Carnevale is reason to visit in February.

Useful Websites

Sardegna Turismo (www. sardegnaturismo.it) Official tourist-board website. First port of call for activities, culture, itineraries, events and accommodation.

ENIT (www.enit.it) Italian State Tourist Board. What to see, do and eat.

Lonely Planet (www. lonelyplanet.com/sardinia) Destination info, bookings, traveller forum and more.

ARST (www.arst.sardegna.it) Regional transport; find timetables and plan your journey.

Trenitalia (www.trenitalia.com) For timetables and prices of rail journeys in Sardinia.

Get Around Sardinia (www. getaroundsardinia.com) Public-transport tips.

Important Numbers

To dial listings in this book from outside Italy, dial your international access code, Italy's country code (🗗39) then the number (including the '0').

Country code	🗗39
International access code	🗗00
Europe-wide emergency	🗗112
Ambulance	🗗118
Fire	🗗115
Police	🗗113

Exchange Rates

Australia	A$1	€0.69
Canada	C$1	€0.67
Japan	¥100	€0.72
NZ	NZ$1	€0.63
UK	UK£1	€1.23
US	US$1	€0.73

For current exchange rates see www.xe.com

Daily Costs

Budget: Less than €120

➡ Dorm bed €20–€25

➡ Double room in a budget hotel €60–€100

➡ Avoid high season (July and August), stay in low-profile regions

➡ Set lunches €15–€20

Midrange: €120–€250

➡ Double room in a midrange hotel €100–€200

➡ Dine in decent local restaurants €25–€45

Top End: More than €250

➡ Luxury doubles in well-known cities and resorts

➡ Relax in hotel spas

➡ Eat superbly in top restaurants, enjoy Sardinia's best wines

Opening Hours

We've provided high-season opening hours; hours will generally decrease in the shoulder and low seasons.

Banks 8.30am to 1.30pm and 2.45pm to 4.30pm Monday to Friday

Bars 7pm to 1am Monday to Saturday

Cafes 7am or 8am to 10pm or 11pm Monday to Saturday

Clubs 10pm to 3am, 4am or 5am Thursday to Saturday

Post offices 8am to 6.50pm Monday to Friday, 8am to 1.15pm Saturday

Restaurants noon to 2.30pm or 3pm and 7.30pm to 10pm or 11pm

Shops 9am to 1pm and 4pm to 8pm Monday to Saturday

Arriving in Sardinia

Cagliari Elmas Airport (p259) ARST buses run roughly every 30 minutes from Elmas airport to Piazza Matteotti (€4, 10 minutes) between 5.20am and 10.30pm. A taxi costs around €20.

Aeroporto Olbia Costa Smeralda (p259) Local bus lines 2 and 10 (€1 or €1.50 if ticket is bought on board) run half hourly between 6.15am and 11.40pm from the airport to central Olbia. A taxi costs around €15.

Fertilia Airport (Alghero; p124) Hourly buses run to/ from Via Cagliari (€1 or €1.50 on board, 25 minutes) between 5am and 11pm. A taxi to the airport costs around €25.

Getting Around

Public transport in Sardinia is reasonably priced but it can be difficult and time-consuming in the island's remoter corners. Services slow to a trickle in the low season.

Bus In most cases buses are preferable to trains. For timetables, visit **ARST** (www.arst. sardegna.it).

Train The main line runs from Cagliari to Oristano, then on to Chilivano-Ozieri where it branches northwest to Sassari and northeast to Olbia. See **Trenitalia** (www.trenitalia.com) for timetables.

Car If you plan to explore, you'll need your own set of wheels in Sardinia. A car is often the only way to access off-the-beaten villages, the mountainous hinterland and uncrowded beaches.

For much more on **getting around**, see p259.

If You Like...

Islands & Beaches

Sardinia's islands, beaches and wind-sculpted seascapes are captivating. Dive into barracuda-filled waters, anchor in hidden bays, and find your own patch of whiter-than-white sand.

Parco Nazionale dell'Arcipelago di La Maddalena Explore pink granite islands, sugar-fine sands and gin-clear water. (p163)

Spiaggia della Piscinas Remote and stunning, this 3.5km swoop of a beach has memorable sunsets. (p66)

Isola dell'Asinara This wildlife-rich island, home to albino donkeys, is best discovered on foot or by bicycle. (p131)

Cala Mariolu Be dazzled by the shimmering white pebbles and aquamarine waters of this tucked-away bay. (p192)

Spiaggia del Principe The Aga Khan loves this gorgeous white crescent lapped by startlingly blue water. (p153)

Spiaggia della Pelosa A ravishing, frost-white sweep of a beach guarded by a Spanish watchtower. (p131)

Is Aruttas A perfect arc of sparkly quartz sand, turquoise sea and total peace. (p98)

Archaeological Digs

Stage your own archaeological explorations on this mysterious island, home to 7000 *nuraghi* (Bronze Age settlements), *pozzi sacri* (sacred wells) and *tombe dei giganti* ('giant's tombs').

Nuraghe Su Nuraxi Sardinia's single Unesco-listed site, and its most famous *nuraghe*, dates to 1500 BC. (p79)

Tiscali Ponder the meaning of this ruined *nuraghe*, hidden in a collapsed cave in the limestone Supramonte. (p191)

Nuraghe di Santa Cristina A beautiful nuraghic complex centred on a Bronze Age *tempio a pozzo* (well temple). (p106)

Serra Orrios Find mystery in the ruined huts and temples of this nuraghic settlement nestled in olive groves. (p190)

Nuraghe di Palmavera A 3500-year-old *nuraghe* with a complex system of dwellings. (p127)

Necropolis del Montessu A prehistoric cemetery set in a rocky amphitheatre. (p68)

Coddu Ecchju This is a fine example of a *tombe dei giganti*, sealed off by stone stele. (p158)

Nuraghe Is Paras This *nuraghe* stands out for its 11.8-metre *tholos* (conical tower). (p186)

Great Outdoors

Climb sea cliffs, breeze across the Med on a board or hike into forest-cloaked mountains; Sardinia thrills with exhilarating landscapes, unique wildlife and boundless outdoor pursuits.

Gola Su Gorropu Strike into the wilderness of the island's grandest canyon, a place of primordial beauty. (p190)

Cardedu Kayak Paddle in off-the-radar spots along the red granite coastline. (p196)

Golfo di Orosei Walk or boat the gulf's sparkling waters in search of little-known bays, grottoes and sea stacks. (p187)

Porto Pollo The beautiful breezes that pummel this north-coast resort are irresistible to windsurfers. (p162)

Cala Gonone Have a high time of it climbing crags and overhangs above the sea. (p191)

Parco Nazionale del Golfo di Orosei e del Gennargentu Hike, bike, canyon, kayak, dive, cave and climb in Sardinia's largest national park. (p187)

Nereo Cave Dive into the deep blue in search of frilly red coral in the Mediterranean's largest underwater grotto. (p125)

La Giara di Gesturi Hike this lush tabletop plateau in search of wild horses. (p80)

Authentic Agriturismi

Go slow with a stint at an *agriturismo* (farm-stay accommodation). Sprinkled across the island, these middle-of-nowhere farmsteads are the ultimate escape, often nestled among oak woods, olive groves and sheep-speckled fields.

Agriturismo Guthiddai This whitewashed retreat sits at the foot of rugged mountains, surrounded by olive trees. (p214)

Agriturismo Su Boschettu Serene farm in Sardinia's agricultural heartland. (p205)

Agriturismo Ca' La Somara Follow the donkeys to this laid-back farm, with tranquil gardens for relaxing moments. (p211)

Agriturismo Testone Sneak away from the crowds at this rustic abode snuggled away in holm oak woods. (p213)

Agriturismo Nuraghe Mannu Gaze out across Cala Gonone at this agriturismo, with a superfriendly welcome and home-grown food. (p215)

Coastal Walks & Rides

Sardinia's soaring cliffs, wild gorges and a coast necklaced with crescent-shaped coves beg exploration on foot or by bicycle.

Selvaggio Blu Go east for the big one – an epic seven-day hike taking in Sardinia's most dramatic coastlines. (p194)

Riviera del Corallo Pedal along the staggering coastal cliffs between Alghero and Bosa for widescreen panoramas. (p125)

Cala Goloritzè Walk from the otherworldly Golgo plateau to

Top: Lighthouse at Olbia (p145)
Bottom: Sardinian orange orchard

this beautiful bay, with unbelievably blue water. (p197)

Funtanamare Cycle to the remote Costa Verde, taking in glassy waters, rugged cliffs and sea stacks. (p62)

Cala Luna Hike from Cala Fuili along cliff tops and through fragrant scrub to this captivating half-moon bay. (p192)

Parco di Porto Conte Revel in stunning seascapes and aromatic flora as you explore on foot or by bike. (p128)

Hilltop Towns & Villages

Winding roads and rivers wend through the patchwork fields, forests and mountains of Sardinia's silent hinterland. Visit hill towns and villages for back-in-time flavour, soul food and swoon-worthy views.

Castelsardo A beautiful medieval centre perched on a hilltop overlooking the sea. (p133)

Ulassai A road corkscrews up to this tiny village crouching beneath jagged mountains. (p198)

Monti Ferru Explore the wonderful nature of this region's villages, but most of all the magnificent local beef and olive oil. (p100)

Orgosolo From the creation of the atomic bomb to the destruction of the twin towers – the murals here pack a powerful political punch. (p181)

San Pantaleo Tiptoe away from the Costa Smeralda's glitz to this pretty stone village surrounded by granite peaks. (p156)

Laconi Peace reigns in this mountain town, where cobbled lanes twist to a verdant woodland park. (p185)

Natural Wonders

Nature has worked wonders in Sardinia – the coastline is indented with bays, honeycombed with grottoes and punctuated by granite rock formations, while canyons carve up the interior.

Grotta di Nettuno Feel the lure of the sea as you descend 654 steps to this cathedral-like grotto. (p128)

Scoglio Pan di Zucchero Sugarloaf Rock is the largest of several *faraglioni* rearing out of glassy blue waters. (p63)

Grotta di Ispinigoli Find a forest of stalagmites (include the world's second tallest) in this mammoth cave. (p189)

Roccia dell'Elefante Bet you didn't think you'd find an elephant near Castelsardo... Novelty factor aside, this rock wonder conceals two Neolithic tombs. (p133)

Il Golgo Peering down into the dark depths of this 270m abyss is enough to bring on vertigo. (p197)

Roccia dell'Orso A weather-beaten lick of granite resembling a bear from certain angles, a dragon from others. (p162)

Food from the Source

Sardinian food is all about simple pleasures – family-run wine cellars, farms selling fresh *pecorino* (sheep's milk cheese), honey and salami, or towns celebrating their bounty at vivacious food festivals.

Cantine Surrau A superslick winery near the Costa Smeralda, famous for its tangy Vermentino whites and full-bodied Cannonau reds. (p155)

Cabras Try salty, flavoursome *muggini* (mullet) and *bottarga* (mullet roe) in this fishing town. (p96)

Durke A fantasy of homemade Sardinian sweets, the best made with just sugar, egg whites and almonds. (p51)

Azienda Agricola Mossa Alessandro Buy tangy salami, creamy goat's-milk ricotta and *fiore sardo pecorino* at this working farm. (p153)

Historic Cities

Carthaginians, Romans, Aragonese and Pisans – all have left their indelible stamp on Sardinia. Rewind the clocks strolling along ramparts, clambering up to citadels and relaxing on church-dotted piazzas.

Alghero Alghero's *centro storico* (historic centre) is a shady labyrinth of honey-coloured *palazzi* (mansions), buffered by walls that on summer evenings are crowded with diners. (p115)

Cagliari Wander the twisting lanes of the medieval citadel Il Castello, lingering as the setting sun lights up its towers and ramparts. (p36)

Oristano Oristano's charming historical centre is full of good eateries and fun bars. (p91)

Iglesias The Iberian atmosphere of Iglesias and its collection of churches make it a fascinating place to explore. (p57)

Olbia Be catapulted back to Roman times contemplating the mighty ships in the Museo Archeologico. (p145)

Nuoro Crouched below Monte Ortobene, this mountain town had its cultural renaissance in the 19th and early 20th centuries. (p171)

Month by Month

TOP EVENTS

Carnevale, February

Pasqua, March/April

Festa di Sant'Efisio, May

S'Ardia, July

Festa del Redentore, August

January

Festa di Sant'Antonio Abate

Bonfires rage in Orosei, Orgosolo, Sedilo and Paulilatino at this festival from 16 to 17 January. Sinister half-human, half-animal *mamuthones* make a mad dash through Mamoiada.

February

Carnevale

Highlights include the burning of an effigy of a French soldier in Alghero, the sinister *mamuthones* in Mamoiada, costumed displays in Ottana and the townsfolk of Bosa inspecting each other's groins.

Sa Sartiglia

Medieval fun abounds at Sa Sartiglia in Oristano, with jousting, horsemen in masquerade and knightly challenges in the lead-up to Shrove Tuesday.

March

Lunissanti Palm Sunday

Palm Sunday is marked by heartfelt processions in the medieval hilltop centre of Castelsardo.

Pasqua

Holy Week in Sardinia is a big deal, with solemn processions and passion plays all over the island. The celebrations in Alghero, Castelsardo, Cagliari, Iglesias and Tempio Pausania are particularly evocative.

Sagra del Torrone

Forget eggs: Tonara in the Barbagia di Belvì gorges on the deliciously nutty local *torrone* (nougat) on Easter Monday (see www.comune-tonara.org).

April

Sagra degli Agrumi

Get juiced with a feast of oranges and lemons at Muravera's zesty Citrus Festival (www.sagradegli-agrumi.it), which happens in mid-April.

Festa di Sant'Antioco

Costumed processions, dancing, concerts and fireworks are held over four days in Sant'Antioco to celebrate the town's patron saint.

May

Festa di Sant'Efisio

On 1 May a wooden statue of St Ephisius is paraded around Cagliari on a bullock-drawn carriage amid colourful celebrations. The saint is carried to Nora, from where he returns on 4 May for yet more festivities.

Cavalcata Sarda

On the second-last Sunday of May, hundreds of locals in traditional costume gather at Sassari to celebrate victory over the Saracens in AD 1000. Horsemen charge through the streets at the end of the parade.

June

Girotonno

Cooking competitions, tastings, concerts and nautical events celebrate Carloforte's famous *mattanza* (tuna catch).

July

S'Ardia

In this ferocious horse race an unruly pack of horsemen race around the chapel at Sedilo.

L'Isola delle Storie, Festival Letterario della Sardegna

Readings, author Q&A sessions and concerts are held in and around Gavoi during its three-day literature festival (see www.isoladellestorie.it).

Festa della Madonna del Naufrago

This mid-July procession takes place off the coast of Villasimius, where a submerged statue of the Virgin Mary is given a wreath of flowers in honour of shipwrecked sailors.

August

Festa di Santa Maria del Mare

Bosa's fishermen pay homage to the Virgin Mary with a river parade of boats bearing her image on the first weekend in August.

Matrimonio Maureddino

On the first Sunday of August, Santadi's costumed townsfolk reenact a Moorish wedding in the central piazza.

I Candelieri

Sassari's must-see festival takes place on 14 August. The high point is the *far-adda,* when the city's nine trade guilds, along with drummers and pipers, parade giant votive candles through the streets.

Festa del Redentore

Horsemen and dancers accompany Sardinia's grandest costumed parade. A torchlit procession winds through Nuoro on 28 August and an early-morning pilgrimage to the statue of Christ the Redeemer on Monte Ortobene takes place the following day.

Festa dell'Assunta

Processions of religious fraternities, men on horseback and women in traditional costume make this mid-August festival in Orgosolo a must.

Time in Jazz

This is Berchidda's big music fest (www.timeinjazz.it) in the second week of August, with jazz jams, dance happenings and dawn concerts.

Narcao Blues Festival

Top blues and jazz performers take to the stage in the small mining village of Narcao for one of Sardinia's top music events (www.narcaoblues.it), in late August.

September

Autunno in Barbagia

Rural villages in Barbagia host foodie events, craft fairs and workshops at this autumn festival, held from September to December.

Festa di San Salvatore

Several hundred young fellows clothed in white set off from Cabras on the Corsa degli Scalzi (Barefoot Race), an 8km dash to the hamlet and sanctuary of San Salvatore.

October

Sagra delle Castagne

The mountain town of Aritzo enlivens late October with a Chestnut Fair, folk music and shows.

November

Rassegna del Vino Novello

Sniff, swirl and drink new wine at this festival held in the piazzas of Milis in early November.

December

Natale

In the run-up to Christmas, many churches set up elaborate cribs or nativity scenes, known as *presepi.* Fireworks displays and concerts ring in the New Year in Alghero.

Itineraries

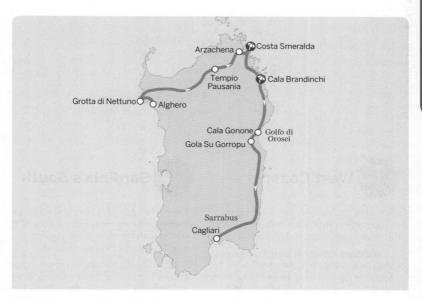

 Essential Sardinia

This best-of-the-best itinerary brings together island's most seductive coastlines, culture and flavours in one easy route.

Warm up with two days in Spanish-style, sea-splashed **Alghero**, unravelling the old town and ramparts, then hop in a boat to head to the cathedral-like **Grotta di Nettuno**.

On day three, wend your way east, pausing for a slice of laid-back village life in alley-woven **Tempio Pausania** and forays into prehistory at the nuraghic sites around **Arzachena**. Wake up to the blissful silence at a rural *agriturismo* (farm-stay accommodation) in Gallura's granite mountains, then spend a couple of days lounging on blissfully secluded coves on the **Costa Smeralda**, the emerald waters of which live up to the hype.

Day six takes you further south, with a picnic break at the utterly sublime **Cala Brandinchi**, then on to the magnificent arc of the **Golfo di Orosei**. Base yourself in **Cala Gonone** and strike out on foot or by car to dramatic, cliff-backed bays, archaeological sites and the immense **Gola Su Gorropu** canyon. Then on day nine, swing south through the mountains of the **Sarrabus** to capital **Cagliari**. Devote your final day to must-see museums and strolls in the hilltop Castello district, and Marina dining.

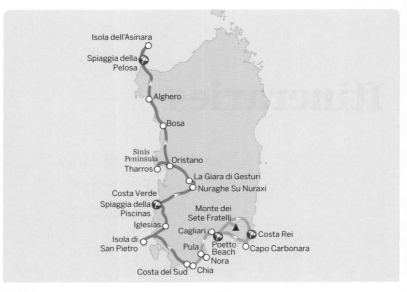

7 DAYS West Coast

A tour of the lesser-known west coast reveals some of Sardinia's most remarkable *nuraghe* and off-the-radar beaches.

Warm up with a day lazing on the white-sand beaches of the **Costa del Sud**, or hop across to the ravishing **Isola di San Pietro** for coastal walks and a lunch of freshly caught tuna. Head north via Sardinia's mining heart, **Iglesias**, to spend a couple of days on the **Costa Verde** and its gloriously deserted beaches – barefoot dune hiking at **Spiaggia della Piscinas** is a must.

On day four, detour to the hinterland to admire the prehistoric marvel that is the Unesco-listed **Nuraghe Su Nuraxi** and glimpse wild horses on the lonesome **La Giara di Gesturi** plateau. Push north on the following day to discover **Oristano** and the Phoenician ruins at **Tharros**, a short hop away on the wild **Sinis Peninsula**.

Day six takes you up to pastel-coloured, alley-woven **Bosa** and its crowning-glory castle, then on a dramatic coastal drive to **Alghero** in time for dinner on the sea walls. Wind out your trip on the silky sands of **Spiaggia della Pelosa** or spotting albino donkeys on the serene **Isola dell'Asinara**.

7 DAYS Sardinia's South

The perfect mix of culture and coast, this south-coast tour contrasts the buzz of the capital with the calm of the mountains and beaches that spread east and west.

Kick off with two days in soulful **Cagliari**, wandering the steep, winding lanes of the medieval Il Castello district and lounging on **Poetto Beach**. Besides checking off trophy sights like the Pisan towers and Museo Archeologico Nazionale, allow time simply to stroll its cafe-rimmed piazzas and boutique-lined lanes.

Day three whisks you on a serpentine coastal drive east, with broad sea and mountain views and pretty coves on every corner. Tiptoe off the map for a spell in the lushly forested heights of **Monte dei Sete Fratelli**. On day four, dive into the iridescent water of the **Capo Carbonara** marine reserve, or simply bliss out on the **Costa Rei**'s flour white beaches.

Spend your last few days swinging west of Cagliari, taking in the Phoenician ruins of **Nora** before more chilled time on the pine-flanked coves of the **Costa del Sud** – **Chia** is the go-to beach for windsurfing, flamingo-spotting and dune walking.

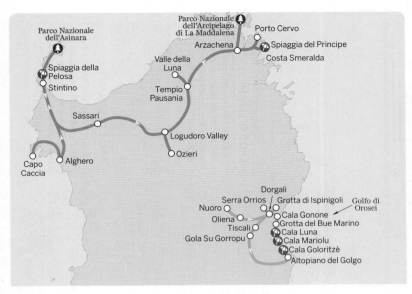

7 DAYS Sardinia's North

With a week on your hands, you can tick off some of the island's most alluring towns and silky white beaches in Sardinia's north.

Begin with invigorating sea views and piazza life in **Alghero**. Day-trip to the dramatic cliffs of **Capo Caccia**. On day three, meander north to isolated **Stintino** and dreamy **Spiaggia della Pelosa**. Or visit the wild **Parco Nazionale dell'Asinara**, home to miniature *asini bianchi* (albino donkeys). Make time for university city **Sassari** on day four, before heading east to tour the Pisan-Romanesque churches of the **Logudoro Valley** and learn about the neolithic treasures of **Ozieri**. Continue your drive northeast on the SS127 to the quaint hill town of **Tempio Pausania**, deep in cork forests, then on to the otherworldly, boulder-strewn **Valle della Luna**.

Explore the *nuraghi* around **Arzachena**, or go island-hopping around the pristine **Parco Nazionale dell'Arcipelago di La Maddalena**. Spend your last day or two on the **Costa Smeralda**, mingling with celebs in **Porto Cervo**, and beach-hopping along its cove-laced coastline to gorgeously secluded bays like **Spiaggia del Principe**.

7 DAYS The Wild East

Be seduced by exhilarating landscapes on this route through the wild Parco Nazionale del Golfo di Orosei e del Gennargentu.

Get set in **Nuoro**, capital of the rugged Barbagia hill country, before hitting the road for **Oliena** to taste its Cannonau wine. Swing east to **Dorgali** on days two and three, a fine base for visiting the **Grotta di Ispinigoli**, home to the world's second-tallest stalagmite, and the nuraghic village of **Serra Orrios**.

From Dorgali, it's a head-spinning drive down to the sweeping bay of **Cala Gonone**, where you can easily spend two days rock climbing, diving or exploring the **Golfo di Orosei** on foot or by kayak. Boat across aquamarine waters to sublime bays, such as **Cala Luna** and **Cala Mariolu**, and the sea cave **Grotta del Bue Marino**.

Packed your walking boots? Spend two days striking out into the wilderness. Hike to the nuraghic village **Tiscali**, and to the **Gola Su Gorropu**, a vast rock chasm. From the weird highland plateau of **Altopiano del Golgo**, further north, mule trails thread down to gorgeous **Cala Goloritzè**, thrashed by astonishingly blue waters.

Off the Beaten Track: Sardinia

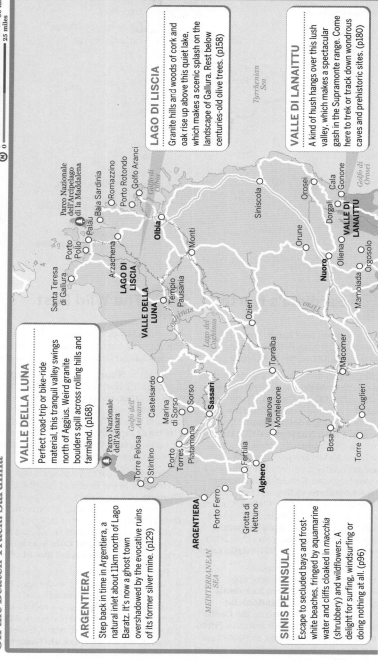

VALLE DELLA LUNA

Perfect road-trip or bike-ride material, this tranquil valley swings north of Aggius. Weird granite boulders spill across rolling hills and farmland. (p168)

ARGENTIERA

Step back in time in Argentiera, a natural inlet about 11km north of Lago Baratz. It's now a ghost town overshadowed by the evocative ruins of its former silver mine. (p129)

SINIS PENINSULA

Escape to secluded bays and frost-white beaches, fringed by aquamarine water and cliffs cloaked in *macchia* (shrubbery) and wildflowers. A delight for surfing, windsurfing or doing nothing at all. (p96)

LAGO DI LISCIA

Granite hills and woods of cork and oak rise up above this quiet lake, which makes a scenic splash on the landscape of Gallura. Rest below centuries-old olive trees. (p158)

VALLE DI LANAITTU

A kind of hush hangs over this lush valley, which makes a spectacular gash in the Supramonte range. Come here to trek or track down wondrous caves and prehistoric sites. (p180)

SORGONO

Deep in the remote, hilly Mandrolisai, Sorgono is surrounded by vast tracts of forest, archaeological sites, and vineyards that produce some of the island's best reds. (p185)

CARDEDU

Often overlooked in favour of Golfo di Orosei beaches further north, this wild and wonderfully undeveloped red granite coastline is a delight to discover on foot or by kayak. (p196)

MONTE DEI SETTE FRATELLI

Leave behind Cagliari's crowds and head to this park's quiet woodlands, granite peaks and waterfalls. (p53)

OASI DI SEU

A dirt track leads to this pristine nature reserve, close to Tharros. Saunter along serene trails through the aromatic Mediterranean scrub and enjoy expansive sea views. (p99)

SPIAGGIA DI PISCINAS

Tricky to get to but worth it, this gorgeous beach on the lonely Costa Verde is a broad ribbon of golden sand, towering dunes and windswept sea. Sheer bliss. (p66)

Map of Sardinia showing locations including Cala Gonone, Urzulei, Arbatax, Baunei, Santa Maria Navarrese, CARDEDU, Tertenia, Villaputzu, MONTE DEI SETTE FRATELLI, Cala Sinzias, Stagno Notteri, Villasimius, Poetto, Golfo di Cagliari, Cagliari, Pula, Chia, Porto Teulada, Teulada, Calasetta, Sant'Antioco, San Pietro, Carloforte, Portovesme, Golfo di Palmas, Iglesias, Carbonia, Capoterra, Riserva Naturale di Monte Arcosu, Monastir, Mandas, Barumini, Tuili, Sadali, Tonara, SORGONO, Parco Nazionale del Golfo di Orosei e del Gennargentu, Lago Omodeo, Abbasanta, Santa Cristina, Riola Sardo, Putzu Idu, SINIS PENINSULA, San Salvatore, Cabras, San Giovanni di Sinis, OASI DI SEU, Oristano, Santa Giusta, Golfo di Oristano, Terralba, Torre dei Corsari, SPIAGGIA DI PISCINAS, Montevecchio, Arbus, Guspini, Ingurtosu, Portixeddu, Buggerru, Masua, Fluminimaggiore, Domusnovas, Funtanamare, Golfo di Gonnesa, Mare di Sardegna, MEDITERRANEAN SEA

Plan Your Trip

Travel with Children

Ah, *bambini* (children)! The Sardinians just love them, so expect pinched cheeks, ruffled hair and warm welcomes galore. And with the island's easygoing nature, gently shelving beaches, caves to explore and prehistoric mysteries straight out of a picture book, travelling here with kids in tow is child's play.

Best Regions for Kids

Alghero & the Northwest
Fantastic child-friendly beaches for all ages, nature parks, fascinating caves and wildlife-watching, and an array of water sports for older kids and teens.

Cagliari
A long town beach, dizzying tower climbing in the historic centre, fun shops and the wonderful *trenino verde* train ride in the countryside.

Olbia & the Gallura
Excellent beaches with entertainment for kids, wildlife excursions, gentle hiking and dolphin-spotting boat trips.

Oristano & the West
Beautiful bird life; water-sport-heavy beaches for teens, and wild, sandy beaches for toddlers.

Nuoro & the East
Cave exploring, climbing, biking and all kinds of activities for older kids and teens; family-friendly campgrounds.

Iglesias & the Northwest
Cavallini (minihorses) roaming on the mountain plateau of La Giara di Gesturi, excellent beaches on the south coast, eerie mines, wondrous caves.

Sardinia for Kids

Like all of Italy, Sardinia is wonderful for children of all ages. Babies and toddlers are cooed over everywhere, while older kids and teenagers can unleash their energy with a host of outdoor activities – from horse riding on the beach to learning to dive and snorkel, kayaking to climbing, wildlife-spotting to coastal hiking.

Still appealingly low-key by comparison with other holiday destinations in Europe, Sardinia has hands down some of the Med's finest beaches. The gently shelving, powder-soft sands on the north, west and south coasts are especially well suited to families. And kids can be kept amused for hours with crystal-clear water to splash around in and sandcastles to build. Most resorts have tree-fringed promenades suitable for buggies, as well as playgrounds and gelaterias.

Beyond the beach. Sardinia's landscapes, history and culture fire little imaginations, especially when a little storytelling is thrown into the mix. Take your children deep into the island's grottoes and caves, to prehistoric sites with names like *tombe dei giganti* (giant's tombs) and Hobbit-like *domus de janas* ('fairy house' chamber tombs). Or plan a fun road trip through boulder-strewn valleys that look freshly minted for a sci-fi film.

Wherever you base yourself, discounts are available for children on public transport and for admission to sights.

Children's Highlights

Beach Fun

➡ **Sinis Peninsula** (p98) Long sandy or tiny pebble beaches, perfect for toddlers.

➡ **Cala Gonone** (p192) Low-key family-oriented resort, with a pine-fringed *lungomare* (seafront promenade), a shady campground and several playgrounds.

➡ **Costa del Sud** (p74) Stretches of sand and shallow, limpid waters along Sardinia's southwest coast.

➡ **Cala Battistoni, Baia Sardinia** (p155) Hair-raising rides and water madness, plus fine sandy beaches.

➡ **Riviera del Corallo, Alghero** (p125) Greenery and umbrellas, sun loungers and kids' play areas.

➡ **Costa Verde** (p66) Gorgeous, dune-backed beaches off the beaten track. Not many facilities but plenty of space to run around.

Energy Burners

➡ **Cardedu** (p196) Kayaking and nautical camping on this remarkable stretch of red granite coast.

➡ **Arborea** (p206) Huge horse-riding resort, with lessons and treks along the beach or through pine woods.

➡ **Golfo di Orosei** (p187) Canoeing, biking, caving, diving and canyoning, all great for teens.

➡ **Palau and Porto Pollo** (p162) These north-coast neighbours offer water sports galore – from windsurfing and kayaking to kids' Bubblemaker diving courses.

➡ **Laguna di Nora** (p76) Canoe expeditions and basic snorkelling.

➡ **Capo Carbonara** (p54) Shallow water and sandy beaches for play and snorkelling.

Nature & Wildlife Encounters

➡ **Sinis Peninsula** (p96) Salt lakes and pink flamingos in spring.

➡ **Parco Nazionale dell'Asinara** (p131) Albino donkeys steal the show at this wildly beautiful national park in the north.

➡ **Parco Naturale Regionale Molentargius** (p45) Protected reed-fringed wetlands with abundant bird life – flamingos, herons, little egrets and the like.

➡ **Stagno S'Ena Arrubia** (p95) Keep binoculars handy to spot flamingos, herons, coots and ospreys.

➡ **La Giara di Gesturi** (p80) Try to spy the shy miniature wild horses that roam this tabletop plateau.

➡ **Capo Carbonara** (p54) A marine reserve with flamingo-filled lagoons and boat trips to the islands.

Rock Stars & Cave Capers

➡ **Roccia dell'Orso, Palau** (p162) Wind-blasted granite formation in the shape of a bear.

➡ **Grotta di Nettuno, Capo Caccia** (p128) Count the 656 steps to the bottom of this glittering, cathedral-like cave.

➡ **Le Grotte Is Zuddas, Santadi** (p69) Marvel at helictites in this spectacular cave system.

➡ **Roccia dell'Elefante, Castelsardo** (p133) Seen the bear rock? Go check out the elephant.

➡ **Grotta di Ispinigoli, Dorgali** (p189) Underground fairyland of stalagmites, including the world's second tallest.

Planning

When to Go

The best time to visit Sardinia with children is from April to June and in September, when the weather is mild, accommodation is plentiful and crowds are fewer. In July and August temperatures soar, prices skyrocket and tourist numbers swell. But if you are tied to school holiday dates, there are still alternatives to the packed coastal resorts. Head inland to an *agriturismo* (farm-stay accommodation), for instance, to give the masses the slip; here you'll find space for the kids to play freely, farm animals, trails to explore and a genuinely warm welcome.

Where to Stay

Resorts up and down Sardinia's coastline are geared towards families. Here the hotels and campsites often have pools, kids' clubs organising activities, and special children's menus. Apartment rentals are often a good bet too, giving you and your family the space and freedom you need – and they often work out cheaper than hotels when you do the sums. Another fine option is an *agriturismo*, which is ideal for active families who fancy getting back to nature and seeing more of Sardinia than just a beach.

It's worth booking in advance whenever possible, and be sure to ask about the hotel's kid policy – many places are happy to squeeze in a cot for free or an extra bed for a nominal charge. Family-friendly accommodation options in this guide are flagged with a ⊞ icon. For more, see the Accommodation chapter.

What to Bring

Most airlines – including Ryanair and easyJet – allow you to carry on a collapsible pushchair for no extra charge (this needs to be tagged at the check-in or bag drop desk). For additional items such as booster seats and travel cots, they often levy a fee of around £10 to £20 per flight. You can take baby food, milk and sterilised water in your hand baggage.

Baby Essentials

You can buy baby formula in powder or liquid form, as well as sterilising solutions such as Milton, at *farmacie*. Disposable nappies (diapers) – *pannolini* – are widely available at *farmacie* and at supermarkets, where you'll find a wider selection. Remember that shop opening hours may differ from your home country, so run out

of nappies on a Saturday evening and you could be in for a messy Sunday.

Fresh cow's milk is sold in litre and half-litre cartons in supermarkets, *alimentari* (food shops) and in some bars. If it is essential that you have milk, you should carry an emergency carton of *lungo conservazione* (UHT).

Car Hire

It is possible to hire car seats for infants and children (usually for a per-day fee) from most car-rental firms, but book them well in advance. Take into account that most compact cars are short on space, so you may struggle to squeeze in your luggage and pushchair in the boot. Check the car's dimensions before booking or consider upgrading to a bigger model.

Getting Around

On trains and ferries children under the age of four generally travel for free, although without the right to a seat or cabin berth; for children between four and 12, discounts of 50% are usually applied.

Sardinian trains are seldom very busy, but in high season it's advisable to book seats. You'll also need to book car seats if you're planning to hire a car.

Note that coastal and mountain roads can be very curvy and travel sickness is a serious prospect, so be prepared.

Kids love the *trenino verde,* a narrow-gauge train that chugs through some of Sardinia's most spectacular and inaccessible countryside.

FOOD, GLORIOUS FOOD

Eating out with the kids is pretty stress free in Sardinia, particularly in the coastal resorts, where kids are made to feel very welcome in hotel restaurants. There are few taboos about taking children to restaurants, even if locals with little ones in tow tend to stick to the more popular trattorias – you'll seldom see children in an expensive restaurant.

Even if there is no children's menu, most places will cheerfully tailor a dish to appeal and serve a *mezzo porzione* (half portion). Very few restaurants have *seggioloni* (high chairs), so either bring a fabric add-on for normal chairs or stick your wiggly toddler on your knee and hope for the best. Likewise, few places have baby-changing facilities, though the staff will almost always try and find a space for you (sometimes rolling a tray table into the toilets for you!).

Foodwise, your children are bound to find something they'll love eating here. Spaghetti, of course, abounds, as do Sardinian takes on pasta like shell-shaped *malloreddus* and ravioli-like *culurgiones* filled with ricotta. Ice cream is a great way of bribing flagging kids, ditto pizza, though most places only serve the latter in the evening.

Regions at a Glance

Sardinia may be an island, but it sure is a big one. Even with your own wheels you may be surprised how long it can take to get from A to B, so careful route planning helps.

The capital Cagliari strikes a perfect balance with its blend of culture and coast. Swinging southwest brings you to the Costa del Sud, the dune-dotted Costa Verde, and verdant countryside with must-see *nuraghi* (Bronze Age fortified settlements). The northwest seduces with Spanish soul in Alghero, as well as shimmering white beaches and grottoes. Hop over to the island's northeast for celebrity glamour on the gorgeous, cove-speckled Costa Smeralda and to tour Gallura's granite heartland. In the mountainous east, the cliffs, peaks and the bluest of seas will have you itching to climb, hike, cycle, kayak and more.

Cagliari & the Sarrabus

Culture
Food
Outdoors

Medieval Palazzi

Nothing says Cagliari like the medieval Il Castello citadel, with its grandstand views, Pisan towers and pastel-fronted palazzi. Rococo churches, a Roman amphitheatre and a stellar archaeological museum map out the island's past.

Shellfish & Sweets

Foodies are in their element with fresh fish in Marina's buzzing restaurants, alfresco shellfish on Poetto Beach, Sardinian sweets at pavement cafes and award-winning wines in Serdiana.

Coastal Walks

A coastal road threads through to the 6km sands of Poetto Beach, fringed with lagoons dotted with pink flamingos in winter. The beaches, crystal-clear waters and cape diving are draws further east.

p34

Iglesias & the Southwest

History
Beaches
Islands

Time Travel

Revisit the Bronze Age at Nuraghe Su Nuraxi, explore Phoenician and Roman history by diving to Nora's submerged ruins, and flick back to 3000 BC touring *domus de janas* (fairy houses) at Necropolis del Montessu.

Hidden Coastlines

This swath of coastline is wildly beautiful: from Costa Verde's 30m-high dunes to the cobalt blue waters of the Costa del Sud, and the mind-blowingly lovely Spiaggia della Piscinas.

Island-Hopping

On Isola di San Pietro, thrill at Eleonora's falcons at Cala Fico, explore palazzi-dotted Carloforte and try Sardinia's best tuna. The seafaring past is evoked in Isola di Sant'Antioco's Phoenician ruins.

p56

Oristano & the West

Beaches
Food
Outdoors

Beautiful Bays

Flour white beaches and bluer-than-blue water: few coastlines are as compelling as the Sinis Peninsula. Escape the world on Is Aruttas' bleached sands or on Isola di Mal di Ventre.

Local Flavours

Cabras for the island's best *bottarga* (mullet roe), Seneghe for its olive oil and *bue rosso* beef, Milis for its sweet oranges, the vineyards for crisp Vernaccia wines... Sardinia's west is foodie heaven.

Summits & Surf

On this western swath of the island, clamber up volcanic Monti Ferru, surf wave-thrashed Putzu Idu and trot through Arborea's flatlands and pinewoods on horseback. The lagoons teem with bird life, from herons to flamingos.

p89

Alghero & the Northwest

History
Coast
Outdoors

Catalan Culture

Long part of Catalonia, Alghero radiates a Spanish air, its honey-coloured seawalls enclosing cobbled lanes and Gothic *palazzi*. Take a *passeggiata* (evening stroll) along the seafront.

Natural Wonders

The coastal road weaves around to broad bays and Capo Caccia, where cliffs plunge to the fairy-tale Grotta di Nettuno. Go north to Spiaggia della Pelosa, a gorgeous lick of white sand with impossibly blue waters.

Unique Wildlife

Head to Isola dell'Asinara to spot *asini bianchi* (white donkeys), silky-haired mouflon and falcons; to Bosco di Monte Lerno to spy Giara horses; and to Le Prigionette Nature Reserve's forests for a Noah's Ark of wildlife.

p113

Olbia, the Costa Smeralda & the Gallura

High Life
Coast
Interior

Celebrity Sands

The Costa Smeralda is the place to daydream about a billionaire's lifestyle as you float in an emerald sea past palatial villas and superyachts. Porto Cervo and Porto Rotondo are celeb-spotting central.

Crystal Waters

The Costa Smeralda is scalloped with beautiful coves and fjordlike inlets. Beach-hop south to San Teodoro's frost white beaches, or north to the ravishing Arcipelago di La Maddalena.

Vineyards & Hill Towns

Gallura's rugged granite interior is a staggering contrast to the coast. Weave through thick cork-oak woods and vineyards to alley-woven hill towns like San Pantaleo and Tempio Pausania.

p144

Nuoro & the East

Outdoors
Coast
Mountains

Cliffs & Canyons

This is hiking and climbing paradise. Cala Gonone's cliffs are a must-climb, while hikers won't want to miss a trek deep into the cavernous Gola Su Gorropu canyon.

Dazzling Coves

Half-moon Cala Luna, pearly Cala Mariolu, breathtaking Cala Goloritzè – everyone has their favourite Golfo di Orosei cove. The dreamiest bays are strung out between cliffs and are best discovered on foot, by boat or kayak.

Peak Performance

In the remote interior, mountains rear spectacularly above deep valleys, holm oak forests and stuck-in-time villages. A helter-skelter of roads leads you to the Gennargentu's lofty peaks and Barbagia's wilds.

p170

On the Road

Cagliari & the Sarrabus

Best Places to Eat

Best Places to Stay

Why Go?

Built high and mighty around a rocky citadel, Cagliari gazes out to the glistening Med, basks in southern sunshine and looks proudly back on almost 3000 years of history. Sardinia's cultured, open-minded capital makes a fine base if you're seeking more than the classic sun-and-sea mix, with a clutch of museums, baroque churches and fortifications begging exploration.

Still a busy, working port, Cagliari hasn't been prettified for the benefit of tourists and is all the more interesting for it. Sightseeing aside, this city is all about simple pleasures, be it fresh seafood in a Marina trattoria, crowd-watching at a pavement cafe or a stroll through Il Castello's medieval alleyways.

Slightly east of town you find yourself in a different world. The mountainous hinterland of the Sarrabus is an untamed, silent wilderness, and the magnificent salt-white beaches of Villasimius and the Costa Rei are all but deserted outside of the peak summer months.

Road Distance (km)

	Cagliari	Castiadas	Costa Rei	Muravera
Castiadas	47			
Costa Rei	60	13		
Muravera	56	27	30	
Villasimius	43	20	17	47

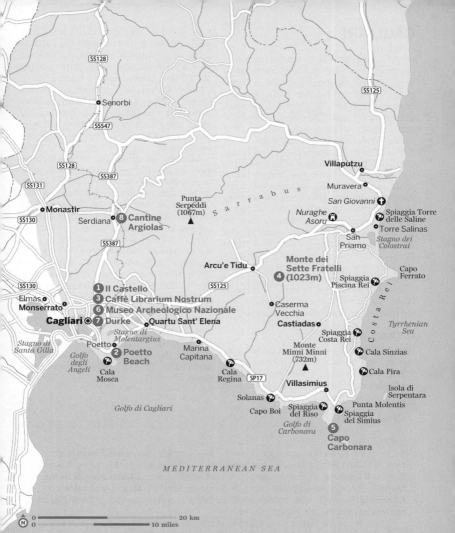

Cagliari & the Sarrabus Highlights

1 Discover the nooks and crannies of **Il Castello** (p37), Cagliari's medieval citadel.

2 Sunbathe by day and party the night away at **Poetto Beach** (p40).

3 Sip a sundowner at hilltop **Caffè Librarium Nostrum** (p49) as the city is dramatically illuminated.

4 Don your walking boots and head for the pine-scented hills of **Monte dei Sete Fratelli** (p53).

5 Dive into the lush blue waters off the **Capo Carbonara** (p54), a marine reserve.

6 Enjoy a fascinating romp through Sardinian history at the artefact-packed **Museo Archeologico Nazionale** (p37).

7 Give in to temptation at old-world **Durke** (p51), a wonderland of traditional Sardinian sweets.

8 Sample the pick of the region's wines or join a cookery class at **Cantine Argiolas** (p50) in Serdiana.

CAGLIARI

POP 157,000

Forget flying: the best way to arrive in Cagliari is by sea, the city rising in a helter-skelter of golden-hued *palazzi* (mansions), domes and facades up to the rocky centrepiece, Il Castello. When DH Lawrence arrived in the 1920s, he compared the Sardinian capital to Jerusalem: '...strange and rather wonderful, not a bit like Italy.'

Yet, although Tunisia is closer than Rome, Cagliari *is* the most Italian of Sardinia's cities. Vespas buzz down tree-fringed boulevards and locals hang out at cafes tucked under the graceful arcades in the seafront Marina district. Up in Il Castello, sunset is prime-time viewing in the piazzas, when the soft evening light illuminates pastel facades and the golden fortress walls like a fresco painting. Everywhere you wander, Cagliari's rich history is spelled out in Roman ruins, museums, churches and galleries.

Edging east of town brings you to Poetto Beach, the hub of summer life with its limpid blue waters and upbeat party scene.

History

Founded by the Phoenicians in the 8th century BC, the city was first developed by the Romans, who carved a vast amphitheatre out of the rocky hillside and made the area into one of the Mediterranean's main trading ports. But it was not until the Carthaginians took control of what they called Karel or Karalis (meaning 'rocky place') around 520 BC that a town began to emerge.

Julius Caesar declared Karalis a Roman municipality in 46 BC. For centuries it remained a prosperous port, heading the grain trade with mainland Italy, but with the eclipse of Rome's power came more turbulent times.

Vandals operating out of North Africa stormed into the city in AD 455, only to be unseated by the Byzantine Empire in 533. By the 11th century, weakening Byzantine influence (accentuated by repeated Arab raids) led Cagliari and the other districts to become virtually autonomous.

In 1258 the Pisans took the town, fortified the Castello area and replaced the local population with Pisans. A similar fate awaited them when the Catalano-Aragonese took over in 1326. The Black Death swept through in 1348, with frequent repeat outbreaks in the succeeding decades.

With Spain unified at the end of the 15th century, the Catalans were subordinated to the Spaniards. Cagliari fared better than most of the island under Spanish inertia, and in 1620 the city's university opened its doors.

CAGLIARI IN...

Two Days

Begin your first day with a postcard view of Cagliari from the **Torre dell'Elefante**, or from its Pisan twin, the **Torre di San Pancrazio**. From here, wander the narrow, twisting lanes of **Il Castello**, filled with neighbourly chatter, to the ornate **Cattedrale di Santa Maria**. In the afternoon, trace the island's nuraghic past at the **Museo Archeologico Nazionale**. Toast your first day over cocktails on the panoramic terrace of **Caffè Librarium Nostrum** as the city begins to twinkle.

On day two, wake up in style over coffee at 19th-century **Antico Caffè**, followed by a languid stroll through fountain-dotted greenery at the **Orto Botanico**. Just around the corner sits Cagliari's **Roman amphitheatre**. Lunch on fresh fish in the Marina district and spend the afternoon mooching around the boutiques and speciality shops. **Piazza Yenne** is a lively spot for an alfresco aperitif.

Four Days

Rise early on day three and head to **Mercato di San Benedetto** for picnic goodies. Take your treasures to **Poetto Beach**, where you can laze, swim or windsurf. If birdwatching is more your scene, explore the **Parco Naturale Regionale Molentargius** on foot or by bike.

Both the pristine beaches of **Villasimius** and one of Sardinia's top wineries, **Cantine Argiolas**, in Serdiana, make great day trips for day four. Or strap on your walking boots to hike the granite mountains and wildlife-rich woodlands around **Monte dei Sette Fratelli**.

The dukes of Savoy (who in 1720 became kings of Sardinia) followed the Spanish precedent in keeping Cagliari as the vice-regal seat, and it endured several anxious events (such as the 1794 anti-Savoy riots). From 1799 to 1814 the royal family, forced out of Piedmont by Napoleon, spent time in Cagliari protected by the British Royal Navy.

Cagliari continued to develop slowly throughout the 19th and 20th centuries. Parts of the city walls were destroyed and the city expanded as the population grew. Heavily bombed in WWII, Cagliari was awarded a medal for bravery in 1948.

Reconstruction commenced shortly after the end of the war and was partly complete by the time Cagliari was declared capital of the semiautonomous region of Sardinia in the new Italian republic in 1949. A good deal of Sardinia's modern industry, especially petrochemicals, has since developed around the lagoons and along the coast as far as Sarroch in the southwest.

In November 2013, Cagliari was given a confidence boost when it was short-listed for European Capital of Culture 2019. Watch this space.

⊙ Sights

Cagliari's key sights huddle in four central districts: Il Castello, Stampace, Marina and Villanova. The obvious starting point is the hilltop Il Castello area, home to a group of fine museums at the Citadella dei Musei and affording terrific views of the cityscape.

To the west, high up the hill, is Stampace, where most of the action spirals around Piazza Yenne. Elsewhere you'll find a number of important churches, a botanical garden and Cagliari's rocky Roman amphitheatre.

Bordered by Largo Carlo Felice to the west and seafront Via Roma, the characterful Marina district is a joy to explore on foot, not so much for sights, of which there are few, but for the atmosphere of its dark, narrow lanes crammed with artisan shops, cafes and trattorias.

In the 19th century Cagliari sprawled eastwards under the Piedmontese; their legacy, Villanova, is a showcase of wide roads and imposing piazzas. Rising above the district, a large public park covers the slopes of Monte Urpinu. On the other side of the mountain, the bird-rich Stagno di Molentargius salt marshes attract birdwatchers.

A BIG PUSHOVER

Stampace was Cagliari's medieval working-class district, where Sards lived huddled in the shadow of the mighty castle. In the 14th century, when the Aragonese were in charge, Sards were forbidden to enter the castle after nightfall. Those caught were mercilessly thrown off the castle walls, with the benediction *stai in pace* (rest in peace), a phrase that presumably gave rise to the name Stampace.

★ **Il Castello** HISTORIC QUARTER
(Map p42) This hilltop citadel is Cagliari's most iconic image, its domes, towers and *palazzi*, once home to the city's aristocracy, rising above the sturdy ramparts built by the Pisans and Aragonese. Inside the battlements, the old medieval city reveals itself like Pandora's box. The university, cathedral, museums and Pisan palaces are wedged into a jigsaw of narrow high-walled alleys. Sleepy though it may seem, the area harbours a growing crop of boutiques, bars and cafes that attract students, hipsters and bohemian types.

The neighbourhood is known to locals as Su Casteddu, a term also used to describe the whole city. The walls are best admired (and photographed) from afar – good spots include the Roman amphitheatre across the valley to the northwest and Bonaria to the southeast.

★ **Museo Archeologico Nazionale** MUSEUM
(Map p38; www.archeocaor.beniculturali.it; Piazza dell'Arsenale; adult/reduced €4/2; ⊙9am-8pm Tue-Sun) Of the four museums at the Citadella dei Musei, this is the undoubted star. Sardinia's premier archaeological museum displays artefacts spanning millennia of ancient history, including a superb collection of pint-sized nuraghic *bronzetti* (bronze figurines) which, in the absence of any written records, are a vital source of information on Sardinia's mysterious nuraghic culture (approximately 1800–500 BC). The museum takes a chronological spin, deftly moving from pre-nuraghic times to the Bronze and Iron Ages, the Phoenicians and Romans.

In all, about 400 nuraghic bronzes have been discovered, many in sites of religious importance, leading scholars to conclude

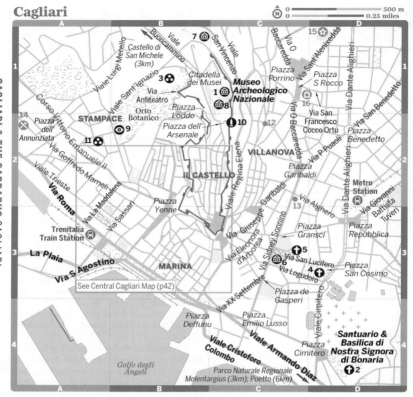

that they were probably used as votive offerings. Depicting tribal chiefs, warriors, hunters, mothers and animals, the figurines are stylistically crude but remarkably effective. There are even little models of the *nuraghi* (Bronze Age fortified settlements).

Since March 2014, the museum has showcased several of the Giganti di Monte Prama. Towering over 2m, these giant sandstone sculptures were unveiled after years of careful restoration. Dating to the 8th and 9th centuries BC, these owl-eyed archers, boxers and wrestlers are the most prized nuraghic sculptures ever found. More are on display in the Museo Civico in Cabras.

Besides precious bronzes, the **ground floor** showcases a fine stash of pre-nuraghic stone implements and obsidian tools, rudimentary ceramics and funny round fertility goddesses, a model tophet (sacred Phoenician or Carthaginian burial ground for children and babies), alongside delicate debris such as terracotta vases, glass vessels, scarabs and jewellery from ancient Karalis (Cagliari), Sulcis, Tharros and Nora.

The **1st and 2nd floors** contain more of the same but are divided by region and important sites rather than by age. Among the highlights are some Roman-era mosaics, a collection of Roman statues, busts and tombstones from Cagliari, and displays of coins.

★**Cattedrale di Santa Maria** CATHEDRAL
(Map p42; www.duomodicagliari.it; Piazza Palazzo 4; ☉7.30am-noon & 4-8pm Mon-Sat, 8am-1pm & 4.30-8.30pm Sun) Cagliari's graceful 13th-century cathedral stands proud on Piazza Palazzo. Except for the square-based bell tower, little remains of the original Gothic structure: the clean Pisan-Romanesque facade is a 20th-century imitation, added between 1933 and 1938. Inside, the once-Gothic church disappears beneath a

Cagliari

rich icing of baroque decor, the result of a radical late-17th-century makeover. Bright frescoes adorn the ceilings, and the three chapels on either side of the aisles spill over exuberantly with sculptural whirls.

The third chapel to the right, the Cappella di San Michele, is perhaps the pinnacle of the baroque genre. A serene St Michael, who appears (in baroque fashion) to be in the eye of a swirling storm, casts devils into hell.

At the central door, note the two stone pulpits, sculpted by Guglielmo da Pisa between 1158 and 1162. They originally formed a single unit, which stood in Pisa's Duomo until the Pisans donated it to Cagliari in 1312. It was subsequently split into two by the meddlesome Domenico Spotorno, the architect behind the 17th-century baroque facelift, and the big stone lions that formed its base were removed to the altar where they now stand.

On the other side of the altar is the entrance to the Aula Capitolare, the crypt where many Savoy tombs are conserved. Carved out of rock, the barrel-vaulted chamber is an impressive sight with its mass of sculptural decoration and intricate carvings.

Pinacoteca Nazionale　　　GALLERY
(Map p38; www.pinacoteca.cagliari.beniculturali. it; Piazza dell'Arsenale; adult/reduced €4/2.50; ⏱9am-8pm Tue-Sun) FREE Above and behind the archaeological museum, this gallery showcases a prized collection of 15th- to 17th-century art. Many of the best works are *retablos* (grand altarpieces of the kind commonly found in Spain), painted by Catalan and Genoese artists for local churches. Of those by known Sardinian painters, the four works by Pietro Cavaro, father of the so-called Stampace school and arguably Sardinia's most important artist, are outstanding. They include a moving *Deposizione* (Deposition) and portraits of St Peter, St Paul and St Augustine.

Also represented are the painter's father, Lorenzo, and his son Michele. Another Sardinian artist of note was Francesco Pinna, whose *Pala di Sant'Orsola* hangs here. These images tend to show the influence of Spain and Italy, rather than illuminating the Sardinian condition. However, there is a brief line-up of 19th- and early-20th-century Sardinian painters, such as Giovanni Marghinotti and Giuseppe Sciuti.

Museo d'Arte Siamese　　　GALLERY
(Map p38; www.museicivicicagliari.it; Piazza dell'Arsenale; adult/reduced €2/1; ⏱10am-8pm Tue-Sun, to 6pm in winter) Cagliari's medieval heart is an unlikely place for a collection of Asian art, but that's exactly what you find here. Donated to the city by local engineer Stefano Cardu, who had spent many years in Thailand, the collection is highly eclectic. Alongside Ming- and Qing-era Chinese porcelain vases, you'll find silk paintings, Japanese statuettes, Burmese sculpture and some truly terrifying Thai weapons.

Torre dell'Elefante　　　TOWER
(Map p42; www.camuweb.it; Via Università; adult/reduced €3/2; ⏱10-7pm Tue-Sun summer, 9am-5pm winter) One of only two Pisan towers still standing, the Torre dell'Elefante was built in 1307 as a defence against the threatening Aragonese. Named after the sculpted elephant by the vicious-looking portcullis, the 42m-high tower became something of a horror show, thanks to its foul decor. The crenellated storey was added in 1852 and used as a prison for political detainees. Climb to the top for far-reaching views over the city's rooftops to the sea.

The Spaniards beheaded the Marchese di Cea here and left her severed head lying

WORTH A TRIP

POETTO BEACH

An easy bus ride from the city centre, Cagliari's fabulous Poetto Beach is one of the longest stretches of sand in Italy. Extending 6km beyond the green Promontorio di Sant'Elia, it's an integral part of city life, particularly in summer when much of the city's youth decamps here to sunbathe by day and party by night. The long, sandy strip is lined with funfairs, restaurants, bars and discos, many of which also act as *stabilmenti balneari* (private beach clubs). These offer various facilities, including showers and changing cabins, as well as renting out umbrellas and sunloungers – prices start at €15 for an umbrella and two sunloungers.

The southern end of the beach is the most popular, with its picturesque Marina Piccola, yacht club and **outdoor cinema** (July and August only). Looming over the marina, the craggy Promontorio di Sant'Elia is known to everyone as the **Sella del Diavola** (Devil's Saddle). According to local legend, the headland was the scene of an epic battle between Lucifer and the Archangel Michael. In the course of the struggle Satan was thrown off his horse and his saddle fell into the sea where it eventually petrified atop what was to become the headland. Although much of the headland is now owned by the military and closed to the public, there are several paths that offer great walking.

In summer Poetto Beach is lined with bars, snack joints and restaurants, known to locals as *chioschi* (kiosks). Things get really busy here between November and March (mollusc season), when shacks serving sea urchins and mussels are set up by fishermen along the beach road. You're charged according to the number of shells left on your table.

To get to Poetto hop on bus PF or PQ from Piazza Matteotti.

around for 17 years! They also liked to adorn the portcullis with the heads of executed prisoners, strung up in cages like ghoulish fairy lights.

Torre di San Pancrazio
TOWER

(Map p38; Piazza Indipendenza; adult/reduced €3/2; ⊘10am-7pm Tue-Sun summer, 9am-5pm winter) Over by the citadel's northeastern gate, this 36m-high tower is the Torre dell'Elefante's twin. Completed in 1305, it is built on the city's highest point and commands expansive views of the Golfo di Cagliari.

Antico Palazzo di Città
PALACE, MUSEUM

(Map p42; www.museicivicicagliari.it; Piazza Palazzo 6; adult/reduced €4/2.50; ⊘10am-9pm summer, to 6pm winter) Housed in what was Cagliari's town hall from medieval times to the 19th century, the beautifully restored Antico Palazzo di Città has been converted into this museum. It contains a small, well-edited collection of Sardinian textiles, ceramics, paintings and engravings. The basement level displays contemporary art.

Museo del Duomo
MUSEUM

(Map p42; www.museoduomodicagliari.it; Via del Fossario 5; adult/reduced €4/2.50; ⊘10am-1pm & 4.30-7.30pm Sat & Sun) Further cathedral treasures are displayed at this compact museum. One standout is the *Trittico di Clemente VII,* which was moved here from the cathedral for safe keeping. This precious 15th-century painting in oil on timber has been attributed to the Flemish painter Rogier van der Weyden, or to one of his disciples. Another important work is the 16th-century *Retablo dei Beneficiati,* produced by the school of Pietro Cavaro.

Palazzo Viceregio
PALACE

(Map p42; Piazza Palazzo 2; ⊘8.30am-2pm & 3-8pm Mon-Fri, 10am-2pm & 4-6pm Sat) Just steps from the cathedral is this pale lime *palazzo,* once home to the Spanish and Savoy viceroys. Today it serves as the provincial assembly and stages regular exhibitions and summer music concerts.

Ghetto degli Ebrei
NEIGHBOURHOOD

(Map p42) In the Ghetto degli Ebrei (Jewish Ghetto), the area north of the Torre dell'Elefante, between Via Santa Croce and Via Stretta, the maze of narrow streets appears little changed since medieval times. Under Spanish rule the Jewish community was expelled in 1492 and today little remains except the name, applied to a restored former barracks, the **Centro Comunale d'Arte e Cultura Il Ghetto** (Map p42; Via Santa Croce 18; adult/reduced €3/2; ⊘9am-8pm Tue-Sun), which hosts temporary exhibitions, many with a Sardinian slant.

In the wake of the Jewish expulsion, the **Chiesa di Santa Croce** (Map p42; Piazzetta Santa Croce) was built over the ghetto's former synagogue.

Galleria Comunale d'Arte
GALLERY

(Map p38; www.galleriacomunalecagliari.it; Viale San Vincenzo 2; adult/reduced €6/2.60; ◷10am-9pm Wed-Mon summer, 10am-6pm daily winter) Housed in a neoclassical villa north of Il Castello, this gallery zooms in on modern Sardinian art, including works by island artists like Tarquinio Sini (1891–1943). His humorous *contrasti* (contrasts) showing frumpily dressed Sardinian girls standing beside glamorous, coiffed flappers, explore the social tensions between traditional Sardinian ways and a rapidly modernising world. Works by Giuseppe Biasi (1885–1945), depicting Sardinian life in rich oils and bold brushstrokes, are another highlight. The gallery's palm-dotted garden commands terrific views of Cagliari's skyline.

The gallery also displays an excellent selection of contemporary works, and the **Collezione Ingrao**, comprised of more than 500 works of Italian art from the mid-19th century to the late 20th century. Frequent temporary exhibitions are also held to showcase works by contemporary artists.

Bastione San Remy
LOOKOUT

(Map p42) The monumental stairway that ascends from busy Piazza Costituzione to Bastione San Remy is the most impressive way to reach Il Castello; save your legs by taking the panoramic elevator. Built between 1899 and 1902, the lookout is a mix of neoclassical and Liberty styles and affords sweeping views over Cagliari's jumbled rooftops to the Mediterranean.

Piazza Yenne
PIAZZA

(Map p42) The focal point of the Marina district, and indeed of central Cagliari, is Piazza Yenne. The small square is adorned with a statue of **King Carlo Felice** to mark the beginnings of the Carlo Felice Hwy (SS131), the project for which the monarch is best remembered. On summer nights, Piazza Yenne heaves as a young crowd flocks to its bars, gelaterias and pavement cafes.

Chiesa di Sant'Anna
CHURCH

(Map p42; Piazza Santa Restituta; ◷7.30-10am & 5-8pm Tue-Sun) Largely destroyed during WWII and painstakingly rebuilt afterwards, this sand-coloured church is basically baroque, but the Ionic columns give it a neo-classical edge. It was undergoing restoration at the time of research.

Museo del Tesoro e Area Archeologica di Sant'Eulalia
MUSEUM

(Map p42; Vico del Collegio 2; adult/reduced €5/2.50; ◷10am-1pm & 4-7pm Tue-Sun) In the heart of the Marina district, this museum contains a rich collection of religious art, as well as an archaeological area, which extends for up to 200 sq metres beneath the adjacent **Chiesa di Sant'Eulalia**. The main drawcard here is a 13m section of excavated Roman road (constructed between the 1st and 2nd centuries AD), which archaeologists think would have connected with the nearby port.

In the upstairs treasury you'll find all sorts of religious artefacts, ranging from exquisite priests' vestments and silverware through to medieval codices and other precious documents. Fine wooden sculptures abound, along with an *Ecce homo* painting, depicting Christ, front and back, after his flagellation. The painting has been attributed to a 17th-century Flemish artist.

Palazzo Civico
LANDMARK

(Map p42; Via Roma) Overlooking Piazza Matteotti, the neo-Gothic Palazzo Civico, also known as the Municipio, is home to Cagliari's city council. Capricious, pompous and not a little overbearing, it was built between 1899 and 1913, and faithfully reconstructed after bombing in 1943. The upstairs chambers contain works by a number of Sardinian artists, including Pietro Cavaro. Admission is by appointment only.

Chiesa di Santo Sepolcro
CHURCH

(Map p42; Piazza del Santo Sepolcro 5; ◷9am-1pm & 5-8pm) The most astonishing feature of this church is an enormous 17th-century gilded wooden altarpiece housing a figure of the Virgin Mary.

ℹ MUSEUM PASS

If you are planning on visiting more than one of Cagliari's Musei Civici (Civic Museums), it's well worth investing in a museum pass. Available at the museums, the pass covers the Galleria Comunale d'Arte (p41), the Museo d'Arte Siamese (p39) and the Antico Palazzo di Città (p40). An adult/reduced ticket costs €8/4. Visit www.museicivicicagliari.com for further details.

Central Cagliari

CAGLIARI & THE SARRABUS CAGLIARI

Cripta di Santa Restituta CRYPT
(Map p42; Via Sant'Efisio; ⏰10am-1pm Tue-Sun)
FREE This crypt has been in use since pre-Christian times. It's a huge, eerie, natural cavern where the echo of leaking water drip-drips. Originally a place of pagan worship, it became the home of the martyr Restituta in the 5th century and a reference point for Cagliari's early Christians. The Orthodox Christians then took it over – you can still see remnants of their frescoes – until the 13th century, when it was abandoned.

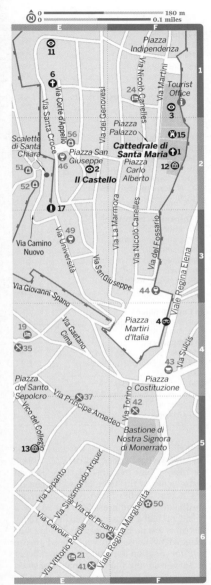

Chiesa di San Michele CHURCH

(Map p42; Via Ospedale 2; ⊙8am-11am & 6-9pm Mon-Sat, 8am-noon & 7-9pm Sun) Although consecrated in 1538, this church is best known for its lavish 18th-century decor, considered the finest example of rococo in Sardinia. The spectacle starts outside with the ebullient triple-arched baroque facade and continues through the vast colonnaded atrium and on into the magnificent octagonal interior, with six heavily decorated chapels radiating out from the centre, topped by a grand, brightly frescoed dome. Of particular note is the sacristy, with its vivid frescoes and intricate inlaid wood.

Before you go inside, take a minute to admire the massive four-columned pulpit in the atrium. This was built and named in honour of the Spanish emperor Carlos V, who is said to have delivered a stirring speech from it before setting off on a fruitless campaign against Arab corsairs in Tunisia. The octagonal interior is quite magnificent, with six heavily decorated chapels radiating out from the centre, topped by a grand, brightly frescoed dome.

Chiesa di Sant'Efisio CHURCH

(Map p42; Via Sant'Efisio) Despite its unassuming facade, the Chiesa di Sant'Efisio is of considerable local importance, not for any artistic or architectural reasons but rather for its ties to St Ephisius, Cagliari's patron saint. A Roman soldier who converted to Christianity and was later beheaded for refusing to recant his faith, St Ephisius is the star of the city's big 1 May festivities. An effigy of the saint that is paraded around the city on a beautifully ornate *carozza* (carriage) is kept here. The baroque interior is sadly off limits to the public.

Over the centuries, the saint has stood the city in good stead, saving the populace from the plague in 1652 – when the church recieved its marble makeover – and repelling Napoleon's fleet in 1793 by stirring up the storm that sent the fleet packing.

At the side of the church is the entrance to the crypt where St Ephisius was supposedly held before being executed in Nora (near Pula). It's marked in stone – *Carcer Sancti Ephysii M* (Prison of the Martyr St Ephisius) – and retains the column where Ephisius was tied during his incarceration.

In WWII the crypt was used as an air-raid shelter, a task it wasn't up to, since many died while holed up here in February 1943. It's interesting to make out the wartime graffiti that covers the walls.

Anfiteatro Romano ARCHAEOLOGICAL SITE

(Map p38; www.anfiteatroromano.it; Viale Sant'Ignazio; ⊙closed for restoration) Cagliari's most

Central Cagliari

impressive Roman monument is this amphitheatre. Dating back to the 2nd century AD, it is carved out of rock on the Buon Cammino hill, near the northern entrance to Il Castello. Although much of the original theatre has been cannibalised for building material, enough has survived to pique the imagination. The amphitheatre was closed for restoration at the time of writing, but it's worth taking a look from the outside. It is expected to reopen in late 2014.

In its heyday, crowds of up to 10,000 people – practically the entire population of Cagliari – would gather to watch gladiators battle each other and the occasional wild animal. In summer, the amphitheatre occasionally hosts concerts.

Villa di Tigellio
ARCHAEOLOGICAL SITE

(Map p38; Via Tigellio; adult/reduced €2/1; ◎ 9am-5pm daily) These remains of three Roman houses date to the 1st century BC. Legend has it that Tigellio Ermogene – a famous Sardinian poet and musician, and a close a friend of Julius Caesar – lived here. Today the ruins are pretty overgrown and are surrounded by houses, so you'll need to use your imagination to picture the magnificent mosaics, columns and baths that once stood here.

Orto Botanico
GARDENS

(Map p38; Viale Sant'Ignazio da Laconi 11; adult/reduced €4/2; ◎ 8.30am-1.30pm Mon-Sat winter, 8.30am-6pm Mon-Sat summer) One of Italy's most famous botanical gardens, the Orto Botanico was established in 1858. Today it extends over 5 hectares and nurtures 3000 species of flora. Leafy arches lead to trickling fountains and gardens bristling with palm trees, cacti and *ficus* trees with huge snaking roots. Specimens from as far afield as Asia, Australia, Africa and the Americas sidle up to the local carob trees and oaks. Littering the gardens are a Punic cistern, a Roman quarry and an aqueduct.

Basilica di San Saturnino   CHURCH

(Map p38; Piazza San Cosimo; ⊙ 9am-1pm Tue-Sat) One of the oldest churches in Sardinia, the Basilica di San Saturnino is a striking example of Palaeo-Christian architecture. Based on a Greek-cross pattern, the domed basilica was built over a Roman necropolis in the 5th century, on the site where Saturninus, a much revered local martyr, was buried. According to legend, Saturninus was beheaded in 304 AD during emperor Diocletian's anti-Christian pogroms.

In the 6th century San Fulgenzio da Ruspe, a bishop in exile from Tunisia, built a monastery here. In 1098 this was reworked into the current Romanesque church by a group of Vittorini monks from Marseille. Since then the basilica has undergone various refurbishments, most notably after it was stripped in 1662 to provide building material for the Cattedrale di Santa Maria and, most recently, after it sustained severe bomb damage in WWII.

Exmà   GALLERY

(Map p38; www.camuweb.it; Via San Lucifero 71; adult/reduced €3/2; ⊙ 9am-1pm & 4-8pm Tue-Sun) Housed in Cagliari's 18th-century *mattatoio* (abattoir), Exmà is a delightful cultural centre. A permanent exhibition details the restoration of the abattoir, but it's best known for its contemporary art shows and photography exhibitions. In summer, there are frequent open-air music concerts.

Chiesa di San Lucifero   CHURCH

(Map p38; Via San Lucifero 78; ⊙ 10am-12.30pm & 5-8pm Sat, 10.30am-12.30pm Sun, weekdays on request) Below this baroque church is a 6th-century crypt where the tomb of the early Archbishop of Cagliari, St Lucifer, rests. In earlier times the area had been part of a Roman burial ground. It's not always open to the public, but its austere 17th-century facade is worth a quick look from the outside.

★ Santuario & Basilica di Nostra Signora di Bonaria   CHURCH, LOOKOUT

(Map p38; www.bonaria.eu; Piazza Bonaria 2; donations welcome; ⊙ 6.30am-noon & 4.30pm-

---

WORTH A TRIP

CALLING ALL BIRDWATCHERS

Slightly east of Cagliari, heading towards Quartu Sant'Elena, lie the protected reed-fringed wetlands of the **Parco Naturale Regionale Molentargius**. A housing estate forms an incongruous backdrop for these freshwater and brackish pools, which attract nesting, migrant and wintering birds in their thousands. With a little luck you may well spot pink flamingos, purple herons, little egrets, marsh harriers, sandwich terns and black-winged stilts from the observation points.

The reserve is best explored on foot or by bicycle. Get informed before you head out at the **visitor centre** (📞 070 3791 9201; www.parks.it/parco.molentargius; Edificio Sali Scelti, Via La Palma) on the eastern fringes of town. Dawn and dusk are prime-time viewing for twitchers.

7.30pm) Crowning the Bonaria hill, around 1km southeast of Via Roma, is this hugely popular pilgrimage site. Devotees come from all over the world to pray to *Nostra Signora di Bonaria,* a wooden statue of the Virgin Mary and Christ, kept in a niche behind the altar, which is said to have saved a 14th-century Spanish ship during a storm. To the right of the sanctuary is the much larger basilica, which still acts as a landmark for returning sailors.

The sanctuary was originally part of a much bigger fortress complex built by the Catalano-Aragonese in 1323. Little remains of the original compound, apart from the truncated bell tower, which originally served as a watchtower, and the Gothic portal. Building began in 1704, but the money ran out and the basilica wasn't officially finished until 1926.

You'll find yet more model boats, as well as other ex-voto offerings and a golden crown from Carlo Emanuele I in the sanctuary's **museum**, accessible through the small cloister. There are also the mummified corpses of four plague-ridden Catalano-Aragonese nobles whose bodies were found miraculously preserved inside the church.

When the Catalano-Aragonese arrived to take Cagliari in 1323, it became clear it would be no easy task. So they sensibly set up camp on the fresh mountain slopes of Montixeddu, which came to be known as

Bonaria (from *buon'aria* meaning 'good air'). In the three years of the siege, the camp became a fortress with its own church.

After ejecting the Pisans and taking the city in 1335, the Aragonese invited Mercedari monks from Barcelona to establish a monastery at the Bonaria church, where they remain to this day.

The Bonaria monks were kept well employed for centuries ransoming Christian slaves from Muslim pirates, and they are credited with saving the Genoese community of Tabarka in Tunisia and bringing them to Isola di San Pietro. But what makes this a place of international pilgrimage is the statue of the Virgin Mary and Christ. Legend has it that the statue was washed up after being cast overboard by Spanish seamen caught in a storm in the 14th century, and today mariners still pray to the Madonna for protection on the high seas. Above the altar hangs a tiny 15th-century ivory ship, whose movements are said to indicate the wind direction in the Golfo degli Angeli.

Castello di San Michele　　CASTLE
(Via Sirai; adult/reduced €3/2; ⊗10am-1pm & 4-7pm Tue-Sun) Lifted by a hill high above the city, this stout three-tower Spanish fortress northwest of the centre commands incredible city and sea views. Set in serene grounds, the 10th-century castle was built to protect Santa Igia, capital of the Giudi-

cato of Cagliari, but is most famous as the luxurious residence of the 14th-century Carroz family. It now hosts art and photography exhibitions. Take bus 5 from Via Roma to the foot of the hill, then walk 800m to the castle.

🏃 Activities

Not surprisingly, water sports are big at Poetto, and you can generally hire canoes at the beach clubs. The Golfo di Cagliari is littered with the wrecks of WWII ships, which makes it an excellent place for divers to explore.

Windsurfing Club Cagliari　　WATER SPORTS
(⏻070 37 26 94; www.windsurfingclubcagliari.org; Viale Marina Piccola) From its base at Marina Piccola, this centre offers a range of water sports courses. A course of six lessons for windsurfing/catamaran/freestyle costs €160/220/500 respectively; the lessons vary in length – see the website for details. Four hours' surfing instruction will cost you €60. Special courses with reduced rates are available for children aged six to 15.

Morgan Diving　　SCUBA DIVING
(⏻337 564354; www.morgandiving.com) This outfit arranges dives to a number of wrecks (prices range from €40 to €110) and is also authorised to conduct dives in the marine reserve of Villasimius. The company is based

---

MASSIMO CARLOTTO'S ALLIGATOR

Massimo Carlotto's life reads like the plot of one of his crime novels...because it *is* the plot of one of his books.

At 19, during Italy's 'years of lead', he witnessed the murder of Margherita Magello, a 25-year-old student who was stabbed 59 times. The events that followed became the novel *Il Fuggiasco* (The Fugitive). Covered in Magello's blood, Carlotto ran to fetch the police, who accused him of the killing. He was later sentenced to 18 years' imprisonment. In 1993, after an international campaign, he was released with a full pardon from the president of Italy.

While in prison, Carlotto found the true-life material for the explicit crime novels he now writes. His most famous series is the Alligator, which Carlotto claims was developed from real legal cases.

The protagonist is loosely modelled on Carlotto himself; he even drives the Škoda Carlotto once drove (because many people say it is the least-stopped car in Italy). The nickname comes from the character's (and Carlotto's) favourite cocktail – seven parts Calvados to three parts Drambuie, crushed ice and a slice of apple – invented by a barman in Caffè Librarium Nostrum in Cagliari, where Carlotto now lives. The cocktail's fame has since spread to bars in Rome, Milan and Naples. It's said that nobody can drink more than four.

Five of Carlotto's books have been translated into English, including *The Fugitive* (2008), *Death's Dark Abyss* (2007) and *The Goodbye Kiss* (2006). Order his books at www.massimocarlotto.it.

TO MARKET!

Early-risers can join locals for a mooch around one of Cagliari's bustling morning food markets from Monday to Saturday. You can pick up all sorts of Sardinian goodies – seafood, tangy salami, *pecorino* the size of wagon wheels, horse steaks, you name it – at historic food market, **Mercato di San Benedetto** (Map p38; www.mercatosanbenedetto. com; Via San Francesco Cocco Ortu; ☺7am-2pm Mon-Sat). For a more intimate vibe, try the delightful **Mercato di Santa Chiara** (Map p42; Scalette di Santa Chiara; ☺7am-2pm Mon-Sat) and brush up your *Italiano* at stalls laden with fresh fish, fruit and bread.

Sundays in Cagliari are best for flea market and antique finds. On the first, second and fourth Sunday of the month, Cagliaritani go bargain hunting at **Piazza del Carmine** antique and collectors market.

at Marina Capitana, 14km east of Cagliari, but you can make arrangements over the phone.

Boardwalk PROMENADE
Dotted with palms and fountains, Cagliari's new boardwalk hugs the seafront, with breezy views back to the Marina district. It's a relaxed place for a jog, stroll or bike ride away from the buzz of the city centre.

⛵ Courses

One World Language Centre LANGUAGE
(Map p38; ☎070 67 02 34; www.oneworldcagliari. com; Via Sidney Sonnino 195; 20hr class from €149) Brush up your Italian with a course at this reputable language school, which takes an interactive approach and offers lessons for all levels. The centre can help arrange homestays (from €210 per week) and apartment rooms (from €160 per week).

L'Accademia LANGUAGE, COOKING
(Map p38; ☎328 8811464; www.laccademia.com; Via San Giovanni 34; 15/20hr class €220/250, individual class per hr €33) Just steps from Via Roma, this central school takes a hands-on approach to learning Italian, offering the chance to combine language skills with cultural immersion activities such as city tours, Italian movie screenings and traditional Sardinian dinners.

☞ Tours

City Tour Cagliari BUS TOUR
(Map p42; www.citytourcagliari.com; adult/reduced €10/8; ☺9.30am-7.30pm) This open-topped bus does an hour's loop of the key landmarks and sights, with multilingual commentary available. The whistle-stop tour takes in major landmarks and sights including Bastione San Remy, the Anfiteatro Romano and Torre di San Pancrazio. Departures are hourly from Piazza Yenne.

Sardinia Tourist Guide CITY TOUR
(☎178 6041520, 349 4558367; www.sardiniatouristguide.it) Based in Selargius, 12km northeast of town, these expert guides run a three-and-a-half-hour tour of Cagliari, which takes in highlights like Poetto Beach, the Sella del Diavola (Devil's Saddle), the Basilica di Bonaria and Il Castello. They also arrange archaeological tours (for instance to Nora) and outdoor excursions such as canyoning in the Flumendosa and an ascent of Monte Corrasi.

✯ Festivals & Events

Cagliari puts on a good show for Carnevale, in February, and during the Easter Holy Week, when a hooded procession takes place between the Chiesa di Sant'Efisio and the cathedral up in Il Castello.

Festa di Sant'Efisio RELIGIOUS
Pilgrims descend on the city in droves for this saintly celebration, held from 1 to 4 May. On the opening day Cagliaritani pour into the streets to greet the effigy of St Ephisius, Cagliari's patron saint, as it's paraded round the streets on a bullock-drawn carriage. As the costumed procession melts away, a hardcore retinue accompanies the statue on its 40km pilgrimage to Nora. Get the best views from the grandstand seating around Piazza Matteotti and Largo Carlo Felice. Tickets for the stands (€15 to €25) are sold at Box Office Tickets (p50).

✗ Eating

In a city where even daily staples such as bread and cheese are elevated to a near art form, *mangiare bene* (eating well) is

DON'T MISS

FAVOURITE SNACK SPOTS

Le Patate & Co (Map p42; Scalette Santo Sepulcro 1; fries €2.50, mains €7.50-12; ⊙11.30am-3pm & 6pm-midnight, closed Thu evening) Antonio knocks up the freshest fries in town – thin, crisp and not overly salty. Sit on the terrace at the top of the steps when the sun's out.

Isola del Gelato (Map p42; Piazza Yenne 35; ice creams €1.50-4; ⊙6am-2am daily) A hugely popular hang-out with ice-creamy treats including semifreddo and sorbet.

Gocce di Gelato e Cioccolato (Map p42; Piazza del Carmine 21; ice creams & desserts €2-5; ⊙noon-10pm winter, to 1am summer) Stop by here for totally divine handmade gelati, desserts (try the millefeuille), spice-infused pralines and truffles.

Locanda Caddeo (Map p42; Via Sassari 75; snacks €2.50-7; ⊙noon-3pm & 7-11pm Mon-Sat, 7-11pm Sun) A cool, gallery-style haunt for focaccia, pizza by the slice and freshly prepared salads.

I Sapori dell'Isola (Map p42; Via Sardegna 50; ⊙7.30am-1.30pm & 4.30pm-8.30pm Mon-Sat) Pop into this friendly deli for top quality Sardinian bread, pastries, salami, cheese, *bottarga* (mullet roe), olive oil, wine and more.

considered a given. The Cagliaritani combine their love of food and socialising at the table, in both humble backstreet trattorias and top-end restaurants. Marina's labyrinthine lanes are chock-full of restaurants, trattorias, bars and takeaways. Some places are obviously touristy but many are not and are popular with the dining locals. Other good eat streets include Via Sassari and Corso Vittorio Emanuele.

There's a certain formality to life here, so it's always best to make a reservation, especially on busy weekend evenings. Things really get going around 9.30pm, but in summer people tend to dine later. Bear in mind that many of the better restaurants close for at least part of August.

Pizzeria Nansen
PIZZERIA €

(Map p42; ☑070 667 03 35; Corso Vittorio Emanuele II 269; pizza €5-10; ⊙11.30am-2.30pm & 6.30-11.30pm Tue-Sun) The pizzas fly out of the oven quicker than you can say *delizioso* at this family-run pizzeria. And they're terrific, too – thin, crisp and flavoursome.

Enò
SARDINIAN €

(Map p42; ☑070 684 82 43; www.enorestaurant.it; Vico Carlo Felice 12; meals €20-25; ⊙7.30am-midnight daily) Bag a table on the terrace of this sleek bistro-cum-wine bar. Sardinian classics like *culurgiones* (ravioli) in herby tomato sauce and baked sea bream pair well with one of 200 different Italian wines.

Ci Pensa Cannas
SARDINIAN €

(Map p42; ☑070 66 78 15; Via Sardegna 37; meals €15-25; ⊙noon-3pm & 7-10.30pm Mon-Sat, noon-

3pm Sun) Skip past some of the more touristy joints on Via Sardegna and head for this no-frills, homespun trattoria. The welcome is genuine and the food modestly priced and generous, be it pasta dishes like *spaghetti ai ricci* (with sea urchins), steaks or seafood.

★ St Remy
SARDINIAN €€

(Map p42; ☑070 65 73 77; www.stremy.it; Via Torino 16; meals €30-35; ⊙12.30-3pm & 7.30-10pm Mon-Fri, 7.30-10.30pm Sat) Tucked away on a side street, St Remy keeps the mood intimate in a vaulted, limewashed space with stone arches. The menu puts a creative spin on Sardinian flavours, with homemade pasta preluding mains like John Dory cooked in a white wine-black olive sauce – all cooked to a T and presented with panache.

Per Bacco
SARDINIAN €€

(Map p42; ☑070 65 16 67; www.enoperbacco.it; Via Santa Restituta 72; meals €25-35; ⊙8.30-11.30pm Mon-Sat) Hidden in the alleys of Stampace is this friendly, low-key find, with stone walls and cheek-by-jowl tables. The chef Sabrina allows ingredients to shine in simple, season-focused dishes. You might begin with, say, antipasti like Cabras *bottarga* (mullet roe) with artichokes, followed by *primi* like *lorighittas ai ricci* (ring-shaped Sardinian pasta with sea urchins) and *secondi* like saffron-infused sea bream.

Ristorante Luigi Pomata
SEAFOOD €€

(Map p42; ☑070 67 20 58; www.luigipomata.com; Viale Regina Margherita 14; meals €40-50; ⊙1-3pm & 8-11pm Mon-Sat) There's always a good buzz at this minimalist bistro, with pared-down decor and chefs skilfully preparing super-fresh sushi at the bar by the entrance. The menu goes with the seasons, but expect such Sardinia-inflected taste sensations as pan-seared filet of red Carloforte tuna with braised red onion and Cannonau salsa. The €15 business lunch is a snip.

Martinelli's
MODERN ITALIAN €€
(Map p42; ☎ 070 65 42 20; www.martinellis. it; Via Principe Amedeo 18; meals from €35; ☺ 8.30pm-midnight Mon-Sat) Simplicity is the ethos underpinning this intimate, subtly lit bistro in the heart of the Marina district. Service is friendly without being overbearing, and the menu plays up seasonal, winningly fresh seafood along the lines of *fregola* (semolina pasta) with clams and sea bass cooked in vernaccia wine and olives.

Antica Cagliari
SARDINIAN €€
(Map p42; ☎ 070 734 01 98; www.anticacagliari. it; Via Sardegna 49; meals €25-40; ☺ 12.30-3pm & 8-11pm Wed-Mon) A cut above most restaurants in the Marina district, this beamed restaurant always has a good buzz. Go for Sardinian dishes like *fregola* with shellfish or whatever fish is fresh that day. Reserve ahead to snag one of the few tables on the pavement terrace.

Man.Gia
ITALIAN, PIZZERIA €€
(Map p38; ☎ 070 204 19 40; www.mangiasenzaglutine.it; Via Mameli 196; meals €25-35; ☺ 6pm-midnight Tue-Sat) Waving the flag as Sardinia's first gluten-free restaurant, Man.Gia also does a roaring trade in pizzas, snacks like crostini and bruschette, pasta and fish. Seasonal standouts like *fregola* with asparagus, sea urchins and *bottarga* add a nice pinch of regional flavour. The look and vibe are laid-back, and they even do gluten-free beer.

Crackers
TRADITIONAL ITALIAN €€
(Map p42; ☎ 070 65 39 12; Corso Vittorio Emanuele 193; meals from €30; ☺ 12.30-2.30pm & 8.30-10.30pm Thu-Tue) A corner of Piedmont in Sardinia, Crackers specialises in northern Italian classics such as *brasato al Barolo* (meat stewed in Barolo wine) and boiled meats served with mustard. There's also a wide range of risottos, some excellent vegetable antipasti, and a thoughtful wine list.

Ristorante Ammentos
SARDINIAN €€
(Map p42; ☎ 070 65 10 75; Via Sassari 120; meals €20-30; ☺ 1-2.30pm & 8-11pm Thu-Tue (closed Wed)) Dine on authentic Sardinian fare in rustic surrounds at this popular trattoria.

Culurgiones in herby tomato sauce are a delicious lead to succulent meat dishes such as wild boar or goat stew.

Dal Corsaro
SARDINIAN €€€
(Map p42; ☎ 070 66 43 18; www.dalcorsaro.com; Viale Regina Margherita 28; meals €40-55; ☺ 1-2.30pm & 8-11pm Tue-Sun) Stiff tablecloths, silver wine buckets and elegant couples set the scene at Cagliari's bastion of fine dining. Sardinian ingredients are highlighted in creative dishes such as *raviola di cipolla e pecorino semi stagionato* (onion ravioli with mature *pecorino* cheese) and roast octopus with lemongrass salsa. The two-course lunch is a steal at €16.

🍸 Drinking & Nightlife

Head up to Il Castello for sundowners with a dress-circle view of Cagliari. The bar scene is centred on buzzy Piazza Yenne and Corso Vittorio Emanuele, although in summer the party scene spirals around Poetto.

Antico Caffè
CAFE
(Map p42; www.anticocaffe1855.it; Piazza Costituzione 10; ☺ 7am-2am) DH Lawrence and Grazia Deledda once frequented this grand old cafe, which opened its doors in 1855. Locals come to chat over leisurely coffees, frilly crêpes and salads. There's a pavement terrace, or you can settle inside amid the polished wood, marble and brass.

Caffè Libarium Nostrum
BAR
(Map p42; Via Santa Croce 33; ☺ 7.30am-2am Tue-Sun) Offering some of the best views in town, this modish Castello bar has panoramic seating on top of the city's medieval ramparts. If the weather's being difficult, make for the brick-lined interior and order yourself an Alligator cocktail, created in honour of the hero of Massimo Carlotto's novels. There's occasional live music.

Caffè degli Spiriti
BAR
(Map p42; www.caffedeglispiriti.com; Bastione San Remy; ☺ 10am-3am) Grab a hammock, lie

---

EATING ON THE HOOF

For a delicious packed lunch go into one of the neighbourhood *salumerie* (delicatessens) and ask for a thick cut of *pecorino sardo* (Sardinian *pecorino* cheese) and a slice or two of smoked ham in a freshly baked *panino* (bread roll).

SERDIANA

About 25km north of Cagliari, the pretty agricultural town of Serdiana is home to one of Sardinia's most celebrated wine producers, the award-winning **Cantine Argiolas** (☑070 74 06 06; www.argiolas.it; Via Roma 28-30, Serdiana; tour with tasting €13-28; ☻tours at 11am & 3pm Mon-Fri, 10.30am Sat) 🍃. You can visit the winery by calling ahead and organising a 1½-hour guided tour; the basic €13 tasting tour includes a tasting of four different wines – among them a tangy Vermentino white and a full-bodied Cannonau red. For an additional €3 the wines are matched with bread, cheese and salami.

For even more insight, you could hook onto a tasting followed by a cookery class (€90 to €95) and enjoy the results with some top Argiolas wines drawn from the cellar. You'll learn how to make specialities like *fregola* (semolina pasta) with clams or ravioli filled with ricotta and spinach.

From Cagliari take the SS554 north and after about 10km follow the SS387 for Dolianova. After another 10km take the turn-off for Serdiana.

back and enjoy the Il Castello views and vibe at this lounge bar on the Bastione San Remy. Inside, it's all black and brick; outside, happy drinkers sit on black leather sofas drinking cocktails, listening to jazzy beats and munching pizzas at tables fashioned from studded wooden doors. DJs regularly work the decks.

Emerson   LOUNGE
(www.emersoncafe.it; Viale Poetto 4; ☻9am-1am summer, 11am-5pm winter) Near the fourth bus stop, and one of the most popular of the seafront *chioschi*, this swank place is a bit of everything. Part cocktail lounge, part restaurant and part beach club, it dishes up everything from pasta to *aperitivi*, live music and sunloungers.

Caffè Svizzero   CAFE
(Map p42; Largo Carlo Felice 6; ☻7am-9pm Mon-Sat) At the bottom of Largo Carlo Felice, this Liberty-style place has been a stalwart of Cagliari cafe society since the early 20th century. Anything from tea to cocktails is on offer in the frescoed interior, founded by a group of Swiss almost 100 years ago.

Ritual Caffè   BAR
(Map p42; Via Università 33; ☻8am-3pm Mon, 8am-2am Tue-Fri, 7pm-2am Sat) This arty cafe is hewn out of the limestone rock face. Seek out a snug alcove in the vaulted stone interior for drinks and occasional live music and DJ beats.

Il Merlo Parlante   PUB
(Map p42; Via Portoscalas 69; ☻8pm-2am daily) Cagliari's nearest thing to a student pub, this is a boisterous place with lager on tap, rock

on the stereo, and a young up-for-it international crowd.

Caffè dell'Elfo   CAFE, BAR
(Map p42; Salita Santa Chiara, 4-6 Piazza Yenne; ☻1-3pm & 8pm-2am Mon-Sat) Named after its little elves, this sweet, petite cafe serves tasty *piadine* (flatbread sandwiches) by day. It's a warm, relaxed wine bar by night.

☆ Entertainment

For information on what's going on in town, ask at the tourist office or pick up a copy of the local newspaper *L'Unione Sarda*. Online, you'll find listings at www.sardegna-concerti.com (in Italian). Most of Cagliari's big concerts are held over the summer.

Cagliari has a lively performance scene, comprising classical music, dance, opera and drama. The season generally runs from October to May, although some places also offer a summer line-up of events.

Box Office Tickets   TICKET OUTLET
(Map p42; ☑070 65 74 28; www.boxofficesardegna. it; Viale Regina Margherita 43) Buy major events tickets here, including those for the summer season of stand-up comedy, music and dance at the Anfiteatro Romano.

Teatro Lirico   THEATRE
(Map p38; ☑070 408 22 30; www.teatroliricodi-cagliari.it; Via Sant'Alenixedda) This is Cagliari's premier venue for classical music, opera and ballet. The line-up is fairly traditional but quality is high and concerts are well attended.

Exmà   CULTURAL CENTRE
(Map p38; ☑070 66 63 99; Via San Lucifero 71) Hosts a year-round series of small-scale

concerts, mainly jazz and chamber music. In summer the action moves to the outside courtyard.

🔒 Shopping

Cagliari has a refreshing absence of overtly touristy souvenir shops, although they do exist. Style-conscious shoppers kit themselves out in designer wear on the arcaded Via Roma and boutique-studded Via Giuseppe Garibaldi. Via Giuseppe Mano is dotted with high-street stores as well as snack bars and gelaterias for relaxing between purchases.

You'll find some lovely, low-key artisan shops tucked away in the city's nooks and crannies, particularly in the Marina district.

★**Durke**   CONFECTIONERY
(Map p42; Via Napoli 66; ⊘10.30am-1.30pm & 4.30-8pm Mon-Sat) In Sardinian, *durke* means 'sweet' and they don't come sweeter than this delightful old-fashioned store. Made according to age-old recipes, the sweets here are quite special and some of the best are made with nothing more than sugar, egg whites and almonds. Indulge on fruit-and-nut *papassinos,* moist *amaretti di sardegna* biscuits and *pardulas,* delicate ricotta cheesecakes flavoured with saffron.

Sapori di Sardegna   FOOD
(Map p42; Vico dei Mille 1; ⊘9.30am-9pm) Roberto, his brother and their enthusiastic team do a brisk trade in glorious Sardinian food at this breezy Marina emporium. Stop by here for the finest *pecorino,* salami, *bottarga,* bread, wine and pretty-packed *dolci* (sweets). If you don't have any room in your luggage, staff can arrange to ship orders worldwide.

Antica Enoteca Cagliaritana   WINE
(Map p42; ✆070 66 93 86; Scalette Santa Chiara 21) Wine buffs will enjoy exploring the racks at this specialist wine shop off Piazza Yenne. You can have orders sent anywhere in the world except the US (customs difficulties, apparently).

Sorelle Piredda   FASHION
(Map p42; ✆070 65 07 72; www.sorellepiredda.com; Piazza San Giuseppe 4) For haute couture with history, visit this oh-so-stylish Castello boutique. It's graced with the imaginative designs of the Piredda sisters, whose slinky evening dresses, capes and intricate shawls are inspired by ancient Sardinian motifs and traditional costume.

Loredana Mandas   JEWELLERY
(Map p42; Via Sicilia 31; ⊘9.30am-1pm & 4.30-8pm Mon-Sat) For something very special, seek out this jewellery workshop. You can watch Loredana create the exquisite gold filigree for which Sardinia is so famous, and then maybe buy a piece. A pair of gold earrings will set you back anything from €220 to €2100.

Spazio P   ART
(Map p42; www.spaziop.it; Via Napoli 62; ⊘noon-midnight Tue-Sat) A gallery showcasing contemporary works by up-and-coming artists, with a sleek bar, at the back, for talking art.

ℹ️ Information

Cagliari is dotted with free wi-fi zones, including Piazza Amendola in the Marina district, but annoyingly you can only log in if you have an Italian SIM card (the password is sent to your mobile phone).

TRENINO VERDE

If you're not in a rush, one of the best ways of exploring Sardinia's interior is on the **trenino verde** (✆070 58 02 46; www.treninoverde.com), a slow, narrow-gauge diesel that runs through some of the island's most inhospitable countryside, stopping at isolated rural villages en route. There are four tourist routes: Mandas to Arbatax (5¼ hours, one way/return €20/28); Mandas-Isili-Sorgono (3½ hours, one way/return €15.50/21.50); Macomer to Bosa (two hours, one way/return €11.50/16.50); and Sassari-Tempio-Palau (4½ hours, one way/return €20/28).

Of the tourist routes, the twisting Mandas to Arbatax line is particularly spectacular, crossing the remote highlands of the Parco Nazionale del Golfo di Orosei e del Gennargentu.

From the metro station on Piazza Repubblica in Cagliari, a metro runs to Monserrato where you can connect with trains for Mandas.

The *trenino verde* runs between mid-June and mid-September.

Banks and ATMs are widely available, particularly around the port and station, on Piazza del Carmine and Corso Vittorio Emanuele.

InfoPoint Porto (Map p42; ☑ 070 677 71 87, 338 649 84 98; www.cagliariturismo.it; Molo Sanità, Stazione Marittima; ☺9am-8pm) At the port, this kiosk is handy for city info and maps.

Guardia Medica (☑ 070 52 24 58; Via Talete) For an emergency call-out doctor.

Lamarì (Via Napoli 43; per hr €3; ☺ 8.30am-9pm Mon-Sat) Speedy internet and wi-fi with cheap snacks and drinks on the side.

Main Post Office (Map p42; Piazza del Carmine 27; ☺8am-6.50pm Mon-Fri, 8am-1.15pm Sat)

Ospedale Brotzu (☑ 070 53 92 10; www. aobrotzu.it; Piazzale Ricchi 1) This hospital is northwest of the city centre. Take bus 1 from Via Roma if you need to make a nonemergency visit.

Tourist Office (Map p42; ☑ 070 409 23 06; Palazzo Viceregio, Piazza Palazzo; ☺10am-7pm summer, 10.30am-1.30pm & 3-5.30pm winter) This friendly tourist office in the Castello district is well stocked with city information and maps.

ℹ Getting There & Away

AIR

Cagliari's Elmas airport (p259) is 9km northwest of the city centre. Flights connect with mainland Italian cities: Rome, Milan, Bergamo, Bologna, Florence, Naples, Rome, Turin and Venice. There are flights to European destinations including Barcelona, Brussels, London, Paris, Stuttgart, Vienna and Zurich. In summer, there are additional charter flights.

The main airlines serving Elmas:

Air One (☑ 892444; http://flyairone.com)

Alitalia (☑ 892010; www.alitalia.it)

Easyjet (☑ 199 201840; www.easyjet.com)

Germanwings (☑ 199 257013; www.german-wings.com)

Lufthansa (☑ 199 400044; www.lufthansa.it)

Meridiana (☑ 892928; www.meridiana.it)

Ryanair (☑ 895 8958989; www.ryanair.com)

BOAT

Cagliari's ferry port is just off Via Roma. **Tirrenia** (Map p42; ☑ 892 123; www.tirrenia.it; Via dei Ponente 1) is the main ferry operator in Cagliari, with year-round services to Civitavecchia (€42 to €62 per person), Naples and Palermo (€53 per person). Book tickets at the port or at travel agencies.

BUS

From the main bus station on Piazza Matteotti, **ARST** (Azienda Regionale Sarda Trasporti;

☑800 865042; www.arst.sardegna.it) buses serve nearby Pula (€3, 50 minutes, hourly) and Villasimius (€3.50, 1½ hours, six to eight daily), as well as Oristano (€7, 1½ hours, two daily), Nuoro (€15.50, 2½ to five hours, two daily), Iglesias (€4.50, one to 1½ hours, two daily), Chia (€4, 1¼ hours, 10 daily) and Sassari (€14.50, 3¼ hours, three daily).

Turmo Travel (☑ 078 92 14 87; www.gruppoturmotravel.com) runs a twice daily service to Olbia (€19, 4½ hours) and a daily bus to Santa Teresa di Gallura (€22.50, 5½ hours).

CAR & MOTORCYCLE

The island's main dual-carriage, the SS131 Carlo Felice Hwy, links the capital with Porto Torres via Oristano and Sassari, and Olbia via Nuoro. The SS130 leads west to Iglesias.

The coast roads approaching from the east and west get highly congested in the summer holiday season.

TRAIN

The main **Trenitalia** (www.trenitalia.com) station is located on Piazza Matteotti. Trains from here serve Iglesias (€3.85, one hour, 16 daily), Carbonia (€4.40, one hour, 10 daily), Sassari (€15.75, 3½ to four hours, five daily) and Porto Torres (€16.90, 4¼ hours, one daily) via Oristano (€5.95, one to two hours, 19 daily). A branch line also connects with Olbia (€16.90, 4¼ hours, one daily) and Golfo Aranci (€18.30, five to seven hours, five daily) via Oristano or Chilivani.

ARST (http://arst.sardegna.it, in Italian) runs a metro service from Piazza Repubblica to Monserrato, where you can connect with trains for Dolianova, Mandas and Isili. A single ticket costs €1.20.

ℹ Getting Around

The centre of Cagliari is small enough to explore on foot. The walk up to Il Castello is tough, but there's an elevator at the bottom of the Scalette di Santa Chiara behind Piazza Yenne.

TO/FROM THE AIRPORT

ARST buses run from Piazza Matteotti to Elmas airport (€4, 10 minutes, 32 daily) between 5.20am and 10.30pm. From 9am to 10.30pm departures are every hour and half-past the hour. A taxi will set you back around €20.

BUS

CTM (Consorzio Trasporti e Mobilità; ☑ 070 209 12 10; www.ctmcagliari.it) bus routes cover the city and surrounding area. You might use the buses to reach a handful of out-of-the-way sights, and they come in handy for the Cala Mosca and Poetto beaches. A standard ticket

WORTH A TRIP

A WALK IN THE WOODS

A world away from the urban hustle of Cagliari, **Monte dei Sette Fratelli** (1023m) is the highest point of the remote Sarrabus district. Its granite peaks and woodlands bristling with cork and holm oak, juniper, oleander and myrtle are a haven to wild boar, hawks and golden eagles, and it's one of only three remaining redoubts of the *cervo sardo* (Sardinian deer). Accessible by the SS125, it offers some magnificent hiking, with routes ranging from straightforward strolls to a tough 12km ascent of **Punta Sa Ceraxa** (1016m).

You can pick up a trekking map from the Caserma Forestale Campu Omu, a forestry corps station near the Burcei turn-off on the SS125. Alternatively, contact the **Coop Monte dei Sette Fratelli** (☑ 070 994 72 00; www.montesettefratelli.com; Via Centrale) in Castiadas, a few kilometres inland from the Costa Rei.

From Burcei, a lonely road crawls 8km up to **Punta Serpeddi** (1067m), from where you can gaze out across the whole Sarrabus to Cagliari and the sea.

---

costs €1.20 and is valid for 90 minutes; a daily ticket is €3.

The most useful bus lines are:

Bus 7 Circular route from Piazza Yenne up to Il Castello and back.

Bus 10 From Viale Trento to Piazza Garibaldi via Corso Vittorio Emanuele.

Bus 30 or 31 Along the seafront and up to the sanctuary at Bonaria.

Bus PF or PQ From Piazza Matteotti to Poetto Beach.

CAR & MOTORCYCLE

Parking in the city centre from 9am to 1pm and 4pm to 8pm Monday to Saturday means paying. On-street metered parking – within the blue lines – costs €1 per hour. Alternatively, there's a big car park next to the train station, which costs €1 per hour or €10 for 24 hours. There's no maximum stay.

Driving in the centre of Cagliari is a pain, although given the geography of the town (one big hill), you might consider renting a scooter for a day or two. There's also a **Hertz** (☑ 070 65 10 78; www.hertz.it; Piazza Matteotti 8) on Piazza Matteotti and several car-rental agencies at the airport. Or if you just want to zip about town and over to Poetto, you can rent a Vespa from **Sardegna in Vespa** (☑ 070 24 01 01; www.sardegnainvespa.com; Isola Rent, Elmas airport; Vespa rental per day €52.80).

TAXI

Many hotels and guesthouses arrange airport pick-ups. There are taxi ranks at Piazza Matteotti, Piazza Repubblica and on Largo Carlo Felice. Otherwise you can call the radio taxi firms **Quattro Mori** (☑ 070 40 01 01; www.cagliaritaxi.com) and **Rossoblù** (☑ 070 66 55; www.radiotaxirossoblu.com).

THE SARRABUS

Stretching east and north of Cagliari, the lonely Sarrabus is one of Sardinia's least-populated and least-developed areas. In its centre rise the bushy green peaks of the Monte dei Sette Fratelli, a miraculously wild hinterland where some of the island's last remaining deer wander undisturbed.

East of Poetto the SP17 hugs the coast prettily (if precariously), providing spectacular views of the azure sea scalloped by crescent-shaped coves like Cala Regina, Kal'e Moru and Solanas. A few kilometres short of Villasimius, a winding road veers south along the peninsula to Capo Carbonara, Sardinia's most southeasterly point, where you're more likely to encounter flocks of inquisitive sheep and goats than cars in the low season.

Villasimius & Capo Carbonara

POP 3600

Once a quiet fishing village surrounded by pines and *macchia* (Mediterranean scrub), Villasimius has grown into one of Sardinia's most popular southern resorts and makes a handy base for exploring the fine sandy bays and transparent waters on this stretch of coast. In summer it's a lively, cheerful place, although activity all but dies out in winter.

If you're around on the second Sunday of July, don't miss the Festa della Madonna del Naufrago, a striking seaborne procession to a spot off the coast where a statue of the Virgin Mary lies on the seabed in honour of shipwrecked sailors.

DON'T MISS

DIVING OFF CAPO CARBONARA

Although the tip of the cape remains a military zone off limits to visitors, the azure waters around Capo Carbonara are a **marine reserve** (www.ampcapocarbonara.it), accessible with an authorised diving company. The reserve includes Isola dei Cavoli, Secca dei Berni and Isola di Serpentara just off the coast from Villasimius. **Morgan Diving** (070 80 50 59; www.morgandiving.com), based at the Porto Turistico, Quartu Sant'Elena, is a licensed operator, as is **Air Sub** (070 79 20 33; www.airsub.com; Via Roma 121) in Villasimius. Both outfits lead dives to a number of sites, including the Secca di Santa Caterina, an underwater mountain. Reckon on €36 to €90 for a dive, depending on location and level of difficulty.

◉ Sights

★ Capo Carbonara   CAPE

If you do just one day trip from Villasimius, make it the 15-minute drive south to Capo Carbonara, a protected marine park. The promontory dips spectacularly into the crystal-clear water of the Med. Besides perfect conditions for scuba divers, the area has some gorgeously secluded bays with white quartz sand, backed by cliffs cloaked in *macchia* and wildflowers. Walking trails teeter off in all directions. The drive takes you past the Notteri salt lake, where flamingos and shearwaters flock in winter.

Museo Archeologico   MUSEUM

(Via Frau 5; adult/reduced €3/1.50, combined ticket with Fortezza Vecchia €4/2.50; ☺9am-1pm Tue-Fri, 10am-1pm & 3-6pm Sat & Sun) Villasimius' little archaeology museum harbours a collection of Roman and Phoenician artefacts, as well as various odds and ends recovered from a 15th-century Spanish shipwreck.

Fortezza Vecchia   HISTORIC SITE

(070 793 02 32; Via Frau 5; admission €1, combined ticket with Museo Archeologico €4/2.50) Perched on cliffs close to Capo Carbonara, this ruined 14th-century fortress dates back to when the Aragonese controlled the island. The views are more extraordinary than the stronghold itself. Visits by appointment only.

✷ Activities

In town the main activity is browsing shops and enjoying the atmosphere. Boat tours tend to operate from May to September.

Spiaggia del Riso   BEACH

Just south of town lies Spiaggia del Riso. One of Villasimius' most striking beaches, this beautiful arc of pale golden sand is lapped by azure waters and scattered with granite boulders polished smooth by the sea.

Stagno Notteri   LAGOON

Running all the way to Villasimius, this lagoon often hosts flamingos in winter. On its seaward side is the stunning Spiaggia del Simius beach with its Polynesian-blue waters.

Fiore di Maggio   BOAT TOURS

(393 0733195, 340 4862894; www.fioredimaggio.eu; Località Campulongu; per adult/child incl lunch €45/25) These daily boat tours, departing at 10.30am and returning at 5pm, are a superb way to see the hidden bays and islands of the Capo Carbonara marine reserve. Take your bathers if you fancy a dip.

Harry Tours   BOAT TOUR

(338 3774051; www.harrystours.com) At the Porto Turistico, about 3km outside of the town centre, you can arrange boat tours (€70 per person including lunch) and dives (from €36) to nearby reefs and wrecks.

✗ Eating

Via Roma and Via del Mare are safe bets for a quick pizza, coffee or gelato, and self-caterers can find supermarkets and grocery stores in the resort centre.

Ristorante Le Anforè   MEDITERRANEAN €€

(070 79 20 32; www.hotelleanfore.com; Via Pallaresus 16; meals €30; ☺dinner Tue-Sun) The chef's love of fresh local produce shines through in Sardinian dishes such as *burrida* (marinated dogfish) and spaghetti with *ricci* at this highly regarded restaurant. There's alfresco dining on the verandah overlooking gardens.

Ristorante La Lanterna   SARDINIAN €€

(070 79 00 13; Via Roma 62; meals around €30; ☺closed lunch Mon) With two fishmongers just down the road, it's no surprise that this cordial restaurant specialises in seafood. Specialities such as *fregola* with plump

mussels and clams or baby octopus in spicy sauce go well with a litre of house white (€7.50). In summer you can dine alfresco in the small garden.

ℹ Information

Just off central Piazza Gramsci, the **tourist office** (☑ 070 793 02 71; www.villasimiusweb. com; Piazza Giovanni XXIII; ☻ 8am-8pm Mon-Fri) can provide information on activities in the town.

ℹ Getting There & Around

Buses run to and from Cagliari (€3.50, 1½ hours, six to eight daily) throughout the year.

If you want to rent your own wheels (a good idea, as most of the beaches are a few kilometres out of town), **Edilrent Simius** (☑ 070 792 80 37; www.edilrentsimius.com; Via Roma 77) hires out bikes (€6.50 to €10 per day), scooters (€30 to €55) and cars (€63 to €80).

Costa Rei

Stretching along Sardinia's southeastern coast, the Costa Rei's resorts are fairly nondescript, but the beaches are out of this world. The long sweep of coastline is frosted with pearly white strands of beach, lapped by azure blue water that beggars belief.

From Villasimius, take the SP17 as it follows the coast north. The road actually runs a couple of hundred metres inland, but you can access the signposted beaches via the dirt tracks that branch off the main road. Crystal-clear waters and the occasional snack-cum-cocktail bar await.

About 25km out of Villasimius you hit **Cala Sinzias**, a pretty sandy *spiaggia* with two campsites. Continue for a further 6km and you come to the Costa Rei resort proper, a holiday village full of villas, shops, bars, clubs and a few indifferent eateries. **Spiaggia Costa Rei** is, like the beaches to its south and north, a dazzling white strand lapped by remarkably clear blue-green water.

At the resort, **Butterfly Servic** (☑ 070 99 10 91; www.butterflyservice.it; Via Colombo; ☻ 9am-1pm & 4-7.30pm Mon-Sat, 10am-1pm & 4.30-7.30pm Sun) is an all-purpose agency offering everything from internet access to bike, scooter and car hire, as well as excursions along the coast to the **Parco Settel Fratelli**.

North of the resort, **Spiaggia Piscina Rei** is a continuation of the blinding white sand and turquoise water theme, with a camping ground fenced in just behind it. A couple more beaches fill the remaining length of coast up to **Capo Ferrato**, beyond which drivable dirt trails lead north.

The same ARST buses from Cagliari to Villasimius continue around to Costa Rei, taking about half an hour.

Nuraghe Asoru

Nuraghe Asoru is the best example of a *nuraghe* in southeastern Sardinia, which is largely devoid of archaeological interest. About 5km inland of San Priamo, it stands north of the SS125. Its central *tholos* (conical tower) is in reasonable shape, but it doesn't really compare to Sardinia's more important *nuraghi*.

Muravera & Torre Salinas

POP 5300

On the flood plain of the Fiume Flumendosa (Flumendosa River), Muravera is not an especially interesting place. An agricultural town, it's best known for its citrus fruit, which it celebrates on the second Sunday before Easter with the **Sagra degli Agrumi** (Citrus Fair).

South of town, the lagoons and beaches of Torre Salinas are picturesquely spread out beneath a Spanish watchtower. It's a seemingly untouched area, centred on the **Stagno dei Colostrai**, winter home to flamingos. On the seaward side of the lagoon, **Spiaggia Torre delle Saline** is the first in a line of dazzling beaches that continues north to the mouth of the Fiume Flumendosa.

In Muravera, you can get a decent bite at **Ristorante Pizzeria Su Nuraxi** (☑ 070 993 09 91; www.sunuraxi.com; Via Roma 257; pizzas from €5, meals around €25) on the main road. It's a relaxed place that serves hearty meats and good pizzas.

Three weekday ARST buses run from Cagliari to Muravera (€6, three hours) via Villasimius. There are quicker inland services (€6, one hour 40 minutes, five Monday to Saturday, two Sunday).

Iglesias & the Southwest

Best Places to Eat

➡ Trattoria Pintadera (p61)

➡ Zia Leunora (p76)

➡ Ristorante L'Oasi (p71)

➡ Agriturismo L'Oasi del Cervo (p66)

Best Places to Stay

➡ B&B Mare Monti Miniere (p203)

➡ Hotel Riviera (p204)

➡ Hotel Luci del Faro (p204)

➡ Agriturismo L'Aquila (p203)

Why Go?

Silky beaches, prehistoric treasures, haunting mines – Sardinia's southwest is rich in history and natural beauty. The main drawcard is its thrilling coastline, which stretches from the great untamed sands of the Costa Verde to the cliff-bound coves of the Iglesiente and the seductive bays of the Costa del Sud. Offshore, the Isola di San Pietro and Isola di Sant'Antioco boast their own distinctive charms: San Pietro with its animated and instantly likeable atmosphere, and Sant'Antioco with its earthy character and rich archaeological legacy.

Inland, there's a rather melancholy feel to the area around Iglesias, the southwest's charming main town. This was once the island's mining heartland and the silent hills are today pitted with abandoned mines, many of which have been resurrected as museums and visitor attractions. Further in, the Marmilla's voluptuous green countryside harbours rich archaeological pickings, including Sardinia's greatest *nuraghe* (Bronze Age settlement), the Unesco-listed Nuraghe Su Nuraxi.

Road Distance (km)

	Arbus	Carbonia	Iglesias	Portovesme
Carbonia	57			
Iglesias	34	23		
Portovesme	55	14	21	
Pula	91	70	77	84

IGLESIAS

POP 27,500

Surrounded by the skeletons of Sardinia's once-thriving mining industry, Iglesias is a historic town that bubbles in the summer and slumbers in the colder months. Its historic centre, an appealing ensemble of lived-in piazzas, sun-bleached buildings and Aragonese-style wrought-iron balconies, creates an atmosphere that's as much Iberian as Sardinian – a vestige of its time as a Spanish colony. Visit at Easter to experience a quasi-Seville experience during the extraordinary drum-beating processions.

History

Although named after its churches – Iglesias means churches in Spanish – the town has a long history as a mining centre. The Carthaginians are known to have mined the surrounding area, as did the Romans who extracted silver and lead, and established a mining town, Metalla, in the hills south of modern-day Fluminimaggiore.

Iglesias itself was founded in the 13th century by Ugolino della Gherardesca. A Pisan noble with a shrewd head for business, Ugolino reopened the Roman mines and organised the town, which was originally called Villa di Chiesa, as a Tuscan-style *comune* (self-regulating town) with its own currency, rights and laws. These laws were subsequently codified and recorded in a book known as the Breve di Villa di Chiesa.

The city thrived but in 1324 it fell to the Catalan-Aragonese, who promptly renamed it Iglesias. More seriously, they closed its mines, and for the next 500 years the pits lay abandoned until private entrepreneurs, such as Quintino Sella, revived their fortunes in the 19th century. As a nascent industrial centre in a resurgent and soon-to-be-united Italy, Iglesias once again flourished until WWII and modern economics tolled its death knell in the 1970s.

◉ Sights

Much of the pleasure of visiting Iglesias lies in the small medieval centre. There are no great must-see sights, but the narrow, car-free lanes and suggestive piazzas are in good nick and are much appreciated by locals who flock here to browse the shops and hang out in the bars. It's also in the *centro storico* (historic centre) that you'll find many of the churches that give the city its name.

★**Cattedrale di Santa Chiara**　　CATHEDRAL
(Duomo; Piazza del Municipio) Dominating the eastern flank of Piazza del Municipio, the Cattedrale di Santa Chiara boasts a lovely Pisan-flavoured facade and a chequerboard stone bell tower. The church was originally built in the late 13th century, but it was given a comprehensive makeover in the 16th century, which accounts for its current Catalan Gothic look.

Inside, the highlight is a gilded altarpiece that once held the relics of St Antiochus. This was originally on the Isola di Sant'Antioco but it was bought to Iglesias in the 17th century to protect it from the threat of pirate raids. And although the clerics were later forced to return the relics they managed to hold on to the altarpiece.

Flanking the cathedral on the piazza is the bishop's residence, the **Palazzo Vescovile**, while opposite is Iglesias' neoclassical **Municipio** (town hall). Neither of these buildings is open to the public.

★**Chiesa di San Francesco**　　CHURCH
(Piazza San Francesco; ⊙8am-noon & 4-8pm) From Piazza del Municipio, Via Pullo leads to the dainty rose red trachyte of the Chiesa di San Francesco. Built over a 200-year period between the 14th and 16th centuries, this small church is a wonderful example of Catalan Gothic architecture with its simple austere facade, circular windows and single-nave interior. Flanking the nave are a series of chapels squeezed in between the buttresses.

Chiesa di Santa Maria delle Grazie　　CHURCH
(Piazza Manzoni 7; ⊙6.45am-8pm) Originally constructed at the end of the 13th century, the modest Chiesa di Santa Maria delle Grazie retains little of its original form. About the only surviving element is the base of the medieval facade, which is topped by a pinky baroque structure, added in the 17th and 18th centuries.

Piazza Quintino Sella　　PIAZZA
Iglesias' focal square, Piazza Quintino Sella was laid out in the 19th century in what was at the time a field outside the city walls. It soon became a central meeting place and still today it throngs with people during the evening *passeggiata* (stroll). The statue in the centre commemorates Quintino Sella (of Sella e Mosca wine fame), a 19th-century statesman and champion of the area's mining industry.

Iglesias & the Southwest Highlights

1 Escaping the coastal crowds on the **Spiaggia di Piscinas** (p66), a fabulous, remote beach on the Costa Verde.

2 Coming face to face with wild horses on Sardinia's high plain **La Giara di Gesturi** (p80).

3 Revelling in inspiring sea views at **Capo Sandalo** (p72) on the Isola di San Pietro.

4 Travelling southern Sardinia's magnificent coastal road, the **Strada Panoramica della Costa del Sud** (p74).

5 Poking around Roman ruins at the beautifully sited **Tempio di Antas** (p65), north of Iglesias.

6 Peering into the long-dead past at the **Necropoli di Montessu** (p68), a prehistoric cemetery set in a rocky amphitheatre.

7 Giving yourself up to the sombre, spine-tingling atmosphere of Iglesias' **Settimana Santa** (p61) processions.

8 Delving into the mysteries of Sardinia's nuraghic culture at the **Nuraghe Su Nuraxi** (p79).

Iglesias

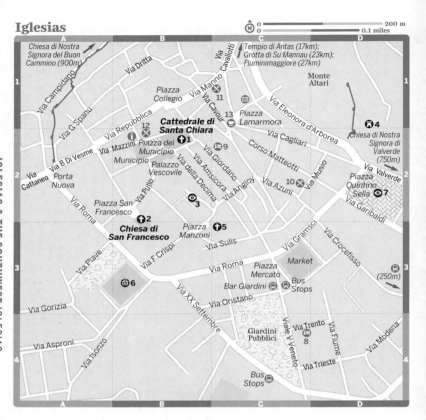

Castello Salvaterra   CASTLE
(Via Montartai) Just off Piazza Quintino Sella, litter-strewn stairs lead to a stout square tower. This is all that remains of Castello Salvaterra, the once-mighty Pisan fortress of Ugolino della Gherardesca. Behind it a path leads along a short section of the town's original crenellated wall.

To get a better idea of what the city looked like before the walls came down, head to Via Campidano, where a stretch of 14th-century wall remains defiantly in place, complete with towers.

Archivio Storico   HISTORIC SITE
(☎078 12 48 50; Via delle Carceri 12; ⊗9am-1pm & 3.30-5.30pm Mon, Wed & Fri) Records illustrating Iglesias' past are kept in the Archivio Storico, the city's historical archive. Of particular interest is the 1327 Breve di Villa di Chiesa, the statute book of the medieval city.

Museo dell'Arte Mineraria
MUSEUM

(☑ 328 8094091; www.museoartemineraria.it; Via Roma 47; adult/reduced €4/2; ☺ 6.30-8.30pm Sat & Sun summer, by appointment rest of year) Just outside the historic centre, Iglesias' main museum is dedicated to the town's mining heritage. It displays up to 70 extraction machines, alongside tools and a series of thought-provoking black-and-white photos. But to get a real taste of the claustrophobic conditions in which the miners worked, duck down into the re-created tunnels. These were dug by mining students and were used to train senior workers until WWII when they were used as air-raid shelters.

Chiesa di Nostra Signora di Valverde
CHURCH

(Via Cappuccini) Next to the town cemetery about 750m from Piazza Quintino Sella, this is another of Iglesias' historic churches. It retains little of its 13th-century structure except for the elegant facade, similar to the Duomo's.

Chiesa di Nostra Signora del Buon Cammino
CHURCH

To the northwest of the town centre, this white 18th-century church is perched on a tall hill commanding lovely views.

🎊 Festivals & Events

Settimana Santa
RELIGIOUS

(☺ Mar/Apr) In the week before Easter Iglesias celebrates its Spanish roots and traditions in a series of dramatic religious processions. Every night between Holy Tuesday and Good Friday, hooded members of religious brotherhoods bear effigies of the Virgin Mary and Christ around town to the tune of a slow, deathly drumbeat.

Estate Medioevale Iglesiente
SUMMER FESTIVAL

(☺ Aug) Iglesias' Medieval Summer comprises a series of themed events that involve much dressing up and flag-waving. Highlights include a huge costumed procession on 13 August.

🍴 Eating & Drinking

★ Trattoria Pintadera
TRATTORIA €€

(☑ 346 6770183; Via Manno 22; meals €30; ☺ 12.30-2pm & 7.30-11pm) A welcoming family-run eatery in the *centro storico,* Pintadera is the sort of place that gives Italian trattorias a good name. In a rustic stone *palazzo* (mansion) you sit down to hearty local pastas – try the ravioli stuffed with

potato and mint – and buttery chargrilled steaks. Great food, a warm atmosphere, and excellent value for money; it's a top choice.

Villa di Chiesa
RISTORANTE, PIZZERIA €€

(☑ 0781 3 16 41; Piazza del Municipio 9-10; meals €30, pizzas €6; ☺ 12.30-3pm & 7.30-11pm Tue-Sun) The elegant confines of Piazza del Municipio set the stage for alfresco dining at this long-standing summer favourite. In winter diners move inside to feast on pizza, pasta and seafood whilst being serenaded by local crooners. Menu stalwarts include *culurgiones* (traditional Sardinian ravioli), and *sebadas* (light pastry filled with cheese and honey).

Gazebo Medioevale
SARDINIAN €€

(☑ 078 13 08 71; Via Musio 21; meals €25-30; ☺ noon-2.30pm & 8-11pm Mon-Sat) A historic local eatery, Gazebo Medioevale looks the part with its exposed-brick walls, stone arches and Sardinian masks. The food is fresh and authentic, with dishes ranging from grilled *tagliata* (steak) to seafood pasta and vegetable couscous. No credit cards.

Caffè Lamarmora
CAFE

(Piazza Lamarmora 6; ☺ 6am-1pm & 3-9.30pm) Occupying a towering 19th-century *palazzo* covered in Liberty-style advertising (these were added in 1904), this landmark cafe is ideally placed for a quick coffee fix.

ℹ Information

Banco BNL (Via Roma 29)

Post office (Vico Mercato Vecchio; ☺ 8.20am-1.35pm Mon-Fri, to 12.35pm Sat)

Tourist office (☑ 0781 27 45 05; www.sportelloiatiglesias.it; Via Mazzini 2; ☺ 10am-noon & 3-6pm Mon-Sat)

ℹ Getting There & Away

BUS

Intercity buses arrive at and depart from Via XX Settembre and Piazza Mercato near the Giardini Pubblici.

Get timetable information and tickets from **Bar Giardini** (Piazza Mercato 10) across the road from the Piazza Mercato stops.

Buses run to Cagliari (€4.50, one to 1½ hours, two daily) and Carbonia (€2.50, 50 minutes, eight daily) as well as closer destinations such as Funtanamare (€1.50, 20 minutes, 11 daily).

CAR & MOTORCYCLE

From Cagliari, it's 55km to Iglesias on the dual-carriageway SS130. Alternatively, you can take the SS195 coastal road from Cagliari to connect with the SS126.

From the north, the SS126 drops south from Oristano to Guspini and then winds through the hills via Arbus and Fluminimaggiore.

TRAIN
Up to eight direct trains run daily to/from Cagliari (€3.85, one hour).

AROUND IGLESIAS

Monteponi Mines

About 2km west of Iglesias, the sprawling, now-abandoned Monteponi mining complex was once one of Sardinia's most important producers of lead, zinc and silver. Extraction on the site started in around 1324 and continued on and off until 1992, when the entire operation transferred to Campo Pisano across the valley.

Regular buses run from Via Cattaneo in Iglesias to the mines (€1, 30 minutes).

Galleria Villamarina   MINE
(☑ 0781 49 13 00; www.igeaspa.it; adult/reduced €8/4.50) Guided visits to Monteponi take in this underground tunnel, which connected the mine's two main shafts: the Pozzo Vittorio Emanuele, which was used for access and the transport of material, and the Pozzo Sella, which served to house water pumps.

Visits were temporarily suspended at the time of writing; see the IGEA website for updates.

Grotta di Santa Barbara

Grotta di Santa Barbara   CAVE
(☑ 0781 49 13 00; www.igeaspaa.it; adult/reduced €12/6) Some 4km from Iglesias, the Grotta di Santa Barbara lies deep within the abandoned San Giovanni mine. The walls of the single enormous chamber are pock-marked with dark-brown crystals and white calcite, while stalactites and stalagmites give the impression of a ghostly underground forest.

Visits were temporarily suspended at the time of writing; see the IGEA website for updates.

Funtanamare

Funtanamare Beach   BEACH
The nearest beach to Iglesias is at Funtanamare (also spelt Fontanamare). A long strip of golden sand backed by dunes and

ⓘ GUIDED MINE VISITS

Visits to the mines in the Iglesias hinterland are run by **IGEA** (☑ 0781 49 13 00; www.igeaspa.it), a regional firm that seeks to promote interest in the area's mining history. Unfortunately, poor financial health has forced the company to temporarily suspend visits to the following sites:

➡ Galleria Villamarina, Monteponi Mines

➡ Grotta di Santa Barbara

➡ Porto Flavia, Masua

➡ Galleria Henry, Buggerru

To check the current situation, contact IGEA directly.

fertile farmland, it's a hugely popular spot, although it rarely gets too crowded, if nothing else because it's so long. Strong winds make it a surfer favourite, particularly when the *maestrale* (northwest wind) is blowing.

Up to 11 daily buses run from Iglesias to the beach (€1.50, 20 minutes), and there's plenty of parking if you want to drive. Buses also continue to a point known as **Plage Mesu**, further south along the same strand.

Domusnovas

Some 10km east of Iglesias, the unremarkable town of Domusnovas sits at the centre of one of Sardinia's top rock-climbing areas. The outlying countryside is peppered with limestone rocks, cliffs and caves, many of which are ideal for sports climbing.

◉ Sights & Activities

Grotta di San Giovanni   CAVE
Four kilometres north of Domusnovas, the Grotta di San Giovanni is well worth checking out. An 850m-long natural cave-gallery adorned with stalactites and stalagmites, it's free to enter and is illuminated between 9am and 9pm. If you're feeling peckish there's a bar-restaurant by the car park at the entrance.

Rock Climbing   ROCK CLIMBING
There are about 500 routes for both novice and experienced climbers. These range from simple, single-pitch walls to tough overhangs, such as the 9a+/b Marina superstar route, which is considered one of

Italy's hardest rock climbs. Experts say climatic and rock conditions are at their best between early autumn and late spring. For more technical information, check out www.climb-europe.com/RockClimbingSardinia.html and www.sardiniaclimb.com.

ⓘ Getting There & Away

Up to 10 daily buses connect Iglesias and Domusnovas (€1.20, 15 minutes).

THE IGLESIENTE

To the north and west of Iglesias, the mountainous landscape is picturesque and strangely haunting. Wild green scrub cloaks the silent hills in a soft, verdant down, while abandoned houses serve as a poignant reminder of the mining communities that once thrived here. The coast is dramatic, offering superb seascapes.

Nebida

From Funtanamare, the SP83 coastal road affords spectacular views as it snakes its way northwards. After 5.5km you come to the small, rather drab village of Nebida, a former mining settlement sprawled along the road high above the sea. The main reason to stop here is to enjoy the mesmerising views from the Belvedere.

◉ Sights

Belvedere   VIEWPOINT
This panoramic terrace, accessible by a cliffside path from Nebida's southern entrance, commands fabulous views. Dominating the seascape is the 133m-high **Scoglio Pan di Zucchero** (Sugarloaf Rock), the largest of several *faraglioni* (sea stacks) that rise out of the glassy blue waters against a backdrop of sheer white cliffs.

The gutted shell of a building you see beneath you is the **Laveria Lamarmora**, a former mineral washing plant.

Spiaggia di Portu Banda   BEACH
About 500m north of Nebida village, a side road leads down to a small pebble beach at **Portu Banda**.

ⓘ Getting There & Away

Local buses run between Iglesias and Masua, stopping off at Nebida (€2, 30 minutes, 11 daily).

Masua

A few kilometres north of Nebida, Masua is another former mining centre. Seen from above, it looks a pretty-ugly prospect, but it's not entirely without interest.

Descending into town, the road leads past an abandoned mining complex to a beach that, while not Sardinia's best, is pleasant enough with its stunning close-ups of the Scoglio Pan di Zucchero. The main drawcard, though, is the mining port of Porto Flavia.

◉ Sights

Porto Flavia   PORT
(☑ 0781 49 13 00; www.igeaspa.it; adult/reduced €8/4.50) A marvel of early-20th-century engineering, Porto Flavia is a port dug into cliffs 50m above the sea. Consisting of two 600m tunnels and a mobile arm, it was used to load zinc and lead ore directly onto cargo ships waiting in the waters below.

To find it, head towards Masua's beach from where a road leads back uphill and around the coast for about 2.5km. At the time of writing visits were temporarily suspended; see the IGEA website for updates.

Built in 1924, Porto Flavia revolutionised the system of shipping minerals from Masua. Before it was built, the mined ore had to be loaded onto boats that had been hauled up onto the beach. These then sailed to Carloforte to transfer their loads to larger cargo vessels. However, Porto Flavia enabled the ore to be transported directly from underground depots to the cargo ships by means of a conveyor belt (in the lower of the two tunnels) and an ingenious mechanical arm.

Cala Domestica

From Masua the SP83 rises quickly in a series of tight turns as it works its way around Monte Guardianu towards Buggerru. Five kilometres before Buggerru, beach lovers should take the signposted turn-off for Cala Domestica.

Cala Domestica Beach   BEACH
A sandy beach wedged into a natural inlet between craggy rocks, Cala Domestica is a heavenly spot. Its shallow blue waters are ideal for a swim whilst surfers can take to the waves that sometimes curl up here. A walk along the rocky path to the right of the beach brings you to a smaller, more sheltered side strand.

Facilities are thin on the ground here – so bring your own shade in summer – but there's a pay car park and a small snack bar.

Buggerru & Portixeddu

POP 1110

A popular resort with a small harbour and a rash of holiday apartments, Buggerru is the biggest village on this stretch of coastline. Set within the natural stone walls of a steep valley, it was established in 1860 and by the early 20th century had developed into an important mining centre with a population of around 6000. For a long time it was accessible only by sea, a fact which forced it into enterprising self-sufficiency – it had its own electricity supply before Cagliari and Sassari, as well as a hospital, a mutual benefit society and a small theatre. It wasn't all roses though, and in 1904 Buggerru's miners downed tools and went on strike – the first ever recorded in Sardinia. Later, the closure of mines in WWI and then in the 1930s forced many migrant workers to leave and the local population to plummet.

A couple of klicks north of Buggerru, the tiny tourist village of Portixeddu boasts a fabulous sandy beach, the Spiaggia di Portixeddu.

◎ Sights & Activities

Galleria Henry   MINE
(☑ 0781 49 13 00; www.igeaspa.it; adult/reduced €8/4.50) A remnant of Buggerru's day as a mining centre, the Galleria Henry is a 1km-long tunnel that was dug in 1865 to allow a small train to transport minerals from underground depots to washing plants.

A highlight of the hour-long gallery tour is the view down to the sea 50m below.

At the time of writing, visits were temporarily suspended; see the IGEA website for updates.

Spiaggia Portixeddu   BEACH
About 2km beyond Buggerru, Spiaggia Portixeddu is one of the best beaches in the area. A long sandy strip, it extends for 3km up to the Rio Mannu, the river marking the end of the Iglesiente coast.

Mormora   BOATING
(☑ 338 9176708) To take to the local waters, this outfit runs boat tours (from €30 per person) and hires out boats (from €90 per half-day plus fuel) from Buggerru's Porto Turistico (Tourist Harbour).

✖ Eating

L'Ancora   TRATTORIA
(☑ 0781 5 49 03; Via degli Asfodeli 6, Portixeddu; meals €25-30; ⊗ daily Jul & Aug, closed Wed) One of the few year-round options in this neck of the woods, L'Ancora is a small family-run trattoria overlooking the beach at Portixeddu. Seafood reigns, so get things started with a rich antipasto before digging into classic crowd-pleasers such as spaghetti with clams and *bottarga* (mullet roe) and fried fish.

❶ Information

Tourist office (☑ 0781 5 40 93; ⊗ 10.30am-12.30pm Tue, Wed, Fri & Sat & 5.30-7.30pm Tue-Sun) Situated on the SP83 coastal road above Buggerru; has information on the town and its environs.

Fluminimaggiore

POP 2960

A pretty but nauseatingly winding 26km stretch of the SS126 leads from Iglesias to Fluminimaggiore, an uninspiring town with a couple of museums and a few modest eateries. It's a disaffected place and, like Orgosolo in central Sardinia, has vented its unhappy condition in murals around the town, many of which hark back to better days with real nostalgia.

The town itself is of little interest, but in its environs you'll find the Grotta di Su Mannau and the Roman Tempio di Antas, both worth a visit.

◎ Sights

Grotta di Su Mannau   CAVE
(www.sumannau.it; adult/reduced €10/6; ⊗ 9.30am-5.30pm Easter-Jun, to 6.30pm Jul-Oct) A few kilometres south of Fluminimaggiore, this is the largest cave system of its sort so far discovered in the Iglesiente. The standard 50-minute tour passes through several lake chambers and the Archaeological Room, so-called because it's thought to have once housed a water temple. Finally you'll reach the Pozzo Rodriguez (Rodriguez Well), home to an impressive 8m column, formed by a stalagmite and stalactite fusing together.

More exciting cave tours are also possible, taking in dramatic chambers like the White Room and the opalescent waters of the Pensile Lake. A six-to-eight-hour tour leads to the cave's crowning glory, the Virgin Room, where you can admire wonderful aragonites and snow white slopes of solidified calcium.

These excursions (from €40 to €80 per person) need to be organised in advance.

★ **Tempio di Antas**   RUINS
(www.startuno.it; adult/reduced €4/3; ⏱10am-1pm & 5-8pm summer, 10am-1pm & 4-7pm winter) An impressive Roman temple set in bucolic scenery 9km south of Fluminimaggiore, the Tempio di Antas has stood in isolation since the 3rd century AD. Built by the emperor Caracalla, it was constructed over a 6th-century-BC Punic sanctuary, which was itself set over an earlier nuraghic settlement. In its Roman form, the temple was dedicated to Sardus Pater, a Sardinian deity worshipped by the nuraghic people as Babai and by the Punic as Sid, god of warriors and hunters.

After lying abandoned for centuries, the temple was discovered in 1836 and extensively restored in 1967. Most impressively, the original Ionic columns were excavated and re-erected. At the foot of these columns you can make out remains of the temple's Carthaginian predecessor, which the Romans cannibalised to erect their version.

From the site several paths branch off into the surrounding countryside. One of them, the **Strada Romana**, leads from near the ticket office to what little remains of the original nuraghic settlement and on to the Grotta di Su Mannau, 2.5km away.

❶ Getting There & Away

Up to 10 daily buses link Iglesias with Fluminimaggiore (€2, 45 minutes). To get to Grotta di Su Mannau and Tempio di Antas, ask the driver to drop you off on the main road, from where you'll have to walk the last couple of kilometres.

COSTA VERDE

One of Sardinia's great untamed coastal stretches, the Costa Verde (Green Coast) extends northwards from Capo Pecora to the small resort of Torre dei Corsari. Named after the green *macchia* (Mediterranean scrub) that covers much of its mountainous hinterland, it's an area of wild, exhilarating beauty and spectacular beaches.

There's no road which follows the entire length of the Costa, so if you're driving northwards from Portixeddu (and you really do need to drive to get the best out of this area), you have to head inland along the SS126 towards Arbus and Guspini.

WORTH A TRIP

CASCATA SA SPENDULA

The wooded countryside around Villacidro, an agricultural town best known for its saffron-based liqueur, harbours a number of striking waterfalls. Chief among these is the Cascata Sa Spendula, where the waters of the Rio Coxinas crash down an imposing rock face en route to the Campidano plain.

To get to the Cascata from Villacidro, head north for Gonnosfanadiga and follow the signs; it's about 1.5km.

Arbus
POP 6490

Sprawled along the slopes of Monte Linas, Arbus' granite old town is home to one of Sardinia's most original museums.

◉ Sights

Museo del Coltello Sardo   MUSEUM
(☎070 975 92 20; www.museodelcoltello.it; Via Roma 15; ⏱9am-12.30pm & 3.30-7.30pm Mon-Fri, by appointment Sat & Sun) FREE Just off Piazza Mercato, the Museo del Coltello Sardo is dedicated to the ancient Sardinian art of knife-making. The museum was founded by Paolo Pusceddu, whose *s'arburesi* (from Arbus) knives are among the most prized on the island. Check out Signor Pusceddu's historic knife collection and, in the entrance courtyard, one of the world's largest penknives.

✖ Eating

Ristorante Sa Lolla   SARDINIAN €€
(☎070 975 40 04; Via Libertà 225; meals around €25; ⏱Thu-Tue) At the bottom of town, Ristorante Sa Lolla is a simple, unpretentious restaurant good for a filling meal of local country fare. Ignore the decorative gnomes and tuck into tasty meat dishes and bowls of steaming pasta.

❶ Getting There & Away

Buses run to Arbus from Cagliari (€4.50, two hours, six daily weekdays, two Sunday), although it's a pretty long haul.

Montevecchio

Surrounded by wooded hills and granite peaks, Montevecchio was once home to a massive mining complex. This has long since closed and although most people have left, there's still a small village with a handful of inhabitants.

From Montevecchio, the SP65 twists its way through the great green wilderness towards Torre dei Corsari. En route keen hikers can summit **Monte Arcuentu** (785m), one of the last preserves of the *cervo sardo* (Sardinian deer).

◉ Sights

Miniera Montevecchio   MINE

(☑070 97 31 73; www.minieramontevecchio.it; adult/reduced €5/3.50; ☻) At its height in 1865, the Montevecchio complex was Italy's most important zinc and lead mine, employing up to 1100 workers. It remained operative until 1991, since when it has been kept alive as a visitor attraction.

Guided tours take in the mines as well as the Palazzo della Direzione (Management Building), machinery-repair workshops and workers' housing. For booking and details of the monthly visiting times check the website.

✕ Eating

Agriturismo Arcuentu   SARDINIAN €

(☑349 2930241, 070 975 81 68; Località Monte Arcuentu; meals €20-25; ☻booking required) Six kilometres out of Montevecchio, the Agriturismo Arcuentu is a great place to stop for a royal Sardinian feast. Afterwards walk off your meal on the slopes of Monte Arcuentu. You'll see a sign for the *agriturismo* (farmstay accommodation) off the SP65 between Montevecchio and Torre dei Corsari.

★**Agriturismo L'Oasi del Cervo** SARDINIAN €€

(☑347 3011318; www.oasidelcervo.com; Località Is Gennas; meals €25-30; ☻booking required) This working farm is as authentic as it gets. Once you've successfully navigated the 2.5km dirt track (follow the signs off the SP65) and are safely seated at the long wooden table, you're treated to an abundant farmhouse spread of tangy cheeses, cured meats, pastas, succulent roasts and homemade *dolci* (sweets).

Agriturismo L'Aquila   SARDINIAN €€

(☑347 8222460; www.agriturismolaquila.com; Località Is Gennas; meals €25-30; ☻booking required) An isolated farm in the green hills northwest of Montevecchio, this welcoming farm-stay serves delicious country fare and traditional Sardinian desserts. To reach the farm, follow the signs off the SP65 and head up the dirt track for a couple of bumpy kilometres.

Torre dei Corsari

Marking the northernmost point of the Costa Verde, Torre dei Corsari is the area's main

---

COSTA VERDE BEACHES

Difficult to get to but blissfully free of unsightly development, the Costa Verde's beaches are among the wildest and most beautiful in Sardinia. The two most famous are Spiaggia di Scivu and Spiaggia di Piscinas, both signposted off the SS126.

Spiaggia di Scivu A 3km lick of fine sand backed by towering dunes and walls of sandstone, Spiaggia Scivu is the most southerly of the Costa Verde's beaches. To get there take the SS126 and head towards Arbus (if heading north) or Fluminimaggiore (if heading south) and follow the signs about 12km south of Arbus.

These direct you onto a narrow mountain track that leads into the scrub-covered southern heights. After about 13km you eventually arrive at a parking area, where there's a kiosk and freshwater showers in summer. From here, it's a few hundred metres' walk to the beach.

Spiaggia di Piscinas This magnificent beach is a picture of unspoilt beauty. A broad band of golden sand, it's sandwiched between a windswept sea and a vast expanse of dunes flecked by hardy green *macchia* (Mediterranean shrubbery). These towering dunes, known as Sardinia's desert, rise to heights of up to 60m.

The beach is signposted off the SS126 and accessible via Ingurtosu and a 9km dirt track. Once you exit the SS126 for Ingurtosu, the road descends through a valley lined with the abandoned buildings and machinery of a crumbling 19th-century mining settlement.

Facilities at the beach are limited but in summer one or two beach bars offer showers, umbrellas and sun-loungers.

resort. In itself, it's not an especially attractive place, with bland modern buildings and an ugly concrete piazza, but it does have a good **beach**. Stretching for about 1.5km, the broad band of golden sand is sandwiched between an emerald green sea and a range of mountainous dunes which mushroom back into green scrubland. Overlooking the southern end of the beach is the ruined watchtower from which the town takes its name. The top end of the beach, known as **Pistis**, is a good long walk away or an 8km drive via **Sant'Antonio di Santadi**. There is pay parking at both ends.

Note that Torre dei Corsari is a summer town, so if you're arriving in winter you'll find almost everything shut. That said, you can usually stock up at the **supermarket** (☎070 97 72 45; Piazza Stella Maris; ⊙8am-1pm & 5-8pm) on the central square.

CARBONIA & AROUND

South of Iglesias, the SS126 unfolds into flatter, less-inspiring country as it runs down to the south's second-largest city, Carbonia. Carbonia itself is of little interest but there are a couple of interesting sights in the vicinity.

To the west, Portovesme is the embarkation point for ferries to the Isola di San Pietro.

Carbonia

POP 28,700

A modern town fallen on hard times, Carbonia was constructed by Mussolini between 1936 and 1938 to house workers from the nearby Sirai–Serbariù coalfield. But since mining ceased in the area in 1972 it has struggled and there's really little reason to stop off in the town centre. Rather head out to the Grande Miniera di Serbariù and the Museo del Carbone.

◎ Sights

Museo del Carbone   MUSEUM
(☎0781 6 27 27; www.museodelcarbone.it; Grande Miniera di Serbariù; adult/reduced €6/4; ⊙10am-7pm daily summer, 10am-6pm Tue-Sun winter) Housed in Carbonia's decommissioned coal mine (the Grande Miniera di Serbariù) this fascinating museum provides a chastening look into the life of Carbonia's miners. The main exhibition hall displays a collection of machines, photos, equipment and documents, whilst tours into the claustrophobic

mine shafts give a good idea of what it must have been like to work at the coalface.

Monte Sirai   ARCHAEOLOGICAL SITE
(☎0781 6 35 12; SS126 Sulcitana, Località Sirai; adult/reduced €5/3, with guided tour €6/4; ⊙10am-8pm Wed-Sun summer, to 3pm winter) ✍ Monte Sirai, 4km northwest of Carbonia, is crowned by the remnants of a 7th-century-BC fort. Built by the Phoenicians of Sulci (modern Sant'Antioco) in 650 BC, it was taken over a century later by the Carthaginians. Not a lot now remains but among the ruins you can make out the placement of the Carthaginian acropolis and defensive tower, a necropolis, and a *tophet*, a sacred burial ground for children.

ⓘ Getting There & Away

Buses run to/from Via Manno in Carbonia's hilltop centre; for tickets go to Bar Balia at Viale Gramsci 4. Regular services connect with Iglesias (€2.50, 45 minutes), and a host of local towns.

Portoscuso & Portovesme

POP 5240

It doesn't look good as you approach the coast. The enormous chimney stacks of a vast thermoelectric industrial complex rise above the flat landscape, offering a nightmarish landmark and presaging visions of industrial sprawl. But when you reach the coast, you'll discover that the industrial blight is actually at Portovesme, a couple of kilometres east of Portoscuso. Portoscuso itself is an attractive fishing port capped by a Spanish-era tower and surrounded by a tiny warren of agreeable lanes; Portovesme is the main ferry port for the Isola di San Pietro.

There's not a whole lot to do in town other than stroll the colourful streets and enjoy the laid-back atmosphere, but there's a decent sandy **beach** and you can admire views from the 16th-century **watchtower**.

✯ Festivals & Events

Sagra del Tonno   FOOD
(Tuna Festival; ⊙Jun) Held around 13 June, Portoscuso celebrates its local tuna with much festive eating and drinking.

✗ Eating

Ciccittu   PIZZERIA €
(☎0781 51 20 01; Via Vespucci 6; pizzas €6, meals €20-25; ⊙7-10.45pm Wed-Mon) Locals claim this relaxed, congenial eatery serves the best

pizza in town. If that doesn't appeal, there's a full menu of pasta and seafood, including several dishes made with the ubiquitous local tuna.

❶ Getting There & Away

Regular buses run to Portoscuso and neighbouring Portovesme from Iglesias (€2.50, 30 minutes, seven daily) and Carbonia (€2, 35 minutes, nine daily). Buy tickets at the newsagent at Via Giulio Cesare 106.

Saremar (☑0781 50 90 65; www.saremar.it) has up to 15 daily sailings from Portovesme to Carloforte (on the Isola di San Pietro) between 5am and 9.10pm (in summer there's an additional sailing at 11.10pm). The trip takes about 30 minutes and costs €5.50 per person or €17.20 with a small car. Be prepared for queues in summer.

Tratalias

Now a sleepy backwater, Tratalias was once the religious capital of the entire Sulcis area. When Sant'Antioco was abandoned in the 13th century, the Sulcis archdiocese was transferred to the village and the impressive Chiesa di Santa Maria was built. The church today presides over Tratalias' lovingly renovated *borgo antico,* the medieval part of town which was abandoned in the 1950s after water from the nearby Lago di Monte Pranu started seeping into the subsoil. The *borgo* is east of the modern town, off the SS195.

❍ Sights

Chiesa di Santa Maria CHURCH
(Piazza Chiesa; admission incl Museo del Territorio Trataliese €2.50; ⊙9.30am-1pm & 3-5pm Tue-Sun winter, longer hours in summer) Consecrated in 1213, this lovely church is a prime example of Sardinia's Romanesque Pisan architecture. It features a simple facade punctuated by a classic rose window and an austere columned interior. To enter, you have to ask at the nearby Museo del Territorio Trataliese and buy a ticket. Note also that the visiting hours change monthly; for the latest check the local council's website: www.comune.tratalias.ca.it.

Narcao

About 15km northeast of Tratalias, this small town is worth a quick detour for its *murales* (murals), depicting life in the local mines. Its other main attraction is its annual music festival.

✤ Festivals & Events

Narcao Blues Festival MUSIC
(☑0781 87 50 71; www.narcaoblues.it; ⊙Aug) One of Sardinia's top musical events, the Narcao Blues Festival is held in late August. It stages blues, funk, soul and gospel concerts, performed by a cast of top international performers.

Montessu

★Necropoli di
Montessu ARCHAEOLOGICAL SITE
(www.montessu.it; adult/reduced €5/3; ⊙9.30am-6pm Mon, 8.45am-6pm Tue-Sun, to 8pm summer) One of Sardinia's most important archaeological sites, this ancient necropolis occupies a rocky natural amphitheatre in the verdant countryside near Villaperuccio. It dates to the Ozieri period (approximately 3000 BC) and is peppered with primitive tombs known as *domus de janas* (literally 'fairy houses'). Many of these appear as little more than a hole in the wall, although some harbour wonderful relief carvings.

From the ticket booth it's a 500m walk up to the main site. When you first arrive up the stairs from the roadway, to your immediate right is a **Tomba Santuario**, a rectangular foyer followed by three openings into a semicircular tomb area behind. Follow the trail to its right to see a cluster of tombs and then the **Tomba delle Spirali**, where you can clearly make out the raised relief of spirals and symbolic bulls.

To get to the site from Villaperuccio, take the road for Narcao and follow the signs off to the left. It's about 2km.

Santadi

POP 3550
Wine buffs can get to grips with the local vino at Santadi, a busy agricultural centre a few kilometres east of Villaperuccio. The town is home to the biggest winery in the southwest, as well as a small museum. A few kilometres to the south, the Is Zuddas caves are well worth a visit.

❍ Sights

Cantina Santadi WINERY
(☑0781 95 01 27; www.cantinadisantadi.it; Via Cagliari 78; ⊙8am-1pm Mon-Sat & 4.30-6.30pm Tue & Fri) On the road between Santadi and Villaperuccio, this award-winning winery is the place to stock up on local wines. Par-

ticularly good are the highly rated reds Terre Brune and Grotta Rosa.

Museo Etnografico
'Sa Domu Antiga' MUSEUM
(☑ 078 195 59 55; Via Mazzini 37; admission €2.60; ☺ 9am-1pm & 3-5pm Tue-Sun) To get an idea of how villagers lived in the early 20th century, this small museum re-creates a rural worker's typical home.

Le Grotte Is Zuddas CAVE
(☑ 0781 95 57 41; www.grotteiszuddas.com; Località Is Zuddas; adult/reduced €10/7; ☺ 10am-12.15pm & 2.30-6pm summer, shorter hours spring & autumn, closed winter) Five kilometres south of Santadi, the Grotte Is Zuddas is a fascinating cave system. Of particular note are the helictites in the main hall. No one really knows how these weirdly shaped formations were created, although one theory suggests that wind in the cave may have acted on drops dripping off the stalactites.

✦ Festivals & Events

Sa Coia Maurreddina CULTURAL
(Matrimonio Mauritano; ☺ Aug) Like many rural towns, Santadi celebrates its traditions in high style. On the first Sunday of August, townspeople gather for Sa Coia Maurreddina (the Moorish Wedding), a costumed rite accompanied by folk dancing, eating and drinking. At the centre of events, the blushing bride and groom are transported to the main square on a *traccas* (cart) drawn by red bulls.

SOUTHWEST ISLANDS

The southwest's two islands, Isola di Sant'Antioco and Isola di San Pietro, display very different characters. The larger and more developed of the two, Isola di Sant'Antioco boasts little of the obvious beauty that one often associates with small Mediterranean islands, and is less pointedly touristy. Barely half an hour across the water, Isola di San Pietro presents a prettier picture with its pastel houses and bright bobbing fishing boats.

Isola di San Pietro

Boasting an elegant main town and some magnificent coastal scenery, Isola di San Pietro is a hugely popular summer destination.

WORTH A TRIP

VILLAGGIO MINERARIO ROSAS

Immersed in the country near Narcao, the **Villaggio Minerario Rosas** (☑ 0781 185 51 39; www.villaggiominerariorosas.it; adult/reduced €6/4; ☺ 9.30am-6pm summer, 9.30am-noon & 4-6pm winter) is a fascinating museum complex housed in what was once an important lead, copper and zinc mine. The site's rusty mine-head machinery and heavy timber structures set the scene for exhibits illustrating village life and the workings of the mine.

Visits take in the pit's former **Laveria** (Washing Plant) where you can see the heavy machines used to work the minerals, and the underground mine shafts.

There are also nature trails to explore, an on-site restaurant, and accommodation (p204) in the miners' former cottages.

A mountainous trachyte island measuring about 15km long and 11km wide, it's named after St Peter, who, legend has it, was marooned here during a storm on the way to Karalis (now Cagliari). The Romans had previously called it Accipitrum after the variety of falcons that nest here.

San Pietro's unique character and atmosphere come from its Genoese inhabitants, ransomed from the Tunisian *bey* (governor) in 1736. Coral fishers by profession, they had been sent to the island of Tabarka to harvest the precious commodity for the Lomellini family in Genoa. But they were abandoned to their fate and fell into miserable slavery until Carlo Emanuele III granted them refuge on San Pietro. Almost out of spite, North African pirates turned up in 1798 and made off with 1000 prisoners. It took five years for the Savoys to ransom them back. Even today the inhabitants of San Pietro speak *tabarkino,* a 16th-century version of Genoese.

ℹ Getting There & Away

Regular Saremar ferries sail to/from Carloforte, the island's main town, from Portovesme (per person/person plus car €5.50/€17.20, 30 minutes, 15 daily) and Calasetta (per person/person plus car €5.20/15.20, seven daily) on the neighbouring island of Sant'Antioco. There's a **Saremar** (☑ 0781 85 40 05; www.saremar.it; Corso Tagliafico 13) ticket office in Carloforte, just off Piazza Carlo Emanuele III.

Delcomar (☑ 0781 85 71 23; www.delcomar. it) runs up to 7 night services to and from Calasetta. It operates a ticket booth just in front of where the ferries dock. The crossing costs €5/15 per person/person plus car.

ℹ️ Getting Around

From Carloforte, four main roads branch out across the island: the SP101, which heads north to La Punta; the SP102 and 103, which serve the south and the beaches; and the picturesque SP104, which cuts across the island to Capo Sandalo.

BICYCLE

If you haven't got your own car, or even if you have, the ideal way to explore the island is by bike. Distances are not huge, and even if there's some hill work there's nothing too dramatic. You can hire bikes (from €10 per day), as well as scooters (from €20) and cars (from €40) at **D & G Motors** (☑ 329 9429628; Via Piave 4a; ☺ 8.30am-1pm & 3-8pm daily) in Carloforte, on a narrow street back from the seafront.

BUS

On weekdays three daily buses run from Carloforte to La Punta (12 minutes), La Caletta (15 minutes) and Capo Sandalo (18 minutes). Services are increased between mid-June and mid-September.

Carloforte

POP 6240

The very image of Mediterranean chic, Carloforte offers a refined introduction to the island. Graceful *palazzi,* crowded cafes and palm trees line the busy waterfront while, behind, a creamy curve of stately buildings rises in a half moon up the green hillside. There are no great sights in the town as such, but a slow wander through the quaint, cobbled streets makes for a pleasant prelude to an aperitif and a fine seafood meal at one of the town's wonderful restaurants.

⊙ Sights & Activities

Museo Civico   MUSEUM
(☑ 0781 85 58 80; Via Cisterna del Re; adult/reduced €2/1; ☺ 10am-1pm & 4-8pm Tue, 9am-1pm Wed, 4-8pm Thu, 9am-1pm & 3-7pm Fri, 5-8pm Sat, 10am-1pm Sun) Uphill from the seafront, Carloforte's sole museum is housed in a small 18th-century fort, one of the first masonry buildings to be erected on the island. Of chief interest is the Tonnara Room, dedicated to the island's tradition of tuna fishing. Continuing the nautical theme, there's an assortment of boating bric-a-brac and a small collection of Mediterranean seashells.

Carloforte Sail Charter   SAILING
(☑ 347 2733268; www.cscharter.it; Via Danero 52) If you want to take to the sea, this operator has a fleet of sailing boats available for charter with or without a skipper (reckon on from €1500 per week) as well as *gommoni* (lightweight rubber boats) for daily hire (€100 to €150). It also runs island tours (€40 to €60 per person) and sailing courses (from €120 for a weekend course).

Isla Diving   DIVING
(☑ 335 462502; www.isladiving.it; Viale dei Cantieri) One of several centres in Carloforte offering a full range of dives and snorkelling excursions around the island. Bank on from €60 for a dive (including equipment hire) and €33 for a snorkelling trip.

Carloforte Tonnare Diving Center   DIVING
(☑ 349 6904969; www.carlofortediving.org; Località La Punta) Operating out of the island's old tuna-processing plant (the Tonnara), this centre runs dives and snorkelling tours as well as the chance to swim with tuna between May and June.

⌖ Tours

Cartur   BOAT TOUR
(☑ 0781 85 50 60; Molo No 3) Operating out of a booth on the *lungomare* (seafront), Cartur is one of several outfits offering boat tours of the island. Budget for about €30 per person.

✪ Festivals & Events

Il Girotonno   FOOD
(www.girotonno.it; ☺ May/Jun) Dedicated to the *mattanza* (seasonal tuna slaughter), the island's main annual event features cooking competitions, tastings, seminars, concerts and various nautical-themed events. It's held over four days in late May/early June.

Creuza de Mà   MUSIC, FILM
(www.festivalcarloforte.org) This three-day summer festival is dedicated to cinema music with concerts and screenings of films and documentaries. The dates vary from year to year; sometimes it's in September, other years in June or July. Check the website for details.

✕ Eating

Tuna is the king of *tabarkina* cuisine, as island cooking is known. It's on menus throughout the year, but is only available fresh from May to August/September. You'll also be able to sample *cuscus* (a variety of North African couscous) alongside *zuppa di pesce* (fish soup), pesto (made with basil), and Genoese *farinata* (a pizza-style flatbread made from chickpea flour and olives).

⭐**Ristorante L'Oasi** RISTORANTE €€
(📞0781 85 67 01; Via Gramsci 59; meals €25-30; ⊗Mon-Sat & Sun lunch) Dig into honest, home-style island cooking at this friendly unpretentious restaurant. The menu, like most on the island, features seafood and plenty of tuna dishes, whilst the ambience is pleasantly rustic with exposed-stone walls and a wooden ceiling.

**Osteria Della
Tonnara da Andrea** RISTORANTE €€
(📞0781 85 57 34; www.ristorantedaandrea.it; Corso Battellieri 36; meals €35; ⊗12.30-2.30pm & 8-10.30pm Thu-Tue, closed mid-Jan–early Mar) Located at the southern end of the waterfront, this charming restaurant is one of the best places to taste the local tuna (though it's only available in the tuna-fishing season). Signature dishes include *lasagnetta di tonno con gocce di pesto* (tuna and pesto lasagne) and *tonno arrosto alla carlofortina* (roast tuna with tomato sauce). Booking is recommended in summer and credit cards are not accepted.

La Cantina TRATTORIA €€
(📞0781 85 45 88; Via Gramsci 34; meals €25-30; ⊗8am-2pm & 5-10pm daily summer, Tue-Sun winter) A great place to sample the cuisine of Carloforte, La Cantina is a simple, one-room trattoria that spreads outdoors in the summer months, with tables on the pedestrianised street. Taste the *cascá alle verdure* – the local couscous with vegetables – or any of the wonderful seafood offerings.

Al Tonno di Corsa RISTORANTE €€€
(📞0781 85 51 06; www.tonnodicorsa.it; Via Marconi 47; tasting menus €25-35, meals around €45; ⊗12.30-2.30pm & 8-10.30pm Tue-Sun) With its bright dining room and terrace overlooking Carloforte's rooftops, this refined restaurant specialises in fresh seafood and tuna cooked in ways you've probably never seen before – smoked, in *ragù* (meat and tomato sauce), as tripe. Tuna tripe, known locally as *belu,* is not for everyone, but if you're tempted it's cooked in a casserole with potatoes and onions.

Da Nicolo RISTORANTE €€€
(📞0781 85 40 48; Corso Cavour 32; meals around €55; ⊗8-11pm Mon-Thu, 1-3pm & 8-11pm Fri-Sun May-Sep) A bastion of San Pietro cuisine, this island institution sits in elegant splendour on the seafront. Tables are laid out with starched formality in a glass pavilion, ready for diners who come from far and wide to try the magnificent tuna and light, local couscous.

 Drinking & Nightlife

The *lungomare* is the place where it's at. Out of town, the popular Caletta beach is also the scene of summer fun, with beach parties pounding on until dawn.

Barone Rosso BAR
(Via XX Settembre 26; ⊗7pm-2am Wed-Mon & noon-3.30pm in summer) Just off the seafront, Barone Rosso is a popular bar with a kitsch interior, lively tunes and a few streetside tables.

Disco Marlin DISCO
(📞0781 85 01 21; ⊗10pm-4am Sat & Sun Jul, nightly Aug) Dance til dawn at Marlin, a popular disco near the Tonnara at La Punta. You'll really need a taxi, or a lift, to get there.

 Information

Banca di Credito Sardo (Corso Cavour 1) Bank with an ATM.
Tourist office (📞0781 85 40 09; www.prolo-cocarloforte.it; Corso Tagliafico 2; ⊗10am-1pm & 5-8pm Mon-Sat) Another useful source of information is the website www.carloforte.net, although at present it's only in Italian.

La Punta

A quick 5.5km drive north of Carloforte brings you to La Punta, a desolate, windswept point with views over to the offshore Isola Piana. In May and June it's here that you'll witness the frenzied *mattanza,* in front of the Tonnara. A dilapidated set of stone buildings littered with rusty anchors and smelly nets, the island's old tuna-processing plant is now home to the Carloforte Tonnare Diving Center, which, as well as organising dives, also runs guided tours of the old plant; contact the diving centre to organise a time.

Southern Beaches

Most of the island's best beaches are in the south, accessible by the SP103 and 102. **Spiaggia La Bobba** looks onto two great stone columns (Le Colonne) that rise out of the sea, giving the island's southernmost point its name, Punta delle Colonne. Continue westwards and you come to the island's

DON'T MISS

CALA FICO

En route to Capo Sandalo take a minute to stop off at the rocky inlet of Cala Fico, one of the island's hidden beauty spots and, along with **Isola del Corno**, home to a nesting colony of Eleonora's falcons. The bay, resembling a tiny fjord, is flanked by a wall of chipped and cracked white-grey rock that catches the late-afternoon sun and reflects the light onto the seawater, lending it a lovely turquoise colour.

most popular beach, **La Caletta** (also known as Spiaggia Spalmatore), a relatively modest arc of fine sand closed off by cliffs. Further south you can detour to view the spectacular coastline of La Conca.

Capo Sandalo

★**Capo Sandalo**   VIEWPOINT
The westernmost point of the island, Capo Sandalo is a superb vantage point, commanding breathtaking coastal views. From the car park near the lighthouse, a series of marked trails heads through the rocky, red scrubland that carpets the cliffs. It's not exactly hard-core trekking, but you'll feel safer in a pair of walking boots.

Isola di Sant'Antioco

Larger and less exuberant than Isola di San Pietro, Isola di Sant'Antioco is Italy's fourth-largest island (after Sicily, Sardinia and Elba). Unlike many Mediterranean islands it's not dramatically beautiful – although it's by no means ugly – and it exudes no sense of isolation. Instead it feels very much part of Sardinia, both in character and look. The animated main town (Sant'Antioco) is an authentic working port, and the green, rugged interior looks like much of southern Sardinia.

In fact, since Roman times, the island has been physically linked to the Sardinian mainland by bridge – the ruins of the Roman structure lie to the right of the modern road bridge.

❶ Getting There & Around

There are two ways of approaching the island. The simplest is to follow the SS126 south from Carbonia and cross the bridge to the town of

Sant'Antioco. Clunkier but more romantic is the car ferry from Carloforte on Isola di San Pietro to Calasetta.

BICYCLE

In Sant'Antioco town, **Euromoto** (☑ 0781 84 09 07, 347 8803875; http://dueleoni.blogspot.it; Via Nazionale 57; ⊙ 9am-1pm & 4-8pm Mon-Sat) hires out bikes (€10), scooters (€28) and cars (€38), as well as organising guided excursions. These are led by volunteers, so there's no fixed rate, although you're welcome to leave a tip.

BOAT

Ferries sail between Calasetta in the north of the island and Carloforte (per person/person plus car €5.20/15.20, seven daily) on the Isola di San Pietro.

BUS

Buses connect Sant'Antioco (Piazza Repubblica) with Carbonia (€2, 50 minutes) and Iglesias (€3.50, 1¾ hours).

Local buses also run around Sant'Antioco and the rest of the island.

Sant'Antioco

POP 11,500
Although Isola di Sant'Antioco has been inhabited since prehistoric times, the town of Sant'Antioco was founded by the Phoenicians in the 8th century BC. Known as Sulci, it was Sardinia's industrial capital and an important port until the demise of the Roman Empire more than a millennium later. It owes its current name to St Antiochus, a Roman slave who brought Christianity to the island when exiled here in the 2nd century AD.

Evidence of the town's ancient past is not hard to find – the hilltop historic centre is riddled with Phoenician necropolises and fascinating archaeological litter.

◉ Sights

★**Museo Archeologico**   MUSEUM
(www.archeotur.it; adult/reduced €6/3.50; ⊙ 9am-7pm) This great little museum is one of the best in this part of southern Sardinia. It has a fascinating collection of local archaeological finds, as well as models of nuraghic houses and Sant'Antioco as it would have looked in the 4th century BC. Highlights include an impressive pair of stone lions that once guarded the town gates, as was customary in Phoenician towns, and a panther mosaic taken from a Roman *triclinium* (dining room).

Further along the road, and spread over the hill, are the tombs of the necropolis (closed to the public).

Basilica di Sant'Antioco Martire   CHURCH
(Piazza Parrocchia 22; ⊘9am-noon & 7-8pm Mon-Sat, 9-10am & 7-8pm Sun summer, 9am-noon & 3-6pm Mon-Sat, 9-10am & 3-6pm Sun winter) Hidden behind the modest baroque facade is a sublimely simple 5th-century church. To the right of the altar stands a wooden effigy of St Antiochus, a martyr of North African origin who was enslaved by the Romans and later hid out in the basilica's creepy catacombs (guided tours adult/reduced €5/3).

According to legend, Antiochus was condemned to work in the island's lead mines by the Romans after he refused to recant his faith. But he escaped, hidden in a tar barrel, and was taken in by an underground Christian group who hid him in the catacombs.

Accessible only by guided tour, the catacombs consist of a series of burial chambers, some dating back to Punic times, that were used by Christians between the 2nd and 7th centuries. The dead members of well-to-do families were stored in elaborate, frescoed family niches in the walls – a few fragments of fresco can still be seen – while middle-class corpses wound up in unadorned niches, and commoners' bodies were placed in ditches in the floor. A few skeletons lying in situ render the idea a little more vividly.

Tophet   ARCHAEOLOGICAL SITE
(www.archeotur.it; adult/reduced €4/2.50; ⊘9am-7pm) Some 500m from the town's Museo Archeologico, the tophet is an 8th-century-BC sanctuary where the Phoenicians and Carthaginians buried their still-born babies. Before visiting, it's worth checking out the tophet display at the Museo Archeologico to see how the tombs were laid out.

Forte Su Pisu   FORT
(Via Castello; admission €2.50; ⊘9am-8pm summer, 9.30am-1pm & 3-6pm winter) Also known as the Forte Sabaudo, this 19th-century Piedmontese fort marks the highest point in town. Its most famous action took place in 1815 when its garrison failed to fight off a party of North African Saracen raiders. In the ensuing battle, many islanders were killed and more than 130 were taken prisoner.

Museo Etnografico   MUSEUM
(Via Necropoli 24a; admission €3; ⊘9am-8pm summer, 9.30am-1pm & 3-6pm winter) In the town's historic centre, you can investigate age-old living habits at this museum, with its assortment of traditional farm and household implements.

Villaggio Ipogeo   TOMBS
(Via Necropoli; admission €2.50; ⊘9am-8pm summer, 9.30am-1pm & 3-6pm winter) A short hop from the Museo Etnografico, you can visit a series of Punic tombs that once housed the poorest of the town's poor.

🎉 Festivals & Events

Festa di Sant'Antioco   TRADITIONAL FESTIVAL
(www.tuttosantantioco.it; ⊘Apr) Held over four days around the second Sunday after Easter, the festival celebrates the town's patron saint with processions, music, dancing, fireworks and concerts. It is one of the oldest saint's festivities on the island, dating to 1359.

🍴 Eating & Drinking

Rubiu   PIZZERIA, BREWERY €
(www.rubiubirra.it; Viale Trento 2; pizzas €6.50-11; ⊘7pm-1am Wed-Mon) This upbeat and contemporary microbrewery has an easygoing vibe and a terrific selection of home-brewed beers and ales. Staff also whip up tasty salads, platters of local cheese, and creative pizzas with toppings such as smoked *muggine* (mullet) and *bottarga*.

Pizzeria Biancaneve   PIZZERIA €
(☑0781 8 21 28; Corso Vittorio Emanuele 110; pizzas €7.50; ⊘12.30-2.30pm & 6.30-11pm daily summer, Wed-Mon winter) On the main strip into town, this modest place does a roaring trade serving passers-by with pizza.

Renzo e Rita   RISTORANTE, PIZZERIA €€
(☑0781 80 04 48; www.renzoerita.com; Via Nazionale 42; pizzas from €4, meals €25; ⊘6.30pm-1am

---

ℹ COMBINED TICKETS

If you plan on visiting the island's principal sights, there are three combined tickets that will save you a euro or two:

➡ Museo Archeologico, Tophet, Museo Etnografico, Villaggio Ipogeo and Forte Su Pisu (adult/reduced €13/8)

➡ Museo Archeologico and Tophet (adult/reduced €7/4)

➡ Museo Etnografico, Villaggio Ipogeo and Forte Su Pisu (adult/reduced €6/4)

Tickets are available at participating sights.

Thu-Tue summer, 6pm-12.30am Thu-Tue winter) A steady stream of locals keeps the *pizzaioli* (pizza-makers) busy at this cheerful pizzeria-cum-restaurant. Many buy takeaway but if you decide to eat in, it has a big, bright dining room, Britpop on the radio, and a comprehensive choice of pizzas, pastas and traditional seafood staples.

Bar Colombo   BAR
(Lungomare Cristoforo Colombo 94; ⊗ Tue-Sun) A salty fishers' bar down by the seafront. It's not going to win any design awards but with the summer crowds swelling onto the outside pavement, it's a lively place for a beer or two.

Around the Island

Much of the island's hilly hinterland is cloaked by *macchia* with the occasional house dotted around the empty slopes. Most of the better beaches lie to the south of Sant'Antioco.

About 5km out of town, **Maladroxia** is a small resort with a couple of hotels and a pleasant beach and port. Further south, **Spiaggia Coa Quaddus** is a wild and woolly beach about 3km short of **Capo Sperone**, the island's panoramic southernmost point.

On the windy west coast, bathing hot spots include **Cala Lunga** and **Cala Sapone** with wonderful crystal-clear waters.

Calasetta, the island's second town, which was founded by Ligurian families from Tabarka in 1769, is located 10km northwest of Sant'Antioco. There are several beaches in the vicinity, including the lovely dune-backed **Spiaggia delle Saline** (Salina).

A block back from the harbour at Calasetta, **Da Pasqualino** (✆ 0781 8 84 73; Via Regina Margherita 85, Calasetta; meals €30-35; ⊗ Wed-Mon) is a local institution specialising in seafood, serving up dishes prepared with the daily catch. Menu stalwarts include delicate fish *cascà* (couscous) and spaghetti with *bottarga*. Note that it also serves two fixed-price lunch menus – €20 for a meat-based menu, €27 for fish.

SOUTH COAST

The island's southern coast is quite magnificent. The central stretch, known as the Costa del Sud, is a dazzling 20km spectacle of twisting, turning road that winds above rugged cliffs plunging into the tantalising blue sea.

Porto Botte to Porto di Teulada

Stretching along Sardinia's southwestern tip, this tract of coastline is a patchwork of pine woods, lagoons and beaches.

From Sant'Anna Arresi, the SS195 swings south, bypassing Sardinia's southernmost point, Capo di Teulada. Like much of this area, the Capo is occupied by a NATO base and is inaccessible to the public. After 10km, the road branches south towards Porto di Teulada.

There are several beaches along this part of the coast, including **Cala Piombo** and **Porto Zafferano**, accessible only in July and August, and only by boat. You can pick up a boat at the small marina at Porto di Teulada near **Porto Tramatzu** beach.

Spiaggia Porto Pino – the best and busiest of the area's beaches – is at the eponymous resort near Sant'Anna Arresi. A favourite with weekending locals, it's a broad swath of creamy sand lapped by lovely, shallow waters ideal for tentative toddlers and nervous swimmers. There's ample parking and a string of cheerful pizzerias near the parking lot.

A second beach, **Spiaggia Sabbie Bianche**, just south of Porto Pino and accessible on foot, is famous for its soft, silky dunes. However, it's on military land and is off limits outside of July and August.

Costa del Sud

Extending from Porto di Teulada to Chia, the Costa del Sud is one of southern Sardinia's most beautiful coastal stretches.

◎ Sights

★ **Strada Panoramica**
della Costa del Sud   COASTAL ROAD
Running the 25km length of the Costa del Sud, this panoramic road – known more prosaically as the SP71 – snakes along the spectacular coastline between Porto di Teulada and Chia. It's a stunning drive whichever way you do it, with wonderful views at every turn and a succession of bays capped by Spanish-era watchtowers.

Starting in Porto di Teulada, the first stretch twists past several coves as it rises to the high point of **Capo Malfatano**. Along the way, **Spiaggia Piscinni** is a great place for a dip with incredible azure waters.

Beyond the cape, the popular **Cala Teuradda** beach boasts vivid emerald green waters, summer snack bars and a conveniently situated bus stop.

From here the road climbs inland away from the water. For great coastal views, turn off along the narrow side road at Porto Campana and follow the dirt track to the lighthouse at **Capo Spartivento**. From here a series of beaches stretch north – watch out for signposts off the main coastal road to **Cala Cipolla** (a gorgeous spot backed by pine and juniper trees) **Spiaggia Su Giudeu** and **Porto Campana**.

At the end of this stretch you'll see another Spanish watchtower presiding over Chia, the small resort that marks the end of the road.

Chia   VILLAGE

More a collection of hotels, holiday homes and campsites than a traditional village, Chia is a hugely popular summer hang-out. To see what all the fuss is about, head up to the Spanish watchtower and look down on its two ravishing beaches – to the west, the **Spiaggia Sa Colonia**; to the east, the smaller **Spiaggia Su Portu**.

A paradise for windsurfers and sports fans, these sandy beaches play host to the annual **Chia Classic**, a surfing, windsurfing and kitesurfing event held between April and June.

❶ Getting There & Around

From Cagliari, there are up to 10 daily buses to/from Chia (€4.50, 1¼ hours). Then, between mid-June and mid-September, two daily buses ply the Costa del Sud, connecting Chia with Spiaggia Teulada (Porto di Teulada; €3, 35 minutes).

Chia to Santa Margherita di Pula

Unless you're staying at one of the self-contained resort hotels that hog much of this part of the coast you're unlikely to glimpse much of the sea around here. Which is a shame because the 9km of coastline between Chia and Santa Margherita di Pula is one of the most beautiful parts of the southwest of Sardinia: a string of magnificent beaches lapped by crystalline waters and backed by fragrant pine woods.

Buses serve Santa Margherita di Pula from Cagliari (€3.50, one hour, nine daily).

Pula & Around

POP 7140

Some 32km from Cagliari, the village of Pula makes a good base for exploring the southern beaches and the nearby site of Nora. There's little to see in the village itself, apart from a small archaeological museum, but in summer visitors throng to its vibrant cafes and various restaurants, lending it an infectious holiday atmosphere.

◉ Sights

Nora   ARCHAEOLOGICAL SITE
(☑070 920 91 38; adult/reduced incl watchtower €7.50/4.50; ⊙9am-sunset) About 4km from Pula, Nora's ruins are all that remain of what was once one of Sardinia's most powerful cities. Founded by Phoenicians in the 8th century BC, it later became an important Punic centre, and, in the 3rd century AD, the island's Roman capital. It was eventually abandoned in the 8th century as the threat of Arab raids got too much for its nervous citizens.

Highlights include a beautifully preserved Roman theatre and an ancient baths complex, the Terme al Mare.

Upon entry, you pass a single melancholy **column** from the former temple of Tanit, the Carthaginian Venus, who was once worshipped here. Beyond this is a small 2nd-century Roman **theatre** facing the sea. Towards the west are the substantial remains of the **Terme al Mare** (Baths by the Sea). Four columns (a tetrastyle) stand at the heart of what was a patrician villa; the surrounding rooms retain their mosaic floor decoration. More remnants of mosaics can be seen at a temple complex towards the tip of the promontory.

Overlooking the ruins, the **Torre del Coltellazzo** is a 17th-century watchtower set on the site of the Phoenician city's acropolis.

Regular shuttle buses run to Nora from Piazza Municipio in Pula.

Chiesa di Sant'Efisio   CHURCH
(☑340 4851860; ⊙2.30-5.30pm Sat, 10am-noon & 2.30-5.30pm Sun) Before you get to Nora, take a moment to stop at this pint-sized Romanesque church. Dating to the 12th century, it marks the spot where the disgraced Roman commander Ephysius was executed for his Christian beliefs in AD 303. Despite its modest dimensions, it's the scene of great celebrations on 1 May as pilgrims bring the

effigy of St Ephysius here as part of Cagliari's **Festa di Sant'Efisio.**

Laguna di Nora   LAGOON
(📞070 920 95 44; www.lagunadinora.it; adult/reduced €8/6, excursions adult/reduced €25/15; ⊘visitor centre 10am-8pm Jul & Aug, to 7pm Jun & Sep) On the western side of the Nora promontory, you can often spy pink flamingos stalking around the Laguna di Nora. To learn more about the lagoon and its aquatic fauna, pop into the visitor centre, which has a small aquarium and displays dedicated to whales and dolphins. It also runs summer excursions, including snorkelling tours and canoe outings.

Near the entrance to the lagoon are two beaches: the pleasant **Spiaggia di Nora** and, a little further around, the bigger **Spiaggia Su Guventeddu.**

Museo Archeologico   MUSEUM
(Corso Vittorio Emanuele 67; ⊘closed for renovation) Before visiting Nora, a trip to this small museum in Pula will help set the scene. Alongside ceramics found in Punic and Roman tombs, some gold and bone jewellery, and Roman glassware, there's a model of the Nora site and helpful explanations in both English and Italian.

Note that at the time of writing the museum was closed for renovation but was due to be re-opened.

✖ Eating

S'Incontru   RISTORANTE, PIZZERIA €
(📞070 920 81 28; www.sincontrupizzeriaristorante. it; Piazza del Popolo 63; lunch menus seafood/meat/veg €13/10/12, panini €5; ⊘6am-midnight daily summer, closed Thu evening winter) The liveliest of the popular eateries on Piazza del Popolo, this laid-back place is a jack of all trades, as good for a mojito as for a pizza, *pannino* or plate of pasta. For a bargain lunch fill-up, there's a selection of fixed-price menus, including a rare (for Sardinia) vegetarian option.

★ Zia Leunora   RISTORANTE €€
(📞070 920 95 59; Via Trieste 19; meals €30-35; ⊘7.30-11.30pm Thu-Sat & Mon-Tue, lunch Sun) Locals warmly recommend this smart, family-run restaurant. Tucked away in a backstreet in Pula's historic centre, it specialises in seafood and serves a full range of classic fish dishes, including an excellent *risotto del mare* prepared with clams, mussels, scampi, prawns and just a hint of chilli. Service is

friendly and the wood-beamed hall an attractive place to dine.

Zio Dino   PIZZERIA €€
(📞070 920 91 59; Viale Segni 14; pizzas €6, meals €30; ⊘Tue-Sun) With its name graffitied high on the wall, bustling Zio Dino serves a solid menu of pizza staples, seafood and meat dishes.

❶ Information

The best source of information on Pula is the website www.visitpula.info.

❶ Getting There & Away

There are up to 20 daily buses to/from Cagliari (€3, 50 minutes).

CAMPIDANO

An important agricultural zone, the Campidano is a broad, flat corridor of land extending northwest from Cagliari. The dusty yellow landscape can be a little dispiriting, especially on torrid summer days when temperatures soar and the area seems enveloped in a thick grey heat haze, but it's not totally devoid of interest.

Uta & Around

Barely 20km northwest of Cagliari, the farm village of Uta boasts one of southern Sardinia's finest Romanesque churches. To the southwest, you can trawl through the hilltop ruins of a medieval castle and trek through the wooded slopes of Monte Arcosu.

◉ Sights

Chiesa di Santa Maria   CHURCH
A wonderful example of Sardinian Romanesque architecture, this beautifully proportioned church lies east of the main village; follow the brown signs for the Santuario di Santa Maria. It was built around 1140 by Vittorini monks from Marseille and features an elegant, sober facade, an open *campanile* (bell tower) and intricate statuary. Check out the busts of people and animals (real and imaginary) on the band that runs around the exterior.

Castello di Acquafredda   CASTLE
(adult/reduced €4/3.50; ⊘9.30am-6.30pm) About 4km south of Uta, you'll see the fairy-tale image of castle ruins atop an extraordinary

craggy mount. These belong to the Castello di Acquafredda, a 13th-century castle that served as a temporary hideout for Guelfo della Gherardesca when his father Ugolino, the reviled ruler of Iglesias, was imprisoned in Pisa and the family banished. Nowadays, little more than the castle walls remain.

Riserva Naturale
di Monte Arcosu
WILDLIFE RESERVE

(☏ 070 96 87 14; www.ilcaprifoglio.it; admission €5; ⊗ 9am-5pm Sat & Sun) South of the Castello di Acquafredda, the Riserva Naturale di Monte Arcosu is a WWF reserve and one of the few remaining habitats of the *cervo sardo*. Covering the peak of Monte Arcosu (948m), it also harbours wild boar, wildcats and plenty of birds of prey.

ⓘ Getting There & Away

Regular buses run to Uta from Cagliari (€3.50, 45 minutes), although the church is a good 1.5km walk from the village centre. To get to the Castello di Acquafredda and the Riserva Naturale di Monte Arcosu, you'll need your own transport.

San Sperate

Some 12km northeast of Uta, San Sperate is famous for its colourful murals. These present a Daliesque tableau of traditional country life as well as depicting some more modern urban trends (skateboards stretching down a wall like an array of colourful tongues). Highlights include Pinuccio Sciola's epic *Storia di San Sperate* (History of San Sperate; 1997) on Via Sassari.

For a taste of great traditional Sardinian cooking, head to Ada (☏ 070 960 09 72; Via Cagliari 21; meals €25-30, pizzas from €4; ⊗ 12.30-3pm & 8-10.30pm Mon-Sat), a colourful, art-clad eatery. Pastas are handmade and there's an interesting array of antipasti, such as prosciutto with preserved prickly pear. Wash it all down with a glass of local wine or your pick of artisanal beer.

For San Sperate, buses run hourly from Cagliari (€3.50, 30 minutes).

Sanluri

POP 8430

One of the biggest towns in the Medio Campidano province, Sanluri is a bustling agricultural centre. In the 14th century Queen Eleonora d'Arborea lived here for a period and the town was a key member of her opposi-

tion to Catalan-Aragonese expansion. In 1409 island resistance was finally crushed at the Battle of Sanluri, paving the way for centuries of Iberian domination. Unfortunately, little remains to vouch for the town's former glory apart from Eleonora's squat, brooding castle.

◉ Sights

Castello di Sanluri
MUSEUM, CASTLE

(☏ 070 930 71 05; www.castellodisanluri.it; Via Generale Nino Villa Santa 1; adult/reduced €5/2.50; ⊗ 9.30am-1pm & 4.30-8pm summer, 9.30am-1pm & 3.30-7pm winter) Just off Via Carlo Felice, the main thoroughfare, Sanluri's 14th-century castle houses the **Museo Risorgimentale Duca d'Aosta** and its eclectic collection of assorted military paraphernalia. Outside in the garden, you'll see a medieval catapult, whilst inside you're treated to an extraordinary display of objects, from period furniture to military mementos.

To strike out from the castle, bikes are available for hire at the ticket office, costing €1.50 for half a day, €3 for the whole day.

Museo Etnografico Cappuccino
MUSEUM

(☏ 070 930 71 07; Via San Rocco 6; admission €3; ⊗ 9am-noon, 4-6pm or by appointment) Housed in a 17th-century monastery, this small museum displays a varied collection of artefacts and artworks, including obsidian arrowheads, Roman-era coins, farm tools and works of religious art.

ⓘ Getting There & Away

Sanluri is well served by bus with regular connections to/from Cagliari (€4.50, one hour).

Sardara

POP 4270

Some 8km northwest of Sanluri, Sardara is a sleepy town with an attractive stone centre and several interesting archaeological sights. It's also known for its curative waters. The Romans built thermal baths in the nearby locality of Santa Maria de Is Acquas and still today people flock to indulge themselves at the local spa facilities.

◉ Sights

Civico Museo Archeologico
Villa Abbas
MUSEUM

(☏ 070 938 61 83; www.coopvillabbas.sardegna. it; Piazza Liberta 7; admission €2.60, incl Chiesa di Sant'Anastasia €4.50; ⊗ 9am-1pm & 5-8pm Tue-Sun summer, 9am-1pm & 4-7pm Tue-Sun winter)

At the top of the historic centre, the Civico Museo Archeologico Villa Abbas showcases a collection of finds from local archaeological sites. Among the finest pieces are two 8th-century-BC bronze statuettes found on the edge of Sardara in 1913.

Area Archeologico &
Chiesa di Sant'Anastasia ARCHAEOLOGICAL SITE
([Z]070 938 61 83; www.coopvillabbas.sardegna. it; Piazza Sant'Anastasia; admission €2.60, incl Civico Museo €4.50; ⊙9am-1pm & 5-8pm Tue-Sun summer, 9am-1pm & 4-7pm Tue-Sun winter) A few hundred metres from Sardara's museum, the Gothic Chiesa di Sant'Anastasia sits in the midst of what was once a much larger nuraghic temple. The highlight here is the underground well, known as Sa funtana de is dolus (Fountain of Pain), which was an important place of worship between the 11th and 7th centuries BC.

Chiesa di San Gregorio CHURCH
(Piazza San Gregorio) The Chiesa di San Gregorio makes a fetching town landmark. Built between 1300 and 1325 in a mixed Romanesque Gothic style, it boasts a sombre, soaring facade and a pretty rose window.

Castello Monreale CASTLE
About 4km south of Santa Maria de Is Acquas, a dirt road leads to the empty walls of the Castello Monreale. Built in the 13th century by the governor of Arborea, the castle was used as a temporary refuge by troops defeated at the Battle of Sanluri and later, in 1478, as a billet for Catalan-Aragonese troops.

⊙ Getting There & Away

Regular buses connect with Cagliari (€6, 1½ hours).

LA MARMILLA

Northeast of Sardara, the landscape takes on a livelier aspect as dusty plains give way to the undulating green hills of La Marmilla. Named after these low-lying mounds (*marmilla* is derived from *mammellare,* meaning 'breast shaped'), La Marmilla is an area of bucolic scenery and quiet, rural life. It's also one of Sardinia's richest archaeological regions, and it's here, in the shadow of the table-topped high plain known as La Giara di Gesturi, that you'll find the island's best-known nuraghic site, the Unesco-listed Nuraghe Su Nuraxi.

Villanovaforru & Nuraghe Genna Maria

POP 660

On the southern fringes of La Marmilla, Villanovaforru is a manicured, pretty little village that attracts coachloads of visitors to its archaeological sites. The village itself boasts a worthwhile museum, while a short hop to the west is the important *nuraghe* of Genna Maria.

⊙ Sights

Museo Archeologico MUSEUM
([Z]070 930 00 50; www.gennamaria.it; Piazza Costituzione 4; admission €3.50, incl nuraghe €5; ⊙9.30am-1pm & 3.30-7pm Tue-Sun summer, to 6pm winter) Housed in an attractive 19th-century *palazzo* in the village centre, the Museo Archeologico provides a good overview of the area's prehistoric past with finds from many local sites, including Su Nuraxi and Genna Maria. These include enormous amphorae and other pots, oil lamps, jewellery and coins.

Adjacent to the museum, the **Sala delle Mostre** (admission €1.50; ⊙9.30am-1pm & 3.30-7pm Tue-Sun summer, to 6pm winter) hosts temporary exhibitions on local life and history.

Complesso Nuragico
di Genna Maria ARCHAEOLOGICAL SITE
([Z]070 930 00 50; www.gennamaria.it; admission €2.50, incl Museo Archeologico €5; ⊙9.30am-1pm & 3.30-7pm Tue-Sun summer, 9.30am-1pm & 2.30-5pm winter) This nuraghic complex, signposted as the Parco Archeologico, is set on a woody hilltop about 1km out of the village on the road to Collinas. It's a tumbledown site but, archaeologically speaking, one of the most important on the island. It consists of a central tower, around which was later raised a three-cornered bastion. Much later an encircling wall was built to protect an Iron Age village, of which little has survived.

Museo Sa Corona Arrubia MUSEUM
(Museo Naturalistico del Territorio Giovanni Pusceddu; [Z]070 934 10 09; www.sacoronarrubia.it; Località Sa Corona Arrubia; adult/reduced €6/4, incl exhibition €8/6; ⊙2-7pm Mon, 9am-1pm & 3-7pm Tue-Thu, 9am-7pm Fri-Sun) To the northeast of Villanovaforru, near Lunamatrona, this excellent museum showcases the area's flora and fauna, as well as illustrating its ancient history and rural culture. Re-creations of prehistoric sites and dioramas of local habitats bring the subjects to life, whilst information panels explain what you're looking at.

WINDOWS TO THE PAST

For centuries, the locals thought little about the stone towers that scattered the island and many were used as humble shepherds' shelters. Then, 70 years ago, carbon dating revealed that they were in fact Bronze Age fortified settlements, most built between 1800 and 500 BC. In the absence of any written records – a fact that has led scholars to assume that the early Sards never had a written language – the *nuraghi* (stone towers) and *tombe dei giganti* (ancient mass graves, literally 'giants' tombs') provide one of the few windows into the mysterious nuraghic civilisation.

There are said to be up to 7000 *nuraghi* across the island, probably twice that many if you count those still underground. Their exact function has long been debated, but the consensus is that they served as watchtowers and sacred sites for religious rites, as well as being used for celebrations and commercial exchanges.

Early *nuraghi* were simple free-standing structures with internal chambers. Over time, they became bigger – the Nuraghe Santu Antine is the tallest remaining *nuraghe*, at 25m – and increasingly complex with elaborate rooms and labyrinthine passages. Walls were raised around the watchtowers and villagers began to cluster within the walls' protective embrace. The most spectacular example of this is the beehive complex of the Nuraghe Su Nuraxi.

The museum also hosts temporary art exhibitions, many dedicated to local artists.

❶ Getting There & Away

Two weekday buses run to the village from Cagliari (€6, 1¾ hours). There are also services to/from Sardara (€1.20, 15 minutes, five Monday to Saturday) and Sanluri (€2, 30 minutes, two Monday to Saturday).

Barumini & Around

POP 1310

From Las Plassas, the road leads through the soft green landscape to Barumini, a tiny village of stone houses and quiet lanes. The main reason to stop here is to visit the Nuraghe Su Nuraxi but there's also a charming museum and kids will enjoy the nearby Sardinia in Miniatura park.

⊙ Sights

Casa Zapata MUSEUM
(☑070 936 84 76; www.fondazionebarumini.it; Piazza Giovanni XXIII; adult/reduced incl Nuraghe Su Nuraxi €10/6.50; ⊙10am-1hr before sunset) This attractive museum complex occupies the 16th-century residence of the Spanish Zapata family, La Marmilla's 16th-century rulers. The whitewashed villa was originally built over a 1st-millennium-BC nuraghic settlement, which has been skilfully incorporated into the museum's display. You'll also find artefacts from the Nuraghe Su Nuraxi, a section dedicated to the Zapata dynasty, and a small collection of agricultural tools and instruments.

Chiesa di Santa Tecla CHURCH
Guarding the crossroads in the village centre, this 17th-century church sports a lovely, curvaceous rose window.

Parco Sardegna In Miniatura THEME PARK
(☑070 936 10 04; www.sardegnainminiatura.it; adult/reduced €10/8; ⊙9.30am-7pm Apr-Nov) A kilometre west of Barumini, the Parco Sardegna in Miniatura features a miniature reconstruction of the whole island, as well as a biosphere, planetarium and plenty of picnic tables. Note that admission to attractions within the park costs extra.

Castello di Marmilla CASTLE
Lording it over the electric green landscape, the ruins of the 12th-century Castello di Marmilla stand atop a conical hill beside the hamlet of Las Plassas, 3km southwest of Barumini. The hilltop castle was part of a defensive line that the medieval rulers of Arborea built on the frontier with the province of Cagliari.

To get to the castle from Las Plassas, follow the road for Tuili and you'll soon see a path on your left rising up the hill.

❶ Getting There & Away

Two weekday buses run from Cagliari to Barumini (€6, 1¾ hours).

Nuraghe Su Nuraxi

★**Nuraghe Su Nuraxi** ARCHAEOLOGICAL SITE
(☑070 936 81 28; www.fondazionebarumini.it; adult/reduced incl Casa Zapata €10/6.50; ⊙9am-7pm summer, to 4pm winter) In the heart of the

voluptuous green countryside near Barumini, the Nuraghe Su Nuraxi is Sardinia's sole World Heritage site and the island's most visited *nuraghe*. The focal point is the 1500 BC tower, which originally stood on its own but was later incorporated into a fortified compound. Many of the settlement's buildings were erected in the Iron Age, and it's these that constitute the beehive of circular interlocking buildings that tumble down the hillside.

The oldest part of the complex, the Nuraxi tower originally rose to a height of 18.6m and had three floors, each housing a single *tholos* (internal chamber). It was subsequently strengthened in around 1200 BC with the addition of four subsidiary towers and a massive curtain wall.

The first village huts arrived in the Bronze Age, between the 11th and 9th centuries BC, though many of the ruins you see today date to a later period of construction in the 6th and 7th centuries BC. As the village grew, a more complex defensive wall was built around the core, consisting of nine towers with arrow slits. Weapons in the form of massive stone balls have also been unearthed here.

In the 7th century BC the site was partly destroyed but not abandoned. In fact it grew and it was still inhabited in Roman times. Elements of basic sewerage and canalisation have even been identified.

The site was rediscovered by Giovanni Lilliu in 1949, after torrential rains eroded the compact earth that had covered the *nuraghe* and made it look like just another Marmilla hillock. Excavations continued for six years and today the site is the only entirely excavated *nuraghe* in Sardinia. You can get an inkling of the work involved by seeing how many square bricks have been incorporated into the structure – these were deliberately made to stand out so they could be distinguished from the original basalt.

Note that visits are by guided tour only, usually in Italian, and that explanatory printouts are available in English. Queues are the norm in summer when it can get extremely hot on the exposed site.

La Giara di Gesturi & Around

⊙ Sights

★ La Giara di Gesturi   PLATEAU
Northwest of Barumini, La Giara di Gesturi is a high basalt plateau famous for its wild horses and uncontaminated natural beauty. The 45-sq-km plain, much of which is carpeted by *macchia* (Mediterranean scrubland) and woods of oak and cork trees, offers excellent walking and wonderful wildlife-watching.

The principal gateway to the Giara, which is a protected area and off limits to cars, is **Tuili**, though you can also reach it from **Setzu** or **Gesturi**.

Approaching from Tuili, the road climbs in a series of steep switchbacks to a car park at the Giara's southernmost entrance. There's no fee to enter here but rangers ask that you check in at the small **information point** (⌨ 347 830 69 03; ⊙ 8am-7pm summer, to 5pm winter).

From the car park, a well-trodden trail leads to a small lake called **Pauli Mauri**. This is one of several seasonal *paulis* (pools) on the Giara where you just might spot one of the area's indigenous *cavallini* (literally 'mini-horses') as they come out to drink. The best time to try for a sighting is the early morning or late afternoon.

The plateau also has its own microclimate, which fosters an array of unusual flora, best seen in spring, when the ground is covered in heather and the 15 species of orchid are in bloom.

One weekday bus runs from Cagliari to Tuili (€6, 2 hours), although you'll need your own transport to get up to the Giara.

Chiesa di San Pietro   CHURCH
(Tuili) Before you head up to the Giara, check out the Chiesa di San Pietro in Tuili. It's often closed but if you can get inside, it harbours a fine *retablo* (altarpiece) made by the Maestro di Castelsardo in 1500.

Chiesa di Santa Teresa d'Avila   CHURCH
(Gesturi) On the Giara's southeastern flank, the town of Gesturi is dominated by the 30m-high bell tower of the Chiesa di Santa Teresa d'Avila. The faithful flock to this 17th-century parish church to celebrate Gesturi's greatest son, Fra Nicola 'Silenzio' (1882–1958), a Franciscan friar revered for his religious devotion, wisdom and simplicity of life.

♐ Tours

Jara Escursioni   OUTDOORS
(⌨ 348 2924983, 070 936 42 77; www.parcodellagiara.it; Via Tuveri 16, Tuili) Operating out of Tuili, this local outfit leads guided tours of the Giara.

BEN MEYER/GETTY IMAGES ©

Sardinia Outdoors

Outdoor enthusiasts are spoilt for choice in Sardinia. The island's breathtaking coast and rugged interior provide the perfect arena for a whole host of activities, ranging from hiking and climbing to caving, riding and mountain biking. Offshore, pristine waters offer yet more thrills and spills.

Contents

➡ Hiking, Cycling & Riding
➡ Diving & Sailing
➡ Other Watersports
➡ Climbing Highs

Above Rock climbing with a view of the Mediterranean Sea

Hiking, Cycling & Riding

With its hilly terrain, inspiring scenery and extensive network of trails, Sardinia is ideal hiking and cycling country. There is a huge variety of routes, from tough mountain tracks to spectacular coastal paths, and whatever your level of fitness you'll find something to suit. For horse lovers, riding is a popular island activity.

Walking

Only by hitting the trail can you appreciate how big, wild and boundlessly beautiful Sardinia really is.

Halfway up the east coast, the Parco Nazionale del Golfo di Orosei e del Gennargentu (p187) offers sublime walking, with majestic coastline and mountainous hinterland. Popular routes lead to the spectacular gorge of Gola Su Gorropu (p190) and the prehistoric village of Tiscali (p191). For something more hardcore, the seven-day Selvaggio Blu (p194) is a once-in-a-lifetime trek.

Further north, there's great walking on Monte Limbara (p168), near Tempio Pausania, and through Gallura's weird rocky landscape. Near Alghero, Le Prigionette Nature Reserve (p127) is another good area.

To the south, you can hike through the empty, verdant countryside around Monti Ferru (p100) and on La Giara di Gesturi (p80), a huge tabletop plateau.

For a gentle coastal ramble, and the chance to spot Eleonora's falcons, head to Capo Sandalo (p74) on the Isola di San Pietro.

Sardinia is combed with footpaths but routes are often unmarked and tricky to navigate solo. Consider hiring a guide

1. Hikers in Parco Nazionale del Golfo di Orosei e del Gennargentu (p187)
2. Isola Caprera (p165)
3. Cyclist in Parco Nazionale dell'Asinara (p131)

from a local hiking cooperative; a half-day hike will cost around €40.

Cycling

Big skies, sea breezes, your bum in a saddle – there's no better way to escape the crowds and see Sardinia, say cyclists.

For electrifying mountain biking, test your mettle on the remote peaks of the Ogliastra (p194), where hurtling descents plunge through oak forests down to the glistening Med.

If road cycling is more your scene, the SS125 provides a challenging ride as it corkscrews through rugged mountain country between Dorgali (p189) and Santa Maria Navarrese (p196). Over on the west coast, take to the spectacular coastal road that runs south of Alghero to Bosa (p125).

Cycling is also an excellent way of getting around Sardinia's offshore islands such as the Isola di San Pietro (p69) and the uninhabited Isola dell'Asinara (p131).

Bikes are available for hire in most resorts and towns for €10 to €30 per day. For cycling routes and maps, visit www.sardegnaturismo.it.

Horse Riding

If hiking and cycling aren't to your taste, Sardinia also has some fine horse-riding opportunities. The island's biggest equestrian centre is the Horse Country Resort (p206) near Arborea; it offers an extensive range of riding packages. Alternatively you can explore the coast around San Teodoro (p151) and the verdant Isola Caprera (p165) on horseback. Expect to pay about €35 for a 1½-hour hack.

Diving & Sailing

As rich and varied as its landscape, Sardinia's seas are a joy to explore. Sailors can search out hidden coves and island-hop around crystalline coastal waters, whilst divers can take to the deep to investigate underwater grottoes and sunken wrecks.

Diving

One look at Sardinia's azure waters – among the clearest in the Mediterranean – and scuba divers are itching to take the plunge. Awaiting them is an underwater Eden full of caves, gorges, coral and sunken ruins. Tuna, barracuda, groupers, and even turtles, dolphins and (harmless) sharks can sometimes be spotted.

Some of the best diving is off Sardinia's rocky islands, such as the Isola di San Pietro (p69) in the southwest, Isola Tavolara (p151) in the northeast, and the protected waters of Arcipelago di La Maddalena (p163) in the north.

There are plenty of schools offering courses and guided dives for all levels from April to October. Expect to pay roughly €40 for a single-tank dive, €420 for a Professional Association of Diving Instructors (PADI) open-water course and €20 per day for equipment hire.

Sailing

Sailing in Sardinia doesn't have to mean designer outfits and a megayacht on the Costa Smeralda, although that is certainly a part of it.

For idyllic summer sailing, pick up a boat in Carloforte (p70) and set sail for the secluded coves of the Isola di San Pietro. To the north, the

1. Alghero's harbour (p115) **2.** Sailing on the Mediterranean Sea

granite isles and protected waters of the Parco Nazionale dell'Arcipelago di La Maddalena (p163) are another favourite spot. Sailing is also the best, and sometimes the only, way of getting to the top beaches of the Blue Crescent, the awesome stretch of coastline around Cala Gonone (p191).

For lessons, the Sporting Club Sardinia (p162) in Porto Pollo offers a range of courses, as does the Club della Vela (p127) near Alghero. Reckon on from €220 for a basic five-lesson sailing course. To charter a sailing boat, you'll be looking at around €1500 per week, whilst it should cost between €100 and €150 to hire a *gommone* (lightweight rubber boat) for a day.

A good source of information is www. sailingsardinia.it (in Italian), which has links to individual charter companies.

TOP FIVE DIVE SITES

➡ **Nereo Cave** (p125) This cathedral-like cave is the largest underwater grotto in the Mediterranean. Here Alghero's famous frilly red coral flourishes in sun-streaked waters.

➡ **Secca del Papa** (p151) Off Isola Tavolara, this wonderland swirls with groupers, barracuda, morays and sea bream.

➡ **Golfo di Cagliari** (p46) Dive more than 30m into the deep to explore this gulf's fascinating WWII wrecks.

➡ **Carloforte** (p70) Swim with shoals of tuna in underwater caves and gorges.

➡ **Nora** (p75) For a spot of underwater archaeology, dive down to submerged Punic-Roman ruins.

Other Water Sports

Thanks to the constant winds that bluster around the island, Sardinia offers world-class windsurfing and Italy's best surfing. For those who prefer a slower pace, sea kayaking is an ideal way of exploring the coast's many beautiful nooks and crannies.

Windsurfing

Windsurfers from across Europe flock to Porto Pollo (p162), on Sardinia's northeastern coast, to pit themselves against the fierce winds that whistle through the channel between Sardinia and Corsica. Beginners can also try their hand here in the safe, sheltered bay waters.

Other windsurfing hot spots include the beautiful Spiaggia della Pelosa (p131) on the northwestern coast, the protected waters of Spiaggia Mugoni (p127) near Alghero, and Cagliari's Poetto Beach (p40). You'll find windsurf centres across the island offering rig hire and lessons for all levels – bank on up to €20 for an hour's rental and about €160 for a two-day course.

An excellent website for windsurfing holidays in Sardinia is www.planetwindsurfholidays.com.

Surfing

Sardinia's position means that that it gets small- to medium-sized waves throughout the year, particularly on the west coast where swells sweep in from the Med. Winter is the best time but there's also reliable action in spring and autumn.

Committed surfers should make a beeline for the Sinis Peninsula, where waves can reach 4m around the wild Capo Mannu (p98). A favourite beach

1. Isola Budelli (p166), in the Parco Nazionale dell'Arcipelago di La Maddalena
2. Windsurfing
3. Surfers on the Sardinian coast

is Putzu Idu (p98) at San Giovanni di Sinis. Kitesurfing is also popular here, with various schools catering to newbies and hardened vets.

Elsewhere, there's action on the beaches around Chia (p75), and at Buggerru (p64) and Masua (p63) on the Iglesiente coast. In the north, Porto Ferro (p129) is popular with local surfers.

Expect to pay about €20 per day to hire a board.

Kayaking

Few experiences in Sardinia beat paddling to hidden coves at your own speed. Cala Gonone (p191) is a great base for sea kayakers to explore the Golfo di Orosei. Alternatively, head to Cardedu (p196) to take in the dramatic sea stacks and coves of the Ogliastra coast. Kayak rental is about €25 per day.

TOP ADRENALIN RUSHES

➡ **Canyoning in the Gola Su Gorropu** (p190) Sheer drops and gigantic boulders in Europe's Grand Canyon.

➡ **Kitesurfing off Putzu Idu** (p98) Let the wind catch your kite off this dream beach.

➡ **Caving in the Supramonte** (p178) Explore the caves and passageways burrowing through the karst.

➡ **Waterskiing off Isola Caprera** (p165) Hold on as you're catapulted across azure waters.

➡ **Complete the Selvaggio Blu** (p194) Take on Italy's toughest trek on the Golfo di Orosei.

Rock climbing, Selvaggio Blu (p194)

Climbing Highs

With its vertiginous coastline and craggy interior, Sardinia is climbing heaven. Bring your own rope, a head for heights and a copy of Maurizio Oviglia's definitive *Pietra di Luna* climbing guide. The websites www. climb-europe.com and www.sardiniaclimb. com will give you a head start.

Cala Gonone-Dorgali

Cala Gonone (p191) is climbing central, with sheer limestone faces bolted with routes for beginners and advanced climbers. There is a huge variety of climbs in the surrounding countryside, including slabs, steep walls, overhangs, single-pitch climbs and easier multipitches.

Alghero

Go west of Alghero to Capo Caccia for terrific sea-cliff climbing and the Via Ferrata del Cabirol (p128). One of only two *vie ferrate* (trails with permanent cables and ladders) in Sardinia, this moderately difficult traverse offers a superb vantage point for views out to sea.

Ogliastra

An excellent year-round venue, the Ogliastra province has some 800 climbs in grades from 4 to 9b. Hot spots include Baunei (p197), for coastal climbs, and Jerzu (p198), famous for its imposing limestone towers, known locally as *tacchi* (heels).

Isili

The popular centre of Isili (p186) tempts climbers with more than 300 single-pitch sports routes ranging from 5a to 8c+. It's best known for steep 'roof climbing' crags.

Domusnovas

Domusnovas (p62) is a renowned winter climbing centre, peppered with limestone rocks, cliffs and caves. There are about 500 routes for both novice and experienced climbers, ranging from simple, single-pitch walls to tough 9a+/b overhangs.

Oristano & the West

Best Places to Eat

➡ Trattoria Biancospino (p105)

➡ Desogos (p102)

➡ Trattoria Gino (p93)

➡ Agriturismo Sinis (p98)

➡ Sa Peschiera 'e Mar 'e Pontis (p97)

Best Places to Stay

➡ Antica Dimora Del Gruccione (p207)

➡ Hotel Lucrezia (p206)

➡ Eleonora B&B (p206)

➡ Corte Fiorita (p207)

Why Go?

This part of central Sardinia boasts much of what makes the island such a beautiful and intriguing place: sublime beaches, vast tracts of verdant hills, ancient ruins and mysterious nuraghic temples.

In the heart of it all is Oristano, one of Sardinia's great medieval cities. It's a lively place with a gracious historic centre and laid-back atmosphere. A short hop away, the Sinis Peninsula harbours gorgeous beaches and ancient Roman ruins, while, to the north, Bosa charms with its riverside *centro storico* (historic centre).

For an altogether different experience, venture inland for a taste of rural Sardinia. The villages and soaring slopes of Monti Ferru are ripe for foodie touring with their prized local specialities, most notably *bue rosso* beef and extra virgin olive oil.

Festival-goers will also enjoy the area. Oristano hosts colourful carnival celebrations and the small village of Sedilo stages one of Sardinia's most exhilarating events, the extraordinary S'Ardia horse race.

Road Distance (km)

	Bosa	Cabras	Oristano	Sedilo
Cabras	55			
Oristano	59	10		
Sedilo	49	56	46	
Seneghe	43	20	25	35

Oristano & the West Highlights

1 Topping up your tan on the prized quartz sand of **Is Aruttas** (p98) beach.

2 Giving your imagination a workout at the windswept ruins of ancient **Tharros** (p99).

3 Throwing yourself into the carnival madness of Oristano's **Sa Sartiglia** (p93).

4 Surveying Bosa's colourful houses from its brooding hilltop castle, **Castello Malaspina** (p103).

5 Facing up to the Giants of Monte Prama at Cabras' **Museo Civico** (p96).

6 Revelling in soaring views and culinary treasures as you tour **Monti Ferru** (p100).

7 Brushing up on your Bronze Age history at the impressive **Nuraghe di Santa Cristina** (p106).

8 Marvelling at daredevil horse-riding skills at Sedilo's **S'Ardia** (p107) festival.

9 Perfecting your spaghetti-western swagger at **San Salvatore** (p98).

ORISTANO

POP 31,100

With its elegant shopping streets, ornate piazzas, popular cafes and some good restaurants, Oristano's refined and animated centre is a lovely place to hang out. Though there's not a huge amount to see beyond some churches and an interesting archaeological museum, the city makes a good base for the surrounding area.

History

The flat, fertile countryside around Oristano was an important nuraghic centre, but it was the Phoenicians who first put the area on the map. Arriving in the latter half of the 8th century BC, they established the city of Tharros, which later thrived under the Romans and became the de facto capital of western Sardinia.

The city was eventually abandoned in 1070 when its citizens, fed up with continuous Saracen raids, decamped to a more easily defendable inland site, Aristianis (present-day Oristano). This new city became capital of the Giudicato d'Arborea, one of Sardinia's four independent provinces, and the base of operations for Eleonora of Arborea (c 1340–1404). A heroine in the Joan of Arc mould, Eleonora organised the 14th-century war against the Spanish and wrote the *Carta de Logu* (Code of Laws) before succumbing to the plague. With her death, anti-Spanish opposition crumbled and Oristano was incorporated into the rest of Aragonese-controlled Sardinia. It wasn't a good time for the city. Trade collapsed and the city suffered from plague and famine.

The construction of the Cagliari–Porto Torres highway in the 1820s and Mussolini's land reclamation programs gave Oristano a much-needed boost.

⊙ Sights

Oristano's main sights are in the *centro storico* (historic centre), a pretty area of stone houses, sunny piazzas and baroque streets.

★ **Piazza Eleonora d'Arborea**　　PIAZZA

Oristano's elegant outdoor salon sits at the southern end of pedestrianised Corso Umberto I. An impressive, rectangular space, it comes to life on summer evenings when townsfolk congregate and children blast footballs against the glowing *palazzi* (mansions). The city's central square since the 1800s, it's flanked by grand buildings, including the neoclassical **Municipio** (Town Hall). In the centre stands an ornate 19th-century **statue of Eleonora** (Piazza Eleonora d'Arborea), raising a finger as if about to launch into a political speech.

Bargain hunters should drop by on the first Saturday of the month when the piazza hosts an antique market.

★ **Cattedrale di
Santa Maria Assunta**　　CATHEDRAL

(Duomo; Piazza del Duomo; ⊘ 9am-7pm summer, to 6pm winter) Lording it over Oristano's skyline, the Duomo's onion-domed bell tower is one of the few remaining elements of the original 14th-century cathedral, itself a reworking of an earlier church damaged by fire in the late 12th century. The free-standing *campanile* (bell tower), topped by its conspicuous majolica-tiled dome, adds an exotic Byzantine feel to what is otherwise a typical 18th-century baroque complex.

Inside, the look is largely baroque, though the transept chapels survive from the Gothic original. Of the art on display, the work to look for is the *Annunziata* in the Cappella dell'Annunziata. A 14th-century wooden sculpture, it is believed to have been carved by the Tuscan sculptor Nino Pisano.

Chiesa di San Francesco　　CHURCH

(Via Sant'Antonio; ⊘ open for mass only) The 14th-century *Crocifisso di Nicodemo*, considered one of Sardinia's most precious carvings, is the highlight of this 19th-century neoclassical church designed by Cagliari architect Gaetano Cima. Also take a look at the sacristy's 16th-century altarpiece by Pietro Cavaro.

In an earlier form, the church, which was first mentioned in the 13th century, was an important meeting place and, in 1388, it hosted the signing of a peace treaty between Eleonora of Arborea and the Aragonese King Giovanni I.

Museo Antiquarium Arborense　　MUSEUM

(🖉 0783 79 12 62; www.antiquariumarborense.it; Piazza Corrias; adult/reduced incl guided tour of historic centre €5/2.50; ⊘ 9am-2.30pm & 3.30-9pm summer, 9am-8pm Mon-Fri, 9am-2pm & 3-8pm Sat & Sun winter) Oristano's principal museum boasts one of the island's major archaeological collections, with prehistoric artefacts from the Sinis Peninsula and finds from Carthaginian and Roman Tharros. There's also a small collection of *retabli* (painted altarpieces), including the 16th-century *Retablo del Santo Cristo,* by the workshop of

Oristano

Pietro Cavaro, which depicts a group of apparently beatific saints. But look closer and you'll see they all sport the instruments of their tortures slicing through their heads, necks and hearts.

The permanent collection, which includes a scale model of 4th-century Tharros, is displayed on the upper floor. Here you'll find prehistoric obsidian and flint spearheads, axes, bones and a smattering of jewellery from the Sinis Peninsula. More interesting, though, is the stash of finds from Carthaginian and Roman Tharros, which includes ceramics, glassware, oil lamps, amphorae and a range of pots, plates and cups.

Pinacoteca Carlo Contini & Centro di Documentazione Sulla Sartiglia
GALLERY

(Via Sant'Antonio 9; ⊙10.30am-1pm & 5-8.45pm Mon-Sat summer, to 7.30pm winter) **FREE** Oristano's municipal art gallery has a small but interesting collection of Sardinian paint-

ings. Look out for various depictions of the *mamuthones,* the sinister costumed characters that feature in many Sardinian carnival festivities, and Sa Sartiglia, Oristano's headline festival. For more on the festival, pop into the adjacent Sartiglia documentation centre and peruse the collection of festival memorabilia, which includes masks, costumes and an interesting selection of historic photos.

Torre di Mariano II
TOWER

(Piazza Roma) Little survives of the medieval walled town except for this 13th-century tower. Known also as the Torre di Cristoforo, it was the town's northern gate and an important part of the city's defences. The bell was added later in the 15th century.

Torre di Portixedda
TOWER

(⊙10am-noon & 4-6pm Tue-Sun) This tower, just to the east off Via Giuseppe Mazzini, was part of the city's medieval walls, most of

Oristano

◎ **Top Sights**
1 Cattedrale di Santa Maria
   Assunta A4
2 Piazza Eleonora d'Arborea B3

◎ **Sights**
3 Chiesa di San Francesco A3
4 Municipio (Town Hall) B3
5 Museo Antiquarium Arborense B2
6 Pinacoteca Carlo Contini &
   Centro di Documentazione
   Sulla Sartiglia A3
7 Statue of Eleonora B3
8 Torre di Mariano II B2
9 Torre di Portixedda..............................D2

⬛ **Sleeping**
10 B&B L'Arco C3
11 Duomo Albergo B4
12 Eleonora B&B B3
13 Iride Guesthouse..................................C1

⬛ **Eating**
   Josto al Duomo ....(see 11)
14 La Torre B1
15 Ristorante Craf Da Banana.................A2
16 Trattoria Gino B1

⬛ **Drinking & Nightlife**
17 Lola Mundo B3

which were pulled down in the 19th century. It's now used to stage temporary exhibitions.

✦ Festivals & Events

★ **Sa Sartiglia**   CARNIVAL
(☉Feb) Oristano's carnival is the most colourful on the island. It is attended in February by hundreds of costumed participants and involves a medieval joust, horse racing and incredible, acrobatic riding.

✕ Eating

Eating in Oristano is a pleasure, especially if you like fish. There's a good range of reasonably priced restaurants, and the nearby Stagno di Cabras lagoon and Golfo di Oristano ensure a steady supply of fresh seafood. Local staples include mullet *(muggine),* sometimes known as *pesce di Oristano* (Oristano fish), which often appears on menus as *mrecca* (boiled, wrapped in pond grass and then dried and salted). Grilled eel is popular, as are *patelle,* limpet-like dark clams.

La Torre   PIZZERIA €
(☑0783 30 14 94; Piazza Roma 52; pizzas €4.50-10, meals €20-25; ☉noon-3pm & 7-11.30pm Tue-

Sun) This place doesn't look like much from the outside; in fact, it's not so amazing inside either. No matter, it serves the best pizza in town. If you're off pizza but just want to enjoy the hectic atmosphere, there's a full menu of pastas and grilled main courses.

★ **Trattoria Gino**   TRATTORIA €€
(☑0783 7 14 28; Via Tirso 13; meals €25-30; ☉12.30-3pm & 7.30-11pm Mon-Sat) For excellent food and a bustling, authentic vibe, head to this old-school trattoria. Gino's has been on the go since the 1930s and still today it packs them in, as locals and visitors squeeze into the single dining room to feast on tasty seafood and classic pastas. Particularly good is the seafood antipasto and the butter-soft roast *seppie* (cuttlefish).

Josto al Duomo   SARDINIAN €€
(☑0783 77 80 61; www.jostoalduomo.net; Via Vittorio Emanuele 34; meals €35-45, 2-/3-/4-course tasting menu €16/25/43; ☉1-3pm & 8-11pm Mon-Sat) Refined and intimate, this hotel restaurant is gathered around an inner courtyard perfect for alfresco dining. The menu is seasonal but the onus is on creative dishes inspired by traditional Sardinian flavours and served with an artistic eye for detail. For wine aficionados, there's also a strong wine list featuring many interesting island labels.

Ristorante Craf Da Banana   RISTORANTE €€
(☑0783 7 06 69; Via de Castro 34; meals €35; ☉12.30-3pm & 7.30-10.30pm Mon-Sat) Housed in a former 17th-century granary, this brick-vaulted restaurant enjoys a good local reputation. Hearty country fare dominates the menu – try the *panne frattau* (Sardinian bread soup) or grilled *asinello* (donkey) – although there are plenty of seafood options to go for, including spaghetti *alla bottarga* (with mullet roe).

🍷 Drinking & Nightlife

116 Caffè   CAFE
(Via Tirso 116; ☉6.30am-1am Mon-Sat) This modern cafe – think bare wooden floorboards, black and grey tones – is the place for an early evening *aperitivo* accompanied by a pre-dinner snack from the ample buffet spread.

Lola Mundo   CAFE
(Piazza Corrias 14; ☉7am-midnight Mon-Sat) With its piazza seating and relaxing music, this popular *centro storico* (historic centre) cafe is a great spot to hang out over a coffee or aperitif.

🛍 Shopping

Cantina Sociale della Vernaccia WINE
(☎ 0783 3 33 83; www.vinovernaccia.com; Via Oristano 6/A, Rimedio; ⊗ 8am-1pm & 3.30-6.30pm Mon-Fri, 9am-1pm Sat) Oristano is famous for its fortified Vernaccia wine, and this cantina about 4km out of the city centre is the place to buy it. Most of Oristano's local producers bring their grapes here to be crushed, so you can be assured of the quality.

ℹ Information

Farmacia (☎ 0783 7 03 38; Corso Umberto I 49-51; ⊗ 8.30am-1.30pm & 5-8.30pm Mon-Fri) Central pharmacy.

Ospedale San Martino (☎ 0783 31 71; Piazza San Martino) Hospital south of the centre.

Post Office (☎ 0783 36 80 28; Via Mariano IV d'Arborea; ⊗ 8.20am-7.05pm Mon-Fri, 8.20am-12.35pm Sat)

Tourist Office (☎ 0783 368 32 10; www.gooristano.com; Piazza Eleonora d'Arborea 18; ⊗ 8.30am-1pm & 3-6pm Mon-Thu, 8.30am-1pm Fri) Ask for the useful booklet *Oristano in your Pocket*.

ℹ Getting There & Away

BUS

From the main **bus station** (Via Cagliari) direct buses run to/from Santa Giusta (€1.20, 15 minutes, half-hourly), Cagliari (€7, two hours, two daily), Bosa (€6, two hours, five daily) and Sassari (€8, two hours, three daily).

CAR & MOTORCYCLE

Oristano is just off the SS131, which connects Cagliari with Sassari and Porto Torres. Branch highways head off to the northeast for Nuoro and Olbia.

TRAIN

The main train station is in Piazza Ungheria, east of the town centre.

Up to 15 daily trains, some of which involve a change, run between Oristano and Cagliari (€5.95, one to 1½ hours). Direct trains serve Sassari (€10.15, two to 2½ hours, two daily) and Olbia (€11.50, 2¾ hours, three daily); there are additional services but they require a change at Ozieri-Chilivani.

ℹ Getting Around

BUS

The town centre is easily covered on foot, although you'll probably want to use buses to get in from the train station. Take a line 3 bus to Piazza Roma in the historic centre.

Various buses run from Via Cagliari to Marina di Torregrande (€1.20, 15 minutes).

CAR & MOTORCYCLE

Parking is not too difficult if you leave your car a little out of the centre. Blue lines denote pay-display parking. Near the centre it costs €0.80 per hour between 8.30am and 1pm and then from 4pm to 7.30pm Monday to Saturday. Outside these hours it's free.

SA SARTIGLIA: ORISTANO'S MARDI GRAS

Sa Sartiglia is Sardinia's most colourful and carefully choreographed festival. Its origins are unknown but its godlike central figure, the *Su Cumpoidori,* hints at pagan ritual. The jousts and costumes are undoubtedly Spanish, probably introduced by the *giudici* (provincial governors), who were trained at the Court of Aragon. The word 'Sartiglia' comes from the Castilian *sortija,* meaning 'ring', and the central event is a medieval joust in which the *Su Cumpoidori,* the King of the *Sartiglia,* must pierce a star (ring) suspended overhead. The virgin brides who dress the *Su Cumpoidori,* along with his effeminate, godlike status and the throwing of grain, all suggest older fertility rites heralding spring.

The event is held over two days, Sunday and *martedi grasso* (Shrove Tuesday or Mardi Gras). At noon the *Su Cumpoidori* is 'born'. He sits on a table (the altar) and is reverently clothed and masked by the *sas massaieddas* (young virgins). From this point on he cannot touch the ground and is carried to his horse, which is almost as elaborately dressed as he. The *Su Cumpoidori's* white mask is framed by a stiff mantilla on top of which he wears a black top hat. In his hand he carries a sceptre decorated with violets and periwinkles with which he blesses the crowd. It is his task to start the *Sartiglia,* the race to the star, which he does with two other knights, his *segundu* (second) and *terzu* (third), who all try to pierce the star. The more times they strike it, the more luck they bring to the coming year. The last ritual the *Su Cumpoidori* performs is the *Sa Remada,* where he gallops along the course lying on his back. Then the games are open to acrobatic riders who perform feats that draw gasps from the crowd.

TAXI

There are taxi stands at the train station and on Piazza Roma. Alternatively call ☑ 0783 7 02 80 or ☑ 0783 7 43 28.

SOUTH OF ORISTANO

South of Oristano, flat plains extend in a patchwork of wide, open fields interspersed with canals, lagoons and the odd pocket of pine wood. Until Mussolini launched an ambitious drainage and reclamation program in 1919, the area was largely covered with malarial swampland and thick cork forests. Nowadays it's a featureless, and sometimes strange, landscape dotted with sleepy villages and agricultural towns.

Santa Giusta

POP 4850

A bustling agricultural town, Santa Giusta lies on the shores of the **Stagno di Santa Giusta**, Sardinia's third-largest lagoon. Once the Punic town of Othoca, it is best known for its extraordinary basilica, one of the first, and finest, examples of Romanesque architecture in Sardinia.

◎ Sights

★ **Basilica di Santa Giusta**   CHURCH
(⊙7.30am-6.30pm) This landmark Romanesque church is one of Sardinia's architectural jewels. Dating to the early 12th century, it sports a severe sandstone exterior punctuated by blind arcades and a typically Tuscan portal. Inside, three naves are divided by rows of marble and granite columns, several of which probably came from ancient Tharros. Beneath the presbytery, a vaulted crypt houses the relics of St Justa, a 2nd-century martyr who is said to have been executed here during the reign of Diocletian.

For four days around 14 May, the basilica takes centre stage during celebrations of the town's annual **Festa di Santa Giusta**.

Stagno S'Ena Arrubia   LAGOON
Six kilometres to the south of Santa Giusta, the Stagno S'Ena Arrubia is a paradise for birdwatchers – flamingos, herons, coots and ospreys are regularly sighted.

❶ Getting There & Away

Half-hourly buses run to/from Oristano's bus station (€1.20, 15 minutes).

Arborea

POP 4030

Founded by Mussolini in 1928, the quiet town of Arborea bears all the hallmarks of its Fascist inception – severe grid-patterned streets, an immaculate central piazza and an array of fantastical architectural styles. Just a few kilometres northwest, the coastal hamlet of Marina di Arborea is home to a notable equestrian centre.

◎ Sights & Activities

Piazza Maria Ausiliatrice   PIAZZA
Arborea's showcase square, Piazza Maria Ausiliatrice is a beautifully tended space that wouldn't look out of place in a Swiss alpine village. Overlooking it is the clocked facade of the Tyrolean-style **Chiesa del Cristo Redentore**, and, over the road, the art nouveau **Municipio** (Town Hall).

MUB Museo della Bonifica   MUSEUM
(☑0783 80 20 05; Corso Italia 24; admission €4; ⊙10am-noon & 3-6pm Tue-Fri, 10am-12.30pm Sat & Sun) ✔ **FREE** Housed in a renovated mill, Arborea's civic museum charts the reclaiming *(bonifica)* of the land on which the town now sits. There's also a small archaeological section displaying nuraghic and ancient artefacts unearthed at the Necropoli di S'Ungroni and other sites in the vicinity.

Spiaggia di Marina di Arborea   BEACH
The tiny settlement of Marina di Arborea gives onto this long and rarely busy beach. Backed by dense pine woods, the sandy strip extends northwards for several kilometres to the Stagno S'Ena Arrubia lagoon.

Horse Country Resort   HORSE RIDING
(☑0783 8 05 00; www.horsecountry.it; Strada a Mare 24; riding lessons per person from €20) Hidden behind a thick pine wood at Marina di Arborea, 2km northwest of Arborea, this is Sardinia's largest equestrian centre, and one of the most important in Italy with a stable of Arabian, Andalucian and Sardinian horses. You can choose from a number of riding packages with lessons starting at €20 per person. Accommodation (p206) at the resort is also available.

Marceddi

Overlooking the mouth of the **Stagno di Marceddi**, this tiny fishing village is the embodiment of a backwater. For much of the year the only signs of modern life are a few battered cars and the ragged electricity lines flapping over dirt roads. The lagoon, which separates the Arborea plains from the Costa Verde, is an important wildlife habitat, harbouring flamingos, cormorants and herons.

✖️ Eating

Da Lucio SEAFOOD €€
(📞0783 86 71 30; www.ristorantedalucio.it; Via Lungomare 40; meals around €35; ⊙12.30-2.45pm & 8.30-10.45pm Fri-Wed) The pick of Marceddi's waterfront restaurants, this is a prime spot for a delicious seafood feast. Try the octopus salad, or, if they're available, fleshy little sea urchins, followed by *fregola con arselle nera* (small semolina pasta with black clams). For a main course, you can't go wrong with grilled fish.

SINIS PENINSULA

Spearing into the Golfo di Oristano, the Sinis Peninsula feels like a world apart. Its limpid lagoons – the Stagno di Cabras, Stagno Sale Porcus and Stagno Is Benas – and snow-white beaches lend it an almost tropical air, while the low-lying green countryside appears uncontaminated by human activity. In fact, the area has been inhabited since the 5th century BC. *Nuraghi* litter the landscape and the compelling Punic-Roman site of Tharros stands as testament to the area's for-

mer importance. Sports fans will enjoy great surfing, windsurfing and some fine diving.

Although summer is the obvious time to visit, early spring is also wonderful as wildflowers brighten the verdant landscape and flocks of migrating birds swarm to the lagoons. The queen of the show is the gorgeous pink flamingo.

Cabras

POP 9080
Sprawled on the southern shore of the Stagno di Cabras, Cabras is an important fishing town and centre of the island's mullet fishing – the local *bottarga* (mullet roe) is much sought-after and well worth trying. There's little reason to linger, but you'll eat well and the archaeology museum deserves a once-over.

◉ Sights

★ Museo Civico MUSEUM
(📞0783 29 06 36; www.penisoladelsinis.it; Via Tharros 121; adult/reduced €5/4, incl Tharros €8/5; ⊙9am-1pm & 4-8pm summer, 9am-1pm & 3-7pm winter) Cabras' one sight of interest is the Museo Civico, located at the southern end of town. The star attraction here is the so-called Giants of Monte Prama, a series of towering nuraghic figures depicting archers, wrestlers and boxers. Also of interest are finds from the prehistoric site of Cuccuru Is Arrius and Tharros, as well as a collection of obsidian

---

THE GIANTS OF MONTE PRAMA

A group of vast nuraghic figures, the Giants of Monte Prama saw the light of day for the first time in almost 3000 years when they went on show in March 2014.

The sandstone statues, which stand up to 2.5m high, are among the oldest of their type ever discovered in the Mediterranean, dating to the 8th or 9th century BC. They depict archers, boxers and warriors, and have strange, haunting faces with pronounced eyebrows and well-defined noses. Their most distinguishing feature, however, are their hypnotic eyes, which are represented by two concentric circles, thought to symbolise power and magic.

As they stand today, the statues are the result of a painstaking four-year project to piece them together from fragments found at Monte Prama, a low-rising hill between San Salvatore and Riola Sardo. The first fragments were accidentally discovered by a local farmer in 1974 but over the next five years more than 5000 pieces were unearthed, including 15 heads and 22 torsos. So far archaeologists have assembled 25 statues and 13 models of *nuraghi,* and identified pieces for three more figures.

Excavation of the site is ongoing and new discoveries are constantly being made. In May 2014, two blocks of carved sandstone were found, leading archaeologists to venture that the site may have been a temple or sanctuary, rather than a necropolis as they previously thought.

and flint tools said to date back to the neolithic cultures of Bonu Ighinu and Ozieri.

✸✸ Festivals & Events

Festa di San Salvatore
RELIGIOUS

(☉ Sep) To mark the Festa di San Salvatore on the first weekend in September, hundreds of young men participate in the **Corsa degli Scalzi**, a traditional barefoot dash between Cabras and San Salvatore. The run, which is spread over two days, commemorates an episode in 1506, when townspeople rushed to San Salvatore to save a statue of the Holy Saviour from Moorish sea raiders.

Events kick off on the Saturday when the runners, all barefoot and clad in white, accompany the statue along 8km of dusty paths to San Salvatore. But this is only the halfway point, and the next day they retrace their steps and haul the statue back to Cabras for safekeeping at the Chiesa di Santa Maria Assunta.

✗ Eating

Sa Peschiera 'e Mar 'e Pontis
SEAFOOD €€

(☑ 0783 39 17 74; Strada Provinciale 6; menus €25-35; ☉ 1-2.30pm & 8-10.30pm, closed Wed & Sun dinner) Fronting the Pontis fishing cooperative on the road between Cabras and Tharros, this is a fantastic place to sample fresh seafood. The menu changes according to the daily catch but pride of place goes to the local *muggine* (mullet) and prized *bottarga* (mullet roe). Booking is recommended and essential at weekends.

Il Caminetto
SEAFOOD €€

(☑ 0783 39 11 39; www.ristorante-ilcaminetto.com; Via Cesare Battisti 8; meals €35; ☉ 12.30-2.45pm & 8-10.30pm Tue-Sun) Hidden away in the historic centre, this is one of the best-known seafood restaurants in the area. Sit down to island classics such as *muggine affumicato* (smoked mullet) followed by *spaghetti alle arselle e bottarga* (spaghetti with clams and mullet roe) and *burrida* (ray in a spicy tomato sauce).

L'Oliveto
PIZZERIA €€

(☑ 0783 39 26 16; Via Tirso 23; meals €30-35; ☉ 7.30pm-midnight Wed-Mon) Head to this unpretentious restaurant-cum-pizzeria in an olive grove near the northern edge of town for traditional seafood staples and excellent pizza.

ℹ Getting There & Away

Buses run every hour to/from Oristano (€1.20, 15 minutes).

Marina di Torregrande

About 4.5km south of Cabras, the small summer resort of Marina di Torregrande is a favourite hang-out for Oristano's beach-goers. Behind the long, sandy beach, the village presents a familiar seaside scene with suntanned locals parading down a palm-flanked *lungomare* (promenade) and music emanating from bars. Out of season it's a different story and you'll find the holiday homes shuttered and most of the restaurants closed.

The village's one and only building of any historical note is the stout 16th-century **Aragonese watchtower**, after which the resort is named. Once you've seen that, there's not much to do except don your swimmers and head to the beach. You can hire sunloungers and umbrellas there – expect to pay from about €11 per day.

✗ Activities

Eolo
WINDSURFING

(☑ 327 5609844; www.eolowindsurf.com; Lungomare Eleonora d'Arborea) Eolo organises sailing and windsurfing courses, as well as kitesurfing, beach tennis and equipment rental (windsurfs start at €15 per hour).

✗ Eating & Drinking

Da Giovanni
RISTORANTE €€

(☑ 0783 2 20 51; Via Colombo 8; meals €35-40; ☉ 1-3pm & 8-11pm Tue-Sun) In a nondescript setting on the main road out of Marina di Torregrande, this historic local restaurant specialises in creative seafood. Typical of their approach is *lasagnette* (small lasagne) with sardines, mussels, thyme and wild fennel sauce.

BNN Fashion Club
BAR, CLUB

(☑ 338 2357540; www.bnnfashionclub.it; SP94, km1.8; ☉ 11pm-6am summer) A few kilometres inland on the road to Cabras, BNN Fashion Club is a popular bar-cum-disco. Guest DJs serve up a steady backbeat of commercial, house and revival music to a well-dressed summer crowd.

ℹ Getting There & Away

From Oristano, buses run from various stops along Via Cagliari (including the main terminal) to Marina di Torregrande (€1.20, 15 minutes).

San Salvatore

A spaghetti-western film set during the 1960s, the tiny hamlet of San Salvatore is centred on a dusty square and surrounded by rows of minuscule terraced houses, known as *cumbessias*. For much of the year these simple abodes are deserted, as is the rest of the village, but in early September they are opened to house pilgrims for the Festa di San Salvatore, a nine-day celebration focused on the village's pint-sized church.

◉ Sights

Chiesa di San Salvatore   CHURCH
(◷9.30am-1pm year-round & 3.30-6pm Mon-Sat summer) In the centre of the village, the 17th-century Chiesa di San Salvatore stands over a stone *ipogeo* (underground vault) dating to the nuraghic period. This original-ly housed a pagan sanctuary linked to the cult of water, and you can still see a well in the main chamber. It was later converted into a Roman-era church, and the dark stone walls still bear traces of 4th-century graffiti and faded frescoes.

✖ Eating

★**Agriturismo Sinis**   SARDINIAN €
(☎328 9312508, 0783 39 26 53; www.agriturismoilsinis.it; Località San Salvatore; meals €20-32; ◷booking required) Just beyond the turn-off for San Salvatore, the Agriturismo Sinis is a working farm with a superb restaurant. The menu depends on what's available on the day, but the vegetables and fruit are home-grown and the meat, including home-bred *porcetto* (suckling pig), is cooked to perfection on a big outdoor grill. Bookings required.

San Giovanni di Sinis

At the southern tip of the Sinis Peninsula, about 5km beyond San Salvatore, the road passes through the small settlement of San

---

SINIS PENINSULA BEACHES

Within easy striking distance of Oristano, the beaches on the Sinis Peninsula are among the best on the island. Ideally you'll need your own car to get to them, but two weekday buses run from Oristano to Putzu Idu (€2, 55 minutes) with four additional services in July and August.

Is Aruttas One of the peninsula's most famous beaches, Is Aruttas is a pristine arc of white sand fronted by translucent aquamarine waters. For years its quartz sand was carted off to be used in aquariums and on beaches on the Costa Smeralda but it's now illegal to take any. The beach is signposted and 5km west of the road north from San Salvatore.

Putzu Idu Backed by a motley set of holiday homes and beach bars, Putzu Idu's beach sits at the north of the peninsula. It's a picturesque strip of sand that's something of a water sport hotspot with excellent surfing, windsurfing and kitesurfing. To the north, the **Capo Mannu** promontory is battered by some of the biggest waves in the Mediterranean.

Isola di Mal di Ventre This bare, rocky island 10km off the coast owes its strange name (Stomach-ache Island) to the sea-sickness that sailors often suffered while navigating its windy waters. Now uninhabited, it was home to a primitive nuraghic settlement and was later used by Saracen pirates. These days, the only people to visit are holidaymakers keen to search out the beaches on its eastern shores. To get to the island, **Maremania** (☎348 0084161; www.maluentu.it; tours per adult/reduced €25/15; ◷8am-1pm & 3-7pm summer only) is one of several operators running boat tours from Putzu Idu between June and September.

Capo Mannu Windsurf School (☎347 6881793; www.capomannuwindsurf.it; Lungomare Putzu Idu) Runs windsurfing lessons and courses for all levels, as well as hiring out boards and sail rigs. One-hour individual lessons start at €35; rig hire from €15 per hour.

Giovanni di Sinis. Just beyond the car park at the foot of the Tharros access road, you'll see the sandstone **Chiesa di San Giovanni di Sinis** (⊙9am-5pm), one of the two oldest churches in Sardinia (Cagliari's Basilica of San Saturnino is older). It owes its current form to an 11th-century makeover, although elements of the 6th-century Byzantine original remain, including the characteristic red dome. Inside, the bare walls lend a sombre and surprisingly spiritual atmosphere.

Five daily buses run from Oristano to San Giovanni di Sinis (€2.50, 35 minutes), continuing on to Is Aruttas beach (€3, 50 minutes).

Tharros

From San Giovanni di Sinis, the road continues past a strip of pizzerias, bars and cafes up to the Area Archeologica di Tharros, one of Sardinia's most thrilling archaeological sites. Tharros was a major city in ancient times and its ruins today make for a haunting sight as they tumble down the promontory to Capo San Marco, the southernmost point of the Sinis Peninsula. Try to visit early in the morning or just before sunset when the site is at its quietest and most atmospheric.

History

The Sinis Peninsula was already home to a thriving nuraghic settlement when the Phoenicians established a base here in about 730 BC. Their city, Tharros, flourished and was eventually absorbed into the Carthaginian empire. But, as an important naval centre in a strategic position, it was always vulnerable and when the Romans attacked in the 3rd century BC, the city fell to the rampant legionnaires.

Under the Romans, it remained a key naval town and was given a thorough overhaul in the 2nd and 3rd centuries AD. It was eventually abandoned in 1070 after its citizens could take no more of the increasingly aggressive Vandal and Saracen raids. Much of the ancient city was subsequently stripped to build the new capital at Oristano.

Sights

★ **Area Archeologica di Tharros** ARCHAEOLOGICAL SITE
(📞0783 37 00 19; www.penisoladelsinis.it; adult/reduced €5/4, incl tower €6/5, incl Museo Civico Cabras €8/5; ⊙9am-8pm summer, to 5pm win-

OASI DI SEU

A few kilometres out of Tharros, and signposted off the main road, the **Oasi di Seu** is a veritable Eden of Mediterranean flora. Once you've navigated the 3km dirt track to the entrance, you enter a silent world of sandy paths and undisturbed nature. Herby smells fill the air, rising off fragrant masses of *macchia* (scrub), rosemary, dwarf palms and pine trees.

ter) The choppy blue waters of the Golfo di Oristano provide a magnificent backdrop to the ruins of ancient Tharros. Founded by the Phoenicians in the 8th century BC, the city thrived as a Carthaginian naval base and was later taken over by the Romans. Much of what you see today dates to the 2nd and 3rd centuries AD, when the basalt streets were laid, and the aqueduct, baths and other major monuments were built.

As you approach the site it's impossible to see the ruins until you reach the hilltop ticket office. From here follow a brief stretch of *cardo* (the main street in a Roman settlement) until you reach, on your left, the *castellum aquae,* the city's main water reserve. Two lines of pillars can be made out within the square structure. From here the **Cardo Massimo**, the city's main thoroughfare, leads to a bare rise topped by a Carthaginian **acropolis** and a **tophet**, a sacred burial ground for children. Also here are remains of the original nuraghic settlement.

From the bottom of the Cardo Massimo, the **Decumano** runs down to the sea passing the remains of a **Punic temple** and, beyond that, the Roman-era **Tempio Tetrastilo**, marked by its two solitary columns. These are, in fact, reconstructions, although the Corinthian capital balanced on the top of one is authentic.

Nearby is a set of **thermal baths** and, to the north, the remains of a **palaeo-Christian baptistry**. At the southernmost point of the settlement is another set of baths, dating to the 3rd century AD.

For a bird's-eye view of the site, head up to the late-16th-century **Torre di San Giovanni watchtower** (adult/reduced €3/2, incl Tharros €6/5; ⊙9am-8pm summer, to 5pm winter), occasionally used for exhibitions. Here you can look down on the ruins, as well as the **Spiaggia di San Giovanni di Sinis**, a popular beach, which extends on both sides of the tower. There is nothing to stop you wandering down the dirt tracks to Capo San Marco and the lighthouse.

❶ Getting There & Away

In July and August, there are five daily buses for San Giovanni di Sinis from Oristano (€2, 35 minutes).

Parking near the site costs about €2 for two hours, €4 per day.

MONTI FERRU

North and inland of the Sinis Peninsula, the landscape is dominated by the wooded slopes of Monti Ferru. Rising to a height of 1050m (Monte Urtigu), this vast volcanic massif is a beautiful and largely uncontaminated area of ancient forests, natural springs and small market towns. Seneghe produces some of Sardinia's best olive oil, and the island's finest beef, and Milis is famous for its sweet succulent oranges. But more than the towns, it's the glorious verdant countryside that is the main draw. Lonely roads snake over rocky peaks covered in a green down of cork, chestnut, oak and yew trees while falcons and buzzards float on warm air currents overhead. Mouflon and Sardinian deer are slowly being introduced back to their forest habitats after coming close to extinction.

Milis

POP 1590

A one-time Roman military outpost (its name is a derivation of the Latin word *miles,* meaning soldier), Milis is a small and prosperous farming village, surrounded by the orange orchards that have brought it wealth. Its principal sight is the stately Palazzo Boyl but there are also a couple of churches worth a passing glance. Near the eastern entrance to town, the Tuscan-Romanesque **Chiesa di San Paolo** harbours some interesting paintings by 16th-century Catalan artists.

◉ Sights

Palazzo Boyl   HISTORIC BUILDING
(📞0783 5 16 65; Piazza Martiri; ⊘ by appointment only) **FREE** A fine example of Piedmontese neoclassicism, 18th-century Palazzo Boyl dominates Milis' manicured village centre.

Originally a summer residence for the aristocratic Boyl family, in the late 19th and early 20th centuries it became something of a literary meeting place; Gabriele D'Annunzio, Grazia Deledda and Honoré de Balzac all spent time here. Nowadays it houses a small museum dedicated to traditional Sardinian costumes and jewellery.

Opposite the *palazzo,* the 14th-century **Chiesa di San Sebastiano** features an impressive rose window in its Catalan Gothic facade.

Chiesa di San Paolo   CHURCH
Near the eastern entrance to town, the Tuscan-Romanesque Chiesa di San Paolo harbours some interesting paintings by 16th-century Catalan artists.

★ Festivals & Events

Rassegna del Vino Novello   WINE
(Festival of Young Wine; www.vininovelli.com; ⊘Nov) In early November, Milis holds the Festival of Young Wine, a chance for Sardinia's wine producers to show off their best products. You can do the rounds sampling the wines and grazing the food stalls that line the streets.

Seneghe

POP 1820 / ELEV 310M

Seneghe is an essential stop on any gastronomic tour of central Sardinia. A dark stone village with little obvious appeal, it is famous for its extra-virgin olive oil, a one-time winner of the prestigious Premio Nazionale Ercole Olivario award (the Oscars of the Italian olive-oil industry). Beef is another speciality. Russet-red *bue rosso* cows are bred only here and in Modica in Sicily, and gourmets consider the meat to be among the finest in Italy. The village also provides food for the soul, hosting an annual poetry festival.

★ Festivals & Events

Settembre dei Poeti   LITERATURE
(www.settembredeipoeti.it; ⊘ Aug/Sep) Held in late August or early September, the Settembre dei Poeti is a four-day celebration of local and international poetry with readings, Q&A sessions and a poetry slam competition – a thoroughly entertaining, dramatic performance in which adversaries improvise rhyming responses to each other, much like a freestyle rap battle.

HIKE MONTI FERRU

The best way of exploring Monti Ferru is to ditch the car and walk. This scenic route leads up to the summit of Monte Entu, at 1024m one of the highest peaks in western Sardinia. It's not especially demanding, although you should allow about four hours.

You'll need a car to get to the start, which is by the Nuraghe Ruju, outside of Seneghe. From Seneghe, head towards Bonarcado and after a few hundred metres follow the sign for S'iscala. Continue up the road for about 8km to the Nuraghe Ruju picnic area and join the path a few metres down from the car park, in the wood to the left of the stone wall. Heading upwards you'll arrive at an opening, marked by a holm-oak tree, where you should go left. Carry on past the wooden gate until you reach a second metal gate. Go through it and continue until you reach a fork in the trail. Head left for some marvellous views of the coast, as far as Alghero on a clear day. From here you can continue onwards to the foot of the volcanic cone that marks the summit of Monte Entu.

Eating

Sa Tanka   RISTORANTE, PIZZERIA €€
(www.satanka.it; Piazzale Montiferru 3/4; ☉1-3pm & 8-10.30pm Tue-Sun) No place for vegetarians, this unpretentious restaurant by the exit to Narbolia specialises in locally sourced meat. That means antipasti of salamis and cured sausages, meaty pasta sauces and juicy *tagliata* (steak) served with rucola, sweet cherry tomatoes and shards of grated Parmesan. Wood-fired pizzas are also served on Friday, Saturday and Sunday evenings.

🛍 Shopping

**Oleificio Sociale
Cooperativo di Seneghe**   OLIVE OIL
(☏340 0882024, 0785 5 46 65; www.oleificiodiseneghe.it; Corso Umberto I; ☉9am-12.30pm & 5-7.30pm Mon-Fri) To stock up on the town's award-wining olive oil make a beeline for the Oleificio Sociale Cooperativo di Seneghe on the Bonarcado road into town. Prices start at €4 for 0.25L or €7 for 0.5L.

Bonarcado

POP 1620 / ELEV 283M

About 5km northeast of Seneghe, the sleepy village of Bonarcado is home to one of Sardinia's most unlikely pilgrimage sites. According to an edict issued by Pope Pius VII in 1821, anyone who confesses at the tiny **Santuario di Santa Maria Madonna di Bonacattu** between 14 and 28 September will receive full plenary indulgence. The sanctuary, which is little more than a chapel capped by a simple dome, was constructed in the 7th century and modified some 800 years later. There are no official opening hours, but you'll usually find it open.

Nearby, the Romanesque **Chiesa di Santa Maria di Bonacardo** is a rather more imposing affair. Consecrated in 1147, it originally formed part of a medieval monastery.

Santu Lussurgiu

POP 2430 / ELEV 503M

On the eastern slopes of Monti Ferru, Santu Lussurgiu lies inside an ancient volcanic crater. The main point of interest is the small *centro storico*, a tight-knit huddle of stone houses banked up around a natural amphitheatre.

◉ Sights

**Museo della
Tecnologia Contadina**   MUSEUM
(Museum of Rural Technology; ☏0783 55 06 17; www.museotecnologiacontadina.it; Via Deodato Meloni 1; ☉by appointment) Santu Lussurgiu has long been known for its crafts and is still today a production centre for ironwork, woodwork and leatherwork. To learn more about the town's rural way of life and traditions, book a visit to this small museum, which has a comprehensive collection of farm tools, utensils and machines.

🍴 Eating

Sas Benas   SARDINIAN €€
(☏0783 55 08 70; Piazza Giovanni; meals €30-40; ☉1-2.30pm & 8-11.30pm Tue-Sun) With a fireplace and heavy stone vaulting, Sas Benas' two dining rooms provide a suitably rustic setting for traditional country fare. Dishes, which showcase seasonal ingredients and local meats, include much-loved classics such as *pasta con funghi e salsiccia* (pasta with mushrooms and

sausage) and *tagliata di bue rosso* (steak of *bue rosso* beef).

ℹ️ Information

Tourist Office (☎ 0783 55 10 34; Via Santa Croce 9; ⏰ 6-8pm Tue, Thu & Sat) Information is available from this small tourist office in the historic centre.

ℹ️ Getting There & Away

Six weekday buses connect Santu Lussurgiu with Oristano (€3.50, 1½ to two hours).

San Leonardo de Siete Fuentes

ELEV 684M

From Santu Lussurgiu, the road to Cuglieri twists steeply up the eastern flank of Monti Ferru. Before you've gone far, a minor road heads off right (towards Macomer) for San Leonardo de Siete Fuentes, a tiny woodland hamlet famous for its gurgling spring waters. Its grandiose Spanish name is a reference to the seven fountains (*siete fuentes*) through which the water gushes.

In the village centre, a path leads up to the charming 12th-century **Chiesa di San Leonardo**, a Romanesque church that once belonged to the Knights of St John of Jerusalem. Beyond this, trails continue uphill, through the oak and elm woods. It's pretty easygoing walking, ideal for parents with little 'uns.

Cuglieri

POP 3010 / ELEV 483M

Perched high on the western face of Monti Ferru, the farming village of Cuglieri makes an excellent lunch stop.

◎ Sights

Basilica di Santa Maria della Neve CHURCH
A landmark for miles around, the hulking, silver-domed Basilica di Santa Maria della Neve marks the highpoint of the village. According to local tradition it stands on the spot where a bull-drawn cart deposited a statue of the Madonna which had mysteriously washed up on the beach at Santa Caterina di Pittinuri in the early 14th century.

More than the church, though, it's the vast views down to the sea that are the real highlight here.

Eating

★ Desogos TRATTORIA €
(☎ 0785 3 96 60; Via Cugia 6; meals €20; ⏰ noon-2.30pm & 8-11pm daily, booking required for dinner in winter) This welcoming, old-school trattoria in the historic centre is perfect for a fill-up of hearty mountain fare. There is a menu, but it's best to surrender yourself into the hands of the maternal owner who will ply you with a lip-smacking array of cured hams, marinated vegetables, tangy cheeses, pastas and grilled meats.

🛍️ Shopping

Azienda Agricola Peddio OLIVE OIL
(☎ 0785 36 92 54; www.oliopeddio.it; Corso Umberto 87; ⏰ 8.30am-1pm & 3-8pm) On the main road through the village, this is the place to stock up on local olive oil. A litre costs between €7 and €9.

ℹ️ Getting There & Away

There are five weekday buses between Cuglieri and Oristano (€3.50, one hour), and, in July and August, two Sunday services.

Santa Caterina di Pittinuri & Around

Winding down from Cuglieri, the SS292 leads to Santa Caterina di Pittinuri, the main resort on the northern Oristano coast. The town itself is largely made up of summer holiday homes and has little of interest, but there are some fine beaches in the vicinity.

A few kilometres to the south, the **Spiaggia dell'Arco** at **S'Archittu** features a dramatic stone arch that rises 6m above the emerald-green waters. Inland from S'Archittu, and accessible by a signposted dirt track off the SS292, are the scanty remains of the Punic-Roman town of **Cornus**, scene of a historic battle in 215 BC. The isolated site is open to free exploration.

About 3km south of **Torre del Pozzo** (also known as Torre Su Putzu), tracks lead off the main road to **Is Arenas** beach, which at 6km is one of the longest in the area.

From Oristano, buses run to S'Archittu and Santa Caterina (€2.50, 40 minutes, five Monday to Saturday, plus two on Sunday in July and August).

BOSA & AROUND

From Santa Caterina di Pittinuri, the SS292 winds northwards to Bosa, a pretty medieval town topped by a formidable hilltop castle. Close by, Bosa Marina provides beach access, while inland, Macomer is a workaday agricultural centre and important transport hub.

Bosa

POP 8010

Bosa is one of Sardinia's most attractive towns. Seen from a distance, its rainbow townscape resembles a vibrant Paul Klee canvas, with pastel houses stacked on a steep hillside, tapering up to a stark, grey castle. In front, moored fishing boats bob on a glassy river and palm trees line the elegant riverfront.

Bosa was established by the Phoenicians and thrived under the Romans. During the early Middle Ages it suffered repeat raids by Arab pirates, but in the early 12th century the Malaspina family (a branch of the Tuscan clan of the same name) moved in and built their huge castle. In the 19th century, the Savoys established lucrative tanneries here, but these have since fallen by the wayside.

◉ Sights & Activities

Most of Bosa's sights lie on the north bank of the river Temo. The main strip, Corso Vittorio Emanuele, is one block north of the riverfront and leads to the two central piazzas: Piazza Costituzione and Piazza IV Novembre. South of the river, Via Nazionale runs 3km west to Bosa Marina, the town's seaside satellite.

★**Castello Malaspina**   CASTLE
(☑0785 37 70 43; adult/reduced €5/3; ☺10am–1hr before sunset spring-autumn, 10am-1pm Sat & Sun winter) Commanding huge panoramic views, the hilltop castle was built in 1112 by the Tuscan Malaspina family. Little remains of the original structure except for the skeleton – imposing walls and a series of tough brick towers – and, inside, a humble 4th-century chapel, the **Chiesa di Nostra Signora di Regnos Altos**. This houses an extraordinary 14th-century fresco cycle depicting saints, ranging from a giant St Christopher to St Lawrence in the middle of his martyrdom on the grill.

Note that the castle's opening hours are substantially reduced from November to March, so if you want to visit in that period, it's best to phone ahead.

★**Museo Casa Deriu**   MUSEUM
(☑0785 37 70 43; www.bosaonline.com; Corso Vittorio Emanuele 59; adult/reduced €4.50/3; ☺10am-1pm & 3-5pm Tue-Sun, longer hours summer) Housed in an elegant 19th-century townhouse, Bosa's main museum showcases local arts and artisanal crafts. Each of the three floors has a different theme relating to the city and its past: the 1st floor hosts temporary exhibitions and displays of traditional hand embroidery; the 2nd floor displays the *palazzo's* original 19th-century decor and furnishings; and the top floor is dedicated to Melkiorre Melis (1889–1982), a local painter and one of Sardinia's most important modern artists.

Cattedrale dell'Immacolata   CATHEDRAL
(Piazza Duomo; ☺10am-noon & 4-7pm) Bosa's cathedral dates to the early 19th century when it was buillt over an earlier Romanesque church. A rare, if not overly riveting example of rococo (officially called Piedmontese baroque), it boasts an imposing marble altar and several frescoes by the 19th-century artist Emilio Scherer.

Museo Delle Conce   MUSEUM
(☑0785 37 70 43; Via Sas Conzas; adult/reduced €3.50/2.50; ☺10am-1pm & 3-6pm summer, 10am-1pm Mon-Fri, 3-6pm Sat & Sun winter) On the south bank of the river, this museum occupies the town's former tanneries which were still in business until after WWII. On the ground floor you can see the original stone tanks where the leather hides were washed; upstairs, explanatory panels and a small collection of photos and old tools illustrate the whole tanning process.

Chiesa di Sant'Antonio Abate   CHURCH
A short walk from Ponte Vecchio on the southern side of the river is the little Chiesa di Sant'Antonio Abate. Featuring a 16th-century Gothic facade in red trachyte stone, it's only open during the festival dedicated to St Antonio Abate on 16 and 17 January and again at Carnevale.

**Cattedrale di
San Pietro Extramuros**   CATHEDRAL
(admission €1; ☺9.30am-12.30pm Tue-Sat & 4-7pm Sat & Sun, shorter hours winter) Two kilometres

Bosa

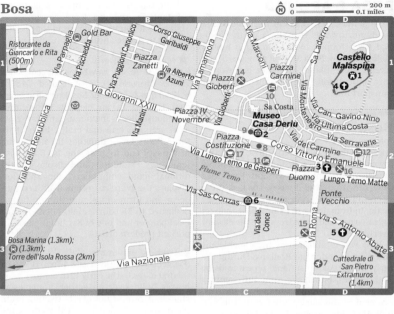

Bosa

◎ Top Sights
1 Castello Malaspina	D1
2 Museo Casa Deriu	C2

◎ Sights
3 Cattedrale dell'Immacolata	D2
4 Chiesa di Nostra Signora di Regnos Altos	D1
5 Chiesa di Sant'Antonio Abate	D3
6 Museo Delle Conce	C2

✪ Activities, Courses & Tours
7 Cuccu	D3
8 Esedra Sardegna	C2
9 Strada della Malvasia	C2

🛏 Sleeping
10 Aghinas	C1
11 Corte Fiorita	C2
12 La Torre di Alice	D2

✴ Eating
13 Al Gambero Rosso	C3
14 Pizza al Taglio	C1
15 Sa Pischedda	D3
16 Trattoria Biancospino	D2

🍷 Drinking & Nightlife
17 Caffè I Portici	C2

upstream from the Chiesa di Sant'Antonio Abate is this 11th-century cathedral, said to be the oldest Romanesque church in Sardinia. Originally built in 1073, it was subsequently modified with changes made to the apse in the 12th century and a Gothic facade added a century or so later.

Cuccu SCOOTER, BIKE HIRE
(☏ 0785 37 32 98; Via Roma 5; ⊘ 9am-1pm & 4-8pm) To explore out of town, you can hire scooters (€40 per day) and bikes (€10 per day) at this mechanic on the southern side of the river.

🎫 Tours

Esedra Sardegna TOURS
(☏ 0785 37 42 58; www.esedrasardegna.it; Corso Vittorio Emanuele 64; ⊘ 9.30am-1pm & 4.30-8pm Mon-Sat, 10.30am-1pm Sun) A reliable local operator that offers a wide range of packages, including river cruises, birdwatching excursions, boat tours, guided shop visits, and train trips on the *trenino verde*. Prices vary but are usually between €25 and €35 per person.

Strada della Malvasia WINE TOURS
(☏ 0785 37 70 43; www.stradadellamalvasiadibosa.it; Corso Vittorio Emanuele 59a) Bosa is an important wine centre, renowned for its

dessert wine, Malvasia. To learn more, the Strada della Malvasia can organise guided tastings (from €3.50 per person) and tours of local vineyards.

✪ Festivals & Events

Carnevale
CARNIVAL

(www.bosaonline.com; ☺ Feb) Carnevale kicks off with a burning pyre outside the Chiesa di Sant'Antonio Abate and follows with days of parades, culminating in boisterous celebrations on *martedì grasso* (Shrove Tuesday).

On the Tuesday morning townsfolk dress in black to lament the passing of Carnevale, while in the evening groups of locals dress in white to hunt the *giolzi,* a manifestation of the carnival that is said to hide in people's groins. To find it people hold lanterns up to each other's nether regions shouting '*Giolzi! Giolzi! Ciappadu! Ciappadu!*' (Giolzi! Giolzi! Gotcha! Gotcha!).

Festa di Santa Maria del Mare
RELIGIOUS

(www.bosasardinia.com; ☺ Aug) For four days around the first Sunday of August, Bosa celebrates the Festa di Santa Maria del Mare. Fishers form a colourful procession of boats to accompany a figure of the Virgin Mary from Bosa Marina to the cathedral. Fireworks and folkloristic performances add to the fun.

Festa di Nostra Signora di Regnos Altos
RELIGIOUS

(www.bosaonline.com; ☺ Sep) In the second week of September, streets in the old town are bedecked with huge palm fronds, flowers and *altarittos* (votive altars) to celebrate the Festa di Nostra Signora di Regnos Altos.

✗ Eating & Drinking

Pizza al Taglio
PIZZERIA €

(Via Ginnasio 7; pizza slices from €1.30; ☺ daily) For a quick bite on the hoof, head to this humble, no-frills takeaway and join the locals for a taste of Giovanni's fabulous sliced pizza.

★ Trattoria Biancospino
TRATTORIA €€

(☑ 0785 37 41 85; Corso Vittorio Emanuele 6; meals €25; ☺ 1-3pm & 7-11pm) A cosy little spot near the cathedral, this charming newcomer is a great find. Unlike most traditional trattorias, it serves a menu largely given over to *piatti unici* (single dishes) such as *bue rosso* steak with grilled cheese, veggies and homemade chips. If those don't appeal, you can go for a fail-safe pasta or try something out of

left field like Thai rice with sweet-and-sour vegetables.

Al Gambero Rosso
SARDINIAN €€

(☑ 0785 37 41 50; Via Nazionale 12; meals €25-30; ☺ 12.30-3pm & 7-11pm Thu-Tue) Brimming with regulars, this unpretentious restaurant stands head and shoulders above most of Bosa's eateries with its friendly service and winningly fresh pasta and seafood. Menu stalwarts include pasta with prawns and artichokes and crispy fried *calamari* (squid). Pizzas are delivered bubbling hot from a wood oven.

Sa Pischedda
SEAFOOD €€

(☑ 0785 37 30 65; Via Roma 8; meals €30-35, pizzas €7; ☺ 12.30-3pm & 7.30-11.30pm daily summer, Wed-Mon winter) At the hotel of the same name, Sa Pischedda is one of Bosa's top restaurants. With tables laid out on a romantic riverside verandah and in a stylish back garden, it specialises in fish, both freshwater and seawater, but also does excellent pasta and pizza.

Ristorante da Giancarlo e Rita
SARDINIAN €€

(☑ 0785 37 53 06; www.mannuhotel.it; Viale Alghero 14; meals €30-40; ☺ 1-2.30pm & 8-10.30pm) Despite its unenticing location – in the Hotel Mannu next to a busy petrol station – this restaurant serves fine island food. Fish and seafood feature heavily alongside traditional pastas and typical Sardinian *dolci* (sweets).

Caffè I Portici
CAFE

(Piazza Costituzione 6; ☺ 7am-9pm, later in summer) Good for a leisurely evening drink, Caffè I Portici is a bustling cafe with outdoor tables on Piazza Costituzione, a prime people-watching spot.

❶ Information

Banco di Sardegna (Piazza IV Novembre)

Farmacia (☑ 0785 37 13 32; Corso Vittorio Emanuele 51; ☺ 9am-12.30pm & 4-7.30pm Mon-Fri)

Post Office (Via Pischedda; ☺ 8.20am-7.05pm Mon-Fri, 8.20am-12.35pm Sat)

❶ Getting There & Away

BUS

There are weekday services from the **bus stops** on Piazza Zanetti to Alghero (€3.50, 55 minutes, two daily), Sassari (€6, 2¼ hours, three daily) and Oristano (€6, two hours, five daily). Buy tickets at **Gold Bar** (Via Azuni; ☺ 5am-midnight).

ORISTANO & THE WEST BOSA

CAR & MOTORCYCLE

Bosa is connected to Macomer by the SS129 and to Alghero by the scenic coastal road, the SP105. In central Bosa it's easy to find street-side parking in the modern town, west of the centre.

ℹ️ Getting Around

Frequent buses run from Piazza Zanetti to Bosa Marina (€1.20, 10 minutes).

Bosa Marina & the Coast

At the mouth of the Fiume Temo, about 2.5km from Bosa proper, Bosa Marina is a busy summer resort set on a wide, 1km-long beach. Overlooking the beach is the **Torre dell'Isola Rossa** (⊘ closed for restoration), one of the largest of a series of defensive towers built by the island's Aragonese rulers in the 16th century.

If you have your own transport, you can search out a number of other beaches. Stretching south are the **Spiaggia Turas**, **Spiaggia Porto Alabe** and **Cala Torre Columbargia**. The first two are respectively a 1.5km and 8km drive from Bosa Marina and can get busy in high season. Cala Torre Columbargia is reached via the town of Tresnuraghes and involves some dusty trail driving. It's about an 18km drive from Bosa Marina.

🏃 Activities

Bosa Diving DIVING
(☑ 335 8189748; www.bosadiving.it; Piazza Paul Harris Banchina Commerciale Foce del Temo, Bosa Marina) This established operator offers a series of packages, including guided dives (from €45) and snorkelling excursions (€35). It also hires out canoes (double canoes €10 per hour) and dinghies (for four people from €130 per day).

Trenino Verde TRAIN TOUR
(www.treninoverde.com; ⊘ mid-Jun–Sep) For a different take on the area, the summer-only *trenino verde* (little green train) runs, slowly, between Bosa Marina, Tresnuraghes and Macomer.

The hours vary from year to year, but typically the train departs from Bosa Marina at around 9.15am, arrives at Tresnuraghes an hour later, and pulls into Macomer at about 11.45am. The return trip to Bosa Marina is then by bus.

Return fares: Macomer to Bosa Marina (€16); Bosa Marina to Tresnuraghes (€13.50).

Macomer

POP 10,440

You probably won't want to hang around long in Macomer. It's not an unpleasant place but unless you're passing through, there's really no great reason to stop off.

If you do have some time to kill, the modest **Museo Etnografico** (☑ 0785 74 30 44; Corso Umberto 225; adult/reduced €3.50/2; ⊘ 9.30am-1pm & 4.30-7.30pm Mon-Fri) houses a motley collection of traditional home furnishings and utensils. If it's shut, ask over the road at **Esedra Escursioni** (☑ 0785 74 30 44; www.esedraescursioni.it; Corso Umberto 206), where you can also arrange excursions and train trips on the *trenino verde*.

Macomer is on Sardinia's main north-south rail line with direct trains to/from Oristano (€3.85, one hour, nine daily), Sassari (€7.35, 1½ hours, two daily) and Cagliari (€10.15, two hours, nine daily). A handful of buses head eastwards to Nuoro (€5, 1¼ hours, four daily).

LAGO OMODEO & AROUND

Surrounded by the green hills of the Barigadu, Lago Omodeo is Sardinia's largest man-made lake. Some 22km long and up to 3km wide, it was created between 1919 and 1924 to supply water and electricity to the agricultural lands around Oristano and Arborea. The countryside around it is sparsely populated and rich in archaeological interest with two of central Sardinia's most important nuraghic sites.

Santa Cristina & Paulilatino

⭐ **Nuraghe di Santa Cristina** ARCHAEOLOGICAL SITE
(www.archeotour.net; adult/reduced incl Museo Archeologico-Etnografico Paulilatino €5/2.50; ⊘ 8.30am-sunset) Just off the SS131 north of Oristano, the Nuraghe Santa Cristina is an important nuraghic complex whose extraordinary Bronze Age *tempio a pozzo* (well temple) is one of the best preserved in Sardinia. The worship of water was a fundamental part of nuraghic religious practice, and there are reckoned to be about 40 sacred wells across the island.

On entering the site, the first area you come to is a small village centred on the **Chiesa di Santa Cristina**, an early Christian church dedicated to Santa Cristina. The church and the terraced *muristenes* (pilgrims' huts) that surround it are opened for only nine days a year – for the feast days of Santa Cristina, around the second Sunday in May, and San Raffaele Arcangelo, on the fourth Sunday in October.

From the church, a path leads about 150m to the **well temple**. Dating back to the late Bronze Age (11th to 9th century BC), the *tempio a pozzo* is accessible through a finely cut keyhole entrance and a flight of 24 superbly preserved steps. When you reach the bottom you can gaze up at the perfectly constructed *tholos* (conical tower), through which light enters the dark well shaft. Every 18 years, one month and two days, the full moon shines directly through the aperture into the well. Otherwise you can catch the yearly equinoxes on 21 March and 23 September, when the sun lights up the stairway down to the well.

Over on the other side of the Christian village is the Nuraghe di Santa Cristina, a single 7m-high **tower** set in a peaceful olive grove. This once stood at the heart of a nuraghic village, which was inhabited until the early Middle Ages and whose remains lie littered around the woody glades.

Museo Archeologico-Etnografico   MUSEUM
(www.archeotour.net; Via Nazionale 127, Paulilatino; adult/reduced incl Nuraghe Santa Cristina €5/3.50; ⏱ 9.30am-1pm & 4.30-7pm Tue-Sun summer, 9.30am-1pm & 3-5.30pm Tue-Sun winter) Finds from the Santa Cristina complex are displayed in this museum in Paulilatino, 5km further up the SS131 from the site. As well as archaeological artefacts, you can also browse a collection of farm and domestic implements from tougher rural days.

Nuraghe Losa

★ **Nuraghe Losa**   ARCHAEOLOGICAL SITE
(www.nuraghelosa.net; adult/reduced €5/3.50; ⏱ 9am-1hr before sunset) Just off the SS131 a few kilometres north of Paulilatino, the Nuraghe Losa is one of Sardinia's most impressive *nuraghi*.

S'ARDIA

On 6 and 7 July Sedilo hosts Oristano's most exciting festival, S'Ardia, when nearly 50,000 people pack themselves into the tiny village to see Sardinia's most reckless and dangerous horse race.

It celebrates the Roman Emperor Constantine, who defeated the vastly superior forces of Maxentius at Rome's Ponte Milvio in AD 312. But since then the festival has received a Christian gloss. Legend holds it that Constantine received a vision before the battle, in which he saw a cross inscribed with the words 'In Hoc Signo Vinces' ('in this sign you will conquer'). He took the sign as the insignia for his forces, and the following year he passed an edict granting the Christians religious freedom. So, locally, although not officially, he was promoted to St Constantine (Santu Antinu in the local dialect).

The race circles the Santuario di San Costantino and the stone cross bearing his insignia. One man – the *Prima Pandela* (First Flag) – is chosen to bear Constantine's yellow-brocade standard. He selects two of the best horsemen to ride with him, and they choose three cohorts each. These men will be the *Prima Pandela's* guard and, armed with huge sticks, they will strive to prevent the hundred other horsemen from passing him. To be chosen as the *Prima Pandela* is the highest honour of the village. Only a man who has proven his courage and horsemanship and substantiated his faith can carry the flag.

On 6 July the procession prays in front of the stone cross and the riders are blessed by the parish priest. In theory the priest should start the race, but in practice it is the *Prima Pandela* who chooses his moment and flies off at a gallop down the hill. The other horsemen are after him in seconds, aiming to pass the *Prima Pandela* before he reaches the victory arch. Hundreds of riflemen shoot off blanks, exciting the horses. The stampede towards the narrow entrance of the victory arch is the most dangerous moment, as any mistake would mean running into the stone columns at top speed. In 2002 one rider died. If all goes well, the *Prima Pandela* passes through the arch and races on to circle the sanctuary, to deafening cheers from the crowd.

Sedilo sits 40km northwest of Oristano, on the SS131.

ANTONIO GRAMSCI

A giant of 20th-century political thought, Antonio Gramsci (1891–1937) was one of the founding fathers of Italian communism. Born to a poor family in Ales, he later moved to Ghilarza and then on to Cagliari and Turin.

It was in Turin that his political thoughts came to fruition. A vociferous advocate of trade unionism – at the time Turin was at the forefront of Italian industrialisation – he joined the Socialist Party in 1913 and six years later co-founded the Marxist newspaper *L'Ordine Nuovo*. Internal rifts within the Socialist Party led to division and, in 1921, Gramsci and a group of fellow activists broke away to form the Italian Communist Party. Much influenced by events in Russia – he visited Moscow in 1922 and married a Russian violinist – Gramsci was arrested by the Fascist police in 1926 and sentenced to 25 years in prison. He died in 1937 at the age of 46.

Of Gramsci's ideas, the best known is his theory of hegemony, which holds that to challenge the cultural homogenisation through which the ruling classes maintain control it's necessary for the working class to arm themselves with alternative cultural and aspirational beliefs.

In **Ghilarza** you can visit the **Casa Museo di Antonio Gramsci** (☑0785 5 41 64; www.casagramscighilarza.org; Corso Umberto I 36; ⊙10am-1pm & 4.30-7.30pm Wed-Mon summer, 10am-1pm & 3.30-6.30pm Sat & Sun winter) **FREE**, a small museum in the house where Gramsci lived between 1898 and 1914.

The site's centrepiece is a three-sided keep, around which are three circular towers, two joined by a wall, and one standing alone. The central tower has lost its top floor but still rises to almost 13m. It has been dated to the Middle Bronze Age, about 1500 BC.

Entrance is by way of one of the side towers, which is connected to the main keep by an internal corridor. Passages lead left and right from the corridor to two towers, one fully enclosed, the other open.

Bidoni

On the eastern side of Lago Omodeo, the stony hamlet of Bidoni hides one of Sardinia's strangest museums. The creepy **Museo S'Omo 'e sa Majarza** (The Witch's House; ☑0783 6 9044; Via Monte 9; ⊙on request), signposted as the Museo del Territorio, is dedicated to witches and local folklore and features the reconstruction of a 16th-century witch's cave. Note, however, that at the time of research the museum was closed for renovation.

Bidoni is signposted from Ghilarza, the main town on the western side of the lake.

Fordongianus

POP 930

Southwest of Lago Omodeo, almost at the confluence of the Tirso and Mannu Rivers, sits the small spa town of Fordongianus, most easily reached along the SS388 from Oristano. Founded by the Roman emperor Trajan in the 1st century AD, Forum Traiani as it was then known was an important commercial centre and site of a major baths complex, whose remains are still visitable.

⊙ Sights

Terme Romane　　　　　ROMAN BATHS
(☑0783 6 01 57; www.forumtraiani.it; adult/reduced incl Casa Aragonese €4/2; ⊙9.30am-1pm & 3-6.30pm) The remains of the 1st-century Terme Romane sit on the banks of the river Tirso. In the centre of the complex you'll see a rectangular pool that is still today full of 54-degree spring water. This was originally covered by a barrel-vaulted roof and flanked by an imposing portico, a section of which still stands.

Casa Aragonese　　　　HISTORIC BUILDING
(adult/reduced incl Terme Romane €4/2; ⊙9.30am-1pm & 3-6pm Tue-Sun) A characteristic of Fordongianus is the rusty-red trachyte stone that so many of its buildings are made of. As red as the rest is the lovely late-16th-century Casa Aragonese, a typical Catalan noble house with a columned loggia and Gothic windows and portal. The strange statues outside, also fashioned from the ubiquitous trachyte, are the result of an annual sculpture competition held here.

❶ Getting There & Away

Up to eight weekday buses connect with Oristano (€2.50, 40 minutes).

SLOW IMAGES/GETTY IMAGES ©

The Coast

Stretching for 1850km, Sardinia's extensive coastline is one of Italy's great natural wonders. The beaches are superb and whichever way you look the scenery is amazing – wild seas crash onto remote virgin sands, surreal boulders frame idyllic coves and *macchia*-cloaked cliffs plunge into sparkling turquoise waters.

Contents
➡ **Best Beaches**
➡ **Seaside Hubs**

Above Spaggia Su Giudeu (p75),
Costa del Sud

SLOW IMAGES/GETTY IMAGES ©

The beach at Chia, Costa del Sud **2.** Sand dunes
. Cala Goloritzè

3

Best Beaches

A magnet for summer sun-seekers, Sardinia's beaches are among the best in the Med. From classic crescents of snow white sand to pebbly coves, secluded bays and tracts of golden dunes, they come in all shapes and sizes, whilst their waters dazzle in a thousand shades of blue.

Spiaggia della Pelosa

Spiaggia della Pelosa (p131) is a heavenly vision of beach perfection – a frost white strip of sand fringed by electric blue waters. Overlooking everything is a Spanish watchtower atop a thin, craggy islet.

Cala Goloritzè

No talk of soaring limestone pinnacles and water the colour of blue curaçao can ever do justice to Cala Goloritzè (p197). As you descend an old mule trail, the cliffs suddenly crack open to reveal one of the most astonishingly lovely beaches you'll ever see.

Cala Brandinchi

A thin arc of powder-soft sand lapped by crystalline turquoise waters – it's not hard to see why Cala Brandinchi (p152) is dubbed Sardinia's 'Little Tahiti'.

Spiaggia di Piscinas

Walking barefoot across the 30m-high sand dunes that back onto the sweeping Spiaggia di Piscinas (p66) is a magical sunset experience. The fact that this fantastically wild beach can only be reached by a dirt track adds to the wonderful sense of remoteness.

Chia

Windsurfers, dune walkers and twitchers who come to spy on pink flamingos all rave about Chia (p75) and its sandy beaches. Sheltered by bushes of aromatic juniper bushes, they're the stuff of postcards.

The road to Capo Caccia (p128)

Seaside Hubs

No matter which way you point the compass, you'll find beach after glorious beach in Sardinia. But where to base yourself? Here are some of our favourite coastal hang-outs, whisking you from the action-packed east to the windswept west, the ritzy north to the silky-sanded south.

Cala Gonone

Cala Gonone (p192) is a terrific base for exploring the crescent-shaped bays, cliffs and grottoes of the Golfo di Orosei. Rock climbers wax lyrical about its crags, and families love the resort's blissfully laid-back vibe.

Costa del Sud

Eclipsed by Sardinia's more famous coastlines, the Costa del Sud (p74) is something of an unsung beauty, with fine beaches, plunging cliffs, and neon blue waters. Windsurfers and surfers come for the breeze and waves.

Costa Smeralda

Enjoying the granite seascapes and pink-hued beaches of the Costa Smeralda (p153) doesn't have to cost a mint. Escape Porto Cervo's celeb-hungry crowds for lesser-known bays, or stay inland for the perfect mix of coast and countryside.

Costa Verde

For a taste of Sardinia before the developers moved in, follow dirt tracks to Costa Verde's exhilaratingly beautiful beaches (p66) backed by huge dunes and lush *macchia* (Mediterranean shrubbery). Complete the experience with a stay at at welcoming *agriturismo* (farm-stay accommodation).

Alghero

From Alghero (p115), the road swings north to an array of pine-backed bays, rocky coves and the dramatic Capo Caccia. At Sardinia's northwestern tip lies the dream beach of Spiaggia della Pelosa.

Alghero & the Northwest

Best Places to Eat

➡ Trattoria Lo Romanì (p121)

➡ La Botteghina (p121)

➡ Agriturismo Sa Mandra (p126)

➡ Agriturismo Porticciolo (p129)

➡ L'Antica Hostaria (p138)

Best Places to Stay

➡ Hotel El Faro (p209)

➡ Angedras Hotel (p208)

➡ Tanina B&B (p209)

➡ Villa Las Tronas (p208)

Why Go?

Inspiring natural beauty goes hand in hand with history and urban charm in Sardinia's northwestern corner.

The obvious belle of the ball is the coastline with its brilliant sandy beaches, heady cliffs and hidden rocky coves. But head inland, and surprises await – architectural and archaeological gems litter the sun-bleached countryside, a string of Pisan-Romanesque churches testify to glories past, while tumbledown ruins tell of prehistoric times.

A history of foreign rule has left an indelible mark on the area, not only in bricks and mortar but also in spirit. Alghero, the northwest's main gateway and a one-time Catalan stronghold, has a distinctly Spanish feel, while Sassari owes its cosmopolitan outlook to its past as a Genoese colony. In many ways, the entire area seems less Sardinian than other parts of the island, less rural and less reserved, but no less enchanting for it.

Road Distance (km)

	Alghero	Castelsardo	Porto Torres	Sassari
Castelsardo	57			
Porto Torres	34	30		
Sassari	38	27	17	
Stintino	57	55	25	42

Alghero & the Northwest Highlights

① Diving into Caribbean-coloured waters at the **Spiaggia della Pelosa** (p131).

② Revelling in dreamy sunset views on Alghero's **sea walls** (p115).

③ Spotting albino donkeys on the rocky wilds of the **Parco Nazionale dell'Asinara** (p131).

④ Escaping the crowds and enjoying great walking in **Le Prigionette Nature Reserve** (p127).

⑤ Heading out to the Capo Caccia headland to explore the fairy-tale **Grotta di Nettuno** (p128).

⑥ Seeing where prehistoric cavepeople lived in Ozieri's

Grotta di San Michele (p141).

⑦ Wandering Castelsardo's medieval lanes and looking over to Corsica from the impregnable hilltop **castello** (p133).

⑧ Getting into the festive swing at the **Cavalcata Sarda** (p138), Sassari's great headline festival.

ALGHERO

POP 40,600

One of Sardinia's most beautiful medieval cities, Alghero is the main resort in the northwest. Although largely given over to tourism – its population can almost quadruple in July and August – the town hasn't given up its unique character and it retains a proud and independent spirit. Its animated historic centre is a terrific place to hang out, and with so many excellent restaurants and bars, it makes an ideal base for exploring the beaches and beauty spots of the nearby Riviera del Corallo.

The main focus of attention is the picturesque *centro storico* (historic centre), one of the best preserved in Sardinia. Enclosed by robust, honey-coloured sea walls, this is a tightly knit enclave of shady cobbled lanes, Gothic *palazzi* (mansions) and cafe-lined piazzas. Below, yachts crowd the marina and long, sandy beaches curve away to the north. Presiding over everything is a palpable Spanish atmosphere, a hangover of the city's past as a Catalan colony. Even today, more than three centuries after the Iberians left, a form of medieval Catalan is still spoken, and street signs and menus are often written in both Catalan and Italian.

History

A modern city by Sardinian standards, L'Alguerium (named after algae that washed up on the coast) started life as an 11th-century fishing village. Thanks to its strategic position, it was jealously guarded by its Genoese founders who, despite a brief Pisan interregnum in the 1280s, managed to retain control until the mid-14th century.

Alghero forcibly resisted the Catalan-Aragonese invasion of Sardinia in 1323, but after 30 years of struggle it fell to the Spanish invaders in 1353. Catalan colonists were encouraged to settle here, and after a revolt in 1372 the remaining Sardinians were expelled and relocated inland to Villanova Monteleone. From then on Alghero became resolutely Catalan and called itself Alguer.

Under its Iberian rulers, the town thrived. It became the main Catalan port on the island and in 1501 was raised to the status of city. Fortifications were built to defend it against land and sea attacks. Further adding to its prestige was the arrival of the Holy Roman Emperor (and king of Spain) Charles V in 1541 to lead a campaign against the North African corsairs.

After about 350 years of Spanish rule, the city passed to the Piedmontese House of Savoy in 1720. The next couple of centuries proved hard for it, and by the 1920s its population had fallen to just over 10,000. Heavily bombed in 1943, it remained in pretty poor shape until tourism arrived in the late 1960s, paving the way for the development of the modern new town.

◉ Sights

Most of Alghero's sights are centred on the *centro storico*, which, with its massive sea walls and narrow lanes, is ideal for leisurely, holiday-paced strolling. Prime time is the early evening when crowds swell the dark, medieval alleyways to parade their tans and browse the bright shop windows.

The entire city centre was originally enclosed by defensive walls, but in the 19th century the landward walls were torn down and partially replaced by the **Giardini Pubblici**, a green space which effectively separates the old town from the new.

Torre Porta a Terra   TOWER
(Map p118; ☑ 079 973 40 45; Piazza Porta Terra; adult/reduced €2.50/2; ⊙ 10.30am-1pm & 5.30-8pm summer, 9.30am-1pm & 4-8pm Mon-Fri winter) Near the Giardini Pubblici, the 14th-century Torre Porta a Terra is all that remains of Porta a Terra, one of the two main gates into the medieval city. A stumpy 23m-high tower known originally as Porta Reial, it now houses a small multimedia museum dedicated to the city's past and, on the 2nd floor, a terrace with sweeping, 360-degree views.

To the south, another impressive tower, the **Torre di San Giovanni** (Map p118; Largo San Francesco; ⊙ depends on exhibition) hosts temporary art exhibitions.

★ Sea Walls   WALLS
(Map p116) Alghero's golden sea walls, built around the *centro storico* by the Aragonese in the 16th century, are a highlight of the town's historic cityscape. Running from Piazza Sulis in the south to Porta a Mare and the marina in the north, they are crowned by a pedestrianised path that commands superb views over to Capo Caccia on the blue horizon. Restaurants and bars line the walkway, providing the perfect perch to sit back and lap up the holiday atmosphere.

To walk the walls, also known as the *bastioni,* start at **Torre di Sulis** (Map p118) on the piazza of the same name. This tower originally closed off the defensive line of

Alghero

ALGHERO & THE NORTHWEST ALGHERO

0 _____ 400 m
0 _____ 0.2 miles

Camping La Mariposa (500m)

Fertilia (5km); Airport (10km)

Via Lido

Via Sardegna

Via F Cervi

Via Castelsardo

Via Fermi

Train Station

Via Galilei

Spiaggia di San Giovanni

Via Don Minzoni

Via Paoli

Via Degli Orti

Via G M Angioi

Sassari (38km)

Via Astrodelo

Via Diez

3

Via Garibaldi

Via Gallura

Via XXIV Maggio

2

Via Vittorio Emanuele

Via Catalogna

Via Mazzini

Via Lamarmora

Giardini Pubblici

6

Via Veneto

Via XX Settembre

Via IV Novembre

Via Brigata Sassari

Via Marconi

Via Craveloi

Via Deledda

Via Andreoni

Via Cagliari

Via Satta

Via Enrico

Via Sassari

Via S Agostino

Via Carrabuffas

See Central Alghero Map (p118)

Via Verdi

Via Canepa

Via Palomba

7

Via Petrarca

10

9

Via Pascoli

Via Manzoni

Via Nazioni Unite

Via Lo Frasso

Viale Giovanni XXIII

Via Alcide De Gasperi

Lungomare Dante

Via Gramsci

Sea Walls 1

Via Nazioni Unite

Via Sassari

Via Mattei

Via Fratelli Kennedy

Villanova Monteleone (23km)

Rada di Alghero

5

8

Via Frank

4

Via Lungomare Valencia

Las Tronas

Via Toda

Bosa (46km)

Alghero

⊙ Top Sights
1 Sea Walls...B6

⊕ Activities, Courses & Tours
2 Italiano in Riviera................................C4
3 Nautisub m/n Andrea Padre.............B4

⊜ Sleeping
4 Angedras Hotel....................................C7
5 Villa Las Tronas...................................B7

⊗ Eating
6 Euro Spin Supermarket......................B5
7 Trattoria Maristella.............................B6

⊖ Drinking & Nightlife
8 El Trò...C7
9 L'Arca..B6

⊛ Entertainment
10 Poco Loco..B6

towers to the south of the old town. Continuing northwards along the **Bastioni Cristoforo Colombo**, you'll pass the **Torre di San Giacomo** (Map p118) before arriving on the main stretch, the **Bastioni Marco Polo** where most of the restaurants are lined up.

At the northern tip are two more towers, the **Torre della Polveriera** (Map p118) and **Torre di Sant'Elmo** (Map p118). The last stretch, the **Bastioni della Maddalena**, with its eponymous tower, **Torre della Maddalena** (Map p118), and fort, **Forte della Maddalena** (Map p118), is the only surviving remnant of the city's former land battlements. Just west of the bastion, and overlooking the crowded marina, is **Porta a Mare** (Map p118), the second of Alghero's medieval gateways through which you can access Piazza Civica in the historic centre.

Cattedrale di Santa Maria   CATHEDRAL
(Map p118; Piazza Duomo; ⊙7am-noon & 5-7.30pm) Overlooking Piazza Duomo, Alghero's oversized Cattedrale di Santa Maria appears out of place with its pompous neoclassical facade and fat Doric columns. An unfortunate 19th-century addition, the facade was the last in a long line of modifications that the hybrid cathedral has endured since it was built, originally on Catalan Gothic lines in the 16th century. Inside it's largely Renaissance, with some late-baroque baubles added in the 18th century.

Free guided tours of the cathedral are available between 10am and 1pm and then from 4pm to 6pm Monday to Friday between February and October.

★Campanile   TOWER
(Map p118; ✆079 973 30 41; Via Principe Umberto; adult/reduced €2/free; ⊙10.30am-12.30pm Mon-Fri & 7-9pm Mon & Fri summer, 10.30am-12.30pm Mon, Tue, Thu, Fri & 4-6pm Mon & Fri autumn, on request Nov-May) Of more interest than the interior of the Cattedrale di Santa Maria is its striking *campanile* (bell tower). Accessible through a Gothic doorway on Via Principe Umberto, this tall octagonal tower – the one you see rising above Alghero's rooftops – is a fine example of Catalan Gothic architecture.

Museo Diocesano d'Arte Sacra   MUSEUM
(Map p118; ✆079 973 30 41; Piazza Duomo; adult/reduced €3/2; ⊙10.30am-1pm & 5.30-8pm, shorter hrs Oct & Dec, closed Nov, by appointment Jan-Mar) This museum of religious art, in the former Oratorio del Rosario, houses religious artefacts from the Cattedrale di Santa Maria, including silverware, statuary, paintings and woodcarving.

Look out for the ghoulish reliquary of what is claimed to be one of the *innocenti* (newborn babies slaughtered by Herod in his search for the Christ child). The tiny skull is chilling, but apparently it appealed to Alghero artist Francesco Pinna, who was given it by a Roman cardinal in the 16th century.

Piazza Civica   PIAZZA
(Map p118) Just inside Porta a Mare, Piazza Civica is Alghero's showcase square. In a former life it was the administrative heart of the medieval city, but where Spanish aristocrats once met to debate affairs of empire, tourists now converge to browse jewellery displays in elegant shop windows, eat ice cream and drink at the city's grandest cafe. Caffè Costantino occupies the ground floor of the Gothic **Palazzo d'Albis** (Map p118), where the Spanish emperor Charles V stayed in 1541.

★Chiesa di San Francesco   CHURCH
(Map p118; Via Carlo Alberto) Alghero's finest church is a model of architectural harmony. Originally built to a Catalan Gothic design in the 14th century, it was later given a Renaissance facelift after it partially collapsed in 1593. Inside, interest is focused on the 18th-century polychrome marble altar and a strange 17th-century wooden sculpture of a haggard Christ tied to a column. Through

Central Alghero

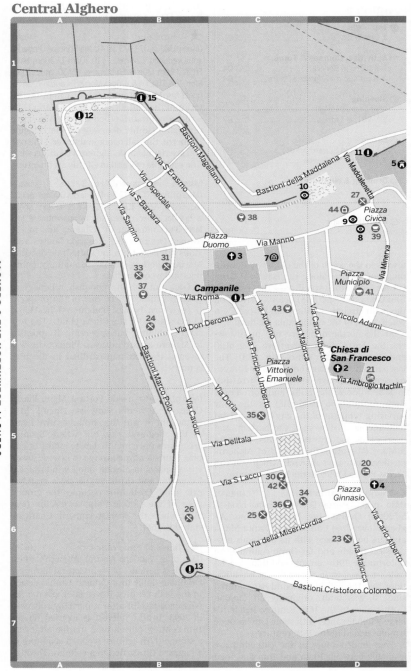

0   100 m
0   0.05 miles

Central Alghero

⊙ Top Sights

1 Campanile	C4
2 Chiesa di San Francesco	D4

⊙ Sights

3 Cattedrale di Santa Maria	C3
4 Chiesa di San Michele	D6
5 Forte della Maddalena	D2
6 Museo del Corallo	F6
7 Museo Diocesano d'Arte Sacra	C3
8 Palazzo d'Albis	D3
9 Piazza Civica	D3
10 Porta a Mare	C2
11 Torre della Maddalena	D2
12 Torre della Polveriera	A2
13 Torre di San Giacomo	B6
14 Torre di San Giovanni	E5
15 Torre di Sant'Elmo	B1
16 Torre di Sulis	E7
17 Torre Porta a Terra	E4

⊕ Activities, Courses & Tours

Cooperativa Itinera	(see 17)
18 Traghetti Navisarda	E1
19 Trenino Catalano	E2

⊜ Sleeping

20 B&B Benebenniu	D5
21 Hotel San Francesco	D4

⊗ Eating

22 Al Refettorio	E4
23 Al Tuguri	D6
24 Angedras Restaurant	B4
25 Borgo Antico	C6
26 Gelateria I Bastioni	B6
27 Il Ghiotto	D2
28 Il Pavone	E6
29 Il Pesce d'Oro	F2
30 La Botteghina	C6
31 Mabrouk	B3
32 Market	F5
33 Osteria Machiavello	B3
34 Spaghetteria Al Solito Posto	C6
35 Trattoria Lo Romanì	C5

⊜ Drinking & Nightlife

36 Baraonda	C6
37 Buena Vista	B3
38 Cafè Latino	C3
39 Caffè Costantino	D3
40 Chez Michel	E7
41 Diva Café	D3
42 Jamaica Inn	C5
43 Mill Inn	C4

⊜ Shopping

Agostino Marogna	(see 8)
44 Boutique Marras	D3
45 Enodolciaria	E4

ALGHERO & THE NORTHWEST ALGHERO

the sacristy you can enter a beautiful 14th-century cloister, the 22 columns of which connect a series of round arches.

The buttery sandstone used in the arcades and columns lends the cloister a special warmth, which makes it a wonderful setting for summer concerts.

Chiesa di San Michele
CHURCH

(Map p118; Via Carlo Alberto) On Via Carlo Alberto, the *carrer major* of the medieval town, the Chiesa di San Michele is best known for its maiolica dome, typical of churches in Valencia, another former Catalan territory. The present tiles were laid in the 1960s, but this doesn't detract from its beauty.

Just before you reach the church you cross Via Gilbert Ferret. This intersection is known as the *quatre cantonades* (four sides), and for centuries labourers would gather here in the hope of finding work.

Beaches

North of the Alghero's yacht-jammed marina, Via Garibaldi sweeps up to the town's long, sandy beaches: **Spiaggia di San Giovanni** and the adjacent **Spiaggia di Maria Pia**. Nicer by far, though, are the beaches near Fertilia. In Alghero you can hire umbrellas and sun-loungers for about €14 per day, as well as windsurfers and canoes.

🏃 Activities

★ Traghetti Navisarda
BOAT TOUR

(☑079 95 06 03; www.navisarda.it; Banchina Dogana; adult/child return €15/8, cave entrance not included; ⊘tours hourly 9am-5pm Jun-Sep, twice daily at 11am & 3pm March-May & Oct) From the port you can take a boat trip along the impressive northern coast to Capo Caccia and the grandiose Grotta di Nettuno cave complex. Traghetti Navisarda is one of a number of operators offering day cruises with lunch and swimming stops, and ferries up to the caves. The round trip, including cave visit, lasts approximately 2½ hours.

Nautisub m/n Andrea Padre
DIVING

(Map p116; ☑079 95 24 33; www.nautisub.com; Via Garibaldi 45; ⊘8.30am-1pm & 4.30-9pm Mon-Sat, 8.30am-12.30pm Sun summer only, shorter hours winter) Operating out of a dive shop, this year-round outfit organises dives (from €45 or €60 including kit hire) and boat tours (from €45), as well as offering kit hire.

Courses

Italiano in Riviera
LANGUAGE COURSE

(Map p116; ☑079 27 50 35; www.italianoinriviera.it; Via Gallura 14) This school runs a series of Italian language courses for all levels. There's also the possibility of combining language studies with classes on the history of art, cookery, wine tasting, and sport.

Individual lessons cost €35 per hour; weekly courses start at €235 per person.

☞ Tours

Cooperativa Itinera
WALKING TOUR

(Map p118; ☑079 973 40 45; Torre Porta a Terra; ⊘9.30am-1pm & 4.30-8pm Mon-Sat) Offers a range of guided tours in and outside of the city, including a 1½-hour walk through the *centro storico*. Tickets (€7.50) are available at the Torre Porta a Terra (p115), the start point for the walk.

Trenino Catalano
TRAIN TOUR

(Map p118; adult/reduced €5/3; ⊘10am-1pm & 4.30-11pm summer, 10am-1pm & 3.30-9pm spring & Sep) A miniature train that chugs around the historic centre. Departures are half-hourly from the port; buy tickets on board.

✷ Festivals & Events

Alghero has a full calendar of festivals and events, though spring and summer are the best times to catch an event. To check what's on, click on the Events link at www.alghero-turismo.it.

Carnevale
CARNIVAL

(www.sardegnaturismo.it; ⊘Feb) During Alghero's carnival festivities, an effigy of a French soldier (the *pupazzo*) is burnt at the stake on *martedì grasso* (Shrove Tuesday) amid much merrymaking.

Sagra del Bogamarì
FOOD

(⊘Feb/Mar/Apr) Alghero locals pay homage to the humble *riccio di mare* (sea urchin) by eating mountainloads of the spiky molluscs. The exact dates vary from year to year but it's usually held between February and March or early April.

Easter Holy Week
RELIGIOUS

(⊘Mar/Apr) Figures of Christ and the Virgin Mary are borne through town in enactments of the *Misteri* (Passion of Christ) and *Incontru* (Meeting of the Virgin with Christ).

Ferragosto
(Feast of the Assumption)   RELIGIOUS

(☺Aug) On 15 August, Alghero celebrates Ferragosto with fireworks, boat races and music.

✕ Eating

Seafood rules in Alghero, a fishing town famous for its lobster, which is often served as *aragosta alla catalana,* catalan-style lobster with tomato and onion.

★ Gelateria I Bastioni   GELATERIA €

(Map p118; Bastioni Marco Polo 5; cones from €2; ☺Mar-Oct) It's only a hole in the wall but this gem of a gelateria dishes up superb ice cream, as well as milkshakes and *granite* (flavoured ice drinks). Particularly fab are the fresh fruit flavours, ideally topped by a generous squirt of whipped cream.

Il Ghiotto   CAFETERIA €

(Map p118; ☎079 97 48 20; Piazza Civica 23; meals €15; ☺6am-midnight) One of the few truly budget places in Alghero. Fill up for as little as €15 from the tantalising lunchtime spread of *panini,* pastas, salads and main courses. There's seating in a dining area behind the main hall or outside on a busy wooden terrace by Porta a Mare.

Spaghetteria
Al Solito Posto   TRADITIONAL ITALIAN €

(Map p118; ☎079 98 00 54; Via Principe Umberto 82; meals €18-20; ☺Wed-Mon) Don't come expecting romance and refined dining. But if you're after a simple pasta fill-up, this popular eatery will do the job. It's a workaday, TV-on-in-the-corner type of place, but the food – pasta with a range of sauces – is good and the bustling vibe is fun.

★ Trattoria Lo Romanì   TRATTORIA €€

(Map p118; ☎079 973 84 79; Via Principe Umberto 29; meals €30; ☺7.30-11.30pm, closed Sun dinner & Mon) Many Alghero restaurants serve *porchetto,* Sardinia's classic spit-roasted pork, but few places cook it to such buttery perfection. The crackling is spot on and the meat sweet and full of flavour. *Porchetto* apart, this is a delightful trattoria. Exposed sandstone walls and soft lighting create a warm, elegant atmosphere, service is attentive, and the fresh island food is excellent.

★ La Botteghina   SARDINIAN €€

(Map p118; ☎079 97 38 375; www.labotteghina. biz; Via Principe Umberto 63; meals €35; ☺12.30-

ℹ FISH ON THE MENU
....

Something to look out for when ordering *aragosta* (lobster) or fish at a restaurant: on most menus, the price of fresh fish is given as per gram (or per *etto,* per 100g), and not for the dish as a whole. If in doubt, check with the waiter and ask to have the fish weighed before ordering.

2.30pm & 7.30-10.45pm Fri-Wed) A stylish *centro storico* restaurant (think white wood decor and brick vaulted ceilings) La Botteghina specialises in simple dishes prepared with seasonal ingredients bought from small local producers. Steaks of *bue rosso* beef, cured meats and Sardinian cheese star on the menu alongside 50cm pizzas and fresh seafood, typically served with *fregola* (small semolina pasta similar to couscous).

Mabrouk   SEAFOOD €€

(Map p118; ☎079 97 00 00; Via Santa Barbara 4; set menu €40; ☺8-11pm Tue-Sun, closed Nov) A cosy seafood restaurant near the cathedral, the Mabrouk is a wonderful place to feast on locally caught fish. What exactly is on the set menu depends on the day's catch, but with several antipasti, three pasta dishes and three main courses included, you won't go hungry.

Il Pesce d'Oro   RISTORANTE, PIZZERIA €€

(Map p118; ☎079 95 26 02; Via Catalogna 12; meals €30, pizzas €5-10; ☺12.30-2.30pm & 7.30-11pm, closed Mon lunch & Wed) A historic Alghero address, this is where the locals come for their weekend meal out. Crowds of cheerful diners squeeze into the sunny-coloured interior to tuck into hearty fish dishes and wood-fired pizzas. For a meal-in-itself pizza, try the house specialty, Pizza Pesce d'Oro, topped with tomato, gorgonzola, sausage, pepper and onion.

Angedras Restaurant   SARDINIAN €€

(Map p118; ☎079 973 50 78; www.angedrasrestaurant.it; Bastioni Marco Polo 41; meals €30-40, lunch menu €16; ☺noon-2.45pm & 7-10.30pm Apr-Oct) Alghero's honey-coloured ramparts set a memorable stage for alfresco dining. This is one of the better restaurants on the walls, serving a largely regional menu of pasta, meat dishes and elegantly presented seafood. At lunch, you can save by going for the €16 menu, which consists of two dishes chosen from the regular à la carte menu.

Al Tuguri
RISTORANTE €€

(Map p118; ☎079 97 67 72; www.altuguri.it; Via Maiorca 113; tasting menus veg/seafood/meat €40/45/45; ⊘12.30-2.30pm & 8.30-11.30pm Mon-Sat; ☑) Quality vegetarian food is something of a novelty in Sardinia, but this is the place to find it. A small, discreet restaurant decorated in traditional rustic style, it serves a dedicated vegetarian menu alongside more traditional fish and meat offerings. Booking is advisable.

Al Refettorio
MEDITERRANEAN €€

(Map p118; ☎079 973 11 26; Vicolo Adami 47; meals €30-35; ⊘12.30-2.30pm & 7.30-11.30pm Wed-Mon) Al Refettorio is a smart wine-bar restaurant with tables under a low stone arch and in a softly lit vaulted interior. There's a strong emphasis on wine, so take the opportunity to sample the local vino, whilst dining on modern Mediterranean fare such as sesame-crusted salmon with red-pepper sauce.

Osteria Machiavello
RISTORANTE €€

(Map p118; ☎079 98 06 28; Bastioni Marco Polo 57; meals €35, fixed-price menus lunch/Sardinian €16/35; ⊘noon-2.45pm & 7-11.30pm Mon-Sat) A popular restaurant on the sea walls, this is a panoramic spot for a leisurely meal. The menu covers most tastes with grilled meats and a number of classic fish dishes. Alongside the à la carte menu, there are also a couple of fixed-price menus, including one for a bargain €16 lunch.

Borgo Antico
SEAFOOD €€

(Map p118; ☎079 973 60 08; Via Zaccaria 12; meals €35; ⊘12.30-2.30pm & 7.30-11pm summer, closed Mon winter) This popular *centro storico* restaurant offers a great location – it's housed in an ex-convent on an atmospheric piazza – and old-school Italian seafood. Bag a squareside table and dive into classics such as *spaghetti alle cozze* (with mussels) and *pesce al sale* (fish baked in salt).

Trattoria Maristella
TRATTORIA €€

(Map p116; ☎079 97 81 72; Via Fratelli Kennedy 9; meals €30; ⊘12.30-2.30pm & 8-11pm, closed Sun dinner) Visitors and locals flock to this bustling little trattoria for reliable seafood and local specialties such as *culurgiones* (ravioli stuffed with potato, *pecorino* and mint) and, in season, spaghetti *ai ricci* (with sea urchins).

Il Pavone
RISTORANTE €€€

(Map p118; ☑079 97 95 84; Piazza Sulis 3/4; meals around €45; ⊘12.30-3pm & 7-11pm summer, closed Sun dinner winter) A city institution, Il Pavone offers the best of both worlds – excellent food and a prime location on Piazza Sulis. Elegant yet relaxed, it serves a comprehensive menu of creative seafood hits, salads, bruschetta and a daily selection of specials at €10. Aperitifs are also served from 11am.

Self-Catering
You can stock up on picnic supplies, fresh meat and fish at Alghero's daily **market** (Map p118; Via Sassari 23; ⊘7am-1pm) near Torre Porta a Terra. Otherwise, there's a **Euro Spin supermarket** (Map p116; Via Lamarmora 28; ⊘8.30am-9pm) overlooking the Giardini Pubblici.

Drinking & Nightlife
Alghero has plenty of drinking options ranging from elegant cafes to romantic waterfront bars, hole-in-the wall cocktail joints, pubs and wine bars. Much of the action is in the *centro storico* but you'll also find places on the sea walls (a favourite spot for sunset views), and the seafront south of Piazza Sulis. In summer many places stay open late, typically to around 2am.

Alghero's clubbing scene is centred on a couple of out-of-town summer clubs. To get to these you'll need your own car or to fork out around €35 for a taxi.

Buena Vista
BAR

(Map p118; Bastioni Marco Polo 47; cocktails €7; ⊘3.30pm-late) Fabulous mojitos go hand in hand with stunning sunset views at this buzzing little bar on the western walls. Upbeat tunes and a cavernous interior add to the friendly, laid-back vibe.

Baraonda
WINE BAR

(Map p118; Via Principe Umberto 75) Exposed stone walls, purple hues and black-and-white jazz photos set the tone at this moody wine bar. In summer sit out on the piazza and watch the world parade by as you get to grips with the extensive wine list.

Chez Michel
CAFE

(Map p118; Piazza Sulis 2; ⊘Tue-Sun) One of several cafes and bars offering ringside seats on Piazza Sulis, this is a prime spot for people-watching and evening drinks. Aperitifs (from €7) are served as well as coffees, cocktails and the occasional DJ set.

L'Arca   CAFE, BAR
(Map p116; ☎ 079 97 79 72; Lungomare Dante 6;
☺ 8am-2am summer, to 10pm Tue-Sun winter)
Cafe by day, rocking music bar by night, this
is an ever-popular hang-out. Inside, DJs conduct the mayhem, while outside, drinkers
swell out onto the crowded seafront.

Cafè Latino   BAR
(Map p118; ☎ 079 97 65 41; Bastioni Magellano
10; cocktails from €4.80; ☺ 9am-2am, closed Tue
winter) Revel in romantic harbour views over
an early evening aperitif at this chic bar on
the sea walls. Overlooking the marina, it has
outside tables and an ample menu of drinks
and snacks, although for a full meal you'd be
better off elsewhere.

Jamaica Inn   PUB
(Map p118; Via Principe Umberto 57; ☺ noon-3pm &
7.30pm-2am) A lively pub in the heart of the
centro storico serving Belgian beers, hamburgers and weekly live music. For an outdoor pew, grab a table on the small terrace
opposite the entrance.

Caffè Costantino   CAFE
(Map p118; Piazza Civica 31; ☺ 7.30am-1.30am,
closed Mon winter) On Alghero's showpiece
piazza, Caffè Costantino is the most famous
cafe in town. It's also one of the busiest, attracting a constant stream of tourists to its
squareside tables. Join them for drinks and
people-watching, but skip the mediocre,
overpriced food.

Diva Café   CAFE
(Map p118; ☎ 079 98 23 06; Piazza Municipio 1;
cocktails €7; ☺ 10am-midnight Mon-Sat) Though
open all day, the Diva shows her true colours
at night when suntanned sippers drop by for
a cocktail on the pretty square.

Mill Inn   PUB
(Map p118; Via Maiorca 37; ☺ Thu-Tue) A cosy
drinking den beneath stone vaults in the
centro storico. It gets busy at weekends and
stages occasional live music.

El Trò   CLUB
(Map p116; ☎ 079 97 99 38; Via Lungomare Valencia
3) A restaurant, bar and disco on the rocks,
El Trò is one of Alghero's historic nightlife
addresses. It serves pizza by the metre and a
regular dose of late-night dance music.

Il Ruscello   CLUB
(☎ 339 235 07 55; SS Alghero-Olmedo; admission
Sat/Sun €13/15; ☺ midnight-late Thu-Sat summer)

One of Alghero's big-name clubs, Il Ruscello
attracts top Sardinian DJs and a clued-up
crowd who dance to house, revival and Latin
tunes. It's about 2km northeast of town on
the road to Olmedo.

La Siesta   CLUB
(Località Scala Piccada; admission €15; ☺ from
midnight Sat summer) About 10km out of town,
this is a big, open-air club with four dance
floors, mainstream tunes and a regular program of live music. If you can't get a lift,
there's sometimes a shuttle bus to the club
from Piazza Sulis, departing at around 1am
or 2am.

☆ Entertainment

Poco Loco   LIVE MUSIC
(Map p116; ☎ 079 98 36 04; www.pocolocoalghe-
ro.com; Via Gramsci 8; ☺ 8pm-2am Tue-Sun) A
historic all-purpose venue with cocktails,
pizza by the metre and regular live music.
Concerts, staged between October and June,
cater to most tastes, although jazz and blues
headline more than most.

🔒 Shopping

Browsing the shop windows on Via Carlo
Alberto, the main shopping strip, is part
and parcel of a trip to Alghero. Throughout
the *centro storico,* the streets are lined with
shops selling foodie treats, designer threads,
tourist tat, and jewellery made from Alghero's famous red coral.

Most shops close over lunch, typically
from around 1pm to 5pm, reopening in the
evening until about 8.30pm. However, in
summer many stay open late, only closing
when the flow of passers-by has dried up.

Enodolciaria   FOOD
(Map p118; ☎ 079 97 97 41; Via Simon 24; ☺ 9.15am-
1pm & 4.30-11pm summer, 9.15am-1pm & 4-8pm
Mon-Sat winter) A local landmark near the entrance to the *centro storico,* this foodie shop
is a gourmet's treat, selling everything from
local liqueurs and island wines to olive oils,
honeys, and packets of *fregola* and *bottarga*
(mullet roe).

Boutique Marras   FASHION
(Map p118; ☎ 079 973 20 85; www.boutique-
marras.com; Piazza Civica 9; ☺ 9.30am-1pm &
4.30-8.30pm Mon-Sat, 5-8.30pm Sun) Antonio
Marras is Alghero's most famous fashion designer – he has worked as artistic director
for Kenzo and is the stylist behind the *I'm*

Isola Barras line. His clothes are among the stylish garments on sale at this elegant boutique, run by Antonio's brother and housed in a medieval *palazzo*.

ⓘ Information

Airport tourist office (☎079 97 71 28; ⊗9am-1pm & 3-7pm Mon-Sat) In the Arrivals hall.

Bar Miramare (☎079 973 10 27; Via Gramsci 2; per hour €5; ⊗8am-noon & 2.30pm-2am) Internet.

BNL Banca (Via Vittorio Emanuele 5)

Farmacia Cabras (☎079 97 92 60; Via Fratelli Kennedy 12; ⊗9am-1pm & 4-8pm Mon-Sat) English-speaking service.

Ospedale Civile (☎079 995 51 11; Via Don Minzoni) The main hospital.

Police station (☎079 972 00 00; Via Fratelli Kennedy 1)

Post office (Map p116; Via Carducci 35; ⊗8.20am-7.05pm Mon-Fri, 8.20am-12.35pm Sat)

Tourist office (Map p118; ☎079 97 90 54; www.alghero-turismo.it; Piazza Porta Terra 9; ⊗8am-8pm Mon-Sat, 10am-1pm Sun) English-speaking staff and tonnes of practical information.

ⓘ Getting There & Away

AIR

Alghero's **Fertilia airport** (☎079 93 50 11; www.aeroportodialghero.it) is 10km northwest of town. It's served by **Alitalia** (www.alitalia.com) and a number of low-cost carriers, including **Ryanair** (www.ryanair.com), which operates flights to mainland Italy and destinations across Europe, including Barcelona, Dublin, Frankfurt, London, Madrid and Paris.

BUS

Intercity buses stop at and leave from Via Catalogna, by the Giardini Pubblici. Buy tickets at the ticket office in the gardens.

Up to 10 daily buses run to Sassari (€2.50 to €3, one hour), where you can pick up connec-

tions to destinations across the island. There are also buses to Porto Torres (€3.50, one hour, five daily) and Bosa (€3.50, 1½ hours, two daily with extra services in summer).

There are no direct links with Olbia. Instead you have to travel via Sassari.

CAR & MOTORCYCLE

From Sassari, 40km away, the easiest route is via the fast-running SS291.

For the 46km to/from Bosa, the best route is along the scenic SP105, one of Sardinia's great coastal roads.

TRAIN

The train station is 1.5km north of the old town on Via Don Minzoni. There are up to 12 trains daily to/from Sassari (€2.20, 35 minutes).

ⓘ Getting Around

Your own feet will be enough to get you around the old town and most other places, but you may want to jump on a bus to get to the beaches.

TO/FROM THE AIRPORT

Hourly buses run to/from Via Cagliari (€1 or €1.50 on board, 25 minutes) between 5am and 11pm.

Two daily **Logudoro Tours** (☎079 28 17 28; www.logudorotours.it) buses run to Cagliari (€20, 3½ hours), Oristano (€16, 2¼ hours) and Macomer (€12, 1¼ hours).

To/from Nuoro, **Redentours** (☎0784 3 03 25; www.redentours.com) has two daily buses (€18, 2¼ hours) for which bookings are required.

A taxi to the airport costs about €25.

BUS

From the bus stops on Via Cagliari, bus line AF runs along the seafront and up to Fertilia. Tickets, available at newspaper stands and *tabacchi* (tobacconists), cost €1, although you can also buy them on board for €1.50.

CAR & MOTORCYCLE

The best place to park in Alghero is at the large free car park along the *lungomare* (seafront) on Via Garibaldi; it's always free and rarely gets so crowded that there's no space.

All the major local and international car-hire companies have booths at Fertilia airport.

Operating out of a hut on the seaward side of Via Garibaldi, **Cicloexpress** (☎079 98 69 50; www.cicloexpress.com; Via Garibaldi; ⊗9am-1pm & 4-8pm Mon-Sat) hires out cars (from €60 per day), scooters (from €30) and bikes (from €5).

TAXI

There's a taxi rank by the Giardini Pubblici at Via Vittorio Emanuele 1. Otherwise you can call for one by phoning **Consorzio Radio Taxi** (☎079 989 20 28).

ⓘ **CENTRO STORICO DRIVING ALERT!**

Note that most of Alghero's historic centre is out of bounds to nonauthorised drivers. If, by mistake, you enter the ZTL (*zona a traffico limitato;* limited traffic zone) you risk a fine, payable to your car-hire company if you're in a rental car.

The ZTL restrictions are lifted between 8am and 10.30am and then again from 2.30pm to 4.30pm Monday to Saturday.

ALGHERO TO BOSA BY CAR OR BIKE

Taking in sensational panoramas, mountain woods and one of Sardinia's great coastal roads, this 108km route offers the best of *il mare* (the sea) and *i monti* (the mountains). It involves some twisting mountain climbing and is best tackled as either a two-day cycle ride or a full-day's road trip.

From Alghero take the inland SS292 road and follow as it winds up towards Villanova Monteleone. Enjoy wonderful views across the water to Capo Caccia, before dipping over a ridge and plunging into deep woods. After 23km you'll reach **Villanova Monteleone** (567m), perched like a natural balcony on the slopes of the Colle di Santa Maria.

Continue on the high road beyond Villanova to enjoy yet more great coastal views as the road bobs and weaves through shady woods. The final 5km climb is far outweighed by the sizzling 10km descent to **Bosa**.

Overnight in Bosa – or at the very least stop to explore its attractive historic centre – before setting off on the return leg, via the spectacular 46km coastal road. There's only one significant climb of 6.2km to 350m, but the effort is offset by the stunning views, and with little to disturb you except for the jangle of goats' bells and the occasional sighting of a bird of prey, it's a superb ride.

There are two swimming spots along the way. The first is just south of **Torre Argentina**, about 4.5km out of Bosa – look for cars parked by the roadside and a path down to the beach. The second is **Spiaggia Speranza**, a rocky beach 8km south of Alghero, where you can lunch on fresh fish at **Ristorante La Speranza** (☑079 957 61 07; SP105 Alghero-Bosa, km 8; meals €35-40; ⊙12.30-2.30pm & 7.30-10.30pm summer, Thu-Tue Oct, weekends only winter) before the final push into town.

RIVIERA DEL CORALLO

Heading northwards from Alghero the coastal road sweeps scenically around to the west, passing through Fertilia, a low-key resort, and Porto Conte, a broad bay sprinkled with hotels and discreet villas. The end of the road, quite literally, is Capo Caccia, a rocky headland famous for its thrilling cave complex, the Grotta di Nettuno. Along the way there are a couple of great beaches and some interesting archaeological sites. Inland, the landscape flattens out and you'll find one of the island's top wine producers as well as a number of hospitable and peaceful *agriturismi* (farm-stay accommodation).

Fertilia

Sandy, pine-backed beaches fringe the coast round to Fertilia, about 5km northwest of Alghero. A rather soulless little town with ruler-straight streets and robust rationalist *palazzi*, its atmosphere comes as something of a surprise to visitors after Alghero's medieval hustle. It was built by Mussolini, who intended it to be the centre of a grand agricultural reclamation project, and who brought in farmers from northeastern Italy. Later postwar refugees arrived from Friuli-Venezia Giulia, bringing with them

an allegiance to the lion of St Mark, symbol of Venice, which adorns the statue at the waterfront.

⊙ Sights & Activities

There's not a great deal to see or do once you've pottered around Fertilia's seafront, but there are a couple of excellent beaches nearby. **Spiaggia delle Bombarde**, a couple of kilometres west of Fertilia, is a local favourite, set amid greenery and well equipped with umbrellas, sun-loungers and a kids play area. If it's too crowded, and it does get extremely busy in summer, you could try the next beach along, **Spiaggia del Lazzaretto**.

Both beaches are signposted off the main road, but if you don't have your own car, the Capo Caccia bus from Alghero passes nearby.

Diving Centre Capo Galera DIVING
(☑079 94 21 10; http://diving.capogalera.com; Località Capo Galera, Fertilia; dives from €20) Signposted off the main road to Capo Caccia, this place organises dives and courses for all levels, as well as superlative cave diving in the Nereo Cave, the biggest underwater grotto in the Mediterranean. Dives start at €20 and full kit hire costs €20.

Accommodation (p208) is also available.

RIVIERA DEL CORALLO: BLOOD RED GOLD

Since ancient times the red coral of the Mediterranean has beguiled and bewitched people. Many believed it to be the petrified blood of the Medusa, attributing to it aphrodisiac and other secret qualities, and fashioning amulets out of it.

Alghero's coast south of Capo Caccia is justifiably called the **Riviera del Corallo** (Coral Riviera). The coral fished here is of the highest quality and glows a dark orangey-red. The strong currents around the headland mean the little coral polyps are short and dense to withstand the drag of the sea, which, in turn, means they have few air pockets – the sign of top-quality coral.

To protect the precious commodity, coral fishing is tightly regulated. It can only be harvested by 25 licensed divers between May and October, and at a depth of no less than 80m. Once harvested, it's sold in chunks, its price varying according to colour, quality and size.

To learn more, head to the **Museo del Corallo** (Map p118; ☑ 079 973 40 45; Via XX Settembre, Villa Costantino; admission €3; ☉ 10.30am-1pm & 5.30-8pm), a small museum dedicated to coral fishing in the area, or to **Agostino Marogna** (Map p118; ☑ 079 98 48 14; www.marognacoralli.it; Piazza Civica 34; ☉ 9.30am-1pm & 4.30-8.30pm Mon-Sat), one of Alghero's finest coral shops. Marogna's signature necklaces are composed of big, round coral beads and often take years to create. To make one smooth red ball results in nearly 60% wastage. As there is only a certain amount of coral for sale each year, staff often have to put these necklaces aside until the new season, when they have to hunt for ex-actly the same shade and quality of coral. Such necklaces can cost as much as €30,000. Most items in the shop go for less, though, with prices starting at around €100.

❶ Getting There & Away

From Alghero, at least five weekday buses run from Via Catalogna to Fertilia (€1.20, 15 minutes). Alternatively, you can take local bus AF.

North of Fertilia

◉ Sights

Necropoli di Anghelu Ruju   ARCHAEOLOGICAL SITE
(admission €3, incl Nuraghe di Palmavera €5; ☉ 9am-7pm summer, 10am-2pm winter) Some 10km northwest of Alghero, just off the road to Porto Torres, lie the scattered burial chambers of the Necropoli di Anghelu Ruju. The 38 tombs carved into the sandstone rock, known as *domus de janas* (fairy houses), date from between 3300 BC and 2700 BC. Most of the sculptural decor has been stripped off and removed to museums, but in some of the chambers you can make out traces of sculpted bull's horns, perhaps symbolising a funeral deity.

Three weekday buses run from Alghero to near the *necropoli* (€2, 25 minutes).

Sella e Mosca   VINEYARD
(☑ 079 99 77 00; www.sellaemosca.com; ☉ guided tour 5.30pm Mon-Sat summer, on request rest of the year) **FREE** Sardinia's top wine producer has been based on this 550-hectare estate since

1899. To learn more about its history and production methods, join the free afternoon tour of the estate's historic cellars and lovingly tended museum. Afterwards, stock up at the beautiful **enoteca** (☉ 8.30am-8pm Mon-Sat summer, to 6.30pm winter). Private tastings can also be organised.

From Alghero, three weekday buses pass by the turn-off for Sella e Mosca (€2, 25 minutes).

✖ Eating

★ **Agriturismo Sa Mandra**   SARDINIAN €€
(☑ 079 99 91 50; www.aziendasamandra.it; Strada Aeroporto Civile 21; meals €35-40; ☉ booking required; ☑) This tranquil *agriturismo* serves fantastic farmhouse food, inspired by the culinary traditions of the mountainous Barbagia region, from where the owners hail. For vegetarians there's a dedicated menu featuring herbed cheeses and fried artichokes, whilst meat lovers can tear into island favourites such as spit-roasted pork or lamb with wild fennel. Book early and come hungry.

To get here head towards the airport and the *agriturismo* is signposted to the right of the SP44.

Agriturismo Barbagia   SARDINIAN €€
(☑ 079 93 51 41; www.agriturismobarbagia.it; Località Fighera, Podere 26; meals €30-35; ☉ booking required) One of several *agriturismi* dotted around the flat countryside north of Fertilia,

this is a charming spot for a royal Sardinian feast. Think starters of cheese, cured hams, and marinated vegetables, traditional pastas such as *malloredus* (semolina dumplings) with sausage in tomato sauce, and juicy lamb and pork roasts.

From Fertilia head north on the SS291, take a right onto the SP44 and then look out for signs on the left.

Nuraghe di Palmavera

Nuraghe di Palmavera   ARCHAEOLOGICAL SITE (admission €3, incl Necropoli di Anghelu Ruju €5; ☺9am-7pm summer, 10am-2pm winter) A few kilometres west of Fertilia on the road to Porto Conte, the Nuraghe di Palmavera is a 3500-year-old nuraghic village. At its centre stands a limestone tower and an elliptical building with a secondary sandstone tower that was added later. The ruins of smaller towers and bastion walls surround the central edifice, and beyond the walls are the packed remnants of circular dwellings, of which there may originally have been about 50.

The circular **Capanna delle Riunioni** (Meeting Hut) is the subject of considerable speculation. Its foundation wall is lined by a low stone bench, perhaps for a council of elders, and encloses a pedestal topped by a model *nuraghe* (Bronze Age settlement). One theory suggests there was actually a cult to the *nuraghi* themselves.

Between April and September, a single weekday bus runs to the site from Alghero (€1.50), otherwise you'll need your own transport.

Porto Conte

Known more poetically as the Baia delle Ninfe (Bay of Nymphs), Porto Conte is a lovely unspoilt bay, its blue waters home to an armada of bobbing yachts and its green shores thick with mimosa and eucalyptus trees.

◉ Sights

Spiaggia Mugoni   BEACH
The main focus of Porto Conte is Spiaggia Mugoni, a hugely popular beach that arcs round the bay's northeastern flank. With its fine white sand and protected waters, it makes an excellent venue for beginners to try their hand at water sports. The **Club della Vela** (☏338 148 95 83) offers windsurfing, canoeing, kayaking and sailing courses, and also rents out boats.

★**Le Prigionette**
Nature Reserve   NATURE RESERVE
(☏079 94 90 60; admission free but ID required; ☺8am-4pm Mon-Sat, 9am-5pm Sun) This reserve, just west of Porto Conte at the base of Monte Timidone (361m), is a beautiful pocket of uncontaminated nature. Encompassing 12 sq km of woodland, aromatic *macchia* (Mediterranean scrub) and rocky coastline, it offers wonderful scenery and excellent walking with a network of well-marked tracks, suitable for hikers and cyclists. All around wildlife flourishes – deer, albino donkeys, Giara horses and wild boar roam the woods, whilst overhead, griffon vultures and falcons fly the skies.

For stirring coastal views head to **Cala della Barca**, a remote cliffside spot overlooking the **Isola Piana**. The easiest and quickest way of getting there is to drive from the reserve's entrance until you come to an open space by a hut – it takes about 20 minutes along the dirt track. Park here and continue on foot for the last kilometre or so.

❶ Getting There & Away

Regular buses run between Porto Conte and Alghero (€1.50, 30 minutes, up to 10 daily between June and September, five rest of year).

Riviera del Corallo & Porto Conte

PARCO DI PORTO CONTE

The **Parco di Porto Conte** (www.parcodiportoconte.it), one of only two regional nature parks in Sardinia, covers 60km of coastline and 53.5 sq km of an area once described by French oceanographer Jacques Cousteau as one of the most beautiful in the Mediterranean.

Its diverse landscape, which ranges from woods and wetlands to tracts of low-lying *macchia* (Mediterranean scrub) and soaring white cliffs, is an important natural habitat, providing sanctuary to 35 species of mammals and 150 of birds.

It offers great walking, particularly in Le Prigionette Nature Reserve (p127) and on the headland running down Porto Conte's eastern flank. One of the best routes leads from a park entrance just off the SS127 near Maristella to **Punta Giglio**, a panoramic point at the south of the promontory. It's about 6km there and back – allow at least three hours – but make the effort and you're rewarded with dazzling sea views over the bay to Capo Caccia.

For further details about the park and its network of paths and cycle tracks check out its website.

Capo Caccia

From Le Prigionette Nature Reserve, the road continues up to Capo Caccia, a dramatic headland that marks the southernmost point of the Parco di Porto Conte. The scenery here is superb as towering white cliffs sheer up from impossibly blue waters and thrilling seascapes unfurl at every turn. For an eyeful, stop off at the signposted viewing point a few hundred metres short of the road's end, and look down on the bay beneath you, and, on the other side, the wave-buffeted Isola Foradada.

◉ Sights & Activities

★ **Grotta di Nettuno**   CAVE
(☑ 079 94 65 40; adult/reduced €13/9; ⊘ 9am-7pm summer, to 3pm winter) Capo Caccia's principal crowd-puller is the Grotta di Nettuno, a haunting, underground fairyland of stalactites and stalagmites. The easiest way to get to the caves is to take the **Navisarda** (Map p118; ☑ 079 95 06 03; www.navisarda.it; Banchina Dogana, Alghero; adult/child return €15/8, cave entrance not included) ferry from Alghero, but for those with a head for heights, there's a vertiginous 654-step staircase, the **Escala del Cabirol**, that descends 110m of sheer cliff from the car park at the end of the Capo Caccia road.

Tours of the caves, which depart on the hour, last around 45 minutes and take you through narrow walkways flanked by forests of curiously shaped stalactites and stalagmites, nicknamed the organ, the church dome (or warrior's head) and so on. At its furthest point the cave extends back for 1km,

but a lot is not open to the public, including several freshwater lakes deep inside the grotto. Note that in bad weather the grotto is closed.

To get to the caves by public transport, a daily bus departs from Via Catalogna (€2, 50 minutes) in Alghero at 9.15am and returns at midday. From June to September, there are two extra runs at 3.10pm and 5.10pm, returning at 4.05pm and 6.05pm.

Via Ferrata del Cabirol   ROCK CLIMBING
(www.ferratacabirol.it) Rock climbers can enjoy exclusive views of the sea on the Via Ferrata del Cabirol, a stunning cliffside route along a series of exposed rock faces. Of medium difficulty, the traverse mainly follows ledges around the rocks but does involve some short vertical ascents. Conditions are best in spring and autumn, though it stays in the shade until 2pm on summer days.

To get here, turn off the Capo Caccia road after 10km, towards the spot that offers views of the Isola di Foradada.

North of Capo Caccia

The road north of Porto Conte leads through the flat, green land known as the Nurra.

◉ Sights

Torre del Porticciolo   BAY
On the coast north of Porto Conte, the Torre del Porticciolo is a tiny natural harbour backed by a small arc of beach and overlooked by a 16th-century watchtower on the northern promontory. High cliffs mount guard on the southern side, and you can explore adjacent coves along narrow walking trails.

Spiaggia di Porto Ferro   BEACH

The Spiaggia di Porto Ferro is a fabulous, unspoilt beach, much loved by local surfers. Hidden behind thick tracts of pine woods about 6km north of Torre del Porticciolo, its 2km of sands and lovely azure waters rarely get as busy as the better-known beaches in the area.

Buses run from Alghero (€3, 45 minutes) twice daily between April and September.

Lago Baratz   LAKE

From Porto Ferro a series of back roads lead 6km inland to Lago Baratz, Sardinia's only natural lake. Surrounded by low hills, the lake attracts some bird life, although the winged fellows tend to hang about the less accessible northern side. Paths circle the lake's marshy banks and there's a 3km dirt track connecting with the Spiaggia di Porto Ferro.

Cantina Sociale di
Santa Maria la Palma   WINERY

(☎ 079 99 90 08; www.santamarialapalma.it; ⊗ 8am-1pm & 3-8pm summer, 8am-1pm & 2.30-6.30pm Mon-Fri, 8am-1pm Sun winter) South of Lago Baratz, the workaday village of Santa Maria la Palma is home to this, the area's second winery after Sella e Mosca. Head to the *enoteca* (wine bar) to browse its extensive selection of reds, whites and spumanti, and fill up with wine straight from the barrel. Guided tours can be arranged on request.

✖ Eating

★ Agriturismo Porticciolo   SARDINIAN €€

(www.agriturismoporticciolo.it; Località Porticciolo; meals €18-32; ⊗ dinner only) This welcoming *agriturismo* serves delicious farmhouse food in a grand barn with wooden beams, rustic decor and a huge fireplace. Portions are generous so you'll need to pace yourself if you want to go much beyond the antipasti and pasta dishes.

THE NORTH COAST

Extending 70km from Sardinia's northwestern tip round to Castelsardo, this stretch of coast encompasses the sublime and the distinctly unsightly.

Leading up to the northwestern peninsula, the flat land to the west of Porto Torres has a desolate feel, especially when the *maestrale* (northwesterly wind) blows in, whipping the *macchia* and bleak rocks. But

OFF THE BEATEN TRACK

ARGENTIERA

For a glimpse into Sardinia's not-so-distant past, head to the haunting backwater of Argentiera. A natural inlet about 11km north of Lago Baratz, it's dominated by the ghostly ruins of its silver mine, once the most important on the island. *Argento* (silver) was first extracted here by the Romans and continued right up to the 1960s when the mine was finally abandoned. The dark-brick mine buildings, now held together by wooden scaffolding, rise in an untidy jumble from a small grey-sand beach. You can't actually go into them, but they make for a stark and melancholy sight.

If you fancy a bite to eat, **Bar Il Veliero** (☎ 079 53 04 71; Via Carbonia 1, Argentiera; panini from €3) is a simple bar set-up a few metres back from the beach. Here you can get *panini,* snacks, or a more substantial plate of pasta.

Argentiera is at the end of the SP18, signposted from Palmadula.

persevere and you'll reach laid-back Stintino, approached via its shimmering *saline* (saltpans), and the fabulous Spiaggia della Pelosa, one of Sardinia's most celebrated beaches.

To the east, the industrial sprawl around Porto Torres, the north coast's busiest port, is far from inviting, but the scenery improves as you push on to Castelsardo. For much of the way, the road is flanked by pine woods, behind which you'll find various isolated beaches. Inland, the flat-topped tablelands of the Anglona, a struggling farm district, lie sandwiched between the Gallura to the east, Logudoro to the south and the small Romangia district to the west.

Stintino

POP 1520

Until the arrival of tourism in the 1960s, Stintino was a remote and forgotten tuna-fishing village. Nowadays it's a sunny little resort, wedged tidily between two ports – one full of bobbing blue fishing boats (Porto Mannu), the other occupied by gleaming white yachts (Porto Minori). Its pastel-painted houses add charm, while its location near the Spiaggia della Pelosa and the Isola dell'Asinara make it an excellent summer base.

Many of Stintino's current residents are descended from the 45 families who established the village in 1885. They originally set up here after being evicted from the Isola dell'Asinara to make way for a new prison and quarantine station. The settlers turned to the sea for their livelihood and the village soon developed a reputation for its tuna hunt, a bloody annual event known as the *mattanza* (slaughter). These days, the town's waters are a favourite with sailors and often host regattas and windsurfing events.

◉ Sights

Museo della Tonnara MUSEUM
(Porto Minori) Stintino's tuna-fishing heritage is documented at this, the town's sole museum. At the time of writing, the museum was closed prior to being transferred to a new location overlooking Porto Minori. The plans for the new building call for six rooms to be ordered like the six chambers of the *tonnara* (the net in which the fish are caught), with documents, photos and computer displays illustrating the centuries-old fishing methods.

Spiaggia Le Saline BEACH
Just south of Stintino a signpost directs you to the abandoned *tonnara* and the Spiaggia Le Saline, once the site of a busy saltworks, now a beautiful white beach. Behind it, marshes extend inland to form the **Stagno di Casaraccio**, a big lagoon where you might just see flamingos at rest.

☞ Tours

Stintino is the main gateway to the Parco Nazionale dell'Asinara, and during summer a regular fleet of ferries operates out of Porto Mannu. From November to April, excursions run on a fairly ad hoc basis with boats only setting out if there are enough people to justify the trip.

Agenzia La Nassa TOURS
(☑ 079 52 00 60; www.escursioniasinara.it; Via Sassari 39; ☉ 9am-12.30pm & 4-7pm) This agency runs a number of tours around Parco Nazionale dell'Asinara. The cheapest option, available between June and September, covers your ferry passage only, leaving you free to walk or cycle within designated areas on the island. More expensive packages include 4WD or bus transport.

Prices range from €18 to €65 per person.

Linea del Parco BOAT TOURS
(☑ 079 52 31 18; www.lineadelparco.it; Porto Mannu; ☉ ticket office 9.30am-12.30pm & 4-7pm) Linea del Parco offers a number of packages including tours by bus or Land Rover, horse rides, and boat excursions. Reckon on from €55 per person for the Land Rover tour. It also hires out bikes for €5 per day.

Mare e Natura TOURS
(☑ 079 52 00 97, 339 9850435; www.marenatura.it; Via Sassari 77, Stintino) Organises land and boat tours of the Parco Nazionale dell'Asinara.

✕ Eating

Albergo Ristorante Silvestrino SEAFOOD €€
(☑ 079 52 30 07; www.hotelsilvestrino.it; Via Sassari 14; meals €35; ☉ 12.30-2.30pm & 7.30-10.30pm, closed Thu winter) On Stintino's main drag, this historic hotel restaurant serves some of the best seafood in town. Its sunny dining hall and small streetside terrace set the stage for timeless creations such as *risotto al nero di seppia* (risotto with black cuttlefish ink) and *fregola ai frutti di mare* (couscous-like pasta with mixed seafood).

Skipper RISTORANTE €€
(☑ 079 52 34 60; Lungomare Cristoforo Colombo 57; meals €25; ☉ Tue-Sun) A long-standing favourite, this casual waterfront bar-cum-restaurant is a jack of all trades. You can sit down on the sea-facing terrace and order anything from coffee and cocktails to seafood pastas, *zuppa gallurese* (a traditional casserole of bread, *ragù*, cheese and meat stock), hamburgers, salads and *panini*.

Lu Fanali TRATTORIA, PIZZERIA €€
(☑ 079 52 30 54; www.lufanali.it; Lungomare Cristoforo Colombo 89; pizzas from €5.50, meals €30; ☉ 7am-midnight) Watch the boats bob by as you dig into reliably good pizzas and seafood staples at Lu Fanali, a friendly, unbuttoned kinda place near Porto Mannu.

ⓘ Information

Agenzia La Nassa (☑ 079 52 00 60; www. escursioniasinara.it; Via Sassari 39; ☉ 9am-12.30pm & 4-7pm) This private agency is your best bet for local information. It can book excursions to the Parco Nazionale dell'Asinara and advise on local accommodation, as well as hire you a bike (per day from €10) or car (from €50).

ℹ Getting There & Away

Between June and mid-September, **Sardabus** (www.sardabus.it) operates five daily buses to/from Alghero's Fertilia airport (€6, 50 minutes).

There are at least four weekday buses (two on Sundays) to Stintino from Porto Torres (€3, 45 minutes) and Sassari (€3.50, one hour, 10 minutes). Services increase between June and September.

Capo Falcone

From Stintino the road continues north to Capo Falcone, a rugged headland peppered with hotels, holiday residences and summer homes.

◎ Sights & Activities

★ **Spiaggia della Pelosa**   BEACH
About 2.5km north of Stintino, the Spiaggia della Pelosa is a dreamy image of beach perfection: a salt white strip of sand lapped by shallow, turquoise seas and fronted by strange, almost lunar, licks of land. Completing the picture is a Catalan-Aragonese watchtower over the water on the craggy Isola Piana.

In July and August the beach gets extremely busy as thousands of beachgoers squeeze onto every available inch of sand, but avoid these peak months and you'll find the crowds far more manageable.

Year-round buses run to the beach from Stintino (€1.20, five minutes, four weekdays, two Sundays). In summer services are considerably increased.

If you have your own wheels, there's limited roadside parking near the beach (within the blue lines) for around €5 per half-day.

Windsurfing Center Stintino   WINDSURFING
(☑079 52 70 06; www.windsurfingcenter.it) On the beach at Pelosa, this outfit rents out windsurfing rigs (from €17 per hour) and canoes (from €10 per hour), as well as offering windsurfing and sailing courses. If that all sounds far too energetic it can also sort you out with an umbrella and sun-loungers (from €20 per day).

Asinara Scuba Diving   DIVING
(☑079 52 71 75; www.asinarascubadiving.com; Viale la Pelosa, Località Porto dell'Ancora) Just before Pelosa beach at the Club Hotel Ancora, this diving centre offers a range of dives around Capo del Falcone and the protected waters of the Parco Nazionale dell'Asinara.

Parco Nazionale dell'Asinara

★ **Parco Nazionale dell'Asinara**   NATIONAL PARK
(www.parcoasinara.org) Named after its resident *asini bianchi* (albino donkeys), the Isola dell'Asinara encompasses 51 sq km of *macchia* (Mediterranean scrub), rocky coastline and remote sandy beaches. The island, Sardinia's second largest, is now a national park, but for years it was off-limits as home to one of Italy's toughest maximum-security prisons.

The only way to reach it is with a licensed boat operator from Stintino or Porto Torres (see p130). Once there, you can explore independently, although access is restricted to certain areas.

The smallest of Sardinia's three national parks, the island is a haven for wildlife, providing a habitat for an estimated 50 to 70 donkeys alongside 80 other animal species, including mouflon (silky-haired wild sheep) and peregrine falcons.

Dotted around its stark landscape are series of abandoned buildings that were once part of the island's notorious *carcere* (prison). Built in 1885, along with a quarantine station for cholera victims, the jail was a kind of Italian Alcatraz and many of Italy's most dangerous criminals did time there, including Neapolitan gangster Raffaele Cutolo and the infamous mafia boss Totò Riina. The prison finally closed in 1997.

The prisoners have long since gone but much of the island remains out of bounds, including the beach at **Cala Sant'Andrea** (a breeding ground for turtles). You can, however, cover the island's highlights on a guided tour. Itineraries vary but most take in the prison at **Fornelli**, **Cala d'Oliva**, the panoramic highpoint of **Punta della Scomunica**, and the beach at **Cala Sabina**.

Note that many tours do not include lunch, so either take a picnic or book a meal at the bar-restaurant at **Cala Reale** (☑346 1737043; set menu €45).

If you're visiting on your own, consider hiring a bike in Stintino and taking that over as there's no public transport on the island.

Porto Torres

POP 22,400

Not one of Sardinia's most alluring towns, Porto Torres is a busy working port

ALGHERO & THE NORTHWEST PARCO NAZIONALE DELL'ASINARA

surrounded by a fuming petrochemical plant. There's no compelling reason to hang around, but if you find yourself passing through – and you might, especially if heading to or from Corsica – there are a couple of worthwhile sights, most notably the Basilica di San Gavino, one of Sardinia's most important Romanesque churches.

Porto Torres had its heyday under the Romans, who founded it as their main port on Sardinia's north coast. It remained one of the island's key ports until the Middle Ages and was capital of the Giudicato di Torres.

◉ Sights

Basilica di San Gavino   CHURCH
(admission & crypt €2, guided tour €3; ⊘ 9am-1pm & 3-7pm summer, to 6pm winter) The uninspiring streets of Porto Torres' modern centre provide the unlikely setting for Sardinia's largest Romanesque church. Built between 1030 and 1080, the basilica is an impressive, and architecturally important structure, notable for its facing apses – it has no facade – and three lateral portals. Its solemn interior is divided by 28 marble columns, pilfered by the Pisan builders from the ancient Roman city, whilst underneath, the crypt is lined with religious statuary and various stone tombs.

The church, which stands on an ancient pagan burial ground, takes its name from one of the great Sardinian saints, the Roman soldier Gavino, who commanded the garrison at Torres in Diocletian's reign. Ordered to put to death two Christian priests, Protus and Januarius, he was converted by them and he himself shared their martyrdom. All three were beheaded on 25 October 304. Evidence for these events is scanty, but the legend of the *martiri turritani* (martyrs of Torres) flourishes.

To get to the basilica follow Corso Vittorio Emanuele south from the port for about 1km, and you'll find it one block to the west.

Museo & Parco Archeologico   MUSEUM, ARCHAEOLOGICAL PARK
(⊘ 079 51 44 33; Via Ponte Romano 99; adult/reduced €3/1.50, free 1st Sun of month; ⊘ 9am-8pm Tue-Sat, 9am-2pm Sun) Near the train station, this complex houses the excavated remains of Turris Libisonis, the ancient Roman port on which the modern city stands. The museum, also known as the Antiquarium Turritano, displays finds from the adjacent archaeological park, including a collection of ceramics, busts, marble statues and mo-

saics. Park highlights include the ruins of an ancient bathing complex known as the Palazzo del Re Barbaro, the mosaiced Domus dei Mosaici, and an impressive Roman bridge.

Guided tours of the site are available and run by the locally run **Ibis Coop** (⊘ 392 838 32 54; www.ibiscoop.com).

✗ Eating

Cristallo   CAFE, PASTICCERIA €
(⊘ 079 51 49 09; Piazza XX Settembre 11; gelati €2.50; ⊘ 7am-midnight Tue-Sun) A local landmark, this bustling bar-cum-*pasticceria* (pastry shop) near the waterfront is good for a typical Italian breakfast (croissant and coffee), light snack or refreshing gelato.

ⓘ Information

BNL (Corso Vittorio Emanuele 20) Bank.
Post office (Via Ponte Romano 83; ⊘ 8.20am-1.15pm Mon-Sat)
Tourist office (⊘ 079 51 50 00; Piazza Garibaldi 17; ⊘ 9.30am-12.30pm & 6-9pm) A helpful office a couple of streets back from the port, just off Corso Vittorio Emanuele.

ⓘ Getting There & Away

BOAT
Tirrenia (⊘ 892 123; www.tirrenia.it) and **Grandi Navi Veloci** (⊘ 010 209 45 91; www.gnv.it) run ferries between Porto Torres and Genoa. Tirrenia services are year-round, while GNV operates between mid-May and September. High-season fares for the 11-hour crossing start at €74.

SNCM (⊘ 079 51 44 77; www.sncmitalia.it) and **La Méridionale** (⊘ in France 491 994 509; www.lameridionale.fr) together operate ferries to/from Marseille (€78 or €141 with a small car, 15 to 17 hours) via Corsica. You can purchase tickets at **Agenzia Paglietti** (⊘ 079 51 41 42; Corso Vittorio Emanuele 19, Porto Torres).

BUS
Buses leave from Via Mare near the porticoes on the waterfront. There are regular buses to Sassari (€2, 30 minutes, hourly), Alghero (€3.50, one hour, five daily) and Stintino (€3.50, 45 minutes, four daily), with extra services in summer. Get tickets from the news-stand near the Cristallo bar on Piazza XX Settembre.

TRAIN
Direct trains run to Sassari (€1.55, 20 minutes, five daily) and Cagliari (€16.90, 3¾ hours, one daily). Additional services run to Cagliari and Olbia via Ozieri-Chilivani.

Castelsardo

POP 5750

An attractive and popular day-trip destination, Castelsardo huddles around the high cone of a promontory jutting into the Mediterranean. Towering over everything is its dramatic *centro storico,* a hilltop ensemble of dark alleyways and medieval buildings seemingly melded onto the grey rock peak.

The town was originally designed as a defensive fort by a 12th-century Genoese family. Named Castel Genoese, it was the subject of much fighting and in 1448 fell to the Spanish, who changed its name to Castel Aragonese. It later became part of the Kingdom of Sardinia under the Piedmontese Savoy dynasty and, in 1767, took its current name, which means Sardinian castle.

◉ Sights

Castello CASTLE
(Via Marconi; admission €2; ⊙ 9.30am-1pm & 3-6.30pm Tue-Sun, longer hours summer) Lording it over the hilltop *centro storico* is the medieval Castello, the centrepiece around which the original town was built. Constructed in the 12th century by the Doria family and home to Eleonora d'Arborea for a period, it commands superb views over the Golfo dell'Asinara to Corsica. It also houses a small museum, the **Museo dell'Intreccio del Mediterraneo** (⌨ 079 47 13 80; Via Marconi; admission €2), dedicated to the basket-weaving for which the town is famous.

Chiesa di Santa Maria CHURCH
(Piazza della Misericordia) Just below the Castello, the medieval Chiesa di Santa Maria is a much-loved local church, venerated for its 14th-century crucifix. One of the oldest crucifixes in Sardinia, this is known as *Lu Cristu Nieddu* (Black Christ) because of the colour the juniper wood has taken on over the centuries.

Cattedrale di Sant'Antonio Abate CATHEDRAL
(church free, crypt & Museo Diocesano €2; ⊙ crypt & Museo Diocesano 10.30am-1pm & 6.30pm-midnight summer) Announcing the presence of the cathedral is its landmark bell tower topped by a brightly tiled cupola. The cathedral itself, which sits on a panoramic terrace, was originally Gothic but a protracted 17th-century remodelling saw the addition of Renaissance and baroque elements.

DON'T MISS

ROCCIA DELL'ELEFANTE: A WONDER ROCK

From Castelsardo, the SS134 Sedini road leads to one of the area's most lovable landmarks, the **Roccia dell'Elefante** (Elephant Rock), a bizarre trachyte rock that looks just like an elephant raising its trunk towards the road. The monolith, the shape of which is the result of nothing more mysterious than wind and rain erosion, has been the source of local interest for millennia as witnessed by the presence of two neolithic tombs (known as *domus de janas* or 'fairy houses') in the hollow interior.

The upper tomb has been damaged by erosion, but the lower one is still in good shape, with four small rooms and a rock carving of a bull's horns.

Inside, the main altar is dominated by the *Madonna in trono col bambino,* a painting by the mysterious Maestro di Castelsardo. More of his works can be seen in the **Museo Diocesano** in the crypt.

Accessible through a door next to the altar, the crypt features a series of small rooms chiselled out of the living rock. These are all that remain of the Romanesque church that once stood here.

⚜ Festivals & Events

Lunissanti RELIGIOUS
(⊙ Mar/Apr) On the Monday after Palm Sunday, the people of Castelsardo celebrate a series of Masses and processions, including a solemn parade through the old town from the Chiesa di Santa Maria.

✗ Eating

La Trattoria da Maria Giuseppe TRATTORIA, PIZZERIA €
(⌨ 079 47 06 61; Via Colombo 6; pizzas €4-10, meals €25; ⊙ 12.30-2.30pm & 7.30-11pm) For a relaxed meal, head to this unpretentious, neighbourhood trattoria near Piazza Pianedda. Locals come here for the excellent wood-fired pizzas, but you can also fill up on pastas, grilled meats and fried local fish.

La Guardiola RISTORANTE €€
(⌨ 079 47 07 55; Piazza Bastione 4; meals €35; ⊙ 12.30-3pm & 7.30-11pm, closed Mon Oct-May) Feast on quality seafood and fabulous 360-degree views at this panoramic hilltop

restaurant. The menu features a number of classic Sardinian meat dishes but it's the well-presented local seafood that really stands out. For a taste, try the ample seafood antipasto.

Cormorano SEAFOOD €€€
(☑079 47 06 28; www.ristoranteilcormorano.net; Via Colombo 5; meals up to €55; ☺12.30-2.30pm & 7.30-10.30pm, closed Mon winter) Behind the unassuming exterior, this restaurant enjoys a stellar reputation for high-end seafood. There's a creative edge to many of the dishes, which include starters such as pickled monkfish with spinach cream and pine nuts, and an array of imaginative pastas such as linguine with scampi and bay leaves.

🛍 Shopping

You can't fail to notice the handicrafts shopping emporia in Castelsardo. As you wander through the old town you'll see women on their doorsteps, creating intricate baskets and other objects of all shapes and sizes.

ℹ Information

Tourist office (☑079 47 02 20; www.castelsardoturismo.it; Via Bastione; ☺9am-1.30pm & 3.30-8.30pm Mon-Fri) In the historic centre.

ℹ Getting There & Away

From just off Piazza Pianedda, buses run to/from Sassari (€3, one hour, 11 weekdays, four Sundays) and Santa Teresa di Gallura (€6, 1½ hours, three daily). Buy tickets from the *edicola* (newsstand) at the corner of Via Trieste and Via Roma.

Around Castelsardo

With your own vehicle you could comfortably take in the following places in a one-day circuit from Castelsardo. If you're relying on public transport it becomes more difficult.

◉ Sights

Chiesa di Nostra Signora di Tergu CHURCH
Tergu, a small village 10km or so south of Castelsardo, is home to a fine Romanesque church, the 12th-century Chiesa di Nostra Signora di Tergu. Built out of wine-red trachyte and white limestone, it sits in a pleasant garden alongside the few visible remains of a monastery that once housed up to 100 Benedictine monks. Of particular note is the church's facade, a pretty ensemble of arches, columns, geometric patterns and a simple rose window.

Museo Domus de Janas MUSEUM
(☑079 58 92 15; Via Nazionale, Sedini; adult/reduced €2.50/1.50; ☺9.30am-1pm & 3-6pm Mon-Fri, 10am-1pm Sat & Sun) Head to the small, sleepy town of Sedini to see one of the area's best-known *domus de janas*. Gouged out of a huge calcareous rock, the prehistoric tomb was lived in by farmers in the Middle Ages and used as a prison until the 19th century. It now houses a small museum displaying traditional farming and household implements.

Four weekday buses run to Sedini from Castelsardo (€2.50, 25 minutes).

Nuraghe Su Tesoru ARCHAEOLOGICAL SITE
In a field off the main road between the Roccia dell'Elefante and Valledoria, you'll pass the Nuraghe Su Tesoru on the left-hand side. More correctly known as the Nuraghe Paddaggiu (meaning haystack in Sardo), this was one of the last *nuraghi* to be built. Only the central tower remains in any recognisable form but originally there were also two lateral towers. It's best admired from the comfort of your own car as stopping on the main road is not exactly convenient.

Valledoria TOWN
About 15km east of Castelsardo, the sprawling town of Valledoria is fronted by beaches that stretch more than 10km east to the small fishing village of Isola Rossa. Up to four weekday buses run from Castelsardo to Valledoria (€2, 25 minutes), although if you can't convince the bus driver to stop at the camping-ground turn-off, you'll have to hitch or walk.

SASSARI

POP 125,700

Sassari, Sardinia's sprawling second city, requires a bit of work. On first sight, it's not an immediately appealing place, but persevere and you'll discover that beneath its rather scruffy veneer lies a proud and cultured university town with an unpretentious atmosphere and a bustling, workaday vibe.

Like many Italian towns it hides its charms behind an outer shell of drab apartment blocks and confusing, traffic-choked roads. But once through to the inner sanctum it opens up, revealing a grand centre of wide boulevards, impressive piazzas and stately *palazzi*. In the evocative and rundown *centro storico,* medieval alleyways hum with Dickensian activity as residents run about their daily business amid grimy facades and hidden churches.

History

The presence of *nuraghi* and ancient ruins in the area around Sassari attest to the presence of settlers in the area long before the city came into being in the Middle Ages. Sassari, or Tathari as it was originally known, was founded by inhabitants of the ancient Roman colony of Turris Libisonis (modern-day Porto Torres) fleeing inland to escape from pirate raids.

It expanded rapidly in the 12th century, growing to become the largest city in the Giudicato di Torres. Eventually, it broke away from the Giudicato and, with support from Genoa, declared itself an autonomous city state in 1294.

But the Sassaresi soon tired of Genoese meddling and in 1321 called on the Crown of Aragon to help rid them of the northern Italians. The Catalan-Aragonese arrived in 1323, but Sassari soon discovered it had leapt from the frying pan into the fire. The first of many revolts against the city's new masters came two years later. It took another century for the Iberians to fully control Sassari.

For a time the city prospered, but waves of plague and the growing menace from Ottoman Turkey sidelined Sardinia, leaving Sassari to slide into decline in the 16th century. A century later the founding of the city's university, Sardinia's first, was a rare highlight in this otherwise grim period.

It wasn't until the middle of the 19th century that Sassari began to take off again, following the modernisation of Porto Torres and the laying of the Carlo Felice highway between the port, Sassari and Cagliari. Since 1945 the city has maintained a slow pace of economic growth. It has also been an industrious producer of national politicians, including former presidents Antonio Segni (1891–1972) and Francesco Cossiga (1928-2010), the charismatic communist leader Enrico Berlinguer (1922–84), and Beppe Pisanu (b 1937), a former interior minister under Silvio Berlusconi.

◉ Sights

★ **Museo Nazionale Sanna**   MUSEUM
(🖉 079 27 22 03; www.museosannasassari.benic-ulturali.it; Via Roma 64; adult/reduced €4/2, free 1st Sun of month; ⊙ 9am-8pm Tue-Sun) Sassari's premier museum, housed in a grand Palla-dian villa, boasts a comprehensive archae-ological collection and an ethnographical section dedicated to Sardinian folk art. The highlight is the nuraghic bronzeware, in-cluding weapons, bracelets, votive boats and figurines depicting humans and animals.

Exhibits are displayed in chronologically ordered rooms, starting with the Sala Pre-istorica, which showcases the island's very earliest Stone Age and neolithic finds. In this and the next room, dedicated to finds from the 3rd-century-BC temple of Monte d'Ac-coddi, you'll find an array of fossils, pottery fragments and bone tools.

Beyond these, the museum opens up in a series of displays dedicated to megalithic tombs and *domus de janas* (fairy houses). Look out for the sophisticated bronzeware, including axe heads and similar tools, jewel-lery and *bronzetti* (bronze figurines).

The next room is given over to the Phoe-nician and Carthaginian eras with some exquisite pottery, gold jewellery and masks. Continuing on, the Roman collection is mostly made up of ceramics and oil burn-ers but there are also some statues and a sprinkling of coins, jewellery and household objects. Off to one side lies a stash of heavy Roman anchors.

The separate ethnographic section has a small collection of Sardinian folk art plus an eclectic array of carpets, saddlebags, embroidered clothes and curious terracotta hot-water bottles.

★ **Piazza Italia**   PIAZZA
Sassari's largest piazza, Piazza Italia, is one of Sardinia's most impressive public spaces. Covering about a hectare, it is surrounded by imposing 19th-century buildings, including the neoclassical **Palazzo della Provincia**, seat of the provincial government and, op-posite, the neo-Gothic **Palazzo Giordano**, now home to the Banca di Credito Sardo. Presiding over everything is a statue of King Vittorio Emanuele II.

The statue was unveiled in 1899 to much pomp and costumed celebration, in antici-pation of the grand event that would become the city's main festival, the Cavalcata Sarda. The piazza also marks the starting point for Sassari's other big jamboree, I Candelieri.

Museo della Brigata Sassari   MUSEUM
(🖉 079 208 51 51; Piazza Castello; ⊙ 8am-4.30pm Mon-Thu, to noon Fri & Sat) **FREE** Sassa-ri is home to one of Italy's most revered army regiments. The Sassari Brigade was

Central Sassari

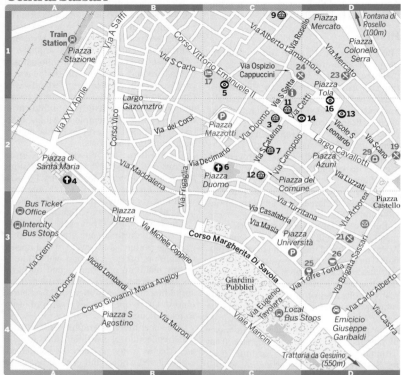

established in 1915 and during WWI established a reputation for bravery in the face of appalling conditions. You can glean something of the suffering they endured in this tiny museum in the regiment's city-centre barracks. Uniforms, photos, documents and other memorabilia testify to the bravery of the Sardinian soldiers, who were thrown into battle against the Austrians in northern Italy.

Corso Vittorio Emanuele II STREET
The main drag through the *centro storico*, Corso Vittorio Emanuele II follows the path of the ancient Roman road from Porto Torres to Cagliari. Little remains from its 13th-century heyday, but there are a few signs of past grandeur. At No 25, **Palazzo Farris** (Corso Vittorio Emanuele II 25) is a 15th-century townhouse currently being restored, whilst, a few metres up, the **Casa di Re Enzo** (Corso Vittorio Emanuele II 42) provides a remarkable Catalan Gothic setting

for a clothes shop. Opposite, the Liberty-style **Teatro Civico** (Corso Vittorio Emanuele II 39) was a 19th-century addition.

Piazza Tola PIAZZA
Just north of Corso Vittorio Emanuele II, Piazza Tola was medieval Sassari's main square where condemned heretics were burned at the stake. Overlooking the charming square is the 16th-century **Palazzo d'Usini**, one of the first Renaissance buildings to be constructed in Sardinia and now home to the city library.

Museo della Città MUSEUM
(adult/reduced €3/2) This museum dedicated to Sassari's history and development is spread over three sites. Its main seat is the 19th-century **Palazzo di Città** (☎079 201 51 22; Corso Vittorio Emanuele II; ⊙10am-1pm & 5-8pm Tue-Sat, 10am-1pm Sun) where exhibits illustrate the city's urban growth, festivals and traditions. A short walk away, **Palazzo**

Central Sassari

Ducale (Piazza del Comune; ⊙9.30am-1pm & 4.30-7.30pm Tue-Fri, 9.30am-1pm Sat), which also doubles as Sassari's city hall, has displays of historic artefacts relating to the palace's former life as an aristocratic 18th-century residence. The third location is **Palazzo della Frumentaria** (Via della Muraglie 1; ⊙10am-1pm & 5-8pm Tue-Sun), a 16th-century grain warehouse that's used to stage temporary exhibitions.

Mus'A Pinacoteca al
Canopoleno GALLERY
(☏079 23 15 60; www.pinacotecamusa.it; Piazza Santa Caterina 4; adult/reduced €2/1; ⊙9am-1.30pm Mon-Fri & 3-5pm Tue) Housed in a 16th-century Jesuit college, Sassari's municipal art collection boasts over 400 paintings from the Middle Ages to the 20th century. Of the religious art on the ground floor, a highlight is Bartolomeo Vivarini's fine triptych, *Madonna con bambino* (1473). Upstairs, works by the likes of Giovanni Lanfranco and Guercino hang alongside landscapes and Flemish still lifes, whilst, up on the 2nd floor, you'll find paintings by 20th-century Sardinian artists.

Duomo CATHEDRAL
(Piazza Duomo; ⊙8.30am-noon & 4-7pm Mon-Sat, 8.30-11.30am & 5-6.45pm Sun) Sassari's Duomo, also known as the Cattedrale di San Nicola, dazzles with its 18th-century baroque facade, a giddy free-for-all of statues, reliefs, friezes and busts. It's all a front, though, because inside the cathedral reverts to its

MONTE D'ACCODDI

Midway between Sassari and Porto Torres, **Monte d'Accoddi** (adult/reduced €3/2; ⊘ 9am-7pm Tue-Sat, 9am-2pm Sun summer, shorter hours rest of year) is a unique archaeological site, centred on a 3rd-millenium-BC temple. Unlike anything else in the Mediterranean (the closest comparable structures are the Mesopotamian ziggurats) the temple was part of a neolithic village which archaeologists estimate existed as early as 4500 BC. Over time, it went through several phases until it appears to have been abandoned around 1800 BC. Soon after, the first *nuraghe* (Bronze Age settlement) began to be raised.

Unfortunately, you don't actually see anything like the Mayan temple you might be imagining. Instead you can just make out a rectangular-based structure (30m by 38m), tapering to a platform and preceded by a long ramp. On either side of the ramp are a menhir and a stone altar believed to be for sacrifices.

true Gothic character. The facade masks a late-15th-century Catalan Gothic body, which was itself built over an earlier Romanesque church. Little remains of this except for the 13th-century bell tower.

Of note inside are the frescoes in the left transept and the Gothic fresco in the second chapel on the right. Also in this chapel is a fine painting of the *Martirio dei SS Cosma e Damiano* (Martyrdom of Saints Cosimo and Damien).

Chiesa di Santa Maria di Betlem   CHURCH
(Piazza di Santa Maria; ⊘ 7am-noon & 4-7pm) With its distinctive dome and proud Romanesque facade, the Chiesa di Santa Maria di Betlem reveals a curious blend of architectural styles. The exterior sports Gothic and even vaguely oriental elements. Inside, the Catalan Gothic vaulting has been preserved, but much baroque silliness has crept in to obscure the original lines of the building. In the lateral chapels stand some of the giant 'candles' that the city guilds parade about town during the 14 August I Candelieri festivities.

Fontana di Rosello   FOUNTAIN
(☑ 079 20 03 45; Piazza Mercato; guided tours €3; ⊘ 9am-7pm) Sassari's most famous fountain,

or what's left of it, sits in a sunken area in the midst of Piazza Mercato, a busy and unsightly traffic junction just outside the city walls. A monumental marble box ringed by eight lion-head spouts and topped by two fine marble arches, it was for a long time the focus of city life. Guided tours are available by calling the number listed.

Festivals & Events

Cavalcata Sarda   PARADE
(⊘ May) One of Sardinia's most high-profile festivals is held in Sassari on the second-last Sunday of May. Thousands of people converge on the city to participate in costumed processions, to sing and dance, and to watch fearless horse-riders exhibit their acrobatic skills.

I Candelieri   HISTORICAL
(⊘ Aug) A big summer festival, held every 14 August. Teams wearing medieval costume and representing various 16th-century guilds bear nine wooden columns (the 'candlesticks') through the town. The celebrations have their origins in 13th-century Pisan worship of the Madonna of the Assumption.

Eating

Eating in Sassari is a real pleasure. Eateries range from cheap student cafes to refined restaurants, and standards are universally high. A local curiosity is *fainè*, a cross between a crêpe and a pancake made from chickpea flour.

Fainè alla Genovese Sassu   SARDINIAN €
(Via Usai 17; fainè from €4; ⊘ 7-11pm Mon-Sat) This bare, white-tiled eatery is Sassari's original purveyor of *fainè*. There's nothing else on the menu, but with various types to choose from – sausage, onions, mushrooms, anchovies – the soft chickpea pancakes are ideal for a cheap, tasty fill-up.

Trattoria L'Assassino   TRATTORIA €
(☑ 079 23 34 63; Via Pettenadu 19; fixed-price menu €20, meals €25; ⊘ 12.30-3pm & 7.30-11pm Tue-Sun) This is a model trattoria in a tiny back lane – go through the arch near the tourist office. Expect plenty of grilled meats, seafood, stuffed snails and traditional pasta staples.

★ L'Antica Hostaria   RISTORANTE €€
(☑ 079 20 00 60; Via Cavour 55; meals €40; ⊘ 1-3pm & 8-11pm Mon-Sat) Hidden behind a discreet exterior, L'Antica Hostaria is one of

Sassari's top restaurants. In intimate surroundings you're treated to inventive dishes rooted in Sicilian and Sardinian culinary traditions. Desserts are also impressive, and there's an excellent list of island and Italian wines.

Le 2 Lanterne
TRATTORIA €€

(📞 329 426 17 06; Via Mercato 28a; fixed-price menus €20-23, meals €25-30; ⊙ daily) Join the locals for a taste of authentic home cooking at this laid-back trattoria near the city walls. The yellow and Pompeiian red decor sets a cheerful mood for honest dishes of *culurgiones* (Sardinian ravioli) with tomato sauce, well-cooked steaks and creamy ricotta desserts.

Trattoria Da Gesuino
TRATTORIA €€

(📞 079 27 33 92; Via Torres 17; pizzas €7, meals €35; ⊙ noon-3pm & 8-11pm Mon-Sat) It's a bit of a walk out from the centre, but Da Gesuino hits the right tone with its relaxed atmosphere, efficient service and excellent food. The menu covers all the usual bases with pasta, risottos, fresh fish and grilled meats. There's also pizza, which is served at both lunch and dinner.

La Vela Latina
TRATTORIA €€

(📞 079 23 37 37; Largo Sisini 3; meals €30; ⊙ 1-2.30pm & 8-10.30pm Mon-Sat) This local favourite is a top spot for traditional island fare. Carnivores with a yen for culinary adventure can go for hard-core meat dishes like *trippa* (tripe) and *cervella* (brain), whilst others can go for more accessible steaks and a tasty selection of seafood antipasti, pastas and risottos.

Il Castello
RISTORANTE €€

(📞 079 23 54 88; Piazza Cavallino de Honestis 6; meals €35; ⊙ closed Wed winter) Just around the corner from Teatro Verdi, this good-looking restaurant has tables laid out in a glass pavilion overlooking a small *centro storico* piazza. Specialty of the house are the grilled meats but you can also dine on great wood-fired pizzas.

🍷 Drinking & Nightlife

With its big student population and busy business community, Sassari has a vibrant cafe culture. You'll find a number of popular spots on Via Roma and further south on Via Torre Tonda, a lively student strip. Many places stay open late and some offer occasional live music.

Accademia
BAR

(Via Torre Tonda 11; ⊙ 7am-midnight Mon-Thu, to 2am Fri & Sat) With an attractive wrought-iron pavilion and buzzing vibe, this is a favourite hang-out in the university district. The cafe gets very busy at lunchtime and on Friday and Saturday nights when it stays open late. If you're lucky, you might also catch a gig here.

Cafè Chiara
CAFE

(Via Torre Tonda 1b; ⊙ 7am-12.45am Mon-Sat) A cosy cafe with low stone ceilings and a few outdoor tables beneath a stretch of 13th-century wall. It's open all day from breakfast through to late and serves a buffet lunch for €8 and happy-hour *aperitivo* for €5.

Caffè Italiano
CAFE

(Via Roma 38/40; ⊙ Mon-Sat) One of the best places on Via Roma is this big, bustling bar with pavement tables and a stylish interior. Business folk lunch here, and young locals come most afternoons to chat over an aperitif.

☆ Entertainment

Teatro Civico
THEATRE

(📞 079 200 80 72; Corso Vittorio Emanuele II 39) Sassari's historic theatre in the Palazzo di Città stages plays, classical-music concerts, film projections and cultural events.

Teatro Verdi
THEATRE, CINEMA

(📞 079 23 94 79; Via Politeama) Teatro Verdi doubles as a cinema when it's not hosting dance performances or opera.

Nuovo Teatro Comunale
THEATRE

(Piazzale Cappuccini) Inaugurated in February 2012, Sassari's largest theatre stages opera, concerts and plays. Check local listings for upcoming performances.

🔒 Shopping

Libreria Dessì Mondadori
BOOKS

(📞 079 201 20 98; Largo Cavallotti 17; ⊙ 9am-8pm Mon-Fri, 9am-1.30pm & 4-8pm Sat) Has a good

ALGHERO & THE NORTHWEST SASSARI

ℹ THEATRE TIP

Sassari's theatres don't tend to move into gear until September or October, after the sting has gone out of the summer heat. For show information, check the local newspaper *La Nuova Sardegna* or contact the theatres directly.

selection of books on Sardinia and a few English-language novels.

ⓘ Information

Banca di Credito Sardo (Piazza Italia 18) In Palazzo Giordano.

Farmacia Piazza Castello (☑ 079 202 90 46; Piazza Castello 2; ☺ 9am-1pm & 4.30-8pm, plus night shift 8pm-9am)

Ospedale Civile SS Annunziata (☑ 079 206 10 00; Via De Nicola 14) Hospital south of the city centre.

Police station (Questura; ☑ 079 249 50 00; Via Giovanni Palatucci 1) The main police headquarters.

Post office (Via Brigata di Sassari 13; ☺ 8.20am-7.05pm Mon-Fri, 8.20am-12.35pm Sat)

Tourist office (☑ 079 200 80 72; Via Sebastiano Satta 13; ☺ 9am-1.30pm & 3-6pm Tue-Fri, 9am-1.30pm Sat) Has information on Sassari and the surrounding area.

ⓘ Getting There & Away

AIR
Sassari shares Alghero's Fertilia airport (p124), about 28km west of the city centre.

BUS
Intercity buses depart from and arrive at Via Padre Zirano, near the Chiesa di Santa Maria di Betlem. There's a small **ticket office** (Via Padre Zirano; ☺ 6.30am-8pm Mon-Sat, 8am-2pm & 5-8pm Sun) by the stops.

Services run to/from Alghero (€2.50 to €3, one hour, 10 daily), Oristano (€8, two hours, three daily), Porto Torres (€2, 30 minutes, hourly) and Castelsardo (€3, one hour, 11 weekdays, four Sundays). Further afield, there are also buses to Nuoro (€8, 1¾ hours, six daily) and Cagliari (€14.50, 3¼ hours, three daily).

For Olbia's port, **Turmo Travel** (☑ 0789 2 14 87; www.gruppoturmotravel.com) has a daily bus (€12, 1½ hours).

CAR & MOTORCYCLE
Sassari is located on the SS131 linking Porto Torres to Cagliari. From Alghero, take the road north towards Porto Torres and then the SS291 east to Sassari. You take the same route from Fertilia airport.

Car hire is available at **Maggiore** (☑ 079 26 04 09; Strada 18, 38, Zona Industriale Predda Niedda) in the industrial zone northwest of the train station.

TRAIN
The main train station is just beyond the western end of the old town on Piazza Stazione. Direct trains run to Cagliari (€15.75, 3¾ hours, three daily), Oristano (€10.15, two to 2½ hours, two daily) and Olbia (€7.35, 1¾ hours, three daily). There are also daily services to these destinations via Ozieri-Chilivani.

Once a week, between mid-June and mid-September, the *trenino verde* (p266) departs from Sassari for the slow panoramic ride to Tempio Pausania (€21.50 return).

ⓘ Getting Around

TO/FROM THE AIRPORT
Up to nine daily buses run from the bus stops on Via Padre Zirano to Fertilia airport (€2.50, 30 minutes).

For the Aeroporto Olbia Costa Smeralda you'll need to catch the train/bus to Olbia and then the city bus to the airport.

BUS
ATP (☑ 079 263 80 00; www.atpsassari.it) orange buses run along most city routes, although you're unlikely to need one in the small city centre. In summer there are also buses to the beaches north of Sassari from the terminus on Via Eugenio Tavolara. Tickets cost €1.20.

CAR & MOTORCYCLE
Parking in Sassari is generally a nightmare. Within blue lines, hourly rates cost up to €0.50 for 30 minutes. Get tickets from traffic wardens, roadside meters or newsagents.

TAXI
You can catch a taxi from ranks on Emiciclo Giuseppe Garibaldi or along Viale Italia and Via Matteotti. To phone for one, call **Taxi Sassari** (☑ 079 25 39 39).

AROUND SASSARI

The most scenic route from Sassari to the coast is the SS200, lined with umbrella pines standing sentry as it passes through the twin market towns of **Sennori** and **Sorso**. These towns are famous for their wine and together produce the sweet Moscato di Sorso-Sennori. A good place to try some is **Da Vito** (☑ 079 36 02 45; http://ristorantedavito.it; Via Napoli 14, Sennori; meals €40; ☺ 12.30-2.30pm & 7-11pm Tue-Sun, 7-11pm Mon), a landmark hotel restaurant in Sennori that's renowned for its delicious seafood.

To the northwest of Sorso, the long sandy beaches at **Platamona Lido** and **Marina di Sorso** are favourites with the Sassaresi, who escape to the coast on hot summer weekends. These cheerful, often crowded, beaches are rather optimistically known as the Sassari Riviera.

To get to the beaches from Sassari take the Buddi Buddi bus (line MP) from Via Eugenio Tavolara. Tickets cost €1.20.

THE LOGUDORO & MONTE ACUTO

Extending south and east of Sassari, this fertile area has been inhabited since nuraghic times and is rich in archaeological interest. It was an important granary for the Roman Empire and still today the landscape is a patchwork of rugged slopes and golden wheat fields – the name Logudoro means 'place of gold'. As the medieval Giudicato del Logudoro, it enjoyed a medieval heyday, and it's to this period that many of the area's impressive churches date. In the heart of the region is the *comune* of Monte Acuto, a collection of village communities sharing a common mountain heritage.

Ozieri

POP 10,900

A prosperous agricultural town, Ozieri sits in a natural hollow, its 19th-century centre sloping upwards from a striking central piazza. The surrounding hills were once home to a number of thriving neolithic settlements and the town has lent its name to a period in prehistory – the Ozieri (or San Michele) culture, which spanned the millennium between 3500 and 2700 BC.

Nowadays, the town's name is also associated with the Premio Ozieri per la Letteratura Sarda, one of Sardinia's major literary awards. The prize, which showcases the work of Italian and Sardinian writers, was originally inspired by the *gare poetiche* (informal poetry wars) held at many at local festivals.

◉ Sights

Museo Archeologico MUSEUM
(☑ 079 785 10 52; Piazza Micca; admission €5, incl Grotta di San Michele €6; ⊙ 9am-1pm & 4-7pm Tue-Sun) Investigate Ozieri's rich archaeological legacy at the wonderful Museo Archeologico, one of Sardinia's best small museums. Housed in an 18th-century convent, it has a small but rich collection, including a couple

WORTH A TRIP

MONTE LERNO

About 8km east of Ozieri, **Lago Lerno** presents a bucolic picture. Although an artificial lake – it was created in 1984 by damming the Rio Mannu – it fits perfectly into the surrounding scenery with grassy slopes gently rising from the still waters and rocky **Monte Lerno** (1094m) looming in the near distance. Nearby, deer, mouflon and wild horses roam in the **Bosco di Monte Lerno** (Monte Lerno Wood). To get to the wood, pass Ozieri, enter Pattada, some 4km east, and continue towards Oschiri. After about 11km, turn right and continue over the Rio Mannu into the northwest reaches of the forest.

of copper ingots (nuraghic settlements were trading copper as far back as the neolithic age), some surprisingly modern-looking tools, and a selection of fine ceramic fragments found in the nearby Grotta di San Michele.

Grotta di San Michele CAVE
(☑ 079 78 76 38; Vicolo San Michele; admission €3, incl Museo Archeologico €6; ⊙ 10am-1pm & 2.30-5.30pm Tue-Sun) Signposted from the top of town, the *grotta* was used as a place to live by the nuraghic people, as well as a tomb and place of cult worship. Excavations in 1914 and then 1949 unearthed pottery, vases and figurines, many of which are now on display at the Museo Nazionale Sanna in Sassari.

Cattedrale dell'Immacolata CATHEDRAL
(Piazza Duomo) Much modified over the centuries, Ozieri's neoclassical Cattedrale dell'Immacolata harbours an important work of art, the *Deposizione di Cristo dalla Croce* (Deposition of Christ from the Cross) by the enigmatic 16th-century artist known as the Maestro di Ozieri.

✕ Eating

La Torre RISTORANTE, PIZZERIA €€
(☑ 079 78 66 95; Via Scarpata del Cantaro 1; meals €30; ⊙ 12.30-3pm & 7.30-11pm Tue-Sun) With its bright, light-filled dining room and central location (a short hop from Piazza Garibaldi) this is a good option for wood-fired pizzas and stylishly presented seafood.

ℹ Information

Local information is available from the summer-only **tourist information point** (✆ 079 78 67 81; www.girandozieri.it; Piazza Garibaldi; ⊙10am-1pm & 4-7pm Tue-Fri, 10am-1pm Sat Apr-Oct) in the main square, Piazza Garibaldi.

ℹ Getting There & Away

By public transport the easiest way to get to Ozieri is by bus from Sassari (€4.50, one hour, seven Monday to Saturday).

Valle dei Nuraghi

To the southwest of Ozieri, the Valle dei Nuraghi (Valley of the Nuraghi) is a verdant area rich in archaeological interest. The fields around the villages of Torralba, Mores, Borutta and Bonarva are littered with the ruins of prehistoric *nuraghi* and *domus de janas*.

◉ Sights

Nuraghe Santu Antine   ARCHAEOLOGICAL SITE
(✆ 079 84 74 81; www.nuraghesantuantine.it; Torralba; adult/reduced €6/4; ⊙9am-sunset) One of the largest nuraghic sites in Sardinia, the Nuraghe Santu Antine sits 4km south of Torralba. The complex is focused on a central tower, which now stands at 17.5m but which originally rose to a height of 25m. Around this, walls link three bastions to enclose a triangular compound. The oldest parts of the *nuraghe* date to around 1600 BC, but much of it was built over successive centuries.

You enter the compound from the southern side and can walk through the three towers, connected by rough parabolic archways. The entrance to the main tower is separate. Inside, four openings lead into the chamber from an internal hall. Stairs lead up from the hall to the next floor, where a similar but smaller pattern is reproduced. Apart from tiny vents there is no light, and the presence of the dark stone is overwhelming. You ascend another set of steps to reach the floor of what was the final, third chamber, now open to the elements.

Back in Torralba, the **Museo della Valle dei Nuraghi** (✆ 079 84 70 10; Via Carlo Felice 143) has a scale model of the *nuraghe* and

---

THE CHURCHES OF THE LOGUDORO

History and architecture buffs should take to the SS597 Olbia road to search out a series of remarkable Romanesque churches.

Approaching from Sassari, the first you come to is the **Basilica della Santissima Trinità di Saccargia** (SS597 Sassari-Olbia km 2; admission €2; ⊙9am-6pm Apr-Oct). A local landmark with its stripy limestone and basalt campanile, the basilica was supposedly built in 1116 on the site of a miraculous revelation. According to legend, the Giudice Constantino di Mariano and his wife camped the night here and received a vision telling them that they were going to have their first longed-for child. The *giudice*, delighted by the news, constructed the church and a neighbouring monastery, which the pope subsequently gave to the Camaldolite monks. Little remains of the monastery, although the dramatically simple church with its blind basalt walls is still in use.

Continuing on from the basilica, you'll pass the abandoned **Chiesa di San Michele di Salvènero**, as you push on to Ardara, 13km away. Ardara was once the capital of the Giudicato di Torres, and a quick turn to the left as you enter the town leads to the brooding mass of the **Chiesa di Santa Maria del Regno** (⊙10am-1pm & 3.30-8pm summer, 3.30-7pm winter). Consecrated in 1107, this grey basalt church features a columned interior and a famous 16th-century *retablo* depicting episodes from the lives of Jesus, Mary and various prophets.

Further east along the SS597, you'll see a turn-off for the **Chiesa di Sant'Antioco di Bisarcio** (guided tours per adult/reduced €3/2; ⊙10am-1pm & 2.30-5.30pm Tue-Sun), one of the largest Romanesque churches in Sardinia, 2km north of the highway. Its campanile was decapitated by a burst of lightning, and much of the facade's decoration has been lost, but the uniquely French-inspired porch and interior convey the impression of its one-time grandeur.

From here you can continue on the SS597 for the tiny **Chiesa di Nostra Signora di Castro** on the banks of **Lago di Coghinas**, or head north along the SS132 to the **Chiesa di San Pietro di Simbranos** at **Bulzi**.

SARDINIA'S CUTTING EDGE

Of all the fine knives made in Sardinia, the most prized is *sa pattadesa* (the Pattada knife), and these days they are only made by a handful of artisans. The classic Pattada knife, first made in the mid-19th century, is the *resolza*, with its so-called myrtle-leaf-shaped blade that folds into a horn handle.

Most of the best artisans only work to order and take at least two days to fashion such a knife, folding and tempering the steel for strength and sharpness. The handle is then carved from a single piece of mouflon (silky-haired wild sheep) horn. If you're looking at a handle that is two parts screwed together, you're not looking at a quality piece. A good knife will cost at least €10 a centimetre.

In the past such knives were made all over the island, but now only a few towns follow the traditional methods. **Pattada** is the most famous, although quality knives are also made in **Arbus**, **Santu Lussurgiu** and **Tempio Pausania**. The classic *s'arburesa* (from Arbus) knife has a fat, rounded blade and is used for skinning animals, while the *lametta* of Tempio Pausania has a rectangular blade good for stripping bark from cork oaks. Of the *pattadesa* knives the best known is the *fogarizzu;* the best *s'arburesa* to look for is the *pusceddu*.

Note that it is illegal in Italy to carry a blade longer than 4cm.

a modest collection of finds from the site. It was closed for renovation at the time of writing.

On weekdays there are up to nine buses from Sassari to Torralba (€3.50, 1½ hours), from where it's a 4km walk to the *nuraghe*.

Dolmen Sa Coveccada
(Mores) FREE To the south of Mores, the majestic Dolmen Sa Coveccada is said to be the largest dolmen (a megalithic chambered tomb) in the Mediterranean. Dating to the end of the 3rd millennium BC, the rectangular construction consists of three massive stone slabs, roofed by a fourth, weighing around 18 tonnes. As it stands, it reaches a height of 2.7m, is 5m long and 2.5m wide.

To reach the Dolmen from Mores, follow signs for Bono and Ittireddu and then, after approximately 6km, turn right at a crossroads. Continue until you see another right turn. Take this and continue on until you get to the end of the road, from where you can continue on foot for about 200m.

Chiesa di San Pietro di Sorres   CHURCH
(Borutta; admission €7 incl Nuraghe di Sant'Andrea Priu; ⊙9.30am-12.30pm & 3.30-6.30pm) This 12th-century Romanesque church commands impressive views from its hillside position overlooking Borutta. The original Pisan church and adjacent abbey had long been abandoned when a community of Benedictine monks moved here in 1955 and set about restoring them to their former glory. The white-and-grey banded facade has three levels of blind arches and is decorated with some lovely elaborate stonework. Of note inside is an intriguing stone Gothic pulpit set on four legs.

Necropoli di
Sant'Andrea Priu   ARCHAEOLOGICAL SITE
(☑348 564 26 11; admission €7 incl Chiesa di San Pietro di Sorres; ⊙10am-1pm & 3-5.30pm, later in summer) About 7km east of Bonorva, the Necropoli di Sant'Andrea Priu lies in lush, verdant countryside. An isolated site (accessible by a narrow potholed road) it is made up of around 20 small grottoes carved into trachyte rock and dating as far back as 4000 BC.

Of the grottoes, the Tomba del Capo, accessible only with a guide, is by far the most interesting. In the early Christian period three of the main rooms were transformed into a place of worship, and partly restored frescoes from the 5th century survive in two of them. Most striking is the fresco of a woman in the *aula* (hall) where the faithful heard Mass.

Rebeccu   VILLAGE
Between the Nuraghe di Sant'Andrea Priu and Bonarva, it's worth taking an hour or so to stop off at Rebeccu, a windswept and largely abandoned medieval hamlet carved into calcareous rock. The village, signposted off the main road, is the unlikely setting for a film festival in mid-August.

Olbia, the Costa Smeralda & the Gallura

Best Places to Eat

➡ Agriturismo Agrisole (p146)

➡ Li Mori (p152)

➡ Jaddhu (p157)

➡ I Frati Rossi (p154)

➡ Agriturismo Saltara (p159)

Best Places to Stay

➡ B&B Lu Pastruccialeddu (p211)

➡ Hotel Panorama (p209)

➡ B&B Petite Maison (p212)

➡ Agriturismo Ca' La Somara (p211)

Why Go?

Costa Smeralda evokes Sardinia's classic images: pearly-white beaches and weird, wind-whipped licks of rock tapering into emerald seas. The stretch of dazzling coast that the Aga Khan bought for a pittance in the 1960s is today the playground of millionaires and A-listers. Come summer, the scandal-hungry paparazzi haunt the marinas, zooming in on oligarchs cavorting with bikini-clad beauties on yachts so big they eclipse the sun.

A few kilometres' drive inland and you could be on another island entirely: here vine-striped hills roll to deeply traditional villages and mysterious *nuraghe* (Bronze Age fortified settlements), silent cork-oak woods and granite mountains. Immune to time and trends, the hinterland is a refreshing contrast to the coast. Hide away in a country *agriturismo* (farm stay) for a few days to appreciate a very different version of the good life.

Further north the Gallura coast becomes wilder, the preserve of the dolphins, divers and windsurfers who splash around in the startlingly blue waters of La Maddalena marine reserve.

Road Distance (km)

	Arzachena	Olbia	Porto Cervo	Santa Teresa di Gallura
Olbia	22			
Porto Cervo	18	25		
Santa Teresa di Gallura	27	49	45	
San Teodoro	49	27	52	76

OLBIA

POP 54,850

Often ignored in the mad dash to the Costa Smeralda, Olbia has more to offer than first meets the eye. Look beyond its industrial outskirts and you'll find a fetching city with a *centro storico* (historic centre) crammed with boutiques, wine bars and cafe-rimmed piazzas. Olbia is a refreshingly authentic and affordable alternative to the purpose-built resorts stretching to the north and south.

History

Archaeological evidence has revealed the existence of human settlement in Sardinia's northeast in the mid-neolithic period (about 4000 BC), but Olbia was almost certainly founded by the Carthaginians in the 4th or

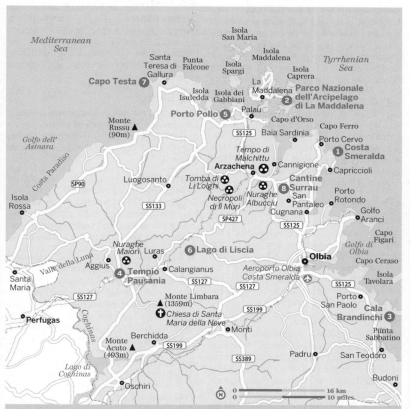

Olbia, the Costa Smeralda & the Gallura Highlights

❶ Hang out with the bronzed, beautiful and superfamous on the **Costa Smeralda** (p153).

❷ Island-hop around the **Parco Nazionale dell'Arcipelago di La Maddalena** (p163) and dive into its jewel-coloured waters.

❸ Lounge on the frosty white sands of **Cala Brandinchi** (p152), nicknamed 'Little Tahiti'.

❹ Explore the endless cork forests around **Tempio Pausania** (p166).

❺ Go with the wind and take to the wild waters off **Porto Pollo** (p162).

❻ Swap the glamour of the coast for the haunting silence of **Lago di Liscia** (p158).

❼ Clamber the weirdly sculptured boulders of **Capo Testa** (p161).

❽ Taste crisp Vermentino whites and rich Cannonau reds in contemporary winery **Cantine Surrau** (p155).

5th century BC. Certainly Carthaginians had been present in the area since the mid-6th century BC as proved by their participation in the Battle of Mare Sardo (a naval battle between Greek colonists from Corsica and a combined Etruscan and Carthaginian fleet in 538 BC, considered by some to be the first ever naval battle in Western waters).

Under the Romans, Olbia became an important military and commercial port – a dozen or so relics of Roman vessels were unearthed in the 1990s. Known as Civita, it went on to become the capital of the Giudicato di Gallura, one of the four independent kingdoms that encompassed Sardinia in the 12th and 13th centuries. But when the Catalano-Aragonese took control, decline set in. Not until the arrival of the highways and railway in the 19th century did the town show signs of life again. The surrounding area was slowly drained and turned over to agriculture and some light industry, and the port was cranked back into operation. Now as a working industrial centre and joint capital of the recently formed Olbia-Tempio province, Olbia is thriving.

◉ Sights

To the south of Corso Umberto, the tightly packed warren of streets that represents the original fishing village has a certain charm, particularly in the evening when the cafes and trattorias fill with groups of hungry locals. A stroll along the *corso*, culminating in a drink on Piazza Margherita, is an agreeable way to spend the evening.

★ Museo Archeologico   MUSEUM
(Isolotto di Peddone; ⊙10am-1pm & 5-8pm Wed-Sun) FREE Architect Vanni Macciocco designed Olbia's strikingly contemporary museum near the port. The museum spells out local history in artefacts, from Roman amulets and pottery to nuraghic finds. The highlight is the relic of a Roman vessel discovered in the old port. A multimedia display recreates the scene of the Vandals burning and sinking such ships in AD 450.

Chiesa di San Simplicio   CHURCH
(Via San Simplicio; ⊙7.30am-1pm & 3.30-8pm) Considered to be Gallura's most important medieval granite church, this Romanesque granite church was built in the late 11th and early 12th centuries on what was then the edge of town. It is a curious mix of Tuscan and Lombard styles with little overt decoration other than a couple of 13th-century frescoes depicting medieval bishops.

Chiesa di San Paolo   CHURCH
(Via Cagliari; ⊙hours vary) Another granite church worth a look is the 18th-century Chiesa di San Paolo, spectacularly topped by a Valencian-style multicoloured tiled dome (added after WWII).

✪ Festivals & Events

L'Estate Olbiese   CULTURAL FESTIVAL
During July and August, outdoor concerts are staged in the city centre as part of the L'Estate Olbiese, a cultural festival that includes concerts, performances, readings and cabarets.

✕ Eating

The bulk of the hotels, restaurants and bars are crowded into the web of narrow streets to either side of Corso Umberto. Cafe life centres on Piazza Margherita and Piazza Matteotti.

Pizzeria Dadino   PIZZERIA €
(☑340 3830176; Via Norvega 47; pizza €5-10; ⊙6.30pm-late) What a delight! This pizzeria has everything going for it – superb pizzas, a cheery family vibe and wallet-friendly prices. It's worth the short trek from the centre.

★ Agriturismo Agrisole   SARDINIAN €€
(☑349 0848163; www.agriturismo-agrisole.com; Via Sole Ruiu, Località Casagliana; menu incl drinks €30; ⊙mid-Jun–mid-Sep) Tucked serenely away in the countryside around 10km north of Olbia, this Gallurese *stazzo* (farmhouse) dishes up a feast of home cooking. Monica, your charming host, brings dish after marvellous dish to the table – antipasti, *fregola* (granular pasta), *porceddu* (roast suckling pig) and ricotta sweets. From Olbia, take the SS125 towards Arzachena/Palau, turning left at the signs at Km327.800.

Bacchus   ITALIAN €€
(☑0789 65 10 00; www.jazzhotel.it; Via degli Astronauti 2; menus €20-40; ⊙12.30-2.30pm & 7.30-10.30pm, closed Sun in winter) Bright, sunny Mediterranean flavours with a pinch of creativity dominate at Bacchus, housed in the Jazz Hotel close to the airport. Go for spot-on antipasti and beautifully cooked fish paired with Sardinian wines. There are gluten-free and vegetarian options.

Olbia

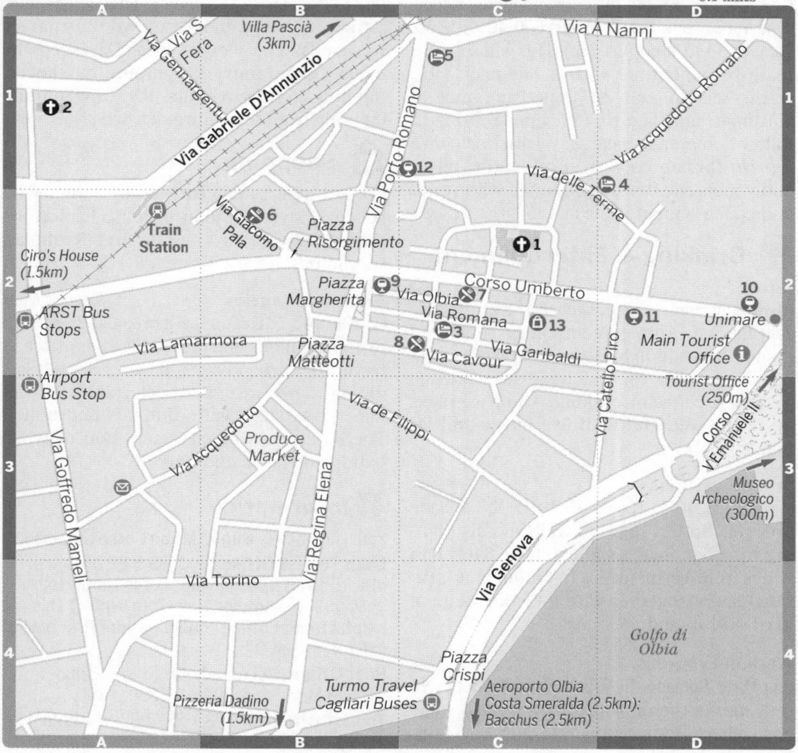

La Lanterna TRADITIONAL ITALIAN €€

(☎0789 2 30 82; www.ristorantelalanternaolbia.it; Via Olbia 13; pizzas €6-16, meals €25-35; ⏲noon-3pm & 6pm-midnight Thu-Tue) The Lanterna distinguishes itself with its cosy subterranean setting of exposed stone and beams. The food is winningly fresh, with Sardinian dishes like handmade *gnochetti* sardi and saffron-infused *fregola* with scorpion fish *ragù* on the menu. The pizza is pretty good, too.

Ristorante da Paolo SARDINIAN €€

(☎0789 2 16 75; enter from Via Garibaldi 18 or Via Cavour 22; meals around €30; ⏲noon-2.45pm & 7-10.45pm Mon-Sat) Stone walls, timber ceilings and coastal paintings give this restaurant a cheery air. Dig into soul food like *zuppa gallurese* (a hearty bread, cabbage and cheese soup), sea bass with *mirto* (myrtle liqueur) and *culurgiones* (Sardinian-style ravioli filled with cheese and potato).

Olbia

Sights

1 Chiesa di San Paolo C2
2 Chiesa di San Simplicio A1

Sleeping

3 Hotel Panorama C2
4 La Locanda del Conte Mameli D1
5 Porto Romano C1

Eating

6 Dolceacqua B2
7 La Lanterna C2
8 Ristorante da Paolo C2

Drinking & Nightlife

9 Enoteca Cosimino B2
10 In Vino Veritas D2
11 KKult D2
12 Work in Progress C1

Shopping

13 Anticas Licanzias C2

Dolceacqua
ITALIAN €€

(📞 0789 196 90 84; http://ristorantedolceacqua. com; Via Giacomo Pala 4; menus €30-40; ⏱ 12.30-2pm & 7.30-10.30pm Tue-Sun) This smart, intimate bistro entices with a laid-back vibe, warm service and an appetising mix of Sardinian and Ligurian cuisine. You might follow homemade pasta, say, with *orata alla liguria* (bream cooked in oil, garlic, olives and wine). The two-course lunch with water and coffee is great value at €15.

 Drinking & Entertainment

KKult
BAR

(www.kkult.com; Corso Umberto 39; ⏱ 8am-3am Tue-Sun) This contemporary split level lounge bar-cafe hybrid has a terrace on Olbia's main drag for watching the world go by over a coffee or cocktail. The pace picks up at the weekend with live music and DJ nights.

In Vino Veritas
WINE BAR

(📞 349 5624071; Corso Umberto 4; ⏱ 8am-midnight) Bottles line the walls at this inviting wine bar. Snag a table to taste Sardinian wines from Vermentinos to Cannonaus, artisanal beers, together with a tasting plate of local *salumi* and *formaggi*.

Work in Progress
BAR

(Via Porto Romano 7; ⏱ 5pm-3am Tue-Sun) No sign marks the door of this relaxed lounge bar, where locals gravitate for cocktails, jazzy music and occasional live music in a slick brick-vaulted interior. There's a courtyard out back for summertime imbibing.

Enoteca Cosimino
WINE BAR

(Piazza Margherita 3; ⏱ 11am-midnight) This popular cafe serves coffee and *cornetti* (croissants) by day, but in the evening it morphs into an elegant wine bar with cocktails and *vino* on the menu.

MUST-TRY GALLURESE DISHES

Zuppa gallurese Layers of bread and cheese drenched in broth and baked to a crispy crust.

Ortidas Fried sea anemones.

Capretto al mirto Roast kid infused with myrtle.

Fregola con cozze e vongole Sardinian granular pasta with mussels and clams.

Mazzafrissa Creamy fried semolina.

Villa Pascià
CLUB

(Via Corea 145; ⏱ 11pm-6am) This glam club attracts a young, upbeat crowd on summer weekends. The pick of local DJs keep the dance floor rammed, pumping out house, hip-hop and Latin beats. It's a five-minute taxi ride from the centre of town.

 Shopping

Corso Umberto is a catwalk to designer labels and stylish Italian fashion. Explore its side streets for arts, crafts and Sardinian specialities.

Anticas Licanzias
FOOD & DRINK

(Via Olbia 42; ⏱ 8.30am-1.30pm & 4.30-8pm) Stop by this fabulous deli and patisserie for bread fresh from a wood oven, *pane carasau* (Sardinian flatbread), and delectable Sardinian sweets laced with almonds and honey. There's also a first-class selection of wine, handmade pasta and olive oil.

ℹ️ Information

You'll find banks with ATMs on Corso Umberto.

Main Tourist Office (📞 0789 5 22 06; www. olbiaturismo.it; Municipio, Corso Umberto; ⏱ 9am-9pm summer, 9am-7pm winter) This helpful tourist office should be your first port of call for info on Olbia.

Post Office (Via Aquedotto 5; ⏱ 8.20am-7.05pm Mon-Fri, 8.20am-12.35pm Sat)

Tourist Office (📞 0789 55 77 32; www.olbi-atempioturismo.it; Via Alessandro Nanni 39; ⏱ 8.30am-2pm Mon, Wed & Fri, 8.30am-2pm & 3-6pm Tue & Thu) This tourist office has stacks of info and brochures on the Olbia-Tempio province.

Unimare (📞 070 2 35 24; www.unimare.it; Via Principe Umberto 1; ⏱ 8.30am-12.30pm & 3.30-7.30pm Mon-Fri, 8.30am-12.30pm Sat) A central travel agent where you can book ferries and flights.

ℹ️ Getting There & Away

AIR

Olbia's **Aeroporto Olbia Costa Smeralda** (📞 0789 56 34 44; www.geasar.it) is about 5km southeast of the centre and handles flights from mainland Italian airports and major European cities. Low-cost operators include Air Berlin, easyJet, Jet2.com and Niki. Destinations served include most mainland Italian airports as well as London, Paris, Madrid, Barcelona, Hamburg, Amsterdam, Vienna and Prague.

BOAT

Olbia's ferry terminal, **Stazione Marittima**, is on Isola Bianca, an island connected to the

TENUTE OLBIOS

The vineyards that ribbon the hillsides on the outskirts of Olbia produce some of the finest Vermentino white wines, as well as a handful of noble reds from the cabernet, Cannonau, merlot and Bovale grapes.

Spread across 60 hectares, the lovingly tended **Tenute Olbios** (☎0789 64 10 03; www.tenuteolbios.com; Via Loiri 83, Località Venafiorita; ☺8.30am-1pm & 3-6pm Mon-Fri) estate whisks visitors through the wine-making process in its 1½-hour guided tours (€10), which head down to the cellar and conclude with a three-wine tasting below the oak ceiling of the granite-walled tasting room. A slightly longer tour (€15) includes a walk through the vines. For an additional €5 per person, you can sample regional cheeses, *salumi* and antipasti. The tours are available in Italian and English and advance booking is recommended, though you are free to pop by to buy wine any time.

Besides a stroll among the vines, this is a beautiful area for an afternoon spent in the Gallura countryside, dappled with oak and pear trees, dotted with lakes and ablaze with wildflowers and broom in spring.

Tenute Olbios is 7km south of the city centre. To get there, take the SP24 and follow the signs.

town centre by the 1km causeway, Banchina Isola Bianca. All the major ferry companies have counters here, including **Moby Lines** (☎199 303040; www.mobylines.it), **SNAV** (☎081 428 55 55; www.snav.it) and **Tirrenia** (☎892123; www.tirrenia.it). There are frequent services – especially during the summer months – to Civitavecchia, Genoa, Livorno and Piombino.

You can book tickets at any travel agent in town, or directly at the port.

BUS

Azienda Regionale Sarda Trasporti (ARST; ☎800 865042, 0789 5 53 00; www.arst.sardegna.it) buses run from Olbia to destinations across the island. Get tickets from **Bar della Caccia** (Via Fiume D' Italia 1; ☺6am-9pm Mon-Sat), just over the road from the main bus stops on Corso Vittorio Veneto; the timetable is posted in the window. Destinations include Arzachena (€2.50, 45 minutes, 12 daily) and Porto Cervo (€3.50, 1½ hours, five daily). Further afield you can get to Nuoro (€9, 2½ hours, eight daily), Santa Teresa di Gallura (€5, 1½ hours, seven daily) and Sassari (€7, 1½ hours, two daily) via Tempio Pausania (€3.50, 1¼ hours, seven daily). There are fewer connections on Sunday.

Turmo Travel (☎0789 2 14 87; www.gruppoturmotravel.com) runs two buses each weekday from Cagliari (€19, 4½ hours), arriving in Piazza Crispi; one continues to Santa Teresa di Gallura. Another daily bus runs from the port to Sassari (€12, 1½ hours). Get tickets at Stazione Marittima or on the bus.

CAR & MOTORCYCLE

Car hire is available at the airport, where all the big international outfits are represented, and at the Stazione Marittima ferry terminal. Bank on about €50 per day for a Fiat Punto.

TRAIN

The station is off Corso Umberto. There are trains to Cagliari (€16.90, four hours, five daily), Sassari (€7.35, two hours, six daily), Golfo Aranci (€2.35, 25 minutes, four daily) and Oristano (€11.50, 2½ hours).

ℹ Getting Around

You are unlikely to need local buses, except for getting to the airport and Stazione Marittima. You can save by buying tickets at tobacconists, some bars or the tourist office; they cost €1/2.50/10 for a single/day/week ticket.

TO/FROM THE AIRPORT

Local bus lines 2 and 10 (€1, or €1.50 if ticket is bought on board) run half hourly between 6.15am and 11.40pm from the airport to Via Goffredo Mameli in the centre. A taxi will set you back around €15.

Several buses for destinations around the island depart from the airport, including a service for Nuoro run by **Deplano** (☎0784 29 50 30; http://deplanobus.com), which operates five times a day from June to September. Tickets cost €12 and journey time is 1¾ hours.

BUS

Local buses are run by **ASPO** (☎0789 55 38 56; www.aspo.it). Bus 9 runs every half hour between Stazione Marittima and the town centre (Via San Simplicio).

CAR & MOTORCYCLE

Driving in Olbia is no fun thanks to a confusing one-way system and almost permanent roadworks. The main strip, Corso Umberto, is closed to traffic between Piazza Margherita and Via Goffredio Mameli. Metered parking (€1 per hour from 8am to 8pm) is available around Olbia, and there is limited free parking by the port – follow the signs.

TAXI
You can sometimes find taxis on Corso Umberto near Piazza Margherita. Otherwise call ☎ 0789 6 91 50.

AROUND OLBIA

Olbia's main beach is the busy **Lido del Sole** (catch bus 5), which is about 6km east of the airport off the main southbound road, the SS125. It's fine for a swim, but far preferable is the swath of white sand at **Pittulongu** or **Sos Aranzos** to the north of town.

Golfo Aranci

POP 2400

Perched on the northern tip of the Golfo di Olbia, Golfo Aranci is a port, straggling resort and fishing village rolled into one. Most people blaze through without a second glance as it's fairly nondescript on the face of things. It's worth considering as a cheaper alternative to the Costa Smeralda, however, if activities like diving, spear-gun fishing and dolphin-spotting rock your boat.

⊙ Sights & Activities

There are three sandy white beaches in town – **Spiaggia Primo**, **Secondo** and the best of the three, **Terzo** (they're translated to First Beach, Second and Third), and with your own transport you can easily get to others. It's also well equipped for families, with a number of public parks and well maintained playgrounds.

Capo Figaro   NATURE RESERVE
Rising up behind the port are the craggy heights of Capo Figaro (340m), which is now a minor nature reserve. Trails criss-cross the *macchia* (Mediterranean scrub), and they lead up to an abandoned lighthouse on the summit, known as *il vecchio semaforo* (old traffic light). It was from here that Guglielmo Marconi sent the first radio signal to the Italian mainland in 1928.

Alpha Diving   DIVING
(☎ 346 3509725; www.alphadiving.it; Piazzetta dei Pescatori 4) Operating out of the port, this European Scuba Agency–accredited diving outfit will set you up for dives around Cape Figaro and Tavolara. A single dive will set you back around €40, a new-diver course €250. The centre also arranges activities such as eco-friendly dolphin-watching excursions (€25) and guided snorkelling (€30).

✖ Eating

Seafood features heavily in the restaurants lined up on and around Via della Liberta. Nearly everywhere closes from November to March.

La Spigola   SEAFOOD €€
(☎ 0789 4 62 86; http://laspigolaristorante.com; Via Colombo 19; meals around €30; ⊙ 10am-10pm Mon-Fri, 9am-11pm Sat & Sun) Skip the rest and go straight for the grilled fish and seafood, from a cracking spaghetti with clams to local lobster, at this friendly beachside restaurant. Bag a table on the terrace for breezy sea views.

OLBIA, THE COSTA SMERALDA & THE GALLURA GOLFO ARANCI

IS SARDINIAN CORK SCREWED?

Do your bit for the Sardinian environment and buy wine with a natural cork. Cork has long been a mainstay of the local economy, but the spread of synthetic bottle stoppers is threatening the industry.

According to a 2006 World Wildlife Fund report, the increased use of plastic corks could lead to the loss of up to three-quarters of the western Mediterranean's cork forests within 10 years.

The impact in Sardinia would be devastating. The island accounts for 80% of Italy's cork production and the industry is a major employer in the northern towns of Calangianus and Tempio Pausania. Each year about 120 quintals of cork bark are harvested, most of it then sold to wine bottlers.

As well as the economic aspect, there are also environmental concerns. Cork harvesting doesn't actually harm the trees – harvesters simply shave the bark off the trunk – but a lack of care might. And if the cork companies don't protect the island's cork forests (and they're unlikely to do so without a vested interest), who will?

ⓘ Getting There & Away

Between June and September six daily ARST buses link Golfo Aranci with Olbia (€2.35, 25 minutes). Trains (€2.35, 25 minutes) also cover the same route, running six times daily year-round.

Sardinia Ferries (☑ 0825 09 50 95; www.sardiniaferries.com) operates frequent daily ferries between Livorno (€53 to €76, six to 10 hours) and Civitavecchia (€54 to €79, 3½ to 6¾ hours) to Golfo Aranci.

SOUTH COAST

The coast reaching south of Olbia is peppered with resorts that heave in summer and slumber in winter. Typical of the type is Porto San Paolo, the main embarkation point for Isola Tavolara, and 11km further south, party-loving San Teodoro.

Porto San Paolo & Isola Tavolara

POP 3200

Porto San Paolo's major attraction lies offshore. Unless you've booked a holiday apartment here, the one real reason to stop off is to catch a boat for Isola Tavolara.

◉ Sights & Activities

★ **Isola Tavolara**   ISLAND
Rising from the sapphire sea like some kind of giant sea creature, this rocky island is a sight to behold. The main draw here is splashing about in the translucent water of the white-sand **Spiaggia Spalmatore**, and admiring the incredible views of Tavolara's heights and mainland Sardinia. You could wander down to the little cemetery to see the graves of Tavolara's kings (the title was bestowed by Carlo Alberto in 1848 after a successful goat-hunting trip).

The island – just 5km long and 1km wide – used to be known as the Island of Hermes, perhaps because you need wings to reach the plateau (565m), which is inhabited only by sea birds and falcons, as well as a few nimble-footed wild goats. The few people who live here reside on the western side on the **Spalmatore di Terra**, where the boats land and there are a couple of beachside snack bars.

Boat Excursions   BOAT TOUR
At Easter time and from July to September, boats depart from Porto Sao Paolo. Outward bound boats leave half-hourly between 9am and 3pm, and return trips set off on the hour between 12.30pm and 6.30pm. The return trip (25 minutes each way) costs €12.50 per person, but longer cruises taking in the smaller Isola Molara and Isola Piana will set you back €25 a head.

Tavolara Diving   DIVING
(☑ 0789 4 03 60; www.tavolaradiving.it; Via Molara 4) Tavolara's craggy coves and crystal-clear waters present some wonderful diving opportunities around the underwater mountain of **Secca del Papa**. If you're interested, reckon on €40 for a single dive and €400 for an Open Water Diver course.

✖ Eating

Il Portolano   ITALIAN €€
(☑ 0789 4 06 70; www.ristoranteilportolano.it; Via Molara 11, Sao Porto Paolo; meals around €40; ☺ noon-2.30pm & 7-10.30pm mid-Apr–mid-Oct) For dreamy sunset views of Isola Tavolara, book a table at chic waterfront Il Portolano, run by Sardinian-Swiss couple Roberto and Claudia. Mediterranean food with the lightest of creative touches is paired with island wines. Seafood is the big deal, be it octopus salad with fresh artichokes and Cabras *bottarga* (mullet roe) or homemade lemon pasta with seabass, almonds and courgette pesto.

San Teodoro

POP 3560

Fun-loving San Teodoro lives to party in summer, its glam beach bars and clubs providing an affordable alternative to the megabucks Costa Smeralda. The model resort is perfect, almost to the point of characterlessness, but its pristine white-sand beaches are glorious. Water sports and boat excursions race you out to sea, while back on dry land trekking, mountain biking and horse riding entice you away from the beach towel.

◉ Sights & Activities

Stagno San Teodoro   NATURE RESERVE
Nestled amid fragrant *macchia* and wind-eroded granite formations, and backing onto La Cinta beach, this lagoon attracts ramblers and birdwatchers. Keep an eye out for bird life including pink flamingos, herons, cormorants, little egrets and kingfishers.

DON'T MISS

SAN TEODORO BEACHES

San Teodoro has some truly glorious beaches, many of which can easily compete with the Costa Smeralda in the beauty stakes. Central **Cala d'Ambra** is pretty, but more striking still is **Spiaggia La Cinta**, 2km to the north, a ribbon of frosty-white sand strung between the topaz sea and the Stagno San Teodoro. It's a popular sports beach, particularly for kitesurfing. Or take your beach towel 9km further north to the stunning crescent-shaped bays of **Lu Impostu** or 1km further on to 'Little Tahiti' **Cala Brandinchi**, separated by a wooded spit of land. Commanding fine views of the limestone hump of Isola Tavolara, **Capo Coda Cavallo**, 13km north of San Teodoro, is a marine reserve and its transparent waters bubble with snorkellers and divers.

Wet Dreams WATER SPORTS
(☎347 9409356, 0784 85 20 15; www.wetdreams.it; Via Sardegna; ⏰9am-1pm & 5-9pm summer) A surf shop on the beach, Wet Dreams offers three-hour introductory kitesurfing sessions for €210. Private instruction starts at €80/100 per hour without/with your own equipment.

Dive Aquarius DIVING
(☎0784 83 41 24; www.diveaquarius.net; Località Capo Coda Cavallo, Villaggio Le Farfalle; s dives from €45) If you fancy taking the plunge in the gin-clear waters of the Tavolara marine park, Dive Aquarius at Capo Coda Cavallo is a safe bet. It offers single dives, night dives, wreck dives, plus the whole shebang of PADI courses.

Maneggio La Cinta HORSE RIDING
(☎338 8228984, 0784 85 10 07; www.maneggiolacintasanteodoro.it; Località La Cinta; 👪) You can saddle up here for a scenic 1½-hour hack (€30) along La Cinta beach.

✕ Eating

Bear in mind that nearly everywhere closes from mid-October to March.

★**Li Mori** SARDINIAN €€
(☎0784 85 10 00; www.agriturismolimori.it; Località Li Mori; meal incl drinks €33; ⏰8-11pm) A genuine slice of rustic island life, Li Mori dishes up a generous spread of Sardinian dishes in a convivial farm setting. Loosen a belt notch for specialities like *malloreddus al sugo di cingiahle* (semolina pasta with wild boar sauce), ravioli, suckling pig roasted to crackling perfection and local *dolci* (sweets) – all washed down with free-flowing wine.

Bal Harbour ITALIAN €€
(☎0784 85 10 52; www.balharbour.it; Via Stintino; meals €30-40; ⏰11am-3am) This supertrendy beachside lounge-restaurant attracts gym-fit guys and girls, who come to pose by the palm-fringed pool by day and sip mojitos to DJ beats by night. The food is surprisingly good, whether you go for a sizzling steak from the Brazilian grill or lighter Italian dishes such as seafood risotto.

La Taverna degli Artisti ITALIAN €€
(☎0784 86 60 60; Via del Tirreno 17; pizzas €5-9, meals around €30; ⏰noon-3pm & 7-11pm) Great seafood and service are on the menu here. Follow garlicky mussels with handmade tagliatelle with scampi and pesto or salt-crusted sea bass. There's also pizza to take away.

Drinking & Nightlife

San Teodoro is the south coast's party central, its lounge bars and clubs attracting the young, bronzed and beautiful in summer from June to September.

Buddha del Mar BAR
(www.buddhadelmar.eu; Piazza Gallura 2; ⏰5am-2am) Summer evenings at this Asian-inspired lounge can resemble an MTV beach party, with the fun fuelled by dancing, cocktails and good vibes.

L'Ambra Night CLUB
(www.ambranight.it; Via Cala d'Ambra; ⏰midnight-6am) Down by the beach, opposite Hotel L'Esagono, this club with an outdoor dance floor rocks to a mainly commercial beat. It occasionally welcomes guest DJ royalty like Sven Väth to the decks.

Luna Glam Club CLUB
(www.lalunadisco.it; Località Stirritoggiu; ⏰midnight-5.30am) Dress to impress the eagle-eyed bouncers and fit in with the glossy 30-plus crowd at this ubertrendy club. It's just south of town, off the exit road from the SS125.

ℹ Information

Tourist Office (☎0784 86 57 67; www.santeodoroturismo.it; Piazza Mediterraneo 1;

⊘ 9am-midnight daily summer, 9am-1pm &
4-7pm Mon-Sat winter) The efficient tourist
office can provide information on local operators and tour guides. Another useful website is
www.visitsanteodoro.com.

ℹ️ Getting There & Away

ARST buses make the run up the coast to Olbia
(€2.50, 40 minutes, six daily, up to nine on
weekdays) and inland to Nuoro (€8, one hour 50
minutes, five daily). Deplano buses also run to/
from Olbia airport (€4, 30 minutes, five daily)
and Nuoro (€10, 1¼ hours, five daily).

COSTA SMERALDA & AROUND

Back in 1962, flamboyant millionaire Karim
Aga Khan and some pals set up a consortium
to buy a strip of beautiful, unspoilt coastline
in northeastern Sardinia from struggling
farmers. Each paid roughly US$25,000 for
their little piece of paradise, and the coast was
christened Costa Smeralda (Emerald Coast)
for the brilliant green-blue hue of its waters.

What a difference 50 years makes. Today US$25,000 would get you (at a push) a
night in the Presidential Suite at Hotel Cala
di Volpe, billionaire jet-setters cruise into
Costa Smeralda's marinas in mega-yachts
like floating mansions, and models, royals,
Russian oligarchs and balding media mo-
guls come to frolic in its waters. Bill Gates
and the Sultan of Brunei, Wayne Rooney and
George Clooney have all been spotted here.

Starting at Porto Rotondo on the Golfo di
Cugnana, about 17km north of Olbia, the Costa stretches for 55km northwards up to the
Golfo di Arzachena. The 'capital' is the yachtie
haven of Porto Cervo, although Porto Rotondo
attracts its fair share of paparazzi attention as
base of Silvio Berlusconi's island operations.

Room rates and temperatures soar in
summer, when beachgoers, yachties and
families flock to the Costa Smeralda.

South of Porto Cervo

Despite the superficial fluff, the Costa Smeralda is quite stunning: the Gallura's granite
mountains plunge into emerald waters in a
succession of dramatic fjordlike inlets.

The Costa starts at the Golfo di Cugnana,
beginning with spectacular views of **Porto
Rotondo**, a second marina developed in
1963 following the success of Porto Cervo.
Resembling an upmarket harbourside sub-
urb of Sydney or San Francisco, Porto Rotondo is where Berlusconi once frolicked
in his Sardinian residence, the pharaonic
Villa Certosa. The resort's attractive seafront promenade is dotted with cafes, pizzerias and chichi lounge bars for sundown
celeb-spotting.

Travelling north, look out for a turn-off
to dreamy **Spiaggia Liscia Ruia**, shortly
before reaching the grand Moorish fantasy
that is the Hotel Cala di Volpe. Next along
is **Capriccioli**, another splendid beach with
crystalline waters and soft sand.

Beyond that you reach the curving
Spiaggia Romazzino, named after the rosemary bushes that grow in such abundance.
Nearby is one of the best beaches on the
Costa, the hard-to-find **Spiaggia del Principe** (also called Portu Li Coggi). Apparently
the Aga Khan's favourite, a magnificent crescent of white sand is bound by unspoilt green
macchia and Caribbean-blue waters. To find
it, follow the signs for Hotel Romazzino, but
before reaching the hotel, turn right at Via degli Asfodeli. Park your car at the barrier and
then walk for the last half a kilometre or so.

Porto Cervo

POP 2100

Porto Cervo is a curious, artificial vision of
Mediterranean beauty. The utopian village
combines Greek, North African, Spanish
and Italian architectural elements, and
the overall effect is pseudo-Moorish with

DON'T MISS

FARM FRESH

Keep an eye out for the *'formaggi e salumi'* sign on the SP59 Arzachena–Porto Cervo
road to find **Azienda Agricola Mossa Alessandro** (☑ 380 3661325; Località La Punga;
⊘ 8am-12.30pm & 4-7pm), a working farm where you can buy creamy goats-milk ricotta,
mature *fiore sardo pecorino* and salami. Alessandro might let you take a peek at the
huge wheels of cheese and racks of salami and pancetta out the back. It's a great place
to pick up picnic supplies.

a touch of the Flintstones. Its perfectly manicured streets are strangely sterile and characterless. Apart from the magnificent coastal scenery that surrounds it, there's nothing remotely Sardinian about Porto Cervo. Instead, it resembles exactly what it is: a purpose-built leisure centre for the super-rich; a kind of Disneyland for Gucci-clad grown-ups.

◎ Sights & Activities

As nearly everyone in Porto Cervo has a boat (it has the best marine facilities on the island), most of the action takes place elsewhere during the day, in the paradisal inlets and on the silky beaches. Things begin to heat up in the early evening when the playboys and -girls come out to browse the boutiques and pose in the piazzas.

Chiesa di Stella Maris   CHURCH
(Piazza Stella Maris; ⊙8.30am-8pm) Perched above Porto Cervo is Michele Busiri Vici's surreal white church with a funnel-shaped bell tower. The church hosts classical music concerts in the summer. Unsurprisingly, it's also done rather well in the donations department, receiving El Greco's impressive *Mater Dolorosa* as a Dutch aristocrat's bequest.

Louise Alexander Gallery   GALLERY
(www.louise-alexander.com; Via del Porto Vecchio 1; ⊙10am-1pm & 5pm-midnight May-Sep) Visit this gallery for temporary exhibitions showcasing works by contemporary artists, such as the recent one zooming in on American portrait sculpturist Barry X Ball. It also sells modern art, so if you're in the market for a Warhol or Lichtenstein, drop them a line.

Piazzetta   PIAZZA
The place to be seen is the Piazzetta, a small square at the centre of a web of discreet shopping alleys. From the piazza, stairs lead to the Sottopiazza and La Passeggiata, both lined with fancy boutiques – Cartier, Gucci, Versace, Prada, Valentino, Moschino – you name it, they're all here.

✖ Eating

Porto Cervo's best restaurants are a quick drive or taxi hop out of town.

La Vecchia Costa   SARDINIAN €
(☑ 0789 9 86 88; Località La Punga; meals €15-25; ⊙noon-2.45pm & 7pm-midnight) This big open-plan restaurant keeps it fresh, seasonal and affordable. Authentic fare such as *lorighit-*

tas (twisted, ring-shaped pasta) in *porcini* lamb sauce and *malloreddus* (Sardinian gnocchi) with crab and mullet roe make this place popular with the locals, so book ahead. It's a five-minute drive from town, on the SP59 between Arzachena and Porto Cervo.

La Briciola   ITALIAN €€
(☑ 0789 9 14 09; Liscia di Vacca; pizza €6-13, meals €30-40; ⊙12.30-2.15pm & 7.30-11pm; ♪) You know you've struck gold when you find a restaurant frequented by locals in a purpose-built resort. With its garden terrace, pleasant service and spot-on pizzas, La Briciola gets it just right. Besides pizza, it does a fine line in pasta (for instance, with *bottarga* and sea urchin), risotti and grilled fish.

Spinnaker   MODERN ITALIAN €€
(☑ 0789 9 12 26; www.ristorantespinnaker.com; Liscia di Vacca; meals around €40; ⊙12.30-2.30pm & 7.30-11.30pm daily Jun-Sep, Thu-Tue Mar-May & Oct) This fashionable restaurant buzzes with a good-looking crowd, who come for the stylish ambience and fabulous seafood. Pair dishes like calamari with fresh artichokes or rock lobster with a local Vermentino white. The restaurant is on the road between Porto Cervo and Baia Sardinia.

Hivaoa   MEDITERRANEAN €€
(☑ 0789 9 14 51; www.ristorantehivaoa.com; Via Della Marina Nuova; pizza €5-12, lunch menu €15, meals €30; ⊙noon-midnight; ♠) Fine dining it is not, but if what you are seeking is a cheerful, affordable, family-friendly place with decent food, Hivaoa hits the mark every time. Go for wood-oven pizza, filling steaks, seafood and pasta dishes.

★ I Frati Rossi   MODERN ITALIAN €€€
(☑0789 9 43 95; www.fratirossi.it; Località Pantogia; meals €40-60; ⊙12.30-2pm & 7.30-10pm Tue-Sun Jan-Oct) This rustic-chic restaurant has broad sea views from its hilltop perch, 3.5km south of Porto Cervo. Local ingredients shine in beautifully cooked and presented dishes such as black tagliatelle with squid and ripe cherry tomatoes. The fish and shellfish platters are astoundingly fresh. Follow the signs up a narrow country lane off the SP59.

♟ Drinking & Nightlife

Porto Cervo's nightlife is a strictly summer-only scene. People-watching is one of the few affordable options, although the moment you sit down at a bar on the Piazzetta you'll be looking at around €10 for a drink. To get in on the real clubbing action,

CANTINE SURRAU

Cantine Surrau (☑0789 8 29 33; www.vignesurrau.it; Località Chilvagghja; ☺10am-9pm Mon-Fri, 10.30am-10pm Sat, 10.30am-9pm Sun) takes a holistic approach to winemaking. Take a spin of the cellar and gallery showcasing Sardinian art before tasting some of the region's crispest Vermentino white and beefiest Cannonau red wines. The standard tasting (€20) gets you three different wines served with *pane carasau* (Sardinian flatbread), cheese, *salumi* and olives, while the €35 tasting consists of five wines, local cheese, salami, *bottarga* (mullet roe) and Sardinian sweets. Find the winery on the road between Arzachena and Porto Cervo.

however, dress to impress and head a couple of kilometres south of town.

Aqua Lounge　　　　　　　　　　LOUNGE
(☑0789 902294; www.aqualounge.it; Piazza Azzurra; ☺10.30am-2am summer) Overlooking the marina, this swanky lounge bar is the place to perhaps celeb watch and play spot the yacht over a cocktail or light bite to eat. Mellow DJ beats and sofa-filled nooks keep the mood relaxed.

Sottovento　　　　　　　　　　CLUB
(www.sottoventoclub.it; Località Sottovento; ☺midnight-5am) Bono, Craig David and Denzel Washington have all been spotted at this exclusive club. Getting in is no party and depends entirely on the whim of the stony-faced bouncers.

Billionaire　　　　　　　　　　CLUB
(www.billionaireclub.it; Via Rocce sul Pevero; ☺11pm-5am) Opened by former Formula One boss Flavio Briatore in 1998, Billionaire's dance floor is like a who's who of the absurdly rich and famous. It stars DJs like Craig David. It's almost impossible to get in unless you happen to know someone or book dinner at the swank restaurant.

Lord Nelson　　　　　　　　　　PUB
(Porto Cervo Marina; ☺5pm-3am) Strangely, for such a swish resort, one of the favourite drinking hang-outs is this nautically themed English-style pub.

❶ Getting There & Away

ARST has up to five bus connections between Porto Cervo and Olbia (€3.50, 1½ hours, five daily).

Between June and September, **Sun Lines** (☑348 2609881; http://sunlineseliteservice. com) buses run at 7.30am, 12.30pm, 3.30pm and 6.30pm from Olbia airport to the Costa Smeralda, stopping at Porto Cervo and various other points along the coast. Tickets cost between €3 and €4.

Poltu Quatu

From Porto Cervo the coast road swings north and west around Capo Ferro headland to Poltu Quatu, a fjordlike inlet flanked by rugged granite cliffs. A jumble of white-washed, terracotta-roofed villas centred on a picture-perfect marina, the resort is easier on the eye than many nearby resorts. Shopping in the boutiques and galleries, dining alfresco and soaking up the views are the main activities.

Orso Diving　　　　　　　　　　DIVING
(☑0789 9 90 01; www.orsodiving.com; ☺summer only) Head to this harbourside outfit to dive in the marine parks of La Maddalena and Tavolara (single dives from €45), snorkel in the fish-filled waters around Isola Caprera (€45), or join a full-day whale-watching excursion (€100). The centre also offers the whole shebang of PADI courses.

Baia Sardinia

POP 200

Follow the meandering road 4km north of Poltu Quatu and you reach Baia Sardinia, just outside the Costa Smeralda but for all intents and purposes a Costa resort like its more famous neighbours.

☀ Activities

Cala Battistoni　　　　　　　　BEACH
Baia Sardinia's major draw is the beach, Cala Battistoni, a fine sweep of pale sand massaged by translucent waters.

Aquadream　　　　　　　WATER PARK
(www.aquadream.it; Località La Crucitta; adult/child €18/12; ☺10.30am-7pm late Jun–early Sep) A surefire winner with the kids, Aquadream has hair-raising slides, flumes and pools to keep children entertained all day.

✕ Eating & Drinking

Most places close from November to Easter.

News Café　　　　　　　　　CAFE €
(Piazza Centrale; ◷8am-2am) In the seafront arcade, this central cafe is a popular meeting point and good for a quick bruschetta at lunchtime and live music and drinks by night.

Casablanca　　　　　　　　ITALIAN €€
(☑339 2940837; www.ristorante-casablanca.it; Piazzetta Principale; meals €30-40; ◷noon-midnight) With a name like Casablanca, you wouldn't expect this restaurant to be any less than romantic. And with candlelit tables and dreamy views out to sea and La Maddalena, it doesn't disappoint. The chef places the accent on freshness and flavour – from salads through to pasta, fish and steaks. Get here for sunset.

Phi Beach　　　　　　　　BAR, CLUB
(www.phibeach.com; Forte Cappellini; ◷1pm-midnight) One of the coast's hottest venues, this is a great place to hang out and watch the sunset. By day it's a regular bathing club with sunloungers and umbrellas to hire, but as the sun goes down it transforms into a cool lounge bar and restaurant. All the while DJs spin chilled sounds in the background.

Ritual　　　　　　　　　　CLUB
(www.ritual.it; Località La Crucitta; ◷11.30pm-5.30am Tue-Sat, to 4.30am Sun & Mon) Just out of town on the road for Porto Cervo, this club is an old favourite. Even if you're not going to dance it's worth a look for the sexy cavernous interior gouged out of the rockside.

❶ Getting There & Away

From Olbia, the Sun Lines bus service to Porto Cervo continues on for 15 minutes to Baia Sardinia.

Cannigione

Some 12km southwest of Baia Sardinia, Cannigione sits on the western side of the Golfo di Arzachena, the largest *ria* (inlet) along this coast. Originally a fishing village established in 1800 to supply the Maddalena islands with food, it grew bigger when coal and cattle ships began to dock at its harbour in the 1900s and is now a prosperous and reasonably priced – if somewhat soulless – resort.

You'll find the best beaches north of Cannigione, including **Tanca Manna**, a good bet for families, with its soft sand and shallow water.

🏃 Activities

Consorzio del Golfo　　　　DIVING
(☑335 7742392; www.consorziodelgolfo.it) Down at the port, there are various operators offering excursions to the Arcipelago di La Maddalena, including Consorzio del Golfo. Bank on €25 to €40 per person.

Areamare　　　　　　　　DIVING
(☑338 8221135; www.areamare.com; Via Vespucci 52) Dive instructor Marco will take you to some of the most beautiful spots around the Arcipelago di La Maddalena. A two-tank dive will set you back €80, six dives around €240 and an Open Water Diver course €420. Discounts are available for advance online bookings.

✕ Eating

La Zattera　　　　　　　ITALIAN €€
(☑333 6839880; www.ristorantelazattera.it; Via Nazionale 86; menus €30; ◷7-11.30pm) As bright and breezy as the sea itself, this restaurant keeps the look cool, with pastel blue and white hues, lanterns and driftwood mirrors. The service is polished and the menu puts little imaginative touches on pasta and fish – all winningly fresh and served with flair.

❶ Information

Tourist Office (☑0789 8 85 10; www.cannigione.org; Via Nazionale 47; ◷9.30am-12.30pm & 5-7pm summer) The helpful Ascor tourist office has bags of information on Cannigione and the surrounding area.

❶ Getting There & Away

Regular ARST buses make the run to Arzachena (€1.20, 10 minutes, four daily Monday to Saturday), Baia Sardinia (€1.50, 30 minutes, three daily Monday to Saturday), Palau (€1.50, 20 minutes, two daily Monday to Saturday) and Olbia (€2.50, one hour, four daily Monday to Saturday).

INLAND FROM THE COSTA SMERALDA

San Pantaleo

Although only about 16km from Porto Cervo, the rural village of San Pantaleo provides a welcome dose of authenticity after the sterile resorts on the coast.

The village sits high up behind the coast, surrounded by gap-toothed granite peaks, and has become something of an artists' haven, speckled with little galleries and craft shops. It is also one of the few Sardinian villages set around a piazza, with a sturdy little church at one end. In summer you'll often find a bustling Thursday market here, and in spring the blossoms make it more photogenic than ever. Year round, it is an attractive place for an aimless amble.

Between 27 July and 30 July San Pantaleo holds its annual knees-up, a weekend of general jollity with traditional Sardinian dancing.

✖ Eating & Drinking

Locanda Sant'Andrea   SARDINIAN €€€
(☑ 0789 6 52 05; www.locandasantandrea.com; Via Zara 43; meals €40-50; ☉ 8am-11pm summer, closed Mon in winter) Near the entrance to the village is this highly regarded restaurant, the menu of which features meat classics such as *porceddu* (suckling pig) and rabbit loin in myrtle sauce. Bookings are recommended.

Caffè Nina   CAFE
(Piazza della Chiesa; ☉ 7am-2am) Take a pew at cosy, stone-walled Caffè Nina and enjoy a glass of Vermentino with some *pecorino* and olives.

❶ Getting There & Away

ARST runs five daily buses to San Pantaleo from Olbia (€2, 35 minutes) and Arzachena (€1.50, 20 minutes).

Arzachena

POP 13,200

Were it not for its position a few kilometres inland from the Costa Smeralda, Arzachena would be overlooked as just another workaday town with a mildly interesting historical centre. Which is pretty much what it is. But with the Mediterranean's most exclusive resorts an easy drive away, it has gone from being a humble shepherds' village in the 1960s to something of a tourist centre.

◉ Sights

Most people use Arzachena as a base for exploring the Costa, but if you want to hang around, action is focused on **Piazza del Risorgimento**, a small piazza with a couple of cafes, and a stone church, the **Chiesa di Santa Maria delle Neve**. A short stroll away is the bizarre **Roccia Il Fungo**,

Mont'Incappiddatu, a mushroom-shaped granite rock at the end of Via Limbara. Archaeologists believe the overarching rock may have been used as a shelter for neolithic tribespeople as long ago as 3500 BC.

✖ Eating

La Terrazza   ITALIAN, PIZZERIA €
(☑ 0789 8 25 75; www.laterrazzaristorantepizzeria.it; Viale Costa Smeralda; pizza €5-10, meals around €30; ☉ noon-2.30pm & 7-11pm Tue-Sun) Wood-fired pizza and cracking seafood are the hallmarks of this popular eatery. Locals come here to grab a bite to eat and chat with the *pizzaiola* (pizza-maker) while out-of-towners sit down to huge helpings of fresh fish and grilled meat.

★ Jaddhu   SARDINIAN €€
(☑ 0789 8 06 36; www.jaddhu.com; Località Capichera; meals €35-45; ☉ 12.30-3pm & 7.30-11pm Apr-Sep) Hidden in granite mountains brushed with olive, myrtle and mastic trees, this *stazzu* (Gallurese stone-built country house) has one of the finest restaurants in the region. Sit on the garden terrace for a fully blown Sardinian feast, from *zuppa cuata* (bread and cheese soup) to swordfish with almonds and candied lime and spot-on *porceddu* (spit-roasted suckling pig) with rosemary potatoes.

The restaurant is part of the Jaddhu Country Resort, situated 5.5km off the SS427 south of Arzachena.

❶ Getting There & Away

Arzachena has good bus connections. ARST services run to/from Olbia (€2.50, 45 minutes, 12 daily), Santa Teresa di Gallura (€3, one hour, five daily) and Palau (€1.50, 25 minutes, five daily). Regular buses also link with the Costa Smeralda resorts, namely Porto Cervo and Baia Sardinia.

Between mid-June and mid-September you can pick up the *trenino verde* (p51) to Tempio Pausania (€11.50, 1½ hours, one daily Tuesday to Friday).

Around Arzachena

Arzachena serves as a springboard to some inland treasures: a series of mysterious *nuraghi* ruins and two *tombe dei giganti* (literally 'giants' tombs'; ancient mass graves).

Nuraghic Sites

What makes Arzachena interesting is the mysterious countryside around it, littered

LAGO DI LISCIA & AROUND

From Arzachena, the SP427 heads inland into the undeveloped and utterly transfixing heart of Gallura. The road bobs and weaves through lush green fields and wood-crested hills as it twists its way up to the agricultural town of **Sant'Antonio di Gallura** en route to **Lago di Liscia**, one of Sardinia's unspoilt secrets. An 8km-long artificial lake, the main source of water for Gallura's east coast, it is set beautifully amid granite-scarred hills and woods of billowing cork and oak trees. The best place to admire it is a picnic spot at a tiny nature reserve, signposted as *olivastri millenari,* above the southern shores. The **olivastri** are a group of wild olive trees that have been growing for thousands of years. Scientists from the University of Sassari have calculated that the biggest, measuring 20m in circumference and reaching a height of 14.5m, is about 3800 years old. Certainly, it's quite a specimen, its gnarled and twisted trunk writhing upwards like something out of *Lord of the Rings*. To get to the site from Sant'Antonio di Gallura follow the road for Luras and Tempio Pausania, then take the turning marked *olivastri millenari*. After a further 10km or so, there's a short, steep dirt track up to the left – the *olivastri* are at the top.

with *nuraghi* and *tombe dei giganti*. The following sites are open from 9am to 7pm daily from Easter to October and in winter on request. Entry costs €3 for a single site, €5 for two and €7.50 to €10 for three. Guided tours in English, German, Spanish and French are available by arrangement.

⊙ Sights

Nuraghe di Albucciu   ARCHAEOLOGICAL SITE
(admission €3; ⊙9am-7pm) This is the nearest *nuraghe* to town, and certainly the easiest to find, on the main Olbia road, about 3km south of Arzachena. It's one of Gallura's finest prehistoric relics and unusual for several reasons, not least for its flat granite roof instead of the usual *tholos* (conical shape) and its warren of what appear to be emergency escape routes.

Tempio di Malchittu   ARCHAEOLOGICAL SITE
(admission €3; ⊙9am-7pm) Accessible via a 2km track from the Nuraghe di Albucciu ticket office, this temple dating back to 1500 BC is one of the few of its kind in Sardinia. The experts can only guess at its original purpose, but it appears it had a timber roof and was closed with a wooden door. From this vantage point you have views over the surrounding countryside, strewn with granite boulders.

Coddu Ecchju   ARCHAEOLOGICAL SITE
(admission €3; ⊙9am-7pm) Taking the Arzachena–Luogosanto road south, you can follow signs to one of the most important *tombe dei giganti* in Sardinia. The most visible part of it is the oval-shaped central stele (standing stone). Both slabs of granite,

one balanced on top of the other, show an engraved frame that apparently symbolises a door to the hereafter, closed to the living. On either side of the stele stand further tall slabs of granite that form a kind of semicircular guard of honour around the tomb.

Li Muri   ARCHAEOLOGICAL SITE
(admission €3; ⊙9am-7pm) This necropolis is a curious site made up of four interlocking megalithic burial grounds, possibly dating to 3500 BC. Archaeologists believe that VIPs were buried in the rectangular stone tombs. At the rim of each circle was a menhir or betyl, an erect stone upon which a divinity may have been represented. To reach Li Muri, turn left (west) for Luogosanto on the Arzachena–Luogosanto road. After about 3km turn right and follow the signs to Li Muri along a dirt track.

Li Longhi   ARCHAEOLOGICAL SITE
(admission €3; ⊙9am-7pm) This *tomba di gigante* is quite striking. The central east-facing stele, part of which was snapped off and later restored, dominates the surrounding countryside from its hilltop location. To reach it, take the SS427 towards Calangianus, turning right after around 3km, then follow the signs.

NORTH COAST

North of Palau, the wind-whipped coast rises and falls like a rocky sculpture, culminating in the lunarlike headland of Capo Testa. Fine beaches stretch out towards Vignola in the west and sunny Santa Teresa di Gallura in the east, the fashionable heart of the summer scene on the north coast. The windy waters are a magnet for wind- and kitesurfers; competitions are often held here, some of which dash across the windy straits to Bonifacio in Corsica.

Santa Teresa di Gallura

POP 5300

Bright and breezy Santa Teresa di Gallura occupies a prime seafront position on Gallura's north coast. The resort gets extremely busy during high season yet somehow manages to retain a distinct local character, making it an agreeable alternative to the more soulless resorts on the Costa Smeralda.

The town was established by Savoy rulers in 1808 to help combat smugglers, but the modern town grew up as a result of the tourism boom since the early 1960s. Santa Teresa's history is caught up with Corsica as much as it is with Sardinia. Over the centuries plenty of Corsicans have settled here, and the local dialect is similar to that of southern Corsica.

◉ Sights & Activities

When they're not on the beach, most people hang out in the centre, lounging on the cafe-lined piazza and admiring the pastel-coloured houses. Otherwise, you can wander up to the 16th-century **Torre di Longonsardo** (admission €2; ⊙10am-12.30pm & 4-7pm Jun-Sep), which overlooks a natural deep port on one side and the entrance to the town's idyllic (but crowded) **Spiaggia Rena Bianca** on the other. If you tire of the beach head down to the **Porto Turistico**, a small enclave of whitewashed villas set round a cloistered courtyard and crowded marina.

At the bottom of Via del Porto you'll find operators running excursions to the Maddalena archipelago. If you want a boat to yourself, you'll have to dig deep into your wallet; prices start at around €1800 per week. There's also excellent diving around Santa Teresa and the islands in the Bocche di Bonifacio.

Blu Dive Center DIVING
(☑338 6808576, 328 7173499; www.bludivecenter.com; Via Nazionale 71; ⊙8am-9pm summer) This professional and super-friendly dive centre offers two-tank dives, wreck dives and snorkelling excursions, as well as the whole shebang

of PADI courses – from discover scuba diving to dive master. You'll be taken to the gorgeously clear waters around La Maddalena marine park, Capo Testa and off the coast of Corsica.

Consorzio delle Bocche BOAT TOUR
(☑0789 75 51 12; www.consorziobocche.com; Piazza Vittorio Emanuele; ⊙9am-1pm & 5pm-12.30am May-Sep) This outfit runs various excursions, including trips to the Maddalena islands and down the Costa Smeralda (summer only). These cost around €42/22 per adult/child and include lunch (excluding drinks).

Centro Sub Marina di Longone DIVING
(☑338 6270054; www.marinadilongone.it; Viale Tibula 11; ⊙9am-7pm summer) For an adventure in the deep blue, check out the offer at this PADI accredited dive centre. Single dives start are €39 and a discovery course 'sea baptism' costs €70.

✗ Eating

Santa Teresa's restaurants open daily in summer and then close completely in winter.

★Agriturismo Saltara SARDINIAN €€
(☑0789 75 55 97; www.agriturismosaltara.it; Località Saltara; meals €34-43; ⊙7.30-10.30pm summer; 🖭) Natalia and Gian Mario welcome you warmly at this *agriturismo*, 10km south of town off the SP90 (follow the signs up a dirt track). Tables are scenically positioned under the trees for a home-cooked feast. Wood-fired bread and garden vegetable antipasti are a delicious lead to dishes like *pulilgioni* (ricotta-filled ravioli with orange zest) and roast suckling pig or wild boar.

Vegetarian menus available on request.

Il Chiostro SEAFOOD €€
(☑334 2128795; www.ilchiostrodelporto.it; Porto Turistico; meals €25-45; ⊙8am-midnight summer) Sunset is prime-time viewing at this welcoming restaurant overlooking the marina, which prides itself on the freshness of its local produce. Try to snag a table on the terrace to eat fish caught that morning – the tuna is superb – or melt-in-the-mouth *porceddu*.

Il Grottino MEDITERRANEAN €€
(☑0789 75 42 32; Via del Mare 14; pizzas €4-12, meals €30; ⊙noon-3pm & 7-11.30pm summer) Il Grottino sets a rustic picture with bare, grey stone walls and warm, low lighting. In keeping with the look, the food is wholesome and hearty with no-nonsense pastas, fresh seafood and juicy grilled meats.

Marlin PIZZERIA, ITALIAN €€
(☎0789 75 45 57; www.ristorante-pizzeriamar-lin.com; Via Garibaldi 4; pizza €4-12, meals €30; ☺noon-3pm & 7pm-midnight summer) Simple, friendly and reasonably priced, Marlin whips up a decent pizza – try the house special with tomato, mozzarella, salmon, prawns and *bottarga* – and does basics like *spaghetti vongole* (with clams) and grilled fish well.

🍷 Drinking & Nightlife

Hang out with the locals at the cafe-bars on Piazza Vittorio Emanuele. Between May and October regular concerts are staged at the Porto Turistico among the boutiques and expensive cafes.

Caffè Mediterraneo CAFE
(Via Amsicora 7; ☺8am-midnight Mon-Thu, 7am-3.30am Fri-Sun) With its arched windows, polished wood bar and jazzy beats, this stylish cafe attracts a young, good-looking crowd.

Join them for a lunchtime *panino* (sandwich; €3.50) or a cool evening cocktail.

Bar Central 80 BAR
(Piazza Vittorio Emanuele; ☺6am-3am) Right on the main square, this central hub swells with happy holidaymakers until the early hours. Grab an outside table and enjoy ringside views of the piazza with your drink.

Estasi's CLUB
(Località Buoncammino; ☺11pm-6am) Towards Palau, 3km south of town, is Santa Teresa's nightlife hub, centred on this outdoor club, where DJs and the occasional band crank up the party vibe in summer.

🛍 Shopping

You'll find plenty of boutiques and jewellery shops in town. The pedestrianised Via Umberto and Via Carlo Alberto, leading south from Piazza Vittorio Emanuele, host a nightly market in summer.

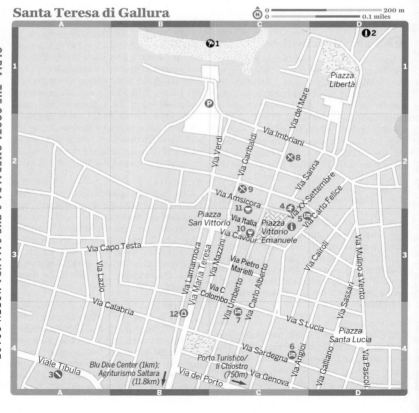

Santa Teresa di Gallura

Mascheras
ARTISANAL

(Via Maria Teresa 54; ⊘9.30am-1pm & 4.30-7.30pm) Watch Signor Maura at work, skilfully carving traditional Sardinian carnival masks, at this tiny shop. His intricate masks include the wooden *boes* and *merdules* (character masks; from €130) typical of Ottana. There's also a range of cheaper wooden knick-knacks.

ℹ Information

Tourist Office (☑0789 75 41 27; www.comunesantateresagallura.it; Piazza Vittorio Emanuele 24; ⊘9am-1pm & 5-8pm Mon-Sat) Very helpful, with loads of information.

ℹ Getting There & Around

BOAT

Santa Teresa is the main jumping-off point for Corsica. Two companies run car ferries on this 50-minute crossing to Bonifacio, although between November and March services are drastically reduced.

Saremar (☑199 118877; www.saremar.it) has three daily departures each way (two at weekends between October and mid-March). A one-way adult fare in high season is €10 and a small car costs up to €37. Taxes add another €8 to the price.

Between the end of March and late September, **Moby Lines** (☑199 303040; www.mobylines.it) operates four daily crossings. Adult tickets cost around €19, a car around €31.

BUS

Departing from the bus terminus on Via Eleonora d'Arborea, ARST buses run to/from Arzachena (€3, one hour, five daily), Olbia (€5, 1½ hours, seven daily), Castelsardo (€5, 1¼ hours, two daily) and Sassari (€7, 2½ hours, three daily).

Turmo Travel (☑0789 2 14 87; www.grup-poturmotravel.com) operates a daily service to/from Cagliari (€23, 5½ hours), as well as a summer service to Olbia airport (€8, 1½ hours, six daily June to September) via Arzachena and Palau.

Other summer services are provided by **Caramelli** (☑079 67 06 13; www.caramellitours.it), which runs a daily bus to/from Porto Cervo (€5, 1¼ hours) via Palau (€2, 30 minutes) and Baia Sardinia (€4.50, one hour).

CAR & MOTORCYCLE

Santa Teresa di Gallura is at the northernmost end of the SS133b and on the SP90, which runs southwest to Castelsardo.

There are numerous rental agencies in Santa Teresa di Gallura, including **Just Sardinia** (☑0789 75 43 43; www.justsardinia.it; Via Maria Teresa 26), which has bikes (from €10 per day), scooters (€25) and cars (€65).

Around Santa Teresa di Gallura

If you've got transport it's worth exploring the long sandy beaches around Santa Teresa. East of town is the Conca Verde, a wild stretch of coastline covered with bushy umbrella pines. Along here you can try **La Marmorata** (8km) or **La Licciola** (11km).

Head 10km in the other direction (west) and you'll arrive at the long, sandy **Rena Maiore**, backed by appealing, soft dunes. ARST buses to Castelsardo can drop you at the turn-off. Further on are the beaches of **Montirussu**, **Lu Littaroni** and **Naracu Nieddu**, none of them very busy even in high summer. Finally, you'll come to the little seaside resort of **Vignola Mare**, the heart of kitesurfing territory.

Capo Testa

Four kilometres from Santa Teresa, this extraordinary granite headland seems more like a sculptural garden. Giant boulders lie strewn about the grassy slopes, their weird and wonderful forms the result of centuries of wind erosion. The Romans quarried granite here, as did the Pisans centuries later.

The place also has a couple of beaches. **Rena di Levante** and **Rena di Ponente** lie either side of the narrow isthmus that leads out to the headland itself.

Right on Rena di Ponente you can rent surfing gear, beach umbrellas and sunloungers.

Porto Pollo & Isola Dei Gabbiani

Seven kilometres west of Palau, windsurfers and kitesurfers converge on Porto Pollo (also known as Portu Puddu) and Isola Dei Gabbiani, where stiff breezes and crystalline waters create the best conditions on the island.

Along the beachfront you'll find various outfits hiring out kit and offering lessons. **Sporting Club Sardinia** (☑0789 70 40 01; www.portopollo.it) takes you windsurfing, kitesurfing and sailing, and has a chilled bar for post-water-sport drinks and gigs. Expect to pay €90 for two 90-minute windsurfing lessons, €260 for a block of five kitesurfing lessons, and €6/18/25/30 for an hour's kayak/windsurf/boat/kite rental. Four 30-minute kids' windsurfing lessons cost €100.

Another reputable choice is **Pro Center MB** (☑0789 70 42 06; www.procenter.it; Baia dei Delfini), where two-hour windsurfing/kitesurfing tas ter sessions cost €69/160 and two-day cou rses including equipment hire and lessons cost €190/280. It also has a wide range of wi ndsurfing courses for kids, as well as kite, windsurf, SUP and kayak hire.

Buses on the Palau–Santa Teresa di Gallura route stop off at the signposted road junction, f rom where you have to walk about 2km.

Palau

POP 4500

Palau is a lively summer resort, its streets lined with surf shops, boutiques, bars and restaurants. It's also the main gateway to Arcipelago di La Maddalena's granite islands and jewel-coloured waters. Out of town, the coast is famous for its bizarre weather-beaten rocks, like the Roccia dell'Orso, 6km east of Palau.

◉ Sights & Activities

Fortezza di Monte Altura   FORT
(adult/reduced €3/2; ⊘guided tours hourly 10.15am-12.15pm & 3.15-7.15pm summer, closed winter) Standing sentinel on a rocky crag, this sturdy 19th-century bastion was built to help defend the north coast and Arcipelago di La Maddalena from invasion – something it was never called on to do. A guided 45-minute tour leads you to watchtowers and battlements with panoramic views out to sea. The fortress is signposted off the SS125, 3km west of town.

Roccia dell'Orso   LOOKOUT
(adult/reduced €2/1; ⊘9am-7.30pm daily, to 9pm in summer; ⛴) This weather-beaten granite sculpture sits on a high point 6km east of Palau. The Roccia dell'Orso (Bear Rock) looks considerably less bearlike up close, resembling more – dare we say it? – a dragon. Analogies aside, the granite formations are extraordinary, as are the far-reaching views of the coast from up here.

Petag   BOAT TOUR
(☑0789 70 86 81; www.petag.it) Down at the port, this is one of several outfits offering boat excursions around the Maddalena islands. Trips cost around €35 per person and include lunch and time to swim on well-known beaches.

Nautilus   DIVING
(☑340 6339006, 0789 70 90 58; www.divesardegna.com; Piazza Fresi 8) There's some excellent diving in the marine park. This PADI-accredited centre runs dives to 40 sites, with single dives starting at around €50. Kids' Bubblemaker courses are available.

✖ Eating

As elsewhere along the coast, nearly all restaurants close their doors from November to Easter.

Del Porticciolo   SARDINIAN €
(☑0789 70 70 51; Piazza del Comune 7; pizzas €3-7, meals around €20; ⊘noon-2pm & 7.15-10.30pm Sat-Thu summer) Locals swear by the authentic antipasti, pasta and fresh fish at this no-frills harbourside restaurant. Stop by for a good-value lunch, or in the evening when chefs fire up the pizza ovens.

C'era una Volta   ITALIAN €€
(☑0789 70 66 04; www.ristoranteceraunavoltapalau.it; Piazza del Molo 22; ⊘noon-2.30pm & 7-11pm summer) On the road down to the harbour, C'era una Volta is unassuming on the face of things, but don't be fooled. There's always a good buzz and warm welcome, and the food is some of Palau's best – follow fresh pasta with the catch of the day simply grilled, and homemade desserts.

La Gritta

ITALIAN €€€

(☑ 0789 70 80 45; www.ristorantelagritta.it; Località Porto Faro; meals €70-80; ☺ 12.30-2.30pm & 7.30-10.30pm summer) One for special occasions, La Gritta is a memorable place to dine. Floor-to-ceiling windows and a terrace allow you to take in the wondrous coastal scenery while the superbly presented seafood combines modern techniques with Italian ingredients. Cheese buffs will enjoy a selection of up to 20 different cheeses, while everyone will appreciate the classic Sardinian desserts.

ℹ Information

Tourist Office (☑ 0789 70 70 25; www.palauturismo.com; Palazzo Fresi; ☺ 9am-1pm & 4-8pm summer, 9am-1pm Mon-Fri, plus 3-5pm Tue & Thu winter) The multilingual staff at the tourist office can provide information about the surrounding area, including the Arcipelago di La Maddalena.

ℹ Getting There & Away

BOAT

Car ferries to Isola Maddalena are operated by **Saremar** (☑ 199 118877; www.saremar.it) and **Delcomar** (☑ 0781 85 71 23; www.delcomar.it). Saremar runs crossings every half hour between 7.30am and 7.30pm. Delcomar runs six night crossings between 12.30am and 5.30am and then has crossings roughly hourly from 8.15am to 11.15pm. The 15-minute crossing costs between €5 and €6 per passenger and €8 and €14 for a small car.

BUS

There are ARST buses connecting Palau with Olbia (€3, 1¼ hours, eight daily), Santa Teresa di Gallura (€2, one hour, five daily) and Arzachena (€1.50, 25 minutes, five daily).

In summer, **Nicos-Caramelli** (☑ 079 67 06 13; www.caramellitours.it) buses run frequently to nearby destinations like Isola dei Gabbiani (€2, 40 minutes), Porto Pollo (€1.50, 35 minutes), Capo d'Orso (€1.20, 20 minutes), Baia Sardinia (€3, 35 minutes) and Porto Cervo (€3, 50 minutes).

In the same summer period, **Turmo Travel** (☑ 0789 2 14 87; www.gruppoturmotravel.com) buses connect Palau with Olbia airport (€6, 50 minutes, six daily).

TRAIN

The *trenino verde* runs from Palau port to Tempio Pausania (€18.50, 1¾ hours, two daily Thursday and Friday) from mid-June to mid-September. It's a slow ride along a narrow-gauge line through some great countryside.

PARCO NAZIONALE DELL'ARCIPELAGO DI LA MADDALENA

One of Sardinia's most ravishing beauty spots, the Arcipelago di La Maddalena provides some spectacular, windswept seascapes. Nelson and Napoleon knew the archipelago well, as did that old warhorse Giuseppe Garibaldi, who bought Isola Caprera for his retirement.

A national park since 1996, **Parco Nazionale dell'Arcipelago di La Maddalena** (www.lamaddalenapark.it) consists of seven main islands and 40 granite islets, as well as several small islands to the south. The seven principal islands are the high points of a valley, now underwater, that once joined Sardinia and Corsica. When the two split into separate islands, waters filled the strait now called the Bocche di Bonifacio. Over the centuries the prevailing *maestrale* (northwesterly wind) has helped to mould the granite into the bizarre natural sculptures that festoon the archipelago.

The area is an important natural habitat, and although national-park status has imposed protection, the ecosystem remains fragile. For this reason, developments were still under way to create a joint Italian-French marine park, the **Parco Marino Internazionale delle Bocche di Bonifacio** (www.pmibb.com) at the time of writing. Parco Nazionale dell'Arcipelago di La Maddalena has been on the tentative list of Unesco World Heritage Sites since 2006.

Isola Maddalena

POP 11,900

Just over the water from Palau, the pink-granite island of Maddalena lies at the heart of the archipelago. From the moment you dock, you'll be taken by the urbane character of the place, its cobbled piazzas and infectious holiday atmosphere.

Until the end of the 17th century the island's small population lived mainly in the interior, farming a meagre living out of the poor soil. But when the Baron des Geneys arrived with the Sardo-Piedmontese navy in 1767 to establish a naval base they gladly gave up their hilltops and relocated to the growing village around Cala Gavetta, now La Maddalena's main port.

Parco Nazionale dell'Arcipelago di La Maddalena

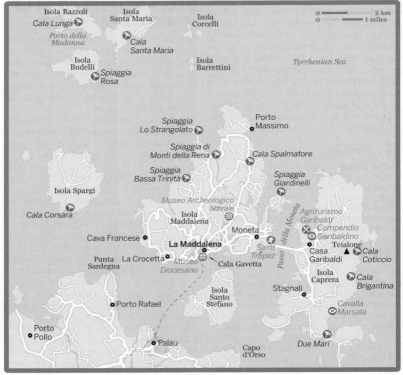

◉ Sights & Activities

Beyond the harbour, the island's drawcard is its startlingly lovely seascapes. Divers sing the praises of the sapphire waters here, which are among the cleanest in the Med and teem with marine life. A 20km panoramic road circles the island, allowing easy access to several attractive bays such as **Giardinelli**, **Monti della Rena**, **Lo Strangolato** and **Cala Spalmatore**.

Museo Diocesano   MUSEUM
(Via Baron Manno; donations welcome; ⊘10am-1pm & 3-8pm Tue-Sun) FREE You could pass half an hour or so inspecting the religious bits and bobs at this museum in the back of the modern Chiesa di Santa Maria Maddalena.

Museo Archeologico Navale   MUSEUM
(✆0789 79 06 33; Località Mongiardino; admission €4; ⊘by appointment 9.30am-12.30pm & 3.30-6.30pm) About 1km out of town, on the road to Cala Spalmatore, this museum exhibits finds from a 1st-century shipwreck. The two modest rooms are presided over by an impressive reconstructed cross-section of the Roman vessel containing more than 200 amphorae.

Saint Tropez   WATER SPORTS
(✆0789 72 77 68, 335 6545214; Via Benvenuto Cellini 36) If larking around on water skis, a wake board or canoe in the calm waters of the Passo della Moneta appeals, try Saint Tropez, located near the bridge over to Isola Caprera.

Elena Tour   BOAT TOUR
(✆333 5254415, 0789 73 93 07; www.elenatour.it; Via Eleonora d'Arborea 24) Elena Tour runs relaxed cruises to the fabulous hidden beaches and smaller, lesser-known islands of Arcipelago di La Maddalena, with plenty of time for chilling and swimming. Reckon on around €40 per person for a full-day tour including lunch. Itinerary details are on the website.

Fratelli Cuccu BICYCLE RENTAL
(📞0789 73 85 28; www.fratellicuccu.it; Via Amendola 8; ⊙9am-8pm) Rental companies line up along Via Amendola on the waterfront. Among them is Fratelli Cuccu, which rents out bikes, scooters, cars and dinghy boats. Quad excursions are also available.

✖ Eating & Drinking

Most of the best eating options are in La Maddalena town. Strolling around its lively centre is the main evening activity, perhaps stopping for a coffee along Via Vittorio Emanuele or a cold beer in Piazza Garibaldi, hub of the evening *passeggiata* (stroll). Nearly every place closes from November to March.

Trattoria Pizzeria L'Olimpo PIZZERIA €
(📞0789 73 77 95; Via Principe Amedeo 45-47; pizzas €6, meals €25; ⊙noon-2pm & 7-10.30pm summer) It's worth hunting down this popular trattoria in the bland streets east of the centre. The food is excellent – pizzas and the usual array of pastas, grilled meats and seafood – and the friendly service a pleasure.

Sottovento SEAFOOD €€
(📞0789 73 77 49; www.ristorantilamaddalena.it; Via E Dandolo 9; meals €35-45; ⊙noon-2.30pm & 7-11.30pm, closed Mon winter) Sardinian home cooking is on the menu at bistro-style Sottovento, a short stroll north of the harbour. Go for seafood antipasti, handmade pasta and fresh fish and you won't be disappointed.

ℹ Information

Tourist Office (📞0789 73 63 21; www.comune.lamaddalena.ot.it; Via XX Settembre; ⊙8.30am-1.30pm & 3.30-5.30pm Mon & Wed, 8.30am-1.30pm Tue, Thu & Fri) The tourist office, to the right of the port as you face seawards, has limited information on the archipelago; opening hours should be taken with a pinch of salt as they change frequently.

ℹ Getting There & Away

There are ferries to La Maddalena from the mainland. They arrive (and leave) at separate points along the waterfront.

ℹ Getting Around

Turmo Travel operates two island bus services, both departing from Via Amendola on the waterfront. One goes to the Compendio Garibaldi complex on Isola Caprera, and the other heads around the island, passing the Museo Archeologico Navale and several beaches, including Cala Spalmatore and Spiaggia Bassa Trinita.

Isola Caprera

Giuseppe Garibaldi's 'Eden', Isola Caprera is a wild, wonderfully serene island, covered in green pines which look stunning against the ever-present seascape and ragged granite cliffs. The road east out of La Maddalena town takes you through desolate urban relics to the narrow causeway that spans the Passo della Moneta between Isola Maddalena and Isola Caprera.

◉ Sights & Activities

Green, shady Caprera is ideal for walking, and there are plenty of trails weaving through the pine forests. There's a stairway right up to the top of the island (212m) where you'll find the **Teialone** lookout tower. As you wander, keep an eye out for seabirds like royal seagulls and cormorants, and peregrine falcons.

The island's rugged coast is indented with several tempting coves. Many people head south for fine sands and turquoise-blue waters at **Due Mari** bays. You could, however, head north of the Compendio Garibaldino for about 1.5km and look for the walking trail that drops down to beautifully secluded **Cala Coticcio**. Marginally easier is **Cala Brigantina** (signposted), southeast of the Garibaldi complex.

★**Compendio Garibaldino** MUSEUM
(adult/reduced €6/3; ⊙9am-8pm Tue-Sun) Giuseppe Garibaldi, professional revolutionary and all-round Italian hero, bought half of Caprera in 1855 (he got the rest 10 years later). He made it his home and refuge, the place he would return to after yet another daring campaign in the pursuit of liberty. The Compendio Garibaldino is an object of pilgrimage for many Italians. Visits, by guided tour in Italian only, take in the rustic elegant rooms, the garden cemetery and a small but touching collection of Garibaldi memorabilia.

The red-shirted revolutionary first lived in a hut that still stands in the courtyard while building his main residence, the **Casa Bianca**. You enter the house proper by an atrium adorned with his portrait, a flag from the days of Peru's war of independence and a reclining wheelchair donated to him by the city of Milan when he became infirm a couple of years before his death. You then proceed through a series of bedrooms where he and family members slept. The kitchen had its own freshwater pump, a feat of high

OLBIA, THE COSTA SMERALDA & THE GALLURA ISOLA CAPRERA

technology in such a place in the 1870s. In what was the main dining room are now displayed all sorts of odds and ends, from binoculars to the general's own red shirt. The last room contains his death bed, facing the window and the sea, across which he would look longingly, dreaming until the end that he might return to his native Nice.

Outside in the **gardens** are Garibaldi's rough hewn granite tomb and those of several family members (he had seven children by his three wives and one by a governess).

Cavalla Marsala   HORSE RIDING
(☑ 347 2359064; Località Stagnali, Isola di Caprera) Cavalla Marsala's hacks along the beach and through the fragrant *macchia* are particularly atmospheric in the early evening. Reckon on on €35 for a 1½-hour trek.

✖ Eating

Agriturismo Garibaldi   SARDINIAN €€
(☑ 0789 72 74 49; meals €30; ⊙ noon-2pm & 7.30-10pm May-Sep) Housed in the buildings where Garibaldi's farmers used to live, this *agriturismo* is a top spot to feast on traditional Sardinian food. The farm produces all its own honey, vegetables, lamb and pork, all of which appear on the delicious fixed menu. Reservations are essential. To get here follow the signs left after crossing the bridge over from Isola Maddalena.

Other Islands

The five other main islands can only be reached by boat. Numerous excursions leave from Isola Maddalena, Palau and Santa Teresa di Gallura and approach the islands in various combinations. Alternatively, you can hire motorised dinghies and do it yourself.

Since NATO bid the **Isola Santo Stefano** farewell in 2008, it is once again a green, tranquil escape. **Isola Spargi**, west of Isola Maddalena, is necklaced by sandy coves and inlets. One of the best is **Cala Corsara**, where the sea is topaz blue. To the north lies a trio of islands: **Isola Budelli**, **Isola Razzoli** and **Isola Santa Maria**. With your own boat and time to paddle about you could explore all sorts of little coves and beaches. On tours it's likely you'll sail past the gorgeous **Spiaggia Rosa** (Pink Beach) on Isola Budelli, so-called because of the sand's unique pink tinge; it's now protected and access to its environmentally threatened sands and waters is forbidden. Other popular stops include fjord-like **Cala Lunga** on Isola Razzoli and the

often-crowded **Cala Santa Maria** on the island of the same name. The beautiful stretch of water between the three islets is known as the **Porto della Madonna** and is on most waterborne itineraries through the archipelago.

THE INTERIOR

Away from the preening millionaires on the beach, Gallura's granite interior is remote and resolutely rural. In fact, it was this fertile hinterland that attracted the waves of Corsican migrants who settled here to farm the cork forests and plant the extensive Vermentino vineyards. Cork has long been a mainstay of the local economy.

Tempio Pausania
POP 14,300

Elevated above the hot Gallurese plain and surrounded by dense cork woods, Tempio Pausania stays cool and calm even in the height of summer. Joint capital of the Olbia-Tempio province, it's an unpretentious spot with a rustic *centro storico* and a laid-back pace of life.

The town was founded by the Romans in the 2nd century BC, and was developed to become an administrative centre of the medieval Giudicato di Gallura. Tempio Pausania's heyday came under the Spanish and then the Savoys, when many of the churches that adorn the town's grey stone centre were constructed. These days it's a relaxed place to hang out and the surrounding countryside is perfect for touring. Nearby Monte Limbara provides numerous trekking opportunities.

◉ Sights

Cattedrale di San Pietro   DUOMO
(Piazza San Pietro; ⊙ 8am-12.30pm & 3-8pm) This granite cathedral is the town's imposing centrepiece. All that remains of the 15th-century original is the bell tower and main entrance. Across the square, the **Oratorio del Rosario** dates to the time of Spanish domination of the island.

Chiesa del Purgatorio   CHURCH
(Piazza del Purgatorio; ⊙ 9am-noon) This modest 17th-century church, presiding over Piazza del Purgatorio, has an intriguing history. The story goes that a member of the noble Misorro family was found guilty of carrying out a massacre on this very spot. To expiate his sins, the pope ordered the man to fund

Tempio Pausania

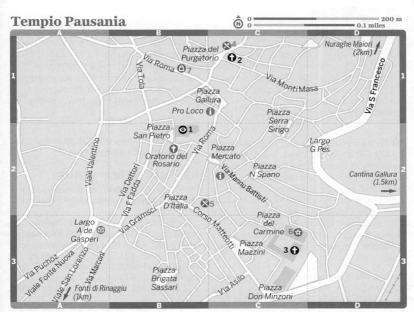

the building of this church, where to this day it is the custom of townspeople to come and pray after a funeral.

Convento Degli Scolopi   CONVENT
(Piazza Mazzini) Tempio is replete with churches, and an indication of the town's former importance lies in the presence of the 17th-century Convento degli Scolopi. It's now a college and not open to the public, but you can wander the serene cloister if the gates are open.

Fonti di Rinaggiu   SPRING
Since Roman days Tempio has been known for its springs; the Fonti di Rinaggiu is a pleasant 1km walk southwest from the centre (take the shady Viale San Lorenzo and follow the 'Alle Terme' signs).

Cantina Gallura   WINERY
(☎ 079 63 12 41; www.cantinagallura.com; Via Val di Cossu 9; ◷ 8am-noon & 2-6pm Mon-Fri, 9am-1pm Sat) For liquid sustenance of a more alcoholic nature, head 1.5km east of town to this cantina, where you can stock up on the local DOCG Vermentino di Gallura.

✨ Festivals & Events

Tempio has a whole host of festivals and events, from music concerts to folklore parades and key religious festivals.

Carnevale (in February) is big here, with flamboyant costumed parades in the build-up to Lent, as is **Easter**. On Good Friday members of *confraternita* (religious brotherhoods) dress up in sinister-looking robes and hoods for the **Via Crucis** night procession. The musical **Festival d'Estate** runs from July to mid-August.

✕ Eating

On tree-shaded Piazza d'Italia and Piazza Gallura you'll find a couple of cafes with alfresco seating where you can grab an espresso, *panino* or pizza.

LUNAR LANDSCAPES

A few kilometres northwest of Aggius towards Trinita d'Agultu you reach the **Valle della Luna**. It's a surreal and evocative landscape, where huge granite boulders spill across rolling hills and farmland like giants' marbles. The lookout point on the SP74 commands fantastic views of the surrounding countryside, honeycombed with bizarrely sculpted rocks. The valley is a fantastic place for a cycle ride, and the road through here down to the coast is tremendously scenic.

★ **Trattoria Gallurese**   SARDINIAN €
(☑ 079 639 30 12; Via Novara 2; set menu €15, meals €20-25; ☺ noon-3pm & 7-10pm) This simple homespun trattoria serves a warm welcome and genuine Gallurese soul food. Go traditional with *cinghiale* (wild boar) slow-cooked in Cannonau red wine or *pecora alla gallurese* (Gallurese-style lamb). Delicious tiramisu with a shot of homemade wild-mint liqueur is the perfect coda to a meal.

Ristorante Il Purgatorio   SARDINIAN €€
(☑ 079 63 43 94; Piazza del Purgatorio 9; meals around €45; ☺ 12.30-2pm & 7.30-9.30pm Wed-Mon) One of the best restaurants in town, this stone-walled restaurant serves earthy seasonal fare and fresh seafood. Menu stalwarts include *cinghiale in umido* (wild-boar stew) and *ravioli carciofi e bottarga* (ravioli with artichokes and mullet roe).

☆ Entertainment

Teatro del Carmine   THEATRE
(☑ 079 67 15 80; Piazza del Carmine) A variety of performances, ranging from operetta to classical concerts, can be enjoyed here, especially during the summer Festival d'Estate.

🛍 Shopping

Casa Mundula   ARTISANAL
(Via Roma 102; ☺ 10am-1pm & 4-8pm Mon-Sat) This atmospheric store is a one-stop shop for cork-based knick-knacks, ceramics, filigree jewellery and hand-crafted knives, as well as Sardinian specialities such as *pane carasau,* local honey and wine, Carloforte tuna and the like.

ℹ Information

Post Office (Largo A de Gasperi; ☺ 8.20am-7.05pm Mon-Fri, 8.20am-12.35pm Sat)
Pro Loco (☑ 079 63 12 73; Piazza Gallura 2; ☺ 10am-1pm & 4-7pm Mon-Fri, 10am-1pm Sat) An extremely friendly information office.
Tourist Office (☑ 079 639 00 80; www.comune.tempiopausania.ot.it; Piazza Mercato 3;

☺ 9am-1pm & 4-8pm Mon-Sat, 10am-1pm Sun) Run by helpful, multilingual staff.

ℹ Getting There & Away

From Olbia (€3.50, 1¼ hours) there are seven daily ARST buses on weekdays to Tempio and three on Sunday.

The train station, a downhill walk from the centre, comes to life for the summertime **trenino verde** (☑ 070 58 02 46; www.treninoverde.com) to/from Sassari (€14.50, 2½ hours, one daily Thursday and Friday), Arzachena (€11.50, 70 minutes, one daily Tuesday to Friday) and Palau (€18.50, 1¾ hours, two daily Thursday and Friday).

Around Tempio Pausania

Nuraghe Maiori

Two kilometres north of town on the SS133 road to Palau is the **Nuraghe Maiori** (admission with/without guided visit €3.50/2.50; ☺ 9am-7pm), signposted off to the right and immersed in billowing cork woods. As the name suggests (*maiori* means 'major'), it is a good deal bigger than many of the simple ruined towers that dot the countryside around here.

A trail leads through fragrant herb gardens to the tower, which has a chamber on each side, and a ramp to a third, open room at the back. Stairs to the left allow you to walk to the top. It's pitch black inside the chambers, so bring a headlight – or ask to borrow a torch – to spot clusters of rare and tiny lesser horseshoe bats.

Monte Limbara

Some 17km southeast of Tempio, the jagged summit of Monte Limbara (1359m) dominates the gritty landscape. The easiest way to reach it is to drive. From Tempio, head south out of town past the train station and follow the SS392 road for Oschiri. After 8km you will hit the left turn-off for the mountain.

The initial stretch takes you through thick pine woods. As you emerge above the treeline, a couple of *punto panoramico* (viewing spots) are indicated, from where you have terrific views across all of northern Sardinia. One is marked by a statue of the Virgin Mary and child, near the simple **Chiesa di Santa Maria della Neve**.

The road then flattens out to reach the viewing point of Punta Balistreri (1359m), where the RAI national TV network has stacked its relay and communication towers. The air is cool and refreshing, even on a midsummer's day, and the views west towards Sassari and beyond and north to Corsica are breathtaking.

Calangianus & Around

Archaeology devotees might want to make the short drive to Calangianus, Sardinia's cork capital, situated about 10km east of Tempio. Its **Tomba dei Giganti di Pascaredda** is among the best preserved in the area.

Nearby, the small town of **Luras** is worth a quick stopover for a look at the **Dolmen de Ladas**, a megalithic tomb (burial chamber) that dates to approximately 3000 BC. The **Museo Etnografico Galluras** (www.galluras. it; Via Nazionale 35a; adult/reduced €5/2.50; ⊙by appointment) celebrates the area's rural traditions with a collection of agrarian tools and a reconstructed village house. Among the displays, look out for Sa Femina Accabadora, a gruesome hammer traditionally used to put the terminally sick out of their misery in a practice of rural euthanasia.

Aggius & Luogosanto

Cowering at the foot of granite peaks, Aggius is a deeply traditional village, clustered around a historic centre of twisting lanes and squat stone houses. It's famous for its choral music and carpets, the latter tradition dating back to the 1900s, when 4000 looms were busy in the area. You can see the looms, and the richly brocaded costumes worn for festive occasions, alongside displays on cork and granite, at the **Museo Etnografico 'Olivia Carta Cannas'** (www.museodiaggius.it; Via Monti di Lizu 6; adult/reduced €4/3; ⊙10am-1pm & 3-7pm).

For a more sinister peek at Aggius' past, stop by the **Museo del Banditismo** (www. museodiaggius.it; Via Pretura; adult/reduced €4/3; ⊙10am-1pm & 4-6pm). Housed in the former magistrates' court, the museum zooms in on banditry in Gallura (still a problem until the 1990s), with a collection of arms, police reports and snapshots of the island's most wanted outlaws.

From Aggius it's possible to loop round northwest onto the SS133 towards remote **Luogosanto** (Holy Place). It's a pretty place that's peppered with churches, the grandest of which is the **Basilica di Nostra Signora di Luogosanto**, built in 1227. Pope Onorio III gave it the title of basilica when he sanctioned its Holy Door which, like the one at St Peter's in Rome, is walled up and only opened every seven years. There's an even older church here, the **Chiesa di San Trano**, which was built to honour the 6th-century St Trano and is moulded into the granite rock.

Lago di Coghinas, Oschiri & Berchidda

Those with wheels could make another excursion south of Monte Limbara. Once down from the mountain, turn left on the SS392 and head south for Oschiri. The road skirts the western side of the Limbara massif, passing through cork oak and pine woods, crests the Passo del Limbara (646m) and then begins its descent. After about 12km the green gives way to scorched straw-coloured fields and the blue mirror of the artificial Lago di Coghinas comes into view.

Just before the bridge over the lake, a narrow asphalted road breaks off east towards Berchidda around the northern flank of **Monte Acuto** (493m), the woody hill where Eleonora d'Arborea hid out for a period in the 14th century. **Berchidda** is a fairly nondescript farming town with a strong wine tradition. You can find out about local wine-making and taste some of the area's Vermentino at the modern **Museo del Vino** (www.muvisardegna.it; adult/reduced €3/2.50; ⊙9am-1pm & 3-6pm Tue-Fri, to 7pm Sat & Sun) right at the top of town. The best time to visit is August, when Berchidda holds its weeklong **Time in Jazz** (www. timeinjazz.it, in Italian) festival, a multicultural event showcasing anything from string quartets to piano soloists and saxophonists.

At the **Cantina del Vermentino** (⊘0789 4 40 12; www.vermentinomonti.it; Via San Paolo 2, Monti; ⊙8.30am-1pm & 2.30-7pm Mon-Fri, 8.30am-1pm Sat) in **Monti**, just over 15km east of Berchidda, taste and buy some of the region's finest wines, including the crisp Vermentino di Gallura, Sardinia's only DOCG-rated wine.

A daily ARST bus passes through Berchidda en route from Nuoro (€7, 1¼ hours) to Olbia (€3, two hours).

Nuoro & the East

Why Go?

Nowhere is nature such an overwhelming force as in the wild, wild east, where the Supramonte's imperious limestone mountains roll down to the Golfo di Orosei's cliffs and startling aquamarine waters. Who knows where that winding country road might lead you? Perhaps to deep valleys concealing prehistoric caves and *nuraghi* (Bronze Age fortified settlements), to the lonesome villages of the Barbagia steeped in bandit legends, or to forests where wild pigs snuffle amid centuries-old holm oaks. Neither time nor trend obsessed, this region is refreshingly authentic.

Outdoor action is everywhere: along the coast where you can drop anchor in a string of pearly white bays, up in the cliffs where you can multipitch climb above the sea, on old mule trails best explored by mountain bike, and at peaks and ravines only reachable on foot. True, the Costa Smeralda attracts more celebrities, but we think you'll agree that the real rock stars and rolling stones are right here.

Best Places to Eat

➡ Il Portico (p175)

➡ Gologone (p180)

➡ Nascar (p196)

➡ Agriturismo Nuraghe Mannu (p193)

Best Places to Stay

➡ Agriturismo Guthiddai (p214)

➡ Lemon House (p216)

➡ Hotel L'Oasi (p215)

➡ Casa Solotti (p213)

Road Distance (km)

	Aritzo	Cala Gonone	Nuoro	Orosei
Cala Gonone	85			
Nuoro	53	32		
Orosei	88	20	35	
Tortolì	65	54	72	69

NUORO

POP 36,400

Once an isolated hilltop village and a by-word for banditry, Nuoro had its cultural renaissance in the 19th and early 20th centuries when it became a hotbed of artistic talent. Today museums in the historic centre pay homage to local legends like Nobel Prize–winning author Grazia Deledda, acclaimed poet Sebastiano Satta, novelist Salvatore Satta and sculptor Francesco Ciusa.

The city's spectacular backdrop is the granite peak of Monte Ortobene (955m), capped by a 7m-high bronze statue of the Redentore (Christ the Redeemer). The thickly wooded summit commands dress-circle views of the valley below and the limestone mountains enshrouding Oliena opposite.

History

Archaeologists have unearthed evidence of prehistoric nuraghic settlements in the Nuoro area. A popular theory maintains that the city was established when locals opposed to Roman rule grouped together around Monte Ortobene. But little is known of the city before the Middle Ages, when it was passed from one feudal family to another under the Aragonese and, later, Spain.

By the 18th century the town, by now under Piedmontese control, had a population of around 3000, mostly farmers and shepherds. A tough, often violent, place, it rose in rebellion in 1868 when citizens burned down the town hall to protest attempts to privatise public land (and thus hand it to the rich landowners). This action, known as Su Connuttu, no doubt confirmed the new Italian nation's view of the whole Nuoro district as a 'crime zone', an attitude reflected in its treatment of the area, which only served to further alienate the Nuoresi and cement their mistrust of authority.

Nuoro was appointed a provincial capital in 1927. It quickly developed into a bustling administrative centre. Although the traditional problem of banditry has subsided and the town presents a cheerful enough visage, Nuoro remains troubled, as high unemployment forces many young people to leave in search of work.

◉ Sights & Activities

Museo Etnografico Sardo MUSEUM
(www.isresardegna.it; Via Antonio Mereu 56; adult/reduced €3/1; ⊙9am-1pm & 3-6pm Tue-Sun summer, 10am-1pm & 3-5pm Tue-Sun winter) Zooming in on Sardinian folklore, this museum harbours a peerless collection of filigree jewellery, carpets, tapestries, rich embroidery, musical instruments, weapons and masks. The highlight is the traditional costume display – the styles, colours and patterns speaking volumes about the people and their villages. Look out for fiery red skirts from the fiercely independent mountain villages, the Armenian-influenced dresses of Orgosolo and Desulo finished with a blue-and-yellow silk border, and the burkalike headdresses of the ladies of Ittiri and Osilo.

Other rooms display life-size exhibits from the region's more unusual festivals. These include Mamoiada's sinister *mamuthones* (costumed characters), with their shaggy sheepskins and scowling masks, and Ottana's *boes* (men masked as cattle), with their tiny antelopelike masks, huge capes and furry boots.

Museo d'Arte GALLERY
(MAN; www.museoman.it; Via S Satta 15; adult/reduced €3/2; ⊙10am-1pm & 3-7pm Tue-Sun) Housed in a restored 19th-century townhouse, the Museo d'Art is the only serious contemporary art gallery in Sardinia. Its permanent collection boasts more than 400 works by the island's top 20th-century painters, including Antonio Ballero, Giovanni Ciusa-Romagna, Mario Delitalia and abstract artist Mauro Manca. Local sculptors Francesco Ciusa and Costantino Nivola are also represented. The gallery also hosts more wide-ranging temporary exhibits, usually held on the ground and top floors.

Chiesa di San Carlo CHURCH
(Piazza San Carlo; ⊙hours vary) To see a bronze copy of Francesco Ciusa's *La Madre dell'Ucciso* (Mother of the Killed), which won a prize at the Venice Biennale in 1907, you should visit the pink chapel Chiesa di San Carlo.

Museo Deleddiano MUSEUM
(www.isresardegna.it; Via Grazia Deledda 42; adult/reduced €3/1; ⊙9am-1pm & 3-6pm Tue-Sun summer, 10am-1pm & 3-5pm Tue-Sun winter) Up in the oldest part of town, the birthplace of Grazia Deledda (1871–1936) has been converted into this lovely little museum. The rooms, full of Deledda memorabilia, have been carefully restored to show what a well-to-do 19th-century Nuorese house actually looked like. Best of all is the material relating to her Nobel prize – a congratulatory telegram from the king of Italy and prize-giving ceremony

Nuoro & the East Highlights

1 Walk on the wild side in the **Gola Su Gorropu** (p190), Europe's Grand Canyon.

2 Drop anchor at the hidden coves and secluded beaches of the **Golfo di Orosei** (p187), lapped by brilliant aquamarine waters.

3 Take a scenic drive along the serpentine **SS125** (p188) for captivating views of the mountains and Med.

4 Marvel at the mysterious nuraghic ruins of **Tiscali** (p191) high in the limestone Supramonte.

5 Leave the world behind as you explore the weird highland plain of the **Altopiano del Golgo** p197).

⑥ Enjoy exhilarating coastal climbing in **Cala Gonone** (p191), cooling off with a dip in the bluest of seas.

⑦ Scale the hidden heights in the hills around **Ulassai** (p198).

photos which show her, proud and tiny, surrounded by a group of stiffly suited men.

There's also a storeroom piled with sacks of wheat and legumes, an internal courtyard, and a large kitchen crammed with pots and pans.

Chiesa della Solitudine   CHURCH
(Viale della Solitudine) Although she lived 36 of her 65 years in Rome, Deledda's life was consumed by Nuoro and its essential dramas. Fittingly, she was brought home to be buried in the plain granite church of the Chiesa della Solitudine. You will find her granite sarcophagus to the right of the altar.

Piazza Satta   PIAZZA
A brief walk up Via Satta leads to Piazza Satta, a small square dedicated to the great poet **Sebastiano Satta** (1867–1914), who was born in a house here. To celebrate the centenary of his birth, sculptor Costantino Nivola gave the square a complete makeover in 1967. Nivola whitewashed the surrounding

houses to provide a blank backdrop for his curious work – a series of granite sculptures planted in the piazzalike menhirs. Each sculpture has a carved niche containing a small bronze figurine (a clear wink at the prehistoric *bronzetti*) depicting a character from Satta's poems.

Parco Colle Sant'Onofrio   PARK
(Via Sant'Onofrio) A short wander uphill from the centre of town brings you to the quiet Parco Colle Sant'Onofrio, which commands broad mountain views. From the highest point you can see across to Monte Ortobene and, further south, to Oliena and Orgosolo.

Museo Archeologico Nazionale   MUSEUM
(www.museoarcheologiconuoro.it; Via Mannu 1; adult/reduced €2/1; ⊙9am-1pm Tue-Sat, plus 3-5.30pm Tue & Thu) This museum presents a romp through the region's archaeological sites. Finds from the surrounding province range from ancient ceramics and fine *bronzetti* to a drilled skull from 1600 BC

Nuoro

and Roman and early medieval artefacts. Anyone with more than a passing interest in nuraghic culture will enjoy the reconstruction of a prehistoric temple and ancient bronze laboratory.

Cattedrale di
Santa Maria della Neve CATHEDRAL
(Piazza Santa Maria della Neve) A big, pink wedding cake of a church, the 19th-century Cattedrale di Santa Maria della Neve is one of 300 or so Italian churches dedicated to the Madonna della Neve. The cathedral's facade is a big flouncing neoclassical spread, giving onto a single-nave interior. Of note inside is *Disputa de Gesù Fra i Dottori* (Jesus Arguing with the Doctors), a canvas attributed to the school of Luca Giordano and located between the first and second chapels on the right.

The so-called Mary of the Snow earned her name after she supposedly appeared to Pope Liberius in a dream and told him to build a church on the site where it would snow the next morning. It promptly snowed the next day and the Pope commissioned what was to become the Basilica di Santa Maria Maggiore in Rome.

Nuoro

⛪ Festivals & Events

Sagra del Redentore RELIGIOUS
The Sagra del Redentore (Feast of Christ the Redeemer) in the last week of August is the main event in Nuoro. It's one of Sardinia's most exuberant folkloric festivals, attracting costumed participants from across the island and involves much parading, music-making and dancing. On the evening of 28 August a torchlit procession, starting at the Chiesa della Solitudine, winds its way through the city.

🍴 Eating

The main street is Corso Garibaldi, which bisects a warren of tidy lanes, where you'll find several restaurants and popular cafes.

La Locanda Pili Monica ITALIAN €
(☑ 0784 3 10 32; Via Brofferio 31; meals €15-20; ⊗ 12.30-2.45pm & 8.30-10.30pm Mon-Sat) It's all about the food at this friendly, down-to-earth trattoria, and the €9.20 set lunch is a bargain. Bag a table and you're in for a treat – think antipasti, fresh pasta and grilled steaks, washed down with a litre (€6) of highly quaffable house wine.

Premiata Pasticceria Il
Golosastro PASTICCERIA €
(Corso Garibaldi 173-5; cakes & pastries €1.50-4; ⊗ 8am-1.30pm & 4-8pm Mon-Sat, 8am-1.30pm Sun) As fine as lace, the intricately crafted local cakes here are *almost* too pretty to eat. Award-winning *patisseur* and baker Giovanni Pedduzza creates delicious sweets made with honey and almonds, *formaggelle* (mini Sardinian-style cheesecakes) and dainty pastry bouquets – all totally divine.

Il Portico SARDINIAN €€
(☑ 0784 23 29 09; www.ilporticonuoro.it; Via Monsignor Bua 13; meals €40; ⊗ 12.30-2.30pm & 8-10.45pm Thu-Tue) You'll receive a heartfelt welcome at this restaurant, where abstract paintings grace the walls and jazzy music plays. Behind the scenes, a talented husband-and-wife team rustle up a feast of local fare like *spaghetti ai ricci* (spaghetti with sea urchins) and fresh gnocchi with lamb *ragù*. Save room for the delectable caramel-nougat semifreddo.

Il Rifugio SARDINIAN €€
(☑ 0784 23 23 55; Via Antonio Mereu 28-36; meals €30; ⊗ 12.45-3pm & 7.45-11.30pm Thu-Tue) One of Nuoro's most popular eateries, this jovial restaurant has won a faithful following for its creative brand of local cooking. Typical

dishes include *capretto* (roasted kid) with artichokes and *pecora alla nuorese con cipolline* (Nuoro lamb with onions). And all at very reasonable prices.

Monti Blu
MEDITERRANEAN €€

(✆ 0784 23 14 43; www.montiblunuoro.com; Piazza Satta 8; meals €25-40; ⊙1-2.45pm & 8-11pm Tue-Sun) Clean, bright Mediterranean flavours shine through in regional dishes such as *tagliata di tonno* (sliced tuna steak with rocket and *pecorino*) at this stylish little restaurant. You can round out a meal in the tea room and stock up on *pecorino*, salami and preserves in the deli.

Agriturismo Testone
SARDINIAN €€

(✆ 0784 23 05 39; www.agriturismotestone.com; Via Verdi 49, Testone; meals €25-30; ⊞) You'll feel immediately part of *la famiglia* at this *agriturismo* (farm stay), which rests in peaceful solitude in the countryside, 20km northwest of Nuoro. The welcome is heart-felt, mealtimes are cheerful, communal affairs, and the mostly home-grown food is terrific. The farm rears lamb and produces its own *formaggi, salumi*, honey, sweets and wine.

Drinking & Nightlife

Nuoro has a lively cafe scene. Take your pick of the pavement terraces in the historic centre for drinks and light bites.

Caffè Tettamanzi Bar Mayore
CAFE

(Corso Garibaldi 71; ⊙6am-3am, closed Sun morning) Going strong since 1875, Nuoro's oldest cafe is something of a local institution. The interior recalls a more glamorous age, with frescoes, marble tables and deep velvet armchairs where you can read works by Grazia Deledda and Sebastiano Satta. Snag a chair outside for crowd-watching and *panini* (sandwiches).

Bar Nuovo
BAR, CAFE

(Piazza Mazzini 6; ⊙7am-midnight) Right on Piazza Mazzini, this is an excellent place to park yourself with a cool beer and watch the world go by. It's equally good for the morning paper, midday gelato and evening aperitif.

Shopping

Corso Garibaldi is studded with fashion boutiques, and springs to life with an antiques market on the second Saturday of the month.

Galleria Il Portico
ARTS & CRAFTS

(Piazza del Popolo 3; ⊙10am-1pm & 4.30-7.30pm Mon-Sat, 10am-1pm Sun) This art gallery showcases works by contemporary artists such as Antonio Corriga, Vittorio Calvi and Franco Carenti. Oils and watercolours predominate here, and prices generally range from a few hundred euros up to several thousand.

Coltelli Sardi
HANDICRAFTS

(www.coltellisardi.com; Corso Garibaldi 53; ⊙9am-1pm & 4.30-8pm) True to Nuoro's pastoral heritage (not to mention those dastardly bandits), Francesco Piredda crafts exquisite Sardinian knives, including the famous Pattada jackknife with a myrtle-leaf-shaped blade that is carved from mouflon or ram horn. They'll set you back between €50 and €250.

ⓘ Information

The train and bus stations are down Via Lamarmora, the extension of Corso Garibaldi.

For banks with ATMs and bookshops, head to Corso Garibaldi. The **main post office** (⊙8.20am-7.05pm Mon-Fri, 8.20am-12.35pm Sat) is on Piazza F Crispi.

Tourist Office (✆ 0784 44 18 23; www.provincia.nuoro.it; Piazza Italia 7; ⊙8.30am-2pm Mon-Fri, plus 3.30-7pm Tue) Has plenty of useful information on Nuoro and environs.

ⓘ Getting There & Away

BUS

ARST (✆ 0784 29 08 00; www.arst.sardegna.it) buses run from the **bus station** on Viale Sardegna to destinations throughout the province and beyond. These include Dorgali (€3, 45 minutes, six daily), Orosei (€3, one hour, 10 daily), La Caletta (€4.50, one hour, seven daily), San Teodoro (€8, one hour 50 minutes, five daily), Baunei (€6, two hours, four daily), Santa Maria Navarrese (€7, two hours 25 minutes, five daily) and Tortolì (€6, two hours 40 minutes, five daily). There are also regular buses to Oliena (€1.50, 20 minutes) and Orgosolo (€2, 35 minutes). Two daily nonstop buses connect with Cagliari (€15.50, 2½ to five hours).

For Olbia, there's an ARST bus (€8.50), and **Deplano** (✆ 0784 29 50 30; www.deplanobus.it) also runs up to five daily buses to Olbia airport (€12, 1¾ hours) via Budoni (€6, one hour) and San Teodoro (€6, 1¼ hours).

For Alghero, **Redentours** (✆ 0784 3 03 25; www.redentours.com) has two daily buses (€18, 2¼ hours), for which bookings are required.

CAR & MOTORCYCLE

The SS131DCN cross-country, dual-carriage highway between Olbia and Abbasanta (where it runs into the north–south SS131 Carlo Felice highway) skirts Nuoro to the north. Otherwise, the SS129 is the quickest road east to Orosei and Dorgali. Several roads head south for Oliena, Orgosolo and Mamoiada.

TRAIN

The **train station** is west of the town centre on the corner of Via Lamarmora and Via G Ciusa Romagna. Trains run from Nuoro to Macomer (€3.10, 1¼ hours, seven daily Monday to Saturday), where you can connect with mainline Trenitalia trains to Cagliari (from Macomer €10.15, 2¼ hours, nine daily).

ℹ Getting Around

Local **ATP** (☑ 0784 3 51 95; www.atpnuoro.it) buses 2 and 3 can be useful for the train station and the ARST bus station, and bus 8 from Via Manzoni for heading up to Monte Ortobene (€1.50). Tickets for city routes cost €1 and are valid for 90 minutes.

You can call for a **taxi** (☑ 0784 20 33 76) or try to grab one along Via Lamarmora.

NORTH OF NUORO

North of Nuoro, the forgotten and lonely countryside harbours a couple of wonderful archaeological sites. They're not easy to get to – even with a car you'll be wondering where on earth you're heading – but persevere and you'll be amply rewarded. Few people make it out here and there are no better places to experience the mystery and isolation of Sardinia's silent interior.

Monte Ortobene

About 7km northeast of Nuoro is the granite peak of **Monte Ortobene** (955m), capped by a 7m-high bronze statue of the Redentore (Christ the Redeemer), strewn with weird and wonderful granite boulders, and covered in thick woods of ilex, pine, fir and poplar. A favourite picnic spot, the mountain is the focus of Nuoro's annual festival, the **Sagra del Redentore**. On 29 August, the brightly clothed faithful make a pilgrimage here from the cathedral, stopping off for mass at the **Chiesa di Nostra Signora del Monte**, and then again under the statue.

The statue was raised in 1901 in response to a call by Pope Leo XIII to raise 19 statues of Christ around Italy to represent the 19 centuries of Christianity. Since then the statue, which shows Christ trampling the devil underfoot, has been an object of devotion to pilgrims who attribute all manner of cures and interventions to it.

The views across the valley to Oliena and Monte Corrasi are at their most breathtaking from the viewpoint near the summit, particularly at dusk when the last light makes the limestone peaks blush pink. To get to the summit by public transport, take local bus 8 from Via A Manzoni in Nuoro.

Fonte Sacra Su Tempiesu

Set in dramatic hill country near the dusty town of Orune, the **Fonte Sacra Su Tempiesu** (www.sutempiesu.it; adult/reduced €3/2; ☺ 9am-7pm summer, to 5pm winter) is a sophisticated nuraghic well temple. Curiously, its name has nothing to do with the temple's prehistoric origins but is a reference to a farmer from Tempio who came across it in 1953. The temple displays a strange keyhole-shaped entrance with stairs leading down to the well bottom, and it's oriented in such a way that on the day of the summer solstice sunlight shines directly down the well shaft.

Water brims to the top of the stairs and trickles down a runnel to another small well, part of the original, more primitive temple that was built around 1600 BC. The newer temple, dating to about 1000 BC, is a (partially restored) masterpiece. Above the well and stairs rises an A-frame structure of carefully carved interlocking stones of basalt and trachyte (sealed watertight with lead). The stone was transported from as far away as Dorgali. No other such structure has been found in Sardinia, and this one (excavation only began in 1981) was for centuries hidden by a landslide that had buried it back in the Iron Age.

Getting here is a problem if you don't have your own transport. Head for Orune, 18km northeast of Nuoro (turn off the SS131DCN highway at the Ponte Marreri exit for the 11km climb to the town). From Orune it is a 5km drive southeast down a sometimes precarious dirt track (signposted). Buses run only as far as Orune. From the ticket office you walk 800m downhill to the temple. You may be accompanied by a guide (in Italian).

Bitti & Complesso Nuragico Romanzesu

From Orune the SS389 continues 12km on to the pastoral town of **Bitti**, made famous in recent years by its singing quartet, the Tenores de Bitti. This male-only vocal group is the most famous exponent of the island's

DON'T MISS

EASTERN SARDINIA'S TOP CLIMBS

Maurizio Oviglia's comprehensive *Pietra di Luna* (€50) climbing guide, available in local bookshops and online, is a useful resource.

Cala Fuili Easily accessible bay and good for beginners, with 190 routes from 5a to 8b+, including cliffs above the beach and scores of overhangs in the gorge for all tastes and exposures.

La Poltrona A massive limestone amphitheatre close to central Cala Gonone, with compact rock, 75 bolted routes from grades 4 to 8a and a maximum height of 175m. Mornings get too hot here in summer, so wait until late afternoon.

Cala Luna Fabulous climbing above a beautiful bay, accessed on a two-hour coastal walk from Cala Gonone or by boat. The 57 routes ranging from 5c and 8b+ include some tricky single-pitches in limestone caves with overhangs. Bonus: the rock faces are in the shade most of the day.

Hotel Supramonte Part of the fun is arriving at this breathtakingly sheer 400m cliff face, which is at the narrowest point of the Gola Su Gorropu canyon. A tough 8b multipitch climb, this is one best left to climbers with plenty of experience under their belt.

S'atta Ruia A Dorgali favourite, consisting of a long limestone cliff with vertical walls and overhangs. There are 81 routes from grades 5a to 7b. Climb in the morning for shade.

Biddiriscottai Just before the bay of Cartoe, Biddiriscottai has a stunning mountain setting with dramatic sea views. The sea cliffs and crags rise above a cave. Technical climbing on 50 well-bolted routes ranging from 5b to 8a+.

Ulassai Climbers have a high time of it in Ulassai. The sheer rock faces of the Bruncu Pranedda canyon and the Lecori cliffs provide some 80 routes, including a number of pretty tough ascents.

Aguglia This pinnacle towering above Cala Goloritzè is a superb introduction to multi-pitch climbing. The real challenge is the overhang – the toughest move is a 6b+.

Vascone (big pool) South of Cala 'e Luas, ideal for deep water soloing (DWS), with lots of gorgeous granite to play on.

Isili Famous for its crags and overhangs, Isili is also a magnet for serious rock climbers, with 250 single-pitch sports routes ranging from 5a to 8b.

traditional form of harmonic singing. To learn more, stop off at the **Museo Multimediale del Canto a Tenore** (Via Mameli 57; adult/reduced €2.50/1.50; ⊙ 9.30am-12.30pm & 3-6pm Tue-Sun summer, to 5.30pm winter), where you can listen to recordings of various groups in action.

About 13km beyond Bitti – follow the road towards Budduso – is the **Complesso Nuragico Romanzesu** (admission €3.50; ⊙9am-1pm & 3-7pm daily). Spread over a 7-hectare site in a thick cork and oak wood, this 17th-century BC nuraghic sanctuary comprises several religious buildings and circular village huts. The highlight is the sacred well temple, covered by a typical *tholos* (conical tower) and connected to a semi-elliptic amphitheatre. To make sense of the ruins, there are up to six daily guided tours; most are in Italian but tours in English and German are also offered.

SUPRAMONTE

Southeast of Nuoro rises the great limestone massif of the Supramonte, its sheer walls like an iron curtain just beyond Oliena. Despite its intimidating aspect, it's actually not as high as it seems – its peak, Monte Corrasi, only reaches 1463m – but it is impressively wild, the bare limestone plateau pitted with ravines and ragged defiles. It makes for a raw, uncompromising landscape, made all the more thrilling by its one-time notoriety as the heart of Sardinia's bandit country.

The Supramonte provides some magnificent hiking. But as much of the walking is over limestone, there are often few discernible tracks to follow, and in spring and autumn you should carefully check the weather conditions. You can engage a local guide at one of the cooperatives in Oliena or Dorgali.

Oliena

POP 7420

Few images in Sardinia are as arresting as the magnificent peak of Monte Corrasi (1463m) when the dusky light makes its limestone summit glow. From Nuoro you can see Oliena's multicoloured rooftops cupped in the mountain's palm. The village itself is an unassuming place with a greystone centre, and is a handy base for exploring the Supramonte.

Oliena was probably founded in Roman times, although its name is a reference to the Ilienses people, descendants of a group of Trojans who supposedly escaped Troy and settled in the area. The arrival of the Jesuits in the 17th century was better documented and set the seeds for the village's modern fame. The eager fathers helped promote the local silk industry and encouraged farmers to cultivate the surrounding slopes. The lessons were learnt well, and now Oliena is famous for its beautiful silk embroidery and its blood-red Cannonau wine, Nepente di Oliena. Oliena is also the home town of Gianfranco Zola, English football's favourite Sardinian import, who was born here in 1966.

◉ Sights

Centro Storico HISTORIC CENTRE
The 13th-century **Chiesa di Santa Maria** rises above Piazza Santa Maria, the village's focal point and the site of the Saturday **market**. Nearby is the blessedly simple 14th-century **Chiesa di San Lussorio**. As you wander the steep grey streets, look out for **murals**, including one of a notorious bandit and local lad, Giovanni Corbeddu Sali (1844–98) and, on a pink house near Via Cavour, an old lady dressed in black and bearing a rifle, symbolising the Easter S'Incontru celebrations.

🏃 Activities

The countryside surrounding Oliena provides some awesome trekking for enthusiasts.

Cooperativa Enis ADVENTURE SPORTS
(☑0784 28 83 63; www.coopenis.it; Località Monte Maccione) This highly regarded adventure sports company offers superb guided treks and 4WD excursions into the Supramonte and along the Golfo di Orosei. These include Tiscali (€33), Gola Su Gorropu (€45), Cala Luna (€45) and the Supramonte di Orgosolo and Murales (€45). A packed lunch bumps up the cost by an extra €5.

Barbagia Insolita ADVENTURE SPORTS
(☑0784 28 60 05; www.barbagiainsolita.it; Corso Vittorio Emanuele 48) Takes you trekking to Gola Su Gorropu (€40) and Tiscali (€35), canoeing on the Rio Cedrino (€40), quad biking (€60) and on 4WD escapades through the countryside (€40).

Sardegna Nascosta HIKING
(☑0784 28 85 50; www.sardegnanascosta.it) Arranges trips and treks (€35 to €55 including lunch) with a cultural focus, from hikes to Monte Corrasi, Gola Su Gorropu and the Valle di Lanaittu to canoeing, climbing and caving excursions.

⭐ Festivals & Events

Settimana Santa CULTURAL FESTIVAL
The village is a hive of festive activity during Easter week. The culmination of the weeklong celebrations is the S'Incontru (The Meeting), a boisterous procession on Easter Sunday in which bearers carry a statue of Christ to meet a statue of the Virgin Mary in Piazza Santa Maria.

Autunno in Barbagia CULTURAL FESTIVAL
From September to December, 27 mountain villages in Barbagia take it in turn to host a weekend of events, from cheese-making workshops to exhibitions and craft demonstrations. Residents open their doors to visitors and put on a feast of local fare. It's a great opportunity to buy local produce.

🍴 Eating

Find Su Gologone and Agriturismo Guthiddai by heading towards Dorgali and taking the turning on the right towards Valle di Lanaittu (follow the signs).

Agriturismo Guthiddai AGRITURISMO €€
(☑0784 28 60 17; www.agriturismoguthiddai.com; Località Guthiddai; meals €28-35; ☺7.30-10.30pm; ⊛) Guests are welcomed like family members at this whitewashed *agriturismo*, romantically set between vineyards and olive groves. Home-grown wine, olive oil and vegies appear on the dinner table, and the house speciality is flavoursome *pecora in cappotto* (ewe stew).

Masiloghi SARDINIAN €€
(☑0784 28 56 96; Via Galiani 68; meals €30-35; ☺noon-3.30pm & 7-11.30pm) Housed in a

WORTH A TRIP

VALLE DI LANAITTU

Immerse yourself in the karst wilderness of the Supramonte by hiking, cycling or driving through this enchanting 7km valley, signposted off the Oliena–Dorgali road. Towering limestone mountains, cliffs and caves lord it over the narrow valley, scattered with natural and archaeological wonders. Rosemary and mastic, grapes and olives flourish in the valley, which attracts wildlife such as martens, birds of prey, wild boar and goats.

Archaeology buffs will be in their element discovering sites that have been inhabited since the Middle Neolithic period. Skeletons and funerary objects including pots and bone tools were discovered in the **Grotta Rifugio**, used by the Bonu Ighinu people (4700 to 4000 BC) as a burial ground. During excavations in the 1970s, two female pagan deities, ceramics and cooking utensils were discovered in the **Grotta del Guano** occupied by the neolithic Ozieri people (3800 to 2900 BC).

Close to the *rifugio* (mountain hut) are the must-see **Grotta Sa Oche & Su Ventu** (admission €2; ⊙ 9am-6pm Apr-Sep), two caves linked by a natural siphon. The former is a wild and enchanting cave named 'Cave of the Voice' after the water that gurgles in its secret underground caverns; the latter has some wonderful stalactites and stalagmites, and was a hideout for notorious Sardinian bandit Corbeddu in the late 19th century.

Three hundred metres north of the *rifugio* is the 5-hectare site of **Sa Sedda 'e Sos Carros** (adult/reduced €5/3; ⊙ 9am-6pm summer), with the remains of some 150 *nuraghe* huts. But the most interesting ruin is the circular **Temple of the Sacred Well**, surrounded by stone spouts that would have fed spring water into a huge central basin.

sunny Mediterranean villa on the main road into town, this smart restaurant showcases local art in its rustic dining hall. Go for house specialities like homemade pasta, local lamb and boar stew. There's a verandah for alfresco dining.

★ **Gologone**   SARDINIAN €€€
(☏ 0784 28 75 12; www.sugologone.it; Località Su Gologone; meals around €55; ⊙ 12.30-3pm & 8-10pm) Nestled at the foot of mountains, this rural retreat is a delight, with a bougainvillea-draped terrace for balmy evenings. The local Cannonau red goes well with the Sardinian classics on the menu – *culurgiones* (ravioli), *porceddu* (suckling pig) roasted to crackling perfection on a big open fire, and *seadas al miele* (light pastries with ricotta and bitter honey).

❶ Getting There & Away

ARST runs frequent buses from Via Roma to Nuoro (€1.50, 20 minutes, up to 12 daily Monday to Saturday, six on Sunday).

BARBAGIA

Sardinia's geographic and spiritual heartland is a tough, mountainous area known as the Barbagia. The name derives from the Latin term 'Barbaria' (itself derived from the Greek word *barbaros* – foreign person,

barbarian) which the Romans gave the area after repeatedly failing to subdue it. The dramatic topography and tough-as-hobnail-boots locals kept the legionnaires out, just as they have since kept the outside world at arm's length with their fierce sense of inward-looking pride. Sardinian dialects are widely spoken in the Barbagia villages, and traditional festivities are celebrated with fervour. It's still common to see older women walking down the street wearing traditional black vestments.

Dozens of distinct village communities dot the Barbagia region, which is divided into districts around the Gennargentu. To the north is **Barbagia Ollolai**, to the west **Mandrolisai**, to the southwest the **Barbagia di Belvi**, and in the south there's the **Barbagia di Seulo**. It's a sparsely populated area and travel routes between the towns are usually limited to a single twisty road. Public transport is limited, so it's definitely worth hiring a car if you want to tour the area with any freedom.

At the region's heart are the bald, windswept peaks of the Gennargentu massif, the highest points on the island – ranging from around 1000m to 1834m (Punta La Marmora) – and the centre of the Parco Nazionale del Golfo di Orosei e del Gennargentu, Sardinia's largest national park.

The best sources of information are the tourist offices in Nuoro, Oliena and Dorgali.

Useful maps include Belletti Editore's *Parco del Gennargentu* (1:100,000; €6) and *Nuoro* (1:200,000; €7.50), a map of the province of Nuoro published by Litografia Artistica Cartografica.

Barbagia Ollolai

Orgosolo

POP 4510

High in the brooding mountains, Orgosolo is Sardinia's most notorious town, its name a byword for the banditry and violence that blighted this part of the island for so long. The violence has now largely dried up and the town is attempting, with some success, to reinvent itself as an alternative tourist attraction. Nowadays, it's not unusual to see visitors walking down the main strip photographing the vibrant graffiti-style murals that adorn the village's buildings. But once the day-trippers have gone, the villagers come out to reclaim their streets – the old boys to sit staring at anyone they don't recognise and the lads with crewcuts to race up and down in their mud-splattered cars.

◉ Sights & Activities

Five kilometres to the south of the town, the SP48 local road heads up to the Montes heights. Another 13km south is the **Funtana Bona**, the spring at the source of the Cedrino river. On the way you pass through the tall holm oaks of the **Foresta de Montes**.

Corso Repubblica　　NOTABLE STREET
WWII, the creation of the atomic bomb, the miners strikes of the Iglesiente, the evils of capitalism, women's liberation – Orgosolo is a giant canvas for emotionally charged graffiti. The majority of murals line the main thoroughfare, **Corso Repubblica**, initiated by Professor Francesco del Casino in 1975 as a school project to celebrate the 30th anniversary of the Liberation of Italy. There are now some 200 murals, many of them executed by Casino. Other notable artists include Pasquale Buesca and Vincenzo Floris.

The styles vary wildly according to artist: some are naturalistic, others are like cartoons, and some, such as those on the Fotostudio Kikinu, are wonderfully reminiscent of Picasso. Like satirical caricatures, they depict all the big political events of the 20th and 21st centuries and vividly document the struggle of the underdog in the face of a powerful, and sometimes corrupt, establishment. Italy's own political failings are writ large, including the corruption of the Cassa del Mezzogiorno and Prime Minister Giulio Andreotti's trials for collusion with the Mafia, where speech bubbles mock his court refrain of 'I don't remember'. Even more interesting are the murals depicting recent events. On the corner of Via Monni there are portrayals of the destruction of the two World Trade Center towers (dated 28 September 2001) and the fall of Baghdad (dated 17 April 2003).

Stroll north along Corso Repubblica and you hit **Via Gramsci**, festooned with colourful depictions of revolutionary fighter Che Guevara, and the fathers of communism Marx, Engels and Lenin.

✱ Festivals & Events

Festa dell'Assunta　　PARADE
You'll catch Orgosolo at its best during the Festa dell'Assunta (Feast of the Assumption) on 15 August, when folk from all around the Barbagia converge on the town for one of the region's most colourful processions.

✖ Eating

Corso Repubblica has a few inexpensive cafe-bars and pizzerias.

Cortile del Formaggio　　DELI €
(Corso Repubblica 216; ◷10am-1pm & 3-8pm Mon-Fri summer) The Cortile del Formaggio is

NUORO & THE EAST BARBAGIA OLLOLAI

BOOKS IN THE BARBAGIA

The small Barbagia village of Gavoi (p183) is the most unlikely place to bump into the likes of Jonathan Coe, Nick Hornby and Zadie Smith. But these best-selling British authors are just some of the big-name literary stars who have descended on the village for its annual literary festival.

A rare success story, **L'Isola delle Storie** has gone from strength to strength since it was inaugurated in 2003. For four days in early July, the village is transformed into an outdoor stage, hosting readings, concerts, theatrical performances, screenings and seminars. For more information check out the festival's website, www.isoladellestorie.it.

a tiny courtyard house where you can buy fresh, smoked and roasted varieties of *fiore sardo* – Sardinian *pecorino* made from raw ewe's milk.

Il Portico PIZZERIA €

(☑ 0784 40 29 29; Via Giovanni XXIII; pizza €4-7, meals €16-20; ☉ noon-2pm & 7-10pm Mon-Sat, noon-2pm Sun) An excellent pizzeria-cum-restaurant serving flavoursome, woody pizzas and superb local vegetables and meats, such as *cinghiale in umido* (wild boar stew) with olives. The airy dining room and friendly, smiley service add to the pleasure.

🛈 Getting There & Away

Regular buses make the run to/from Nuoro (€2, 35 minutes, six daily Monday to Saturday, three on Sunday).

Mamoiada

POP 2580

Just 14km south of Nuoro, the undistinguished village of Mamoiada stages Sardinia's most compelling carnival celebrations.

Mamuthones wearing shaggy sheepskins and beastly wooden masks run riot in Mamoiada during February's carnival festivities. If you can't be here then, you can get an idea of what it's all about at the **Museo delle Maschere Mediterranee** (www.museodellemaschere.it; Piazza Europa 15; adult/reduced €4/2.60; ☉ 10am-1pm & 3-6pm Tue-Sun). The exhibit includes a multimedia presentation and garbed mannequins wearing the famous sheepskins.

There are a couple of shops in the village selling the wooden masks worn by the *mamuthones*. Don't expect to pay less than €100 for a good one.

For a quick bite to eat, try **La Campagnola** (☑ 0784 5 63 96; Via Satta 2; pizzas €4.50-6, meals around €25; ☉ noon-2.45pm & 7.30-10.30pm Tue-Sun), a sunny eatery with pizza and pasta on the menu.

🛈 Getting There & Away

Infrequent ARST buses connect with Nuoro (€2, 20 minutes, five daily Monday to Saturday, one Sunday).

Orani & Ottana

The main reason to make a stop in the grey, sleepy village of **Orani** is the **Museo Nivola** (www.museonivola.it; Via Gonare 2; adult/reduced €2.50/1.50; ☉ 9am-1pm & 4-9pm summer, 9am-1pm & 4-8pm winter). The museum celebrates the original sculpture and sand-casting techniques of Costantino Nivola, the son of a local stonemason, who fled Sardinia under Fascist persecution in 1938 and subsequently spent most of his life working in America. Part of the museum was closed for renovation at the time of writing.

Five kilometres south of Orani, the village of **Sarule** sits at the foot of the 1083m Monte Gonare. The village itself doesn't really warrant a stop but a narrow side road to the east leads up to the 17th-century **Santuario di Nostra Signora di Gonare**, a grey buttressed church sitting atop a lone conical hill. It's an important pilgrimage site, and every year between 5 and 8 September villagers celebrate the Madonna di Gonare with horse races, singing and dancing.

More dramatic by far are the carnival celebrations that are held on Shrove Tuesday at **Ottana**, an otherwise lacklustre village con-

---

CARNIVAL IN MAMOIADA

Mamoiada's carnival festivities kick off with the **Festa di Sant'Antonio** on 16 and 17 January. According to myth, Sant'Antonio stole fire from hell to give to man, and to commemorate the fact bonfires are lit across the village. But more than the fireworks, it's the appearance of the *mamuthones*, the costumed characters for which the village is famous, that gives the festival its sinister edge. These monstrous figures re-emerge on Shrove Tuesday and the preceding Sunday for the main Carnevale celebrations. Up to 200 men don shaggy brown sheepskins and primitive wooden masks to take on the form of the *mamuthones*. Weighed down by up to 30kg of *campanacci* (cowbells), they make a frightening spectacle. Anthropologists believe that the *mamuthones* embodied all the untold horrors that rural man feared, and that the ritual parade is an attempt to exorcise these demons before the new spring. The *mamuthones* are walked on a long leash held by the *issokadores*, dressed in the guise of outmoded gendarmes, whose job it is to drive them out of town.

PEAK BAGGER

It's relatively easy to reach Sardinia's two highest peaks from either Fonni or Desulo. You'll find the turn-off for the **Bruncu Spina** trailhead 5km out of Fonni, on the road to Desulo. From here a 10km road winds through treeless territory to the base of a ski lift. One kilometre before the lift you'll see a steep dirt trail to the right, from where a 3km track leads right to the summit (1829m). From here you have broad, sweeping views across the island in all directions. If you're here in winter, there's some modest skiing on these slopes, and a daily lift pass and ski hire costs around €30. For details, see www.bruncuspina.com.

For a view from 5m higher you need to march about 1½ hours south to **Punta La Marmora** (1834m). Although it looks easy enough from Bruncu Spina, you need a good walking map or a guide, as well as sufficient water in summer.

sidered to be the dead centre of Sardinia. Said to rival those of Mamoiada, festivities culminate in a parade of costumed *boes* (men masked as cattle) herded down the streets by their masters, the *merdules* (masked men symbolising our prehistoric ancestors).

Gavoi

POP 3010

Famous for its *fiore sardo* and literature festival, Gavoi is one of Barbagia's prettier villages. It has a pristine historic centre, with a small web of narrow lanes hemmed in by attractive stone houses. Three kilometres to the south, **Lago di Gusana** shimmers amid thick woods of cork, ilex and oak trees.

⊙ Sights & Activities

A popular fishing spot, the lake and surrounding countryside provide plenty of sporting opportunities.

Chiesa di San Gavino   CHURCH
In Gavoi village centre, the Chiesa di San Gavino was built in the 16th century to a Gothic-Catalan design, as evidenced by the plain red trachyte facade and splendid rose window. From the piazza outside the church, cobbled alleyways lead up through the medieval *borgo* (village).

Barbagia No Limits   ADVENTURE SPORTS
(☏ 0784 182 03 73; www.barbagianolimits.it) Barbagia No Limits is a local operator that can organise a whole range of outdoor activities, including trekking (€25 to €45), kayaking (€35), canyoning (€35 to €60), caving and jeep tours (€35 to €65).

✖ Eating

Up in the village proper, the rustic **Ristorante Sante Rughe** (☏ 0784 5 37 74; www.santarughe.it; Via Carlo Felice 2; meals around €30;

⊙12.30-2.30pm & 8-10.30pm Thu-Tue) serves fine local cooking. Speciality of the house is *lu su erbuzzu*, a heart-warming soup of bacon, sausage, cheese and beans flavoured with wild herbs. The cheese selection is a further treat and the pizzas (evenings only) are excellent.

ⓘ Getting There & Away

By bus, there are four weekday ARST connections from Nuoro (€3, one hour 10 minutes) and one on Sunday.

Fonni & Desulo

At 1000m Fonni is the highest town in Sardinia and has a sizeable rural community. It's also a popular base for hikers, who come to explore Sardinia's highest peaks – the Bruncu Spina (1829m) and the Punta La Marmora (1834m).

⊙ Sights

From Fonni, a scenic country road (SP7) wriggles south through parkland and oak forests, with grandiose views of limestone peaks rising out of deeply folded valleys. After 25km you hit **Desulo**, a long string of a town that was once three separate villages. There's nothing much to see but, like Fonni, it provides a good base for hikers, given its proximity to the Gennargentu.

Basilica della
Madonna dei Martiri   BASILICA
(off Piazza Europa) At Fonni's highest point is the imposing 17th-century Basilica della Madonna dei Martiri, one of Barbagia's most important baroque churches. Surrounded by *cumbessias* (pilgrims' huts), it's famous for a revered image of the Madonna that's said to be made from the crushed bones of martyrs. In June it's the focus of Fonni's two

main feast days, the Festa della Madonna dei Martiri on the Monday after the first Sunday in June and the Festa di San Giovanni on 24 June.

Outside the church a couple of trees have been curiously transformed by sculptors into religious scenes, notably one showing the crucified Christ and the two thieves.

✖ Eating

**Ristorante Albergo
Il Cinghialetto**   SARDINIAN €€
(🖉0784 5 76 60; Via Grazia Deledda 193; meals €25-30; ☉12.30-2.30pm & 7.30-10pm Tue-Sun) Down in the modern part of the village is this simple, friendly pick, dishing up meaty Sardinian fare and pizza. An open fire keeps things toasty in winter.

❶ Getting There & Away

From Nuoro, there are ARST buses to both Fonni (€3, 40 minutes, eight daily Monday to Saturday, two Sunday) and Desulo (€4.50, one hour 20 minutes, daily Monday to Saturday).

Barbagia di Belvi

Aritzo

POP 1445

A vivacious mountain resort, Aritzo has been attracting visitors since the 19th century. Its cool climate and alpine character (its elevation is 796m) caught the imagination of the Piedmontese nobility, who came here to hunt boar in its forests. There are plenty of marked walking trails around the village, most of which are fine to walk alone.

The lucrative business of snow gathering put Aritzo on the map. For some five centuries the village held a monopoly on snow collection and supplied the whole of Sardinia with ice. Snow farmers, known as *niargios*, collected the white stuff from Punta di Funtana Cungiada (1458m) and stored it in straw-lined wooden chests before sending it off to the high tables of Cagliari.

◉ Sights & Activities

Museo Etnografico   MUSEUM
(Via Guglielmo Marconi; admission incl Sa Bovida Prigione Spagnola adult/reduced €2.50/2; ☉10am-1pm & 3-7pm Tue-Sun summer, to 6pm winter) You can see some of the historic straw-lined chests used by snow farmers in the Museo Etnografico, a small museum in the village

elementary school. The museum also has a motley collection of traditional costumes and masks, as well as various farm implements and household objects.

**Sa Bovida
Prigione Spagnola**   HISTORIC BUILDING
(Via Guglielmo Marconi; admission incl Museo Etnografico adult/reduced €2.50/2; ☉10am-1pm & 3-7pm Tue-Sun summer, to 6pm winter) Just off the main drag is this 16th-century prison. Built of dark grey schist stone, this chilling jail was used as a maximum-security facility right up until the 1940s.

Chiesa di San Michele Arcangelo   CHURCH
The Chiesa di San Michele Arcangelo retains little of its early Gothic origins. Inside, you'll find an 18th-century pietà and a 17th-century portrait of San Cristoforo. Across the road from the church is a viewpoint from where you can see the fortress-like limestone peak **Monte Texile**, now a protected natural monument.

✯ Festivals & Events

Today the ice the village is most celebrated for is its tangy lemon sorbet, which you can try at the mid-August **Festa de Sa Carapinna**.

On the last Sunday of October, people crowd the streets in search of chestnuts at the **Sagra delle Castagne.**

Barbagia di Seulo

To the south and east of Aritzo, the Barbagia di Seulo sidles up to the rocky heights of the Gennargentu national park. It's a lonesome area of small towns and snaking mountain roads.

From Aritzo, the road southeast winds through the small towns of **Seulo** and **Seui**, the latter of which has a few traditional houses with wrought-iron balconies. Continue upwards towards Ussassai until after about 9km you come to a fork in the road at Cantoniera Arcueri. Follow for Montarbu and after another 9km or so you'll see Sardinia's largest *nuraghe*, the Nuraghe Ardasai, on your left. Built on a rocky outcrop dominating the deep Flumendosa River valley, it's worth a stop for the views. Six kilometres further on is a turn-off for the dense **Foresta di Montarbu**, towered over by the 1304m mountain of the same name. Several kilometres beyond this is the even more impressive **Monte Perda Liana**, at 1293m.

SORGONO

As much for the getting there as the being there, Sorgono rewards
heart of the Mandrolisai, the remote hilly area to the west of the G
is surrounded by huge tracts of forest, full of ilex, cork, chestnut a
vicinity, the **Biru 'e Concas** archaeological site boasts one of the
menhirs in Sardinia, while, in town, the **Cantina del Mandrolis**
IV Novembre 20; ⊙9am-1pm & 3-5.30pm Mon-Fri, 9am-1pm Sat) is on
important wine producers, famous for its beefy reds. You are more than welcome to
the wines before you buy.

By train you can reach Sorgono on the *trenino verde*. If you're driving it's a 25km
twisty drive from Aritzo on the SS295.

From here the road descends, leading
eventually to the southern bank of the **Lago
Alto della Flumendosa**. The main road
skirts the lake eastward for about 10km before crossing over the *trenino verde* tourist
train line a couple of times and reaching the
main Nuoro–Lanusei road.

SARCIDANO

Southwest of Aritzo the rugged mountains
flatten out to the broad Sarcidano plain,
littered with *nuraghi* and other mysterious
prehistoric sites.

Laconi

POP 2090

Straddling the SS128 as it twists south, Laconi is a charismatic mountain town, with a
blissfully slow pace of life and bucolic views
of green, rolling countryside. Its cobbled
lanes hide some genuine attractions, including an intriguing archaeological museum,
the house where Sardinia's only saint was
born, and a castle-topped woodland park.

◉ Sights & Activities

Museo delle Statue Menhir   MUSEUM
(http://menhirmuseum.it; Via Amsicora; adult/
reduced €5/3; ⊙10am-1pm & 3.30-7pm Tue-Sun
summer, to 6pm winter) Occupying an elegant
19th-century *palazzo* (mansion), this delightful museum exhibits a collection of 40
menhirs. Taken from sites across the surrounding area, these stark anthropomor-
phic slabs are strangely compelling. Little
is known of their function, but it's thought
that they were connected with prehistoric
funerary rites. In the backlit gloom they appear all the more mysterious, the shadows

emphasising the faded sculptural relief that
suggests whether they are 'male' or 'female'.

If you find this interesting you may want
to detour to **Pranu Mutteddu** further south,
where you can see them in situ.

Casa Natale di Sant'Ignazio   SHRINE
(Via Sant'Ignazio 58) FREE Tucked down a cobbled lane, this simple two-roomed house is
where St Ignatius was apparently born (he
died in 1781). The back room, with its low
wood ceiling and stone walls, is a good example of what a village house must have
looked like in the 18th century. Here a shrine
to St Ignatius is illuminated by candlelight.
There are no official hours for visitors but
the house is almost always open; if it's not,
ask at the tourist office.

Parco Aymerich   PARK
(⊙8am-8pm summer, to 4pm winter) Continue
past the saint's house on Via Sant'Ignazio
and take the first left to reach this smashing 22-hectare park. Among the exotic trees
(including an impressive cedar of Lebanon
and several eucalyptuses), springs, lakes
and grottoes, you'll find the remains of an
11th-century castle, the **Castello Aymerich**.
From here you have wonderful views across
the park and the greenery surrounding
Laconi.

ℹ Information

Laconi is also one of the few towns in this area
with a **tourist office** (☑0782 86 70 13; Piazza
Marconi; ⊙9am-1pm Mon-Fri). It's over the road
from the neoclassical Municipio (Town Hall) on
the central piazza.

ℹ Getting There & Away

BUS

Bus services to Laconi are fairly limited. There
are connections with Isili (€2, 35 minutes, daily),

minutes, three daliy Monday to
Barumini (€2.50, 35 minutes, two
to Saturday), but most run very
morning or in the late afternoon.

trenino verde (€11, 1¼ hours, one on Tuesday) calls in here on its way north from Mandas.
The station is about 1km west of the town centre.

South of Laconi

Santuario Santa Vittoria

Beyond the small village of Serri, the **Santuario Santa Vittoria** (adult/reduced €4/2, incl Nuraghe Arrubiu & Prano Mutteddu €9/4.50; ☺ 9.30am-1pm & 3-8.30pm summer, to 5pm winter) is one of Sardinia's most important nuraghic settlements, which was first studied in 1907 and later excavated in 1962. What you see today is divided roughly into three zones. The central area, the Recinto delle Riunioni (Meeting Area), is a unique enclave thought to have been the seat of civil power. A grand oval space is ringed by a wall within which are towers and various rooms.

Beyond it is the religious area, which includes a Tempietto a Pozzo (Well Temple), a second temple, a structure thought to have been the Capanna del Sacerdote (Priest's Hut), defensive trenches, and a much later addition, the Chiesa di Santa Vittoria, a little country church after which the whole site is now named. Separated from both areas is the Casa del Capo (Chief's House), so-called

perhaps because it is the most intact habitation, with walls still up to 3m high. Finally, a separate area, made up of several circular dwellings, is thought to have been the main residential quarter. Still, only four of about 22 hectares have been fully uncovered.

Santuario Santa Vittoria is at the end of a scenic road (on one side you look over La Giara di Gesturi (p80), on the other the land rises up towards the Gennargentu).

Nuraghe Is Paras

About 20km south of Laconi, by the sports centre in Isili, the **Nuraghe Is Paras** (adult/reduced €3/2; ☺ 9.30am-12.30pm & 4-7pm summer, 9.30am-12.30pm & 3.30-5pm winter, closed Mon) is notable for its striking *tholos* which, at 11.8m, is the highest in Sardinia.

Nuraghe Arrubiu

Rising out of the Sarcidano plain, about 10km south of Orroli and off the SP10, is the **Nuraghe Arrubiu** (adult/reduced €4/2, incl Santuario Santa Vittoria & Prano Mutteddu €9/4.50; ☺ 9.30am-1pm & 3-8.30pm daily summer, to 5pm winter), which takes its Sardinian name from the red colour of the trachyte stone. This impressive structure, centred on a robust tower, now about 16m high, is thought to have reached 30m. Surrounding it is a five-tower defensive perimeter and the remains of an outer wall and settlement. The artefacts found here indicate that the Romans made good use of it.

SAFE & RESPONSIBLE TREKKING

Before embarking on a walking trip, consider the following points to ensure a safe and enjoyable experience, and help preserve the ecology and beauty of Sardinia.

➤ Pay any fees and possess any permits required by local authorities.

➤ Obtain reliable information about physical and environmental conditions along your intended route (eg from park authorities).

➤ Be aware of local laws, regulations and etiquette about wildlife and the environment.

➤ Walk only in regions, and on trails, within your realm of experience.

➤ Hillsides and mountain slopes, especially at high altitudes, are prone to erosion. Stick to existing trails and avoid shortcuts.

➤ Where there is no toilet, bury your waste. Dig a small hole 15cm (6in) deep and at least 100m (320ft) from any watercourse.

➤ Carry out all your rubbish. You can reduce waste by taking minimal packaging.

➤ Always seek permission from landowners to camp.

➤ Be aware that weather conditions and terrain vary significantly from one region, or even from one trail, to another.

Pranu Mutteddu

Near the village of Goni, **Pranu Mutteddu** (www.pranumutteddu.com; adult/reduced €4/2, incl Nuraghe Arrubiu & Santuario Santa Vittoria €9/4.50; ☺ 9.30am-1pm & 3-8.30pm daily summer, to 5pm winter) is a unique funerary site dating to the neolithic Ozieri culture (between the 3rd and 4th millennia BC). The site is dominated by a series of *domus de janas* (literally 'fairy houses'; tombs cut into rock) and some 50 menhirs, 20 of them lined up east to west, presumably in symbolic reflection of the sun's trajectory. The scene is reminiscent of similar sites in Corsica and is quite unique in Sardinia.

Pranu Mutteddu is a 20km drive east of Senorbì and the SS128, close to the tiny village of Goni. The website pinpoints its exact location.

GOLFO DI OROSEI

For sheer stop-dead-in-your-tracks beauty, there's no place like this gulf, forming the seaward section of the **Parco Nazionale del Golfo di Orosei e del Gennargentu** (www. parcogennargentu.it), Sardinia's largest national park, which takes in the Supramonte plateau and the Golfo di Orosei. Here the high mountains of the Gennargentu abruptly meet the sea, forming a crescent of dramatic cliffs riven by false inlets, scattered with horseshoe-shaped bays and lapped by exquisitely aquamarine waters. Beach space is at a premium in summer, but there's room for everyone, especially in the rugged, elemental hinterland.

Orosei

POP 6150

Scenically positioned at the gulf's northernmost point and surrounded by marble quarries and fruit orchards, Orosei is an unsung treasure. Over centuries the silting of the Rio Cedrino (Cedrino river), Spanish neglect, malaria and pirate raids took their toll on the town, once an important Pisan port. Today the atmospheric historic centre is laced with cobbled lanes that twist to pretty stone-built houses, medieval churches and leafy piazzas for kicking back and watching the world go slowly by.

◉ Sights & Activities

Presiding over Piazza del Popolo is the **Chiesa di San Giacomo**, a Spanish-style church with an imposing neoclassical facade and a series of tiled domes. Its terrace commands views of the mountains rising above a jumble of terracotta rooftops. Across the square, the baroque ochre-hued **Chiesa del Rosario**, with its trio of wooden crosses, wouldn't look out of place in a spaghetti western. The lane leading up from its left-hand side takes you to Piazza Sas Animas and the stone church of the same name, with a vaguely Iberian feel about it. Opposite rises the 15m-high hulk of the **Prigione Vecchia**, also known as the Castello, a tower left over from a medieval castle. The most appealing of all Orosei's churches, though, is the humble yet highly atmospheric 8th-century **Chiesa di San Sebastiano** on Piazza San Sebastiano, with a trio of stone arches and a reed-woven ceiling.

On the fringes of the historic centre, the **Chiesa di Sant'Antonio** dates largely from the 15th century. The broad, uneven courtyard surrounding the church is lined with squat *cumbessias* and has a solitary Pisan watchtower.

✖ Eating & Drinking

S'Hostera SARDINIAN €€
(☎ 380 7014355; www.shosteraorosei.it; Via Grazia Deledda 56; meals €25-35; ☺ 7.30-11pm) A simple trattoria on the face of things, S'Hostera stands head and shoulders above most restaurants in Orosei when it comes to food. The carpaccio, homemade pasta, freshly grilled fish and specialities like *zuppa di pesce* (a rich shellfish stew) and *orata alla vernaccia* (sea bass cooked in white wine) are big on flavour and served with a smile.

Yesterday Bar BAR
(Via Nazionale 48; ☺ 5pm-1am) Troubles indeed seem far away at this arty Beatles-themed bar, set around a pocket-sized courtyard. It's a chilled spot for a snack, cold beer or cocktail.

❶ Information

Tourist Office (☎ 0784 99 83 67; Piazza del Popolo 13; ☺ 10am-12.30pm) Once in town, follow signs for the *centro* to wind up in Piazza del Popolo, where you'll find the local tourist office.

WORTH A TRIP

ROAD TRIPPING

It's well worth getting behind the wheel for the sheer pleasure of driving the 60km of road snaking from **Dorgali** to **Santa Maria Navarrese**. The serpentine, and at times hair-raising, SS125 threads through the mountaintops and the scenery is distractingly lovely: to the right the ragged limestone peaks of the Supramonte rear above the woods, and gorges carve up the broad valley; to the left the mountains tumble down to the bright-blue sea. The views are tremendous as you crest the vertiginous **Genna 'e Silana** pass at 1017m. Shortly afterwards, near the turn-off for Urzulei, you'll spot the sign for **Formaggi Gruthas** (www.gruthas.it; Località Giustizieri) where you can stop to buy farm-fresh *pecorino*, goat's cheese and ricotta. The buttresslike peak of 647m Monte Scoine marks the approach to Santa Maria Navarrese. For a great detour on the return trip, follow signs from Lotzorai towards Talana, then Urzulei. The road twists through an otherworldly canyonlike valley, shadowing a river and passing reddish granite outcrops, vineyards and cactus-dotted slopes, before looping back up to the SS125 at Urzulei.

The drive is perhaps most beautiful in spring when wildflowers cloak the hills and broom adds a splash of gold to the landscape. Aside from the odd hell-for-leather Fiat, traffic is sparse, but you should take care at dusk when wild pigs, goats, sheep and cows rule the road and bring down loose rocks from the heights.

ⓘ Getting There & Away

Several daily buses run to Orosei from Nuoro (€3, about one hour, five daily Monday to Saturday, three daily Sunday) and Dorgali (€2, 25 minutes, two daily Monday to Saturday, one Sunday).

Around Orosei

Orosei Beaches

A strip of pale-golden sand fringed by topaz waters runs 5km south and undergoes several name changes along the way: **Spiaggia Su Barone**, **Spiaggia Isporoddai** and **Spiaggia Osalla**. All are equally tempting and are mostly backed by pine stands, giving you the option of retreating to the shade for a picnic or even a barbecue (facilities are scattered about the pines). Past a big breakwater you can wander from Spiaggia Osalla around to **Caletta di Osalla**, the second stretch of sand after the main beach.

Orosei's beachfront satellite, **Marina di Orosei**, is 2.5km east of the town proper. The beach marks the northern end of the Golfo di Orosei; from here you can see the gulf arched in all its magnificence to the south. The Marina di Orosei beach is closed off to the north by the Rio Cedrino and behind the beaches stretch the **Stagni di Cedrino** lagoons.

More fabulous beaches necklace the coast to the north of Marina di Orosei, including pine-backed **Cala Liberotto** and Cala Gine-pro, which appeals to families with its shallow water and campground. Further north still is **Bidderosa**, which forms part of a nature reserve and never gets too busy because visitor numbers are restricted. A 4km trail leads down to the beach, a dreamy vision of sugar-white sand, flanked by lush pines, eucalypts and juniper, and lapped by cobalt-blue waters. The northern stretch sidles up to another fine beach, **Berchida**.

Galtelli

POP 2450

Crouched at the foot of Monte Tuttavista and hemmed in by olive groves, vineyards and sheep-nibbled pastures, Galtelli is quite the village idyll. Its tiny medieval centre is a joy to wander, with narrow lanes twisting to old stone houses and sun-dappled piazzas. If you fancy tiptoeing off the map for a while, this is the place.

◉ Sights & Activities

Museo Etnografico Sa Domo 'e sos Marras   MUSEUM
(Via Garibaldi 12; adult/reduced €3/2.50; ☺9.30am-12.30pm & 4.30-7.30pm Tue-Sun summer, 10am-noon & 4-6pm winter) Housed in an 18th-century noble villa, the Museo Etnografico Sa Domo 'e sos Marras contains a fascinating collection of rural paraphernalia. There's a loom made out of juniper wood, a donkey-drawn millstone and a small display of children's toys. Upstairs, rooms have been decorated in their original 18th-century style.

Grazia Deledda Trail   WALKING TOUR

The town's main claim to fame is its mention in Grazia Deledda's most famous novel *Canne al Vento* (Reeds in the Wind). The tourist office can advise on Grazia Deledda itineraries which take in the **Chiesa di San Pietro**, a Romanesque-Pisan church near the town cemetery, and the 17th-century **Casa delle Dame Pintor**, the fictional home of the Pintor sisters in *Canne al Vento*, a passionate tale about the demise of a family of aristocratic landowners.

ℹ Information

Tourist Office (☎0784 9 01 50; www.galtelli. com; Via Sassari 12; ☺9am-noon & 4-7pm summer, 10am-noon Tue-Sun winter) Information is available from the tourist office up in the old town.

ℹ Getting There & Away

Up to five daily buses connect Galtelli and Orosei (€1.20, 10 minutes).

Dorgali

POP 8550

Dorgali is a down-to-earth town with a grandiose backdrop, nestled at the foot of Monte Bardia and framed by vineyards and olive groves. Limestone peaks rear above the centre's pastel-coloured houses and steep, narrow streets, luring hikers and climbers to their summits.

For more outdoor escapades, the dramatic Golfo di Orosei and spectacularly rugged Supramonte are within easy striking distance.

◉ Sights & Activities

In town, you can browse the shops selling local craftwork – Dorgali is famous for its leathergoods, ceramics, carpets and filigree jewellery. Once you've done that you've pretty much exhausted Dorgali's opportunities and can turn your attention to the area's great limestone wilderness. There are several outfits in Dorgali that organise 4WD excursions, hikes and caving expeditions.

Museo Archeologico   MUSEUM

(www.museoarcheologicodorgali.it; Via Vittorio Emanuele; adult/reduced €3/1.50; ☺9.30am-1pm & 3.30-6pm, to 7pm Jul & Aug) This modest archaeology museum spells out the region's past in artefacts, from pre-nuraghic to medieval times.

Cooperative Ghivine   ADVENTURE SPORTS

(☎338 8341618, 0784 9 67 21; www.ghivine.com; Via Lamarmora 69/e) This one-stop action shop organises a huge array of activities, from boat tours to free climbing and archaeology expeditions. Trekking highlights include Gola Su Gorropu (€40), Tiscali (€40), Monte Corrasi and the gorgeous bays of Cala Luna and Goloritzè.

Sardinia Bike Travel   MOUNTAIN BIKING

(☎340 290183; www.sardiniabiketravel.com; Via Lamarmora 180) This is the place to slip into the saddle to explore the east coast. Sardinia Bike Travel organises mountain biking excursions that follow old shepherd and charcoal burner trails, and rents out mountain bikes, motorbikes and quads.

✗ Eating

Inexpensive snack bars, pizzerias and patisseries dot the main drag, Via Lamarmora.

Ristorante Colibrì   SARDINIAN €€

(☎0784 9 60 54; Via Gramsci 14; meals €30; ☺12.30-2.30pm & 7-10.30pm) Squirrelled away in an incongruous residential area (follow the numerous signs), this lemon-walled restaurant is the real McCoy for meat eaters. Stars of the menu include *cinghiale al rosmarino* (wild boar with rosemary), *capra alla selvatiza* (goat with thyme) and *porceddu*.

ℹ Information

Proloco Dorgali (☎0784 9 62 43; www. dorgali.it; Via Lamarmora 108b; ☺10am-1pm & 4-8pm Mon-Fri) Can provide information on Dorgali and Cala Gonone, including contact details for local trekking outfits and accommodation lists.

ℹ Getting There & Away

ARST buses serve Nuoro (€3, 50 minutes, eight daily Monday to Saturday, four Sunday) and Olbia (€7.50, two hours 50 minutes, two daily Monday to Saturday, one Sunday). Up to seven (four on Sundays) shuttle back and forth between Dorgali and Cala Gonone (€1.20, 20 minutes). You can pick up buses at several stops along Via Lamarmora. Buy tickets at the bar at the junction of Via Lamarmora and Corso Umberto.

North of Dorgali

Grotta di Ispinigoli

A short drive north of Dorgali, the fairytale-like **Grotta di Ispinigoli** (adult/reduced €7.50/3.50; ☺tours on the hour 10am-6pm summer, 10am-noon & 3-5pm winter) cave is a veritable forest of glittering rock formations, including the world's second-tallest stalagmite (the highest is in Mexico and stands at 40m).

Unlike most caves of this type, which you enter from the side, here you descend 60m inside a giant 'well'- at its centre stands the magnificent 38m-high stalagmite. You can admire the tremendous rock formations, many of them sprouting from the walls like giant mushrooms and broccoli, but forget the souvenir snapshots – photography is forbidden.

Discovered by a shepherd in 1950, the caves weren't explored in earnest until the 1960s. A deep network of 15km of caves with eight subterranean rivers has since been found. Cavers can book tours of up to 8km through one of the various tour organisers in Dorgali or Cala Gonone. Nuraghic artefacts were discovered on the floor of the main well, and Phoenician jewellery on the floor of the second main 'well', another 40m below. On the standard tour you can just peer into the hole that leads into this second cavity, known also as the **Abbisso delle Vergini** (Abyss of the Virgins). The ancient jewellery found has led some to believe that the Phoenicians launched young girls into the pit in rites of human sacrifice.

Linger for dinner and panoramic sunset views at the **Ristorante Ispinigoli** (☑0784 9 52 68; www.hotelispinigoli.com; meals around €30; ⊙noon-3pm & 7.15-9pm Mon-Fri, advance bookings only Sat & Sun), just below the entrance to the cave. Located in Hotel Ispinigoli, the well-known restaurant rolls out local delights such as *fregola con arselle* (Sardinian pasta and clam soup), herb-infused roast kid and a waistline-expanding selection of *formaggi*.

S'Abba Frisca

Around 5km from Grotta di Ispinigoli, on the country road towards Cala Gonone, **S'Abba Frisca** (☑335 6569072; www.sabbafrisca.com; adult/reduced €7.50/5; ⊙9am-noon & 3-7pm summer, by appointment winter) is a veritable trove of ethnographic treasures. It's worth a visit for the gardens alone, bristling with centuries-old olive trees, fragrant *macchia* (Mediterranean scrub) and medicinal plants. Other displays bringing Sardinia's cultural heritage to life include a shepherd's hut built from basalt and juniper, old olive and wine presses, and a traditional *pane carasau* bread oven.

Serra Orrios & S'Ena 'e Thomes

Eleven kilometres northwest of Dorgali, at kilometre 25 on the SP38, is **Serra Orrios** (adult/reduced €5/2.50; ⊙hourly tours 9am-1pm & 3-6pm daily, shorter hours winter), a ruined nuraghic village inhabited between 1500 and 250 BC. Nestled among olive groves, the remains comprise a cluster of 70 or so horseshoe-shaped huts grouped around two basalt-hewn temples: Tempietto A, thought to be used by visiting pilgrims, and Tempietto B, for the villagers. A third temple has also been discovered, leading experts to surmise that this may have been a significant religious centre. There's a diagram near the entrance, which helps to understand the site, as the guided tours are in Italian only.

From here you could continue north to **S'Ena 'e Thomes** (⊙dawn-dusk) FREE, a fine example of a *tomba di gigante* (literally 'giant's tomb'; ancient mass grave) built at the height of the nuraghic period. Situated 3km north of the crossroads on the Nuoro–Orosei road, S'Ena 'e Thomes is signposted to the right. A narrow path winds through marshy farmland to the central, oval-shaped stone stele (3.65m tall and 2.10m wide) which closes off the ancient burial chamber.

South of Dorgali

Gola Su Gorropu

Sardinia's most spectacular **gorge** (☑328 876563; www.gorropu.info; adult/reduced €5/3.50; ⊙10.30am-5pm) is flanked by limestone walls towering up 400m in height. The endemic *Aquilegia nuragica* plant grows here, and at quieter times it's possible to spot mouflon and golden eagles. From the Rio Flumineddu riverbed you can wander about 1km into the boulder-strewn ravine without climbing gear; follow the markers. After 500m you reach the narrowest point, just 4m wide, and the formidable **Hotel Supramonte**, a tough 8b multipitch climb up a vertical 400m rock face.

To hike into the gorge you'll need sturdy shoes and sufficient water. There are two main routes. The most dramatic begins from the car park opposite Hotel Silana at the **Genna 'e Silana** pass on the SS125 at kilometre 183. The 8km trail takes 1½ to two hours one way, so allow at least four hours for the return trek, longer if you plan to

TREKKING TO TISCALI

The hike to Tiscali is pure drama, striking into the heart of the limestone Supra
The trailhead is at the **Sa Barva bridge** over the green Rio Flumineddu, the sam
ing point as the route to Gola Su Gorropu. You'll need sturdy footwear for some easy
hopping, but most of the path – marked with red arrows – is easygoing, and canopies
of juniper and cork oaks afford shady respite. The 7km trail is signposted and takes between 1½ and two hours; allow five hours for the return hike, breaks and a visit to Tiscali.
Time permitting, you can visit the **Domus de Jana Biduai** (⊙dawn-dusk) **FREE** on the
road back to Dorgali. Stepping stones cross the river to this ancient nuraghic tomb.

There are many companies in Oliena, Dorgali and Cala Gonone offering guided tours
to Tiscali. Typically these cost around €40 per person and sometimes include lunch.

spend time exploring the gorge itself. While the descent is mostly easygoing, the climb back up is considerably tougher.

The hike weaves through holm oak woods, boulder-strewn slopes and cave-riddled cliffs. For a bird's-eye perspective of the gorge, you could take the 6km ridge trail from the car park to 888m **Punta Cucuttos**. It takes around 1½ hours one way.

The second and slightly easier route (14km) to Gorropu is via the **Sa Barva bridge**, about 15km from Dorgali. To get to the bridge, take the SS125 and look for the sign on the right for the Gola Su Gorropu and Tiscali between kilometres 200 and 201. Take this and continue until the asphalt finishes after about 20 minutes. Park here and cross the Sa Barva bridge, after which you'll see the trail for the Gola signposted off to the left. From here it's a scenic two-hour hike along the Rio Flumineddu to the mouth of the gorge (four hours return).

If you'd prefer to go with a guide, Sandra and Franco at the **Cooperativa Gorropu** (☑ 0782 64 92 82, 333 8507157; www.gorropu.com; Via Sa Preda Lada 2, Urzulei) arrange all sorts of excursions and activities, from trekking and canyoning to caving and cookery courses; see the website for prices. Their base is in Urzulei, but they also run a small info centre at Genna 'e Silana pass.

Tiscali

Hidden in a mountain-top cave deep in the Valle Lanaittu, the mysterious nuraghic village of **Tiscali** (adult/reduced €5/2; ⊙ 9am-7pm daily summer, to 5pm winter) is one of Sardinia's archaeological highlights. Dating from the 6th century BC and populated until Roman times, the village was discovered at the end of the 19th century. At the time it was rel-

atively intact, but since then grave robbers have done a pretty good job of looting the place, stripping the conical stone-and-mud huts down to the skeletal remains that you see today.

It's an eerie sight: jumbled ruins amid holm-oak and turpentine trees huddled in the twilight of the limestone overhang. The inhabitants of Sa Sedda 'e Sos Carros (p180) used it as a hiding place, and its inaccessibility ensured that the Sards were able to hold out here until well into the 2nd century BC.

Cala Gonone

POP 1280

Climbers, divers, sea kayakers, beachcombers and hikers all find their thrill in Cala Gonone. Why? Just look around you: imperious limestone peaks frame grandstand views of the Golfo di Orosei, sheer cliffs dip into the brilliant-blue sea, trails wriggle through emerald-green ravines to pearly-white beaches. It is quite magnificent. Even getting here is an adventure, with each hairpin bend bringing you ever closer to a sea that spreads out before you like a giant liquid mirror.

Gathered along a pine-shaded promenade, the seaside resort still has the low-key, family-friendly vibe of the small fishing village it once was. August aside, the beaches tend to be uncrowded and the room rates affordable. Bear in mind that the resort slumbers in winter, closing from October until Easter.

⊙ Sights & Activities

Cala Gonone is the perfect launchpad for exploring the gulf's most alluring bays, which are scattered like horseshoes along the coast. The fact that the best beaches and grottoes

...rdinia, you should try to make an excursion along the 20km ...olfo di Orosei by boat. Intimidating limestone cliffs plunge head... ...ed by pretty beaches, coves and grottoes. With an ever-changing ...ebbles, seashells and crystal-clear water, the unfathomable forces ...d to create a sublime taste of paradise. The colours are at their ...hen the sun starts to drop behind the higher cliffs.

...la Gonone you head south to the Grotta del Bue Marino (p193). ...ne cave is **Cala Luna**, a crescent-shaped strand closed off by high cliffs to the s~~~~ ...la Sisine is the next beach of any size, also a mix of sand and pebbles and backed by a deep, verdant valley. **Cala Biriola** quickly follows, and then several enchanting spots where you can bob below the soaring cliffs – look out for the patches of celestial-blue water.

   Cala Mariolu is arguably one of the most sublime spots on the coast. Split in two by a cluster of bright limestone rocks, it has virtually no sand. Don't let the smooth white pebbles put you off, though. The water that laps these beaches ranges from a kind of transparent white at water's edge through every shade of light and sky blue and on to a deep purplish hue.

can only be reached by hiking or dropping anchor gives them added castaway appeal.

Cala Gonone Beaches
BEACH

In town, the small shingle **Spiaggia Centrale** is good for a quick dip, but the finest beaches lie further south. Further along the waterfront is the narrow sandy strip **Spiaggia Palmasera**, interrupted by rocky stretches (watch out for sea urchins). Better for splashing around in the aquamarine sea is **Spiaggia Sos Dorroles**, 1km south, backed by a striking yellow-orange rock wall.

Cala Fuili
BEACH

About 3.5km south of town (follow Via Bue Marino) is this captivating rocky inlet backed by a deep green valley. From here you can hike over the cliff tops to **Cala Luna**, about two hours (4km) away on foot. The trail cuts a scenic path through juniper and mastic trees and is easy to navigate, with triangle-circle symbols marking handy rocks. The coastal views are breathtaking as you approach Cala Luna.

Cala Luna
BEACH

A favourite with rock climbers, this crescent-shaped bay is wildly beautiful, backed by a lush ravine, framed by cave-pitted cliffs and pummelled by exquisite turquoise waters. Linger after the boats have gone and you'll pretty much have the bay to yourself. If your navigation skills are good, you could continue along a tough,

unmarked trail to the striking **Arco Lupiru** rock arch (4km; around 1½ hours) or **Cala Sisine** (11km; four hours). Wild camping on the beaches is not permitted, but the authorities have been known to turn a blind eye to discreet campers.

Cala Cartoe
BEACH

Tucked away 10km to the north of town, this is another gorgeous beach, a silky strip of fine white sand bordered by emerald waters and dense woodland. It gets predictably busy in August, but visit out of season and it will probably be all yours. To get here you'll need a car; take Via Marco Polo from behind the port and follow it to a T-junction; the cove is signposted to the right (north).

Nuraghe Mannu
ARCHAEOLOGICAL SITE

(adult/reduced €3/2; ⏰ 9am-11am & 5-7pm summer, to 5pm Apr-Jun & Sep-Oct, closed Nov-Mar) To get an eagle-eye view over the coast, follow the signs off the Cala Gonone–Dorgali road to this *nuraghe*. After 3km the rocky track peters out at a wild headland where you can see nearly the entire curve of the gulf. The location is romantic, set above a lush gorge and with silver-grey blocks strewn beneath the olive trees. First inhabited around 1600 BC, the tower is a modest ruin, but you can still see niches in the central chamber.

The Romans took a shine to the *nuraghe* and, looking at the traces of former dwellings, you can contrast their geometric forms with the elliptical shapes of their predecessors.

Grotta del Bue Marino CAVE

(adult/reduced €10/5; ⊘ guided tours hourly 10am-noon & 3-5pm summer, 11am-3pm winter, groups only Oct-Mar) It's a scenic 40-minute hike from Cala Fuili, or a speedy boat ride from Cala Gonone, to this enchanting grotto. It was the last island refuge of the rare monk seal (*'bue marino'* or 'sea ox' as it was known by local fishermen). The watery gallery is impressive, with shimmering light playing on the strange shapes and neolithic petroglyphs within the cave. Guided visits take place up to seven times a day. In peak season you may need to book.

Acquario di Cala Gonone AQUARIUM

(www.acquariocalagonone.it; Via La Favorita; adult/reduced €10/7.50; ⊘ 10am-6pm summer) Check out the local marine life before taking the plunge at this shiny new aquarium, designed by architects Peter Chermayeff and Sebastiano Gaias. The 25 tanks bubble with sea horses, jellyfish, rays and – moving into more tropical waters – clownfish and anemones.

☞ Tours

A huge fleet of boats, from large high-speed dinghies to small cruisers and graceful sailing vessels, is on hand at Cala Gonone to whisk you along the beautiful coastline. Boats operate from March until about October – dates depend a lot on demand. Prices vary according to season with 'very high season' being around 11 to 25 August. You can get information at agencies around town or at the booths at the port.

Prima Sardegna ADVENTURE SPORTS

(☑ 0784 9 33 67; www.primasardegna.com; Via Lungomare Palmasera 32; ⊘ 9am-1pm & 4-8pm summer) This is the go-to place for climbing information, assistance and helmet rental (€5). It also arranges guided excursions to Tiscali and Gorropu (€40), as well as hikes and 4WD tours in the Supramonte. Daily bike/scooter/single kayak/double kayak rental costs €24/48/30/55 respectively. Mini cruises along the Golfo di Orosei cost between €35 and €45.

Nuovo Consorzio Trasporti Marittimi BOAT TOUR

(☑ 0784 9 33 05; www.calagononecrociere.it; Porto Cala Gonone) This outfit offers tours including return trips to Cala Luna (€12), Cala Sisine (€18), Cala Mariolu (€26) and Cala Gabbiani (€26). A trip to the Grotta del Bue Marino costs €16.50, including entry to the cave. All tours are around €5 more in July and August. See the website for timetables.

Argonauta DIVING

(☑ 347 5304097, 0784 9 30 46; www.argonauta.it; Via dei Lecci 10) PADI-accredited Argonauta offers a range of water-based activities, including snorkelling tours (€30 adults, €25 kids), scuba diving taster sessions (€60), cavern and wreck dives (€45) and canyoning excursions (€40). They also run PADI Bubblemaker courses for children (€60).

Cielomar BOAT TOUR

(☑ 0784 92 00 14; Località Palmasera) This outfit runs day-long tours along the gulf, costing from €40 per person, as well as hiring out *gommone* (motorised dinghies) for €80 to €120 per day, excluding petrol which usually costs an extra €25 or so.

Dolmen ADVENTURE SPORTS

(☑ 347 6698192; www.sardegnadascoprire.it; Via Vasco da Gama 18, Cala Gonone) Dolmen is a reliable operator running 4WD tours into the Supramonte, canyoning excursions to the Gorropu and boat trips to the Grotta del Bue Marino. Bikes, scooters and dinghies are also available for hire. Call ahead for times and prices.

✖ Eating & Drinking

There are plenty of snack bars, gelaterias and pizzerias on or near the waterfront. Most places close from November to March.

Agriturismo Nuraghe Mannu SARDINIAN €€

(☑ 0784 9 32 64; www.agriturismonuraghemannu.com; off the SP26 Dorgali–Cala Gonone Rd; meals €25-35; ⊘ 8-11pm) Scenically perched above the gulf and nestled amid silvery olive groves, this *agriturismo* puts on a mouth-watering spread. Loosen a belt notch for a feast of home-produced *pecorino*, salami, olives and wine, followed by handmade pasta, succulent roast kid or lamb and (phew!) Sardinian sweets.

Il Pescatore SEAFOOD €€

(☑ 0784 9 31 74; Via Acqua Dolce 7; meals €25-35; ⊘ noon-2.30pm & 7-10.30pm) Fresh seafood is what this authentic place is about. Sit on the terrace for sea breezes and fishy delights, such as pasta with *ricci* and spaghetti with clams and *bottarga* (mullet roe), all washed down with half a litre of the crisp house white (€5).

SELVAGGIO BLU

For serious hikers, the Selvaggio Blu is the stuff of myth: an epic seven-day, 45km trek along the Golfo di Orosei's wild and imperious coastline, traversing thickly wooded ravines and taking in bizarre limestone formations, caves and staggeringly sheer cliffs. Both the scenery and the walking are breathtaking (in every sense of the word!) on what is often hailed as Italy's toughest trek.

The trail follows the starkly eroded – and often invisible – trails of goatherds and charcoal burners, teetering around cliffs that plunge into the dazzlingly blue sea. Because of its challenging terrain, the trek requires a good level of fitness and some climbing experience for the short climbs and abseiling involved. The seven-day duration is based on the assumption that you will walk six to eight hours a day. You'll also need to come prepared with a bivi bag or an ultralight tent, climbing gear (including two 45m ropes), a roll mat, sturdy boots, a compass, map and ample food.

A guide is recommended as the trail is not well signposted and there's no water en route (guides can arrange for it to be dropped off by boat). The website www.selvaggioblu.it (in Italian) will give you itchy feet.

The author of *Arrampicare a Cala Gonone* (€18) and *Il Sentiero Selvaggio Blu* (€16), **Corrado Conca** (☑ 347 2903101; www.corradoconca.it) is Sardinia's hiking and climbing guru, and a brilliant guide for the trek. Bank on paying around €500 per person. Corrado is often up in the hills climbing, so give him plenty of notice.

Road House Blues ITALIAN €€
(☑ 0784 9 31 87; Lungomare Palmasera 28; pizza €5-10, meals €20-30; ☺ noon-midnight) For a swift beer or a bite to eat, this relaxed haunt on the seafront *lungomare* (promenade) is just the ticket. Dig into pizzas named after rock bands – think Parma ham, Pearl Jam – and Sardinian dishes such as homemade pasta with chard and *pecorino*. House wine is a snip at €8 a litre.

Ristorante Acquarius PIZZERIA, SARDINIAN €€
(☑ 0784 9 34 28; Lungomare Palmasera 34; pizza €6-10, meals around €30; ☺ noon-11.30pm) There's always a good buzz at this cheery *lungomare* contender. The pizzas done in a wood-fired oven are spot-on, as is the *porceddu* served with rosemary potatoes. Refresh your palate with a tangy myrtle sorbet.

ℹ Information

You can find information at the very helpful **tourist office** (☑ 0784 9 36 96; www.dorgali.it; Viale Bue Marino 1a; ☺ 9.30am-1.30pm & 3-7pm May-Sep, 9.30am-1.30pm Oct-Apr, 9.30am-8pm Jul & Aug) in the small park off to the right as you enter town.

For trekking and climbing maps and guides, check out **Namaste** (Via Colombo di Gometz 11, Cala Gonone; ☺ 6.40am-1pm & 4-8pm). It stocks Maurizio Oviglia's *Pietra di Luna* (€50), a comprehensive rock-climbing guide covering the Cala Gonone, Jerzu and Baunei areas; Corrado Conca's *Il Sentiero Selvaggio Blu* (€17), covering the stunning seven-day Selvaggio Blu hike; and

La Sardegna in Bicicletta (€13.90) detailing 1000km of cycling routes. You can also pick up walking maps and travel guides here.

ℹ Getting There & Away

Buses run to Cala Gonone from Dorgali (€1.20, 20 minutes, seven daily Monday to Saturday, four Sunday) and Nuoro (€3.50, 70 minutes, six daily Monday to Saturday, three Sunday).

OGLIASTRA

Wedged in between Nuoro and Cagliari, the much smaller province of Ogliastra boasts some of the island's most spectacular scenery. Inland, it's a vertical land of unspoilt valleys, silent woods and windswept rock faces, while the coastal stretches become increasingly dramatic the nearer you get to the Golfo di Orosei.

Getting around the area is fairly slow, particularly inland. Distances are not great, but the mountainous landscape means roads are steep and often very twisty. You can travel by bus, but it would be better to hire a car if you want to get to the more out-of-the-way corners.

Tortolì & Arbatax

POP 10,800

Your impressions of Tortolì, Ogliastra's bustling provincial capital, depend on where you've arrived from. If you've just disembarked from the mainland you might be disappointed with the town's mundane, modern appearance. But if you've just emerged from the heavy silences of the interior you might find the cheery souvenir shops and large roadside hotels a welcome change.

Ferries from Cagliari arrive at Arbatax port, about 4km away down Viale Monsignor Virgilio, and you can also arrange boat tours up the coast to the Golfo di Orosei from here. In summer you can catch the *trenino verde* from the station in Arbatax.

◉ Sights & Activities

Tortolì and Arbatax are resort towns and sights are few and far between. At the port you can arrange boat excursions up the coast to the beaches and grottoes of the Golfo di Orosei. Costs vary but are typically around €40 to €50 per person.

Arbatax Beaches   BEACH
You can hit the beach on either side of Arbatax. You'll find the fine sandy bays and crystal waters of **Spiaggia Orri**, **Spiaggia Musculedda** and **Spiaggia Is Scogliu Arrubius** about 4km south of hotel-dotted Porto Frailis. Or continue even further south to the pristine cliff-flanked cove of **Spiaggia Cala Francese** at **Marina di Gairo**.

Rocce Rosse   NATURAL LANDMARK
If you have a moment in Arbatax, head across the road from the port and behind the petrol station to the Rocce Rosse (red rocks). Like the ruins of some fairy-tale castle, these bizarre, weather-beaten rock formations dropping into the sea are well worth a camera shot or two, framed in the distance by the imperious cliffs of the southern Ogliastra and Golfo di Orosei.

✖ Eating

You'll find a handful of so-so pizzerias and snack bars by the port in Arbatax; nearly all are closed from November to March.

Da Capo   PIZZERIA, ITALIAN €€
(☑0782 62 01 27; www.ristorantedacapo.com; Via E Berlinguer 7; lunch €10-14, menus €25-35; ⊙12.30-2pm & 7-10.30pm Tue-Sun) You'll receive the warmest of welcomes at this family-run restaurant on the fringes of Tortolì. Go for pizzas baked to an original family recipe and Sardinian classics that make the most of what is seasonal – homemade tagliatelle with angler fish and asparagus sauce, filet of beef cooked in Cannonau red wine and the like.

Ittiturismo La Peschiera   SEAFOOD €€
(☑0782 66 44 15; Spiaggia della Cartiera, Arbatax; meals around €30; ⊙1-3pm & 8-10.30pm Jun-Sep) What swims in the Med in the morning lands on plates by lunchtime at this Ittiturismo, run by Tortolì's fishing cooperative. The humble shack may be in the back of beyond, but it's worth going the extra mile for fish this fresh. Follow the signs as you enter town and walk five minutes along a reed-fringed river bank. Reservations are essential.

La Bitta   ITALIAN €€€
(☑0782 66 70 80; www.hotellabitta.it; Località Porto Frailis; meals €40-55; ⊙12.30-2.30pm & 7.30pm) For fine dining in Porto Frailis, you can't beat La Bitta. Dress up smart for exquisitely prepared food – think handmade pasta with skate and dill pesto and macaroni with artichokes, ricotta and *bottarga*.

❶ Information

You can get information from the **tourist office** (☑0782 60 09 00; Via Mameli 22, Tortolì; ⊙8.30am-2pm Mon-Fri) in Tortolì.

On the main strip in Tortolì, **Frailis Viaggi** (☑0782 62 00 21; www.frailisviaggi.it; Via Roma 12, Tortolì; ⊙9am-1pm & 4.30-8pm Mon-Fri) is a useful travel agency where you can book ferry tickets, as well as organise boat excursions (€650 per person) and hire a car.

❶ Getting There & Away

BOAT
The main ferry company serving Arbatax is **Tirrenia** (☑892123; www.tirrenia.it). Ferries sail to/from Genoa (€59, 18 hours, twice weekly), Civitavecchia (€49, 10½ hours, twice weekly) and, from late July to August, Fiumicino (€63, 4½ hours, twice weekly). There are also connections with Cagliari (€33, 5¼ hours, twice weekly) and Olbia (€31.50, 4½ hours, twice weekly).

BUS
ARST buses connect Tortolì with Santa Maria Navarrese (€1.20, 15 minutes, 11 daily Monday to Saturday, two Sunday), Dorgali (€5, one hour 50 minutes, daily Monday to Saturday) and Nuoro (€7, 2½ to three hours, four daily Monday to Saturday), as well as many inland villages. Local buses 1 and 2 run from Arbatax to Tortolì and, in the case of the latter service, to the beach and hotels at nearby Porto Frailis.

TRAIN
Near the port, you'll find the terminus for the **trenino verde** (☑070 58 02 46; www.treninoverde. com), a scenic train that runs between Arbatax

and Mandas (€20, five hours) twice daily, except Tuesday, from mid-June to mid-September. Stops include Lanusei, Arzana, Ussassai and Seui. The route between Arbatax and Mandas is the most scenic on the island, chugging along a gravity-defying track through some of Sardinia's least accessible mountain terrain.

North of Tortolì & Arbatax

Lotzorai

POP 2190

Located about 6km north of Tortolì, Lotzorai is not of enormous interest in itself but it sits behind some glorious pine-backed beaches, such as **Spiaggia delle Rose**. To find the beach, follow the signs to the three camping grounds that are clustered just behind it.

On the country road towards Talana, 4km from Lotzorai, you'll find the farm-style **Ristorante Sant'Efisio** (☑0782 64 69 21; www.hotel-santefisio.com; Località Sant'Efisio; meals €20-30; ⊙12.30-2.30pm & 7.30-9.30pm; 🖫). Choose between the rustic dining room and flowery terrace to relax and enjoy classic regional dishes. Try handmade *culurgiones* filled with fresh cheese and mint, spit-roasted wild boar and *tacculas* (quails wrapped in myrtle) with a local Cannonau red.

Santa Maria Navarrese

At the southern end of the Golfo di Orosei sits the unpretentious and attractive beach resort of Santa Maria Navarrese. Shipwrecked Basque sailors built a small church here in 1052, and then dedicated it to Santa Maria di Navarra on the orders of the Princess of Navarre, who happened to be one of the shipwreck's survivors. The church was set in the shade of a grand olive tree that is still standing – some say it's nearly 2000 years old.

⊙ Sights & Activities

Lofty pines and eucalyptus trees back the lovely beach lapped by transparent water (with more sandy stretches to the south).

About 500m further north of the centre is the small pleasure port, where various operators run cruises up the increasingly wild coastline.

Isolotto di Ogliastra NATURAL LANDMARK
Offshore are several islets, including the Isolotto di Ogliastra, a giant hunk of pink porphyritic rock rising 47m out of the water. The leafy northern end of the beach is topped by a watchtower built to look out for raiding Saracens.

Monte Scoine MOUNTAIN
Rearing above the landscape like a bishop's mitre, the crag of Monte Scoine attracts climbers to its bolted routes (4b to 6b), especially in summer when it stays shady until midafternoon.

Consorzio Marittimo Ogliastra BOAT TOUR
(☑0782 61 51 73; www.mareogliastra.com) The Consorzio Marittimo Ogliastra charges between €35 and €45 per person for tours that take in sea caves and several stunning swimming spots, such as Cala Goloritzè, Cala Mariolu and Cala Sisine. Children pay half price or less.

✘ Eating & Drinking

Nascar ITALIAN €€
(☑0782 61 53 14; www.albergohotelnascar.it; Via Pedras 1; meals around €30; ⊙7.30-10pm) A family-run affair, Nascar stands head and

---

KAYAKING IN CARDEDU

There's no better way to explore Ogliastra's coves, grottoes and rock formations than with Francesco Muntoni, who knows the area like the back of his hand.

In Cardedu, 16km south of Tortolì, you'll find **Cardedu Kayak** (☑0782 7 51 85, 348 9369401; www.cardedu-kayak.com; Località Perda Rubia, Cardedu), where you can spend the day with your paddle slicing rhythmically through the turquoise waters. Francesco caters to kayakers of all levels. His courses cost €150 for five two-hour lessons and, if you would prefer to go it alone, daily kayak rental starts at €25 per person. Be sure to bring your swimming gear in summer. Francesco can help organise longer tours and 'nautical camping' if you fancy fishing from the kayak and sleeping on the secluded beaches.

On request, Francesco can also arrange cycling tours into the fertile valleys surrounding Cardedu, hikes along the striking red granite coastline, and walks up into the surrounding hills, which are littered with fine examples of *domus de janas* (prehistoric chamber tombs).

shoulders above most places in town, with its romantic garden terrace, slick vaulted interior and faultless service. The food is superb, too, with antipasti, fresh pasta and just-caught fish on the menu, all expertly paired with wines from local vineyards.

Bar L'Olivastro
BAR

(☏ 0782 61 55 13; Via Lungomare Montesanto 1; ⊙ 8am-1am) Down by the seafront and set up on shady terraces below the branches of the town's centuries-old olive tree, Bar L'Olivastro is a relaxed spot for a coffee and snack by day, or a cocktail by night. There is occasional live music.

❶ Getting There & Around

A handful of ARST buses link Santa Maria Navarrese with Tortolì (€1.20, 15 minutes, 11 daily Monday to Saturday, two Sunday), Dorgali (€4, 1½ hours, two daily), Nuoro (€7, 2½ hours, four daily Monday to Saturday, two Sunday) and Cagliari (€9.50, four hours, four daily Monday to Saturday).

Baunei & the Altopiano del Golgo

POP 3740

Continuing north along the coast, after about 9km you hit the shepherd's town of Baunei. There's little reason to stop off here, but what is seriously worth your while is the 10km detour up to the Altopiano del Golgo, a strange, other-worldy plateau where goats, pigs and donkeys graze in the *macchia* and woodland. From here a road snakes down to the rock spike of Pedra Longa, a natural monument and also the starting point for Sardinia's star coastal trek, the Selvaggio Blu.

◎ Sights & Activities

★ Cala Goloritzè
BEACH

The last beachette of the gulf, Cala Goloritzè rivals the best. At the southern end, bizarre limestone figures soar away from the cliffside. Among them is jaw-dropping Monte Caroddi or the **Aguglia**, a 148m-high needle of rock beloved of climbers. Follow the signs from the Cooperativa Goloritzè at the Golgo plateau and it's a gentle 4.5km or about an hour's walk down (and a slightly tougher 1½ hours back) to Cala Goloritzè.

Suitable for families, the easygoing hike along an old mule trail takes you through a beautiful limestone canyon shaded by juniper and holm oaks, passing cliffs honeycombed with caves, dramatic rock arches, overhangs and pinnacles en route.

After you've been walking for around 15 minutes you'll get your first tantalising glimpses of the bay and a sea so blue it will make you gasp. Keep an eye out for a traditional sheepfold and the idiosyncratic spike of the Aguglia as you approach the bay. Steps lead down to the half-moon of bone-white pebbles; this is a perfect picnic spot. Bring along your bathers for a dip in the deliciously warm, astonishingly blue waters.

Il Golgo
NATURAL LANDMARK

Follow the signs from Baunei up a 2km climb of impossibly steep switchbacks to the plateau. Head north following the Su Sterru (Il Golgo) sign for less than 1km, then leave your vehicle and walk over to this remarkable feat of nature – a 270m abyss just 40m wide at its base. Its funnel-like opening is now fenced off but, knowing the size of the drop, just peering into the dark opening is enough to bring on the vertigo.

Chiesa di San Pietro
CHURCH

Standing lonesome on the Golgo plateau is this late-16th-century church, a humble construction flanked to one side by *cumbessias* – rough, largely open stone affairs which are not at all comfortable for the passing pilgrims who traditionally sleep here to celebrate the saint's day.

Salinas Escursioni
WALKING

(☏ 340 5665739, 360 692431; www.supramonte-selvaggio.it; Via Pisa 4) If you want to strike out on foot on the old mule trails, into holm oak and juniper woods and along the limestone cliffs of the Supramonte, these guys will help you do it. They arrange guided walks ranging from two-hour hikes to Pedra Longa to the six-day Selvaggio Blu trek.

Cooperativa Goloritzè
HIKING

(☏ 368 7028980; www.coopgoloritze.com) This highly regarded cooperative arranges excursions ranging from trekking to 4WD jeep trips. Many treks involve a descent through canyons, such as the Codula di Luna or the Codula de Sisine, to the Golfo di Orosei's dreamy beaches. Staff at the refuge also organise guides and logistical support for walkers attempting Sardinia's once-in-a-lifetime Selvaggio Blu trek (p194). Prices for the excursions vary depending on the itinerary, which you can agree on beforehand, and how many people are in the group.

DON'T MISS

ON THE TRAIL IN ULASSAI

The dramatic limestone and dolomite cliffs, or *tacchi*, that rear above Ulassai make this fabulous hiking and climbing territory. Trekkers can strike out on foot into the **Bruncu Pranedda** canyon or head 7km southwest to view the totally arresting **Cascata Lequarci** waterfall, with wispy threads that plummet almost 100m over a vertical rock face. The waterfall is at its most spectacular after heavy rainfall. You can make a day of it by bringing a picnic to enjoy in the verdant surrounds of the **Santuario di Santa Barbara**, a quaint Romanesque chapel.

Eating & Drinking

Locanda Il Rifugio   SARDINIAN €€
(✆ 368 7028980; www.coopgoloritze.com; Località Golgo; meals €25-35; ⊘ 1-3pm & 8-11pm summer) Managed by the Cooperativa Goloritzè, this beautifully converted farmstead puts on a generous spread of regional fare such as *ladeddos* (potato gnocchi) and spit-roasted kid and suckling pig, washed down with local Cannonau red.

Inland Ogliastra

Jerzu

POP 3280

Known as the Citta del Vino (Wine Town), Jerzu is famous for its full-bodied Cannonau red wine. The town is set precariously on a mountainside, its steeply stacked buildings surrounded by imposing limestone towers, known as *tacchi* (heels), and some 650 hectares of vineyards. Each year about 50,000 quintals of grapes are harvested to make two million bottles of wine at the **Antichi Poderi di Jerzu** (✆ 0782 7 00 28; www.jerzuantichipoderi.it; Via Umberto 1; ⊘ 8.30am-1pm & 2.30-7pm Mon-Sat), the town's modern cantina. Guided visits and tastings can be arranged by calling in advance.

Ulassai & Osini

POP 1550

Heading north from Jerzu you're in for some scenic treats as the road licks a tortuous path around the titanic mountains to Ulassai, dwarfed by the rocky pinnacles of Bruncu Pranedda and Bruncu Matzei. Although nothing special in itself, this small village is surrounded by some of Sardinia's most thrilling and impenetrable countryside, a vast natural playground for outdoor enthusiasts, with superb rock climbing and trekking.

Sights & Activities

⭐**Grotta di Su Marmuri**   CAVE
(adult/reduced €10/6; ⊘ tours 11am, 2pm, 4pm & 6pm May-Sep, 11am, 2.30pm & 5pm Apr, 11am & 2.30pm Oct) High above Ulassai, the mammoth Grotta di Su Marmuri is a 35m-high cave complex. Visits are by guided tour only (minimum of four people), which take you on a one-hour, 1km walk through an underground wonderland festooned with stalactites and stalagmites – some like humungous drip candles, others as delicate as coral. Whatever the temperature outside, it is always chilly down here, so be sure to bring some extra layers.

Scala di San Giorgio   VIEWPOINT
Accessible from the village of Osini, the Scala di San Giorgio is a vertical gully that takes its name from the 12th-century saint who is said to have divided the rock as he walked through the area proselytising in 1117. From the top you get vast views over the valley to the abandoned villages of **Osini Vecchio** and **Gairo Vecchio**, both destroyed by landslides in 1951.

Stazione dell'Arte Maria Lai   GALLERY
(www.stazionedellarte.it; adult/reduced €5/3; ⊘ 9am-7.30pm summer, to 6pm winter) Housed in the old railway station, the outstanding Stazione dell'Arte Maria Lai showcases the emotive works of the late artist Maria Lai. Born in Ulassai in 1919, Maria was one of Sardinia's most important contemporary artists.

Su Marmuri Cooperative Tessile Artigiana   HANDICRAFTS
(www.sumarmuri.it; Via Funtana Serì; ⊘ 8am-noon & 2-7pm Mon-Sat summer, 8am-noon & 2-6pm Mon-Fri winter) For rugs, towels, curtains and bedspreads bearing Maria's naturalistic designs, head to the Su Marmuri Cooperative Tessile Artigiana. Here you'll find a group of dedicated ladies keeping alive traditional hand-looming techniques and you can see the noisy looms in action. Prices start at around €20 for a hand towel.

Accommodation

Best Places to Sleep

→ Il Cagliarese (p200)

→ The Lemon House (p216)

→ Borgo Alba Barona (p210)

Best B&Bs

→ B&B Lu Pastruccialeddu (p211)

→ Casa Solotti (p213)

→ Eleonora B&B (p206)

Best Boutique Hotels

→ Hotel Panorama (p209)

→ Corte Fiorita (p207)

→ Su Gologone (p214)

Where to Stay

So what's it to be? A B&B housed in a restored *palazzo* (mansion) in Nuoro, a chic apartment in Cagliari's medieval Il Castello district, or a back-to-nature *agriturismo* (farm-stay accommodation) snuggled in the depths of Gallura's holm oak forests? With so many atmospheric places to stay, deciding where to base yourself in Sardinia involves so much more than just choosing a bed for the night.

If you are here for the beaches, the island's your oyster: whether it's to be the serene Costa Verde in the southwest, the silky sands of the Costa del Sud in the south, or the celebrity-style glamour of the Costa Smeralda in the north-east. Up for an adventure? Base yourself in laid-back Cala Gonone, Dorgali or Santa Maria Navarrese in the east for rock climbing, high-altitude hiking, water sports and sensational coastal walks.

With a little careful planning, accommodation need not be eye-wateringly expensive either. Outside of high season (mid-June to August), rates invariably drop, often by as much as 50%, and it's much easier to find something on the spur of the moment. Generally, the further you are from the sea, the cheaper it gets. Note that most hotels close from mid-October to Easter.

Pricing

The price indicators in reviews refer to the cost of a double room with private bathroom – and include breakfast unless otherwise noted. Where half board and full board is included, this is mentioned in the price.

CATEGORY	COST
€	less than €100
€€	€100–€200
€€€	more than €200

Agriturismi

Bracing country hikes, sundowners under the olive trees and waking to the sound of braying donkeys – if the thought of this appeals, you'll feel at home in an *agriturismo*. Often immersed in greenery at the end of long dirt tracks, these family-friendly working farms are for those who value peace and quiet over creature comforts.

Housed in a traditional *stazzo* (farmstead) or stone cottage, rooms are simple and snug – expect to pay between €70 and €100 for a double – and breakfasts are copious. Many *agriturismi* give you the choice of half board (€60 to €80 per person) and dinner tends to be a jolly communal affair, with a feast of farm-fresh vegies, cheese, meat and wine. The only catch is that you'll almost certainly need your own wheels.

To search for your country escape by region, visit www.agriturismodisardegna.it, www.agriturismo.it and www.tuttoagriturismo.net.

B&Bs

Like *agriturismi,* B&Bs often offer good value for money, particularly when compared with the prices of local hotels. There is no islandwide umbrella group for B&Bs, but tourist offices can usually provide contact details. In Cagliari, **Domus Karalitanae** (www.domuskaralitanae.it) offers a comprehensive listing of the city's B&Bs. Online listings are available at www.bed-and-breakfast.it.

On average, budget for about €25 to €45 per person per night in a B&B.

Camping

Campers are well catered for in Sardinia, with most campgrounds scenically located on the coast and offering top-notch facilities like swimming pools, restaurants, supermarkets and kids clubs. If inflatable mattresses are not your thing, many campgrounds have well-equipped bungalows. Prices can be surprisingly high in July and August, when advance bookings are recommended. Expect to pay between €30 and €40 for a site for two people, a car and a tent, and extra for showers and electricity. Campgrounds usually open from Easter to mid-October.

So you can picture yourself waking up on that secluded beach, huh? Wild camping is officially not permitted, but out of the main season and away from the resorts, you can often get away with it, providing you keep the noise down and don't light fires. Always get permission to camp on private property.

You can get lists of campgrounds from local tourist offices or online at www.campeggi.com, www.sardegna.camping.it or www.camping.it.

Hostels

Sardinia's six youth hostels are run by the **Italian Youth Hostel Association** (Associazione Italiana Alberghi per la Gioventù; ☑ 06 487 11 52; http://aighostels.it/en), which is affiliated with **Hostelling International** (HI; www.hihostels.com). You'll need to have an HI card to stay at these hostels. Dorm rates range from €15 to €25, including breakfast. All the hostels also have beds in private rooms, typically costing around €20 per person.

Hotels

Hotels in Sardinia (and their rates) vary wildly, from small, family-run *pensioni* (guesthouses) with just a couple of no-frills rooms to the mammoth resort-style villages on the coast with private beaches, tennis courts, spas, the works. Quality varies enormously and the official star system should be taken with a pinch of salt.

For guaranteed character and boutique style look out for **Charme e Relax** (www.charmerelax.it). This Italian association specialises in small to midsized hotels, usually in unique buildings (monasteries, castles, old inns and so on) or special locations.

Tourist offices have booklets listing all local accommodation, including prices.

CAGLIARI & THE SARRABUS

Cagliari

For charm, value and a good old-fashioned welcome, Cagliari's B&Bs outshine its so-so hotels. Stay central in the Marina and Il Castello districts, or bag a bargain by going the extra mile to Villanova.

★ **Il Cagliarese**   B&B €
(Map p42; ☑ 339 6544083; www.ilcagliarese.it; Via Vittorio Porcile 19; s €45-70, d €60-90; ❋ 🤚) Bang in the heart of Marina district, this snug B&B is a find. Mauro bends over backwards to please and his sister, Titziana, plays the cake

fairy at breakfast with her scrumptious pastries and tiramisu. The immaculate rooms sport homey touches such as embroidered fabrics and carved wooden furnishings.

Casa Marina APARTMENT €
(Map p42; ☑327 3042552; www.bandbcasamarina.it; Via Cavour 52; d €60, breakfast per person €5; ☏) You'll be glad you stumbled across Casa Marina, which gives you home-style comfort and a supercentral location for bargain prices. Just paces from the sights and waterfront, the two roomy, light-drenched, high-ceilinged apartments have been done out with flair, and there's a shared kitchen should you wish to rustle up a snack. Alberto is your affable host.

Hostel Marina HOSTEL €
(Map p42; ☑070 67 08 18; www.hostelmarinacagliari.it; Scalette San Sepolcro 2; dm/s/d/q €22/40/60/100; ☀☏) Housed in a beautifully converted 16th-century monastery, this hostel has oodles of historic charm and original features such as vaulting and beams. Many of the spacious, well-kept dorms overlook the city. Help yourself to fresh bread, fruit and coffee at breakfast. Bike hire, sailing courses and Italian classes can be arranged – just ask.

La Peonia B&B €
(☑070 51 31 64; www.lapeonia.com; Via Riva Villasanta 77; s €50-65, d €72-90; ☀☏) Antonello and Vanna are your kindly hosts at this romantic neo-Gothic abode. Turn-of-the-century interiors with polished wood furnishings are a striking contrast to the sleek, monochrome bathrooms. Bus M from Piazza Matteotti pulls up in front of the B&B, 2.5km northeast of town.

Residenza Kastrum B&B €
(Map p42; ☑348 0012280; www.kastrum.eu; Via Canelles 78; s €50-55, d €70-90, q €120-150; ☀☏) This cosy, characterful B&B has marvellous views over the city rooftops to the gulf from its hilltop Castello perch. The simple, spotless rooms are geared up for families (cots are available). Linger over breakfast and memorable sunsets on the terrace.

Il Girasole B&B €
(Map p42; ☑348 1097278; www.ilgirasole.sardegna.it; Vico Barcellona 6; s €45-55, d €60-75; ☀☏) As bright and cheery as a *girasole* (sunflower), this boho-flavoured B&B is crammed with ethnic knick-knacks and African art. Luca is a happy-go-lucky soul and puts on a

decent spread at breakfast. You're welcome to use the kitchen and unwind in the living room or on the terrace.

La Ghirlanda B&B €
(Map p42; ☑070 204 06 10; www.laghirlandacagliari.it; Via Baylle 7; s €60-65, d €80-100, tr €100-125; ☀☏) Antiques and frescoes whisk you back in time at this handsome 18th-century townhouse in the Marina district. The bright, high-ceilinged rooms are tastefully done out in pastel colours and wooden floors. Breakfast at a nearby bar is included in the price.

Rosso e Nero B&B €
(Map p42; ☑349 7463473; www.rossoenerobeb.it; Via Savoia 6; s €43-49, d €66-73; ☀☏) Stefano goes the extra mile to make you feel at home at this B&B in the Marina district. Sightseeing tips, a beach towel, DVDs – whatever you need, just say the word. The brick-vaulted entrance leads through to sunny, immaculate rooms with ample space. Breakfast is a delight with fresh bread, pastries and strong Italian coffee.

Il Profumo del Mare B&B €
(☑338 1448275; Viale Poetto 196; d €50-76; P☀☏) Behind the nondescript facade is this terrific budget pick, just a pebble's throw from Poetto Beach. Breezy rooms are done out in sky blues, and the terrace has cracking sea views. Antonio happily shares his tips on Cagliari. There's free wi-fi and bike rental. Take bus PF or PQ from Piazza Matteotti to Poetto stop, 50m from the B&B.

T Hotel LUXURY HOTEL €€
(☑070 4 74 00; www.thotel.it; Via dei Giudicati 66; s €119-134, d €139-209, ste €249; P☀☏☒) This hard-to-miss steel-and-glass tower adds a dash of contemporary design to the cityscape. The rooms reveal a linear, modish look, and the spa invites relaxation with its hydrotherapy pool, jets and treatments. From Piazza Matteotti, take bus M to Via Bacaredda and walk 200m.

Suite sul Corso B&B €€
(Map p42; ☑ 349 4469789; www.locandadelcorso.
it; Corso Vittorio Emanuele 8; s €50-80, d €80-120,
tr €130-160; ❄ 🛜) Sleep in style at this boutique B&B just off Piazza Yenne. Exposed
stone, floaty fabrics and glass mosaics lend
warmth to the minimalist-chic rooms, all
with flat-screen TVs and kettles. The triple
even has its own whirlpool. The owner's
quirky photography jazzes up the corridors.

Hotel Miramare BOUTIQUE HOTEL €€
(Map p42; ☑ 070 66 40 21; www.hotelmiramare-
cagliari.it; Via Roma 59; s €76-122, d €98-146, ste
€145-235) This boutique four-star hotel sits
right on the sea-facing Via Roma. Rooms are
individually styled and reach from pared-
down contemporary cool to full-on belle
époque glamour, with crimson walls, span-
gly chandeliers and high wooden beds. Wi-fi
is available and kids under 12 stay free.

Villasimius

Spiaggia del Riso CAMPGROUND €
(☑ 070 79 10 52; www.villaggiospiaggiadelriso.
it; Via Degli Aranci 2; camping 2 people, car & tent
€23-42, 4-bed bungalows €100-160; 🛜) 🞕 Set
in a pine grove near the Porto Turistico, this
big beachside campground has tent pitches,
bungalows, a supermarket and a children's
play area. Booking is absolutely essential in
summer.

Hotel Mariposas HOTEL €€
(☑ 070 79 00 84; www.hotelmariposas.it; Via Mar
Nero 1; s €74-188, d €96-238; P ❄ 🛜 ≋) A short
hop from the beach, this low-slung hotel is
set in glorious flower-strewn gardens. The
spacious rooms all have their own terrace
or balcony, and there's an attractive pool for
whiling away an afternoon.

Stella Maris HOTEL €€€
(☑ 070 79 71 00; www.stella-maris.com; Località
Campulongu; half board per person €170-265;
P ❄ 🛜 ≋) On the road to the Porto Turistico, this is a beautiful resort hotel set in
its own pine wood on a frost white beach.
Rooms are stylish, decorated with Sardinian fabrics and tasteful furniture, and the
gardens and split-level pool are perfect for
some R&R.

Costa Rei

Camping Capo Ferrato CAMPGROUND €
(☑ 070 99 10 12; www.campingcapoferrato.it; Via
Cilea 98; camping 2 people, car & tent €28-38;

TOP 10 AGRITURISMI

The best way to experience authentic Sardinian food is to eat at an *agriturismo* (farm-stay
accommodation). There are hundreds dotted around the island, but these are our faves:

Agriturismo Ca' La Somara (p211) This laid-back farm has beautiful gardens, home-
grown vegetarian fare and friendly donkeys.

Agriturismo Sinis (p206) A genuine working farm on the wild, peaceful Sinis Peninsula, with a relaxed vibe, rustic rooms and superb food.

Agriturismo Testone (p213) Surrounded by oak woods, this is a silent retreat, offering
a warm welcome and a feast of home-grown food.

Agriturismo Porticciolo (p208) A friendly 24-hectare farm near Alghero, with 100 pigs.

Agriturismo Su Boschettu (p205) A blissfully relaxed farmstead nestled amid olive
and fruit trees.

Agriturismo L'Oasi del Cervo (p203) A charming country abode with gorgeous
beaches close by and mood-lifting mountain views.

Agriturismo Guthiddai (p214) A delightful whitewashed retreat in the granite
Supramonte.

Agriturismo Nuraghe Mannu (p215) Look over the spectacular Orosei coast at this
terraced jewel.

Agriturismo Li Scopi (p210) This peaceful *agriturismo* reclines in lovingly tended
gardens and is just a short hop from the dazzling white sands of La Cinta beach.

Agriturismo L'Aquila (p203) Drop off the tourist trail for a spell at this comfortable
and rustic working farm, dishing up a feast of home-grown fare.

Apr-Oct) Pitch a tent under the eucalyptus and mimosa trees at this beachfront campground by the southern entrance to the resort. There's a mini club (summer only) and playground for kids.

Albaruja Hotel HOTEL €€
(070 99 15 57; www.albaruja.it; Via C Colombo; s €85-123, d €132-178; P ❀ ❀) The Albaruja is a cut above most of the hotels on the Costa Rei, with attractive villa-style residences nestled in flowery gardens, a kids playground and a palm-rimmed pool. It's just a two-minute walk from the beach.

IGLESIAS & THE SOUTHWEST

Iglesias

B&B Mare Monti Miniere B&B €
(Map p60; 0781 4 17 65, 348 3310585; www.maremontiminiere-bb.it; Via Trento 10; s €30, d €50-60, tr €65; ❀ ❀) A warm welcome awaits at this cracking B&B. Situated in a quiet side street near the historic centre, it has three cheery and immaculately kept rooms with above-par touches like DVD players and bathrobes. Independent of the main house, there's also a smart studio flat with its own kitchen facilities. Thoughtful extras include beach towels and free bike hire.

La Babbajola B&B B&B €
(Map p60; 347 6144621; www.lababbajola.com; Via Giordano 13; s €27-30, d €54-60) Housed in an aristocratic 19th-century townhouse, this characterful B&B offers homey accommodation in the *centro storico* (historic centre). Its three double rooms are spacious and tastefully furnished with patterned floor tiles, bold colours and attractive period furniture. There's also a kitchen and communal TV room. Two of the three rooms share a bathroom.

The Iglesiente

Hotel Golfo del Leone HOTEL €
(0781 5 49 52; www.golfodelleone.it; Località Portixeddu; s €48-58, d €68-90, tr €84-120, q €105-142; P ❀) Set in its own grounds about 1km inland from Portixeddu beach, this cheery year-round hotel has 14 bright, sea-facing rooms. Service is friendly and the helpful staff can organise horse-riding excursions

in the surrounding countryside. The in-house restaurant serves up decent local food for about €25 per head. Half board is also available.

Agriturismo Fighezia AGRITURISMO €
(348 0698303; www.agriturismofighezia.it; s €55-63, d €70-86, tr €90-114, half board per person €50-83; P) One of several *agriturismi* in the lush green hills behind Portixeddu, this tranquil farm-stay boasts soothing views and rustic cabin-style rooms with terracotta tiles, solid wooden fixtures and private terraces. Dinner is served on a large communal table on the terrace of the main house.

Costa Verde

Agriturismo L'Aquila AGRITURISMO €
(347 8222426; www.agriturismolaquila.com; Località Is Gennas, Montevecchio; r per person €30-35, half board per person €49-57; P ❀) A welcoming bolthole in the green wilderness of the Costa Verde, this authentic *agriturismo* offers modest, no-frills rooms, earthy farmhouse food, and stunning views of the surrounding peaks. To get here from Montevecchio, head towards Torre dei Corsari, then take the signposted exit and follow the dirt track for a couple of bumpy kilometres.

Agriturismo L'Oasi del Cervo AGRITURISMO €
(347 3011318; www.oasidelcervo.com; Località Is Gennas, Montevecchio; half board per person €45-60; P) With 15 modest rooms and a remote location in the midst of *macchia*-cloaked hills, this working farm is a genuine country hideaway. It's all very down to earth but the rooms are comfortable enough, the views are uplifting and the homemade food is delicious. You'll see a sign for the *agriturismo* off the SP65 between Montevecchio and Torre dei Corsari.

Carbonia & Around

La Ghinghetta HOTEL €
(078 150 81 43; www.laghinghetta.com; Via Cavour 26, Portoscuso; s/d €80/100, half board per person €130; May-Oct; ❀ ❀) Overlooking the beach at Portoscuso, this lovely seaside hotel combines charm, comfort and cuisine. It has attractive, nautically themed rooms set in a whitewashed fisher's house, and a highly regarded seafood restaurant (meals €38 to €45).

BAG A BARGAIN

Surf the following websites for great deals on last-minute accommodation in Sardinia:

➡ www.alpharooms.com

➡ www.lastminute.com

➡ www.laterooms.com

➡ www.priceline.com

➡ www.travelsupermarket.com

Villaggio Minerario Rosas HOTEL €
(☑0781 185 51 39; www.villaggiominerariorosas.it; Narcao; s €27-32, d €40-50; P �) This one-time pit village near Narcao has been resurrected as a museum-complex-cum-hotel with guest rooms in the miners' former cottages. The rooms are well sized and rustic with plenty of wood, brick and exposed stone in evidence. The cottages come with kitchen facilities and there's an outdoor area for barbecues and picnics.

Southwest Islands

Isola di San Pietro

Hotel California PENSION €
(☑0781 85 44 70; www.hotelcaliforniacarloforte.com; Via Cavallera 15, Carloforte; s €40-60, d €60-100;) This superfriendly family-run *pensione* is situated in a quiet residential street a few blocks back from the *lungomare* (seafront). It's a modest affair but it's open year-round and the spacious, sun-filled rooms are tastefully decorated and, for the price, exceptional value.

Il Ghiro B&B €
(☑338 2050553; www.carlofortebedandbreakfast.it; Piazza Repubblica 7, Carloforte; s €30-45, d €55-85;) Right in the heart of the action, this tiny B&B overlooks a lively central piazza. Its two small rooms impress with wood-beamed ceilings, oil paintings and cheerful colours. Breakfast is served in the reception area, which sits in what used to be a seamstress's shop.

★**Hotel Riviera** HOTEL €€
(☑0781 85 31 13; www.hotelriviera-carloforte.com; Corso Battellieri 26, Carloforte; s €75-125, d €120-190, ste €250-370;) Housed in a red seafront villa, this swank but relaxed four-star hotel exudes Mediterranean chic. The tiled rooms are cool and light, with four-poster beds, understated furniture and marble-clad bathrooms. Some also have sea views and balconies, though these cost up to €30 extra.

Hotel Hieracon HOTEL €€€
(☑0781 85 40 28; www.hotelhieracon.com; Corso Cavour 62, Carloforte; d with view €150-250, without view €100-170; May-Nov;) A throwback to a smarter age, this seafront hotel occupies a stunning art nouveau mansion. Period furniture and original oil paintings adorn the decent-sized rooms, and there's a tranquil garden where you can snooze under the palm trees. To eat at the hotel restaurant, budget for at least €30.

Isola di Sant'Antioco

SANT'ANTIOCO

Hotel Moderno HOTEL €
(☑0781 8 31 05; www.hotel-moderno-sant-antioco.it; Via Nazionale 82; s €50-60, d €80-100, tr €105-132, q €120-142;) A bright, welcoming hotel on the main road into Sant'Antioco town. Rooms are agreeable with orange-salmon colours and big, comfy beds. Downstairs, the seafood restaurant, Ristorante da Achille (open April to October; tasting menus €40 to €60), has an excellent local reputation.

Hotel del Corso HOTEL €
(☑0781 80 02 65; www.hoteldelcorso.it; Corso Vittorio Emanuele 32; s €49-60, d €69-100;) Well positioned in the town centre, this polished three-star hotel sits over the Cafè del Corso, one of Sant'Antioco's smartest and most popular drinking spots. Rooms are well appointed, if rather characterless.

AROUND THE ISLAND

Campeggio Tonnara CAMPGROUND €
(☑0781 80 90 58; www.campingtonnara.it; Località Cala Sapone; camping 2 people, car & tent €14-53, 2-person bungalows €50-120, 4-person bungalows €60-160; Apr-Oct; P) A well-equipped campground near Cala Sapone on the island's west coast. Ideal for relaxing in natural surrounds, it boasts the full gamut of services from a swimming pool and tennis court to shops and an on-site pizzeria.

Hotel Luci del Faro HOTEL €€
(☑0781 81 00 89; www.hotellucidelfaro.com; Località Mangiabarche; d €108-214, half board per person €79-136; mid-Apr–early Nov; P)

Only a few kilometres outside Calasetta, the well-signposted Luci del Faro stands in glorious solitude on an exposed plain near Spiaggia Grande, the island's best-known beach. Popular with cyclists, it's a relaxed, family-friendly place with simple, sunny rooms, an in-house restaurant and sweeping views.

South Coast

Camping Sardegna
CAMPGROUND €

(📞0781 96 70 13; Località Porto Pino; camping 2 people, car & tent €18-25, 4-person caravans €60-75; ☺ Jun-Sep; 📶) This seasonal campground offers basic facilities and sheltered pitches in a pine grove at Porto Pino. There are few frills but the location is great with the beach right on your doorstep.

Campeggio Torre Chia
CAMPGROUND €

(📞070 923 00 54; www.campeggiotorrechia.it; Via del Porto 21, Chia; camping 2 people, car & tent €23-31, 4-person cottages €65-128; ☺ May-Oct) At the popular summer resort of Chia, this busy campground has shady pitches and a series of cottages a few hundred metres from the beach. The cottages, which sleep up to four, come with a double bedroom, bathroom, kitchen facilities and a living room with sofa bed.

B&B Fiore
B&B €

(📞070 924 60 10; www.bedandbreakfastfiore.it; SS195 km 31; d €60-100; 🅿❄📶) A lovely B&B set amid fruit and palm trees. Its three bright, simply furnished rooms open onto verandahs and you can laze in the garden hammock or walk to the pale-sand beach of Porto d'Agumu 800m away. If driving from Chia to Pula, you'll find the B&B off to the left of the SS195.

★Hotel Baia di Nora
HOTEL €€

(📞070 924 55 51; www.hotelbaiadinora.com; Località Su Guventeddu; d €180-430, half board per person €100-220; ☺ Apr-Oct; 🅿❄📶🏊) On the main road from Pula to Nora, this is a swish resort-style set-up with all the trimmings, including a perfectly tended garden, swimming pool and private beach. Rooms are cool and summery with tiled floors and understated furnishings.

Hotel Villa Madau
HOTEL €€

(📞070 924 90 33; www.villamadau.it; Via Nora 84, Pula; s €68-120, d €80-199, tr €90-225; ❄📶) This friendly three-star hotel is in Pula's historic centre, a short hop from Piazza del Popolo. Rooms are individually decorated but the overall feel is light and summery with cheerful blues and yellows, traditional Sardinian fabrics, and cool polished tiles. Note that the local church bells sound pretty loud in the street-facing rooms.

Forte Village
HOTEL €€€

(📞070 92 15 16; www.fortevillage.com; Santa Margherita di Pula; r from €225; 🅿❄📶🏊) This is the godfather of all southern Sardinian resorts. Hidden in a wooded grove behind high security gates, the 250-sq-km resort is an unapologetic bastion of luxury with bungalows, villas and several hotels. Facilities include 10 swimming pools, 21 restaurants, shops, a nightclub and up to 1km of beach frontage.

La Marmilla

★Agriturismo Su Boschettu
AGRITURISMO €

(📞333 4797401, 070 93 98 84; www.suboschettu.it; Località Pranu Laccu, Pauli Arbarei; B&B per person €35, meals around €20-25) Guests are met with a warm Sardinian welcome at this charming farm-stay, nestled amid olive groves and fruit trees near the town of Lunamatrona. The five guest rooms are fairly functional, but the setting is wonderfully relaxing and the food is local and delicious.

Hotel Funtana Noa
HOTEL €

(📞070 933 10 20; www.hotelfuntananoa.it; Via Vittorio Emanuele III 66-68, Villanovaforru; s/d €45/65, half board per person €50.50; ❄) A tasteful three-star housed in a large *palazzo* (historic mansion) just down from the centre of Villanovaforru. The style is rustic with plenty of heavy timber, antique-style furniture and brick arches. Enjoy summer evenings with drinks in the elegant internal courtyard.

Hotel Su Nuraxi
HOTEL €

(📞070 936 83 05; www.hotelsunuraxi.it; Viale Su Nuraxi 6; s €50, d €70-80, half board per person €40-75; 🅿❄📶) This family-run hotel near the Nuraghe Su Nuraxi makes an ideal base for exploring the Giara di Gesturi and the surrounding countryside. Rooms, which are decorated in a simple country style, are set hacienda-style around a central courtyard, and there's a lovely restaurant where you can dine on filling farmhouse food.

ORISTANO & THE WEST

Oristano

★**Eleonora B&B** B&B €

(Map p92; ☑347 4817976, 0783 7 04 35; www.
eleonora-bed-and-breakfast.com; Piazza Eleonora
d'Arborea 12; s €35-60, d €60-75, tr €75-95; ❋ ☎)
This charming B&B scores on all counts:
location – it's in a medieval *palazzo* on
Oristano's central piazza; decor – rooms are
tastefully decorated with a mix of antique
furniture, exposed brick walls, and gorgeous
old tiles; and hospitality – owners Andrea
and Paola are helpful and hospitable hosts.
All this, and it's excellent value for money.

Iride Guesthouse GUESTHOUSE €

(Map p92; ☑0783 7 04 35, 347 4817976; www.guest-
houseiride.com; Via Vincenzo Bellini 29; s €40-60, d
€60-90; ❋☎) This recently opened guesthouse is ideal for longer stays. About 400m
from Piazza Roma, it has six rooms spread
over two floors, each decorated in a crisp,
modern style and equipped with its own
kitchen facilities. Contemporary paintings
and literary quotes adorn the brightly coloured walls, whilst sunlight pours in through the
street-facing windows. No breakfast.

B&B L'Arco B&B €

(Map p92; ☑0783 7 28 49; www.arcobed-
andbreakfast.it; Vico Ammirato 12; s without bathroom €35-40, d without bathroom €60-65; ❋)
This homey B&B is hidden away in a quiet
cul-de-sac near Piazza Martini. There are
only two guest rooms but they are spacious
and tastefully decorated. Breakfast is served
in the family kitchen, and there's a small terrace upstairs.

Duomo Albergo HOTEL €€

(Map p92; ☑0783 77 80 61; www.hotelduomo.net;
Via Vittorio Emanuele II 34; s €65-80, d €108-135;
❋@) Oristano's top hotel is refined and elegantly understated. Behind its discreet facade, guest rooms reveal a low-key look with
traditional fabrics and cooling white tones.
In summer breakfast is served in an internal
courtyard, whilst gourmets can dine on creative Sardinian cuisine at the hotel's highly
rated restaurant, Ristorante Josto al Duomo.

South of Oristano

Horse Country Resort HOTEL €€

(☑0783 8 05 00; www.horsecountry.it; Strada a
Mare 24, Marina di Arborea; r €100-220, half board
per person €71-128; ☺Mar-Oct; ⓟ❋☎❄) This
big four-star resort is part of Marina di Arborea's famous equestrian centre. Set on
a green site near the beach, it offers a full
range of services with up to 1000 beds, two
swimming pools, a health centre and excellent sporting facilities. Staff can arrange
horse riding and excursions to nearby sites
and the Costa Verde.

Sinis Peninsula

Agriturismo Sinis AGRITURISMO €

(☑0783 39 26 53, 328 9312508; www.agrituris-
moilsinis.it; Località San Salvatore; half board per
person €52-65; ❋) Near the dusty hamlet of
San Salvatore, this working farm offers six
guest rooms and wonderful earthy food.
Rooms are frill free but clean and airy, and
views of the lush garden can be enjoyed
from chairs on the patio.

Agriturismo Su Pranu AGRITURISMO €

(☑0783 39 25 61, 329 8925640; www.agriturismo-
supranu.com; Località San Salvatore; half board per
person €52-65; ❋) Run by the same family as
the Agriturismo Sinis, this farm-stay has six
bright guest rooms decorated in a simple
and neat style. There's a shared terrace outside the rooms that looks onto the garden,
perfect for an afternoon *aperitivo*.

Francesca's House APARTMENT €

(☑340 5017464; www.francescahouse.net; Via
Marconi 11, Riola Sardo; for 2 people €60-70,
for 4 people €80-100; ❋@) This is a lovely
self-contained one-bedroom house, ideal for
those who want a base in the area and to
self-cater. The blue house, which can sleep
up to four, is a cosy set-up with a cane roof,
small courtyard and fully functional wood
oven. Note there's a minimum two-night
stay, and weekly rates are available.

★**Hotel Lucrezia** HOTEL €€

(☑0783 41 20 78; www.hotellucrezia.it; Via Roma
14a, Riola Sardo; s €104-114, d €129-174, ste €219-
274; ❋@) Housed in a 17th-century *cortile*
(courtyard house), this elegant hideaway
has rooms surrounding an inner garden
complete with wisteria-draped pergola, fig
and citrus trees. The decor is rustic chic,
with high 18th-century antique beds, period
furniture and eye-catching tiled bathrooms.
Bikes are provided, and the welcoming staff
regularly organise cooking classes. Note
that there's a three-night minimum stay in
August.

Monti Ferru

⭐ **Antica Dimora Del Gruccione**　HOTEL €
(☑ 0783 55 20 35; www.anticadimora.com; Via Michele Obinu 31, Santu Lussurgiu; s/d €60/90, half board per person €75; ❄ 🛜) It's worth overnighting in Santu Lussurgiu just to stay at this charming hotel. Its rooms are spread over two sites: those in the main 17th-century mansion come with high ceilings, creaking parquet floors and heavy brocade fabrics, whilst those over the road boast a more modern look with art deco style furniture and rooftop views. Don't miss the sumptuous breakfast.

Lago Omodeo & Around

⭐ **Mandra Edera**　HOTEL €
(☑ 320 1515170; www.mandraedera.com; Località Mandra Edera; r per person €61-81, half board per person €81-101; ⊙ mid-Apr–Oct; 🅿 ❄ 🛝) The welcoming, family-friendly Mandra Edera is a lovely ranch-style hotel set amid towering oak trees and fruit orchards. Rooms are in bungalows laid out on neat lawns and there's a smart restaurant as well as a pool and the opportunity for horse riding. The hotel is signposted off the SS131 north of Paulilatino.

Bosa & Around

La Torre di Alice　B&B €
(☑ 329 8570064, 0785 85 04 04; www.latorredialice.it; Via del Carmine 7, Bosa; s €35-45, d €55-70; ❄ 🛜) This is a great budget choice in Bosa's medieval centre. Set in a wonderful old tower house near Piazza Episcopio, its five rooms are neat and comfortable, with low brick-vaulted ceilings, wrought-iron beds and relaxing decor. Breakfast is served at the rustic communal table in the kitchen.

⭐ **Corte Fiorita**　HOTEL €€
(☑ 0785 37 70 58; www.albergo-diffuso.it; Via Lungo Temo de Gasperi 45, Bosa; s €50-120, d €65-180; ❄ @) A so-called *albergo diffuso*, Corte Fiorita has beautiful, spacious rooms in four *palazzi* across town: one on the riverfront and three in the historic centre. No two rooms are exactly the same, but the overall look is rustic-chic with plenty of exposed stonework, wooden beams and vaulted ceilings.

APARTMENT & VILLA RENTALS

If you plan to stay in one place for a week or more, self-catering accommodation can be excellent value. For a two- to four-bed apartment, rates are typically between €350 and €600 per week in low season, €500 to €900 in high season. You'll pay double that for a more luxurious villa with a swimming pool and sea views. Be sure to read the small print for additional charges such as electricity, water, bed linen and final cleaning.

Apartments are generally well located and equipped with kitchenettes and terraces or balconies. Seven nights is usually the minimum stay and some apartments have fixed change-over days. You may be required to pay a deposit of around 30% when you book, and some places require the balance to be settled before arrival.

Pick up lists of apartments and villas for rent at local tourist offices, or find one to suit your style on the following websites:

Costa Smeralda Villas (www.costasmeraldavillas.com) Blow-the-budget villas on the Costa Smeralda with luxury trimmings from tennis courts to pools, lemon orchards to private beaches.

Holiday Lettings (www.holidaylettings.co.uk) Great selection of good-value apartments across the island, all searchable by region.

HomeAway (www.holiday-rentals.co.uk) Features around 1500 self-catering options, from country retreats near Alghero to townhouses in Olbia.

Owners Direct (www.ownersdirect.co.uk) An easy-to-navigate website with a wide array of apartments and villas to suit all budgets.

Rent Sardinia (www.rent-sardinia.com) A good selection of 1000 villas and apartments scattered across the island, searchable by location and other criteria.

Sardegne.com (www.sardegne.com) Lists apartment rentals alongside B&Bs, *agriturismi* (farm-stay accommodation) and hotels.

Aghinas HOTEL €€

(☎ 0785 60 58 27; www.aghinas.com; Piazza Carmine 17, Bosa; s €35-95, d €50-150; ❋ 🤶) This friendly little three-star resides in a *palazzo* at the western edge of the historic centre. There's nothing fancy about the high-ceilinged rooms, which sport cool white tones and traditional Sardinian fabrics, but there's a kitchen for guest use and the location is excellent.

ALGHERO & THE NORTHWEST

Alghero

★**B&B Benebenniu** B&B €

(Map p118; ☎ 380 1746726; www.benebenniu.com; Via Carlo Alberto 70; s €30-75, d €45-90; ❋ 🤶) A home away from home, this laid-back B&B exudes warmth and familiarity. Wonderfully located on a lively *centro storico* piazza, it has generously sized rooms with simple furnishings and plenty of natural light. The owner, Marija, is a delightful host and more than happy to share her local tips and recommendations.

Hotel San Francesco HOTEL €

(Map p118; ☎ 079 98 03 30; www.sanfrancescohotel.com; Via Ambrogio Machin 2; s €48-63, d €78-101, tr €100-135; ❋ @ 🤶) This is one of the few hotels in Alghero's historic centre. Housed in an ex-convent (the monks still live on the 3rd floor) it has plain, comfortable rooms set around a 14th-century cloister

---

ROOM WITH A VIEW

---

where classical-music concerts are staged in summer.

Camping La Mariposa CAMPGROUND €

(☎ 079 95 04 80; www.lamariposa.it; Via Lido 22; camping 2 people, car & tent €20-44, 4-person bungalows €50-80; ☺ Apr-Oct; @) About 2km north of Alghero's centre, this is the nearest campground to town. It enjoys a prime beachside location, and decent facilities, including bike hire, a windsurfing school and diving centre.

★**Angedras Hotel** HOTEL €€

(Map p116; ☎ 079 973 50 34; www.angedras.it; Via Frank 2; s €60-95, d €65-135; P ❋ 🤶) A model of whitewashed Mediterranean elegance, the Angedras – which spells Sardegna backwards – offers cool, white rooms decorated in an understated Sardinian style. There's also an airy terrace good for iced drinks on hot summer evenings. Note that the hotel is a 15-minute walk from the historic centre.

Villa Las Tronas LUXURY HOTEL €€€

(Map p116; ☎ 079 98 18 18; www.hotelvillalastronas.it; Via Lungomare Valencia 1; s €154-297, d €220-407) Live like royalty at this palatial seafront hotel. Housed in a 19th-century palace once used by holidaying royals, it's set in its own lush gardens on a private headland. The rooms are pure fin de siècle with acres of brocade, elegant antiques and moody oil paintings. A spa, with an indoor pool, sauna, hydromassage and gym, invites lingering.

Riviera del Corallo

Capo Galera Diving Centre B&B €

(☎ 079 94 21 10; http://diving.capogalera.com; Località Capo Galera, Fertilia; d €60-110, apt €85-180; 🤶) This popular diving centre provides simple accommodation in a white cliffside villa near Fertilia. As well as an enchanting setting and laid-back atmosphere, it offers several double rooms and apartments for two or six people. Note that there's a four-night minimum stay between July and September.

Agriturismo Porticciolo AGRITURISMO €

(☎ 079 91 80 00; www.agriturismoporticciolo.it; Località Porticciolo; B&B per person €30-50, 4-person apt per week €600-1000; ❋) This 24-hectare working farm offers pleasant year-round accommodation in a series of independent lodges peppered around a large lawn. Decorated in a simple rustic style, they come with kitchen facilities and their own small patios.

★ Hotel El Faro HOTEL €€€

(☑ 079 94 20 10; www.elfarohotel.it; Località Porto Conte 52; s €64-394, d €74-404; **P**★🛜🏊) You'll find this gorgeous, manicured retreat right at the southern tip of Porto Conte. Facilities, which include two pools, a private jetty, spa and gym, are superb; rooms are coolly stylish; and there are heavenly views over to Capo Caccia.

The North Coast

Albergo Silvestrino HOTEL €

(☑ 079 52 30 07; www.hotelsilvestrino.it; Via Sassari 14, Stintino; s €45-70, d €60-110; ☉ closed Dec & Jan; ★🛜) Stintino's oldest hotel is still one of its best. Occupying a hard-to-miss red villa at the sea end of the main street, it offers summery rooms with cool tiled floors and unfussy furniture. Downstairs, the excellent in-house restaurant specialises in local seafood.

Casa Doria B&B €

(☑ 349 3557882; www.casadoria.it; Via Garibaldi 10, Castelsardo; s €30-42, d €57-82; ★🛜) One of a number of B&Bs in Castelsardo's medieval centre, this homey place has all the trappings of a rustic guesthouse: period furniture, wrought-iron bedsteads and wooden ceilings. There are three rooms, each simply decorated, and a 3rd-floor breakfast room with fantastic sea views.

La Pelosetta Residence Hotel HOTEL €€

(☑ 079 52 71 88; www.lapelosetta.it; Capo del Falcone; s €57-110, d €64-170, 4-person apt €46-190; ☉ May-Sep; ★@) Overlooking the Spiaggia della Pelosa, this seasonal three-star hotel sits on one of Sardinia's most celebrated beaches. It has a mix of functionally furnished rooms and self-catering apartments, all with uninterrupted sea views, and an excellent beach-front restaurant.

Sassari

★ Tanina B&B B&B

(Map p136; ☑ 346 1812404; www.taninabandb.com; Viale Trento 14; s/d/tr €30/50/70; 🛜) On a residential street about half a kilometre from Piazza Italia, this is a model B&B. Its three large guest rooms are lovingly maintained and decked out in old-school Italian style with heavy dressers, wrought-iron bedsteads and floral motifs. Each has its own external bathroom and there's a fully equipped communal kitchen for guest use.

Hotel Vittorio Emanuele HOTEL €€

(Map p136; ☑ 079 23 55 38; www.hotelvesassari.it; Corso Vittorio Emanuele II 100-102; s €50-105, d €65-150; ★@🛜) Occupying a renovated medieval *palazzo,* this slick three-star hotel provides corporate comfort at reasonable rates. Rooms are comfortable, if anonymous, and the location, on the main drag in the historic centre, is convenient for pretty much everywhere.

OLBIA, THE COSTA SMERALDA & THE GALLURA

Olbia

Porto Romano B&B €

(Map p147; ☑ 349 1927996; www.bedandbreakfastportoromano.it; Via A Nanni 2; d €60-80; ★🛜) We love the totally chilled vibe and the heartfelt *benvenuto* (welcome) at this homey B&B, which is very close the train station. Light, spacious and well-kept, the rooms have tiled floors and wood furnishings, and some come with balconies. You're welcome to use the shared kitchen and barbecue area.

Ciro's House B&B €

(☑ 0789 2 40 75; www.bbolbia.com; Via Aspromonte 7; s €30-55, d €55-90; 🛜) Eduardo, family and Ciro (the dog) welcome you at this smashing little B&B, 1.5km west of the town centre. Kitted out in a mishmash of styles and sporting colourful tiled bathrooms, the rooms are basic but comfy. Light sleepers may find the street a tad noisy.

★ Hotel Panorama HOTEL €€

(Map p147; ☑ 0789 2 66 56; www.hotelpanoramaolbia.it; Via Giuseppe Mazzini 7; s €99-149, d €109-199, ste €179-225; **P**★) The name says it all: the roof terrace at this friendly, central hotel has peerless views over the rooftops of Olbia to the sea and Monte Limbara. The rooms are fresh and elegant, with gleaming wooden floors and marble bathrooms, and there's a whirlpool and sauna for quiet moments.

La Locanda del Conte Mameli BOUTIQUE HOTEL €€

(Map p147; ☑ 0789 2 30 08; www.lalocandadelcontemameli.com; Via delle Terme 8; s €59-149, d €74-149, tr €114-189; **P**★🛜) Raising the style stakes is this boutique hotel, housed in an 18th-century *locanda* (inn) built for Count

Mameli. A wrought-iron balustrade twists up to chic caramel-cream rooms with Orosei marble bathrooms. An original Roman well is the centrepiece of the vaulted breakfast room.

Around Olbia

Golfo Aranci

★ Borgo Alba Barona   HOTEL €

(☑393 474141292; www.hotelborgoalbabarona.com; Via Sa Curi 25, Località Donigheddu; d €40-60, half board extra per person €25; P ✱ ☎) Up a winding country road, high above the Golfo Aranci, this Gallurese *stazzo* stands in blissful isolation and in beautifully tended gardens. The simple, tiled floored bungalows have spirit-lifting views of the glittering sea and granite mountains. The home cooking is great, too. Turn right after 3km on the SP16 towards Golfo Aranci, following the signs to Località Donigheddu.

Hotel Gabbiano Azzurro   HOTEL €€€

(☑0789 4 69 29; www.hotelgabbianoazzurro.com; Via dei Gabbiani; s €170-295, d €205-355; P ✱ ☲) Overlooking the aquamarine waters of Spiaggia Terzo, the Gabbiano Azzurro is a big, anonymous hotel. But that shouldn't put you off, as the benefits are many: a pool with jetted seats, a sea-view restaurant and a pretty private beach to name a few. Activities, from cookery classes to wine tastings, sport fishing and trekking, can be arranged.

South Coast

Browse for hotels, *agriturismi* and apartments at www.visitsanteodoro.com.

Agriturismo L'Aglientu   AGRITURISMO €

(☑0789 4 10 91; www.turismorurale.org; Via l'Aglientu 1, Porto San Paolo; s €50-80, d €70-100, tr €90-135; P ✱ ☎) ✎ Serene and delightfully green, this farmstead is a fine country escape – you can even buy home-grown organic vegies. The rooms are bright and rustic, with colour-scheme themes like lemon, olive and lilac. There's a laid-back vibe in the living room, where you can peruse the books and games.

Camping San Teodoro
La Cinta   CAMPGROUND €

(☑0784 86 57 77; www.campingsanteodoro.com; Via del Tirreno, San Teodoro; camping 2 people, car & tent €31-39, 4-person bungalows €105-118; ☎) About 800m from the town centre, this popular campground sits in a huge tree-filled plot right on the southern end of La Cinta beach.

Agriturismo Li Scopi   AGRITURISMO €€

(☑338 9766350; www.agriturismoliscopi.com; Li Scopi; d €95-145; P ✱ ☎) Only the rustle of the olive trees and birdsong interrupt the pin-drop peace at this lovely *agriturismo* on the fringes San Teodoro. The bright, spacious tiled-floor rooms open onto verandahs overlooking the well-tended gardens. La Cinta beach is 1.5km away.

Costa Smeralda & Around

South of Porto Cervo

Villaggio Camping
La Cugnana   CAMPGROUND €

(☑0789 3 31 84; www.campingcugnana.it; Località Cugnana; camping 2 people, car & tent €28-30; ☎ ☲) This seaside campground is located on the main road just north of Porto Rotondo. There's plenty to keep the kids amused with a swimming pool, a playground and organised activities. A free shuttle bus can whisk you to some of the better Costa Smeralda beaches.

Hotel Capriccioli   HOTEL €€

(☑0789 9 60 04; www.hotelcapriccioli.it; Località Capriccioli; d incl half board €310-360; P ✱ ☲) In an area dominated by luxury hotel chains, it's a real pleasure to find a welcoming family-run place like Hotel Capriccioli. Right on the Capriccioli beach, it offers bright rooms furnished in typical Sardinian style with wrought-iron beds and classical island fabrics.

Porto Cervo & Around

Prices are hardly bargain basement, but you'll certainly get more for your euro if you stay slightly outside of megabucks Porto Cervo.

La Murichessa   HOTEL €

(☑339 5 316532; www.lamurichessa.it; Località Vaddimala; d €50-100, tr €70-130; P ☎) Planning a peaceful escape? This bucolic country house delivers with views of mountains, centuries-old olive trees and the glinting sea. The big, sunny rooms bear artistic touches like shell-shaped lights. Anna Lisa is a great cook – be sure to try her homemade marmalade at breakfast. To find La Murichessa take the SP59 Porto Cervo–Arzachena road and look carefully for the wooden sign.

★ B&B Costa Smeralda
B&B €€

(📞 0789 9 98 11; www.bbcostasmeralda.com; Lu Cumitoni, Poltu Quatu; d €80-130; ✱@🛜) Tucked in the hills above the fjordlike harbour of Poltu Quatu, 3km north of Porto Cervo, this is an especially charming B&B. Sunlight streams into rooms, which are a blaze of blue and white. There are tantalising sea views from the verandah, where you can enjoy some of Luciana's freshly made breads and pastries at breakfast.

Hotel Le Ginestre
LUXURY HOTEL €€€

(📞 0789 9 20 30; www.leginestrehotel.com; Località Porto Cervo; d incl half board €230-500; P✱🛜≋) In typical Costa style, this hotel has rooms in low-lying ochre buildings interwoven with perfect lawns, palms and bougainvillea. Uniformed staff provide impeccable service, rooms are light and elegant, and there's a pool and beauty centre for R&R. It's 1km south of Porto Cervo.

La Rocca Resort & Spa
LUXURY HOTEL €€€

(📞 0789 93 31 31; www.laroccaresort.com; Località Pulicino, Baia Sardinia; d incl half board €250-480; P✱≋) 🖉 A postcard ensemble of pastel pink villas, green lawns and flower-lined walkways, La Rocca is a plush retreat with cool, summery rooms and excellent facilities. The pool has a natural rocky fountain, and there's a free shuttle bus to take you to the private beach at Cala di Ginepre, 800m away.

Inland from the Costa Smeralda

San Pantaleo

★ Agriturismo
Ca' La Somara
AGRITURISMO €€

(📞 0789 9 89 69; www.calasomara.it; s €60-80, d €80-134; P≋) Donkeys guide the way to this welcoming *agriturismo*, 1km along the road to Arzachena. A relaxed, ramshackle farm, it offers 12 simple guest rooms, and is full of quiet nooks where you can swing in a hammock, stroll in gardens and enjoy back-to-nature spa treatments. Vegetarian dishes prepared with home-grown produce are served in the rustic dining room. Credit cards (and kids) are not accepted.

Locanda Sant'Andrea
HOTEL €€

(📞 0789 6 52 05; www.locandasantandrea.com; Via Zara 36; s €105-149, d €110-193, tr €138-215, q €182-273, half board per person extra €30; P✱🛜≋) Located near the entrance to the village, this tranquil pick has bright, well-kept rooms and a bougainvillea-framed pool. The same family manages the highly regarded restaurant, so breakfast is predictably good and includes homemade cakes and pastries.

Hotel Arathena
HOTEL €€

(📞 0789 6 54 51; www.arathena.it; Via Pompei; d €136-244; P✱@≋) Knotted, gnarled wood beams and ochre-tinted stone walls set the tone at this attractive hotel, while rooms are furnished with terracotta tiles, wood and natural fabrics. Outside, an infinity pool shimmers against a sublime backdrop of green peaks. There is a minimum three-night stay in the high summer season.

Arzachena & Around

★ B&B Lu Pastruccialeddu
B&B €€

(📞 0789 8 17 77; www.pastruccialeddu.com; Località Lu Pastruccialeddu, Arzachena; s €70-100, d €90-120, ste €120-150; P≋) This is the real McCoy, a smashing B&B housed in a typical stone farmstead, with pristine rooms, a beautiful pool and two resident donkeys. It's run by the ultrahospitable Caterina Ruzittu, who prepares the sumptuous breakfasts – a vast spread of biscuits, yoghurt, freshly baked cakes, salami, cheese and cereals.

From Olbia, follow the signs for Arzachena/Palau and the main road Viale Costa Smeralda. After the second set of traffic lights, take the right after the Despar supermarket and follow the signs for approximately 1.5km to Lu Pastruccialeddu.

★ Surrau Turismo Rurale
B&B €€

(📞 339 6788556; www.bebsurrau.it; Località Surrau; s €65-90, d €90-118) Dreamily set above vineyards, with views of granite peaks, this B&B combines rustic touches – tiled floors, wrought-iron bedsteads – with modern simplicity in its peaceful rooms. The ever-charming Emanuele is on hand to prepare breakfast, give tips or serve you a glass of local wine on the verandah at sundown. Heading north out of town, find it at km 347 on the SS125.

Hotel del Porto
HOTEL €€

(📞 0789 8 80 11; www.hoteldelporto.com; Via Nazionale 94, Cannigione; d €98-206, half board per person €63-123; ✱@) Overlooking the marina in Cannigione, this is a good central choice. The breezy rooms are simply decorated with traditional Sardinian fabrics and polished tiles.

Hotel Stazzo Lu Ciaccaru HOTEL €€€
(☑0789 8 19 47, 0789 84 40 01; www.stazzoluci-accaru.it; Località Lu Ciaccaru; d €164-244, ste €180-290; P❋🖥🎿) Hotel Stazzo Lu Ciaccaru is rural romance in a nutshell, with granite-and-wood dwellings sprinkled across grounds planted with centuries-old olive trees. For extra luxury, there's a private villa complete with four-poster bed and own pool – at a price, naturally. Nestled in glorious seclusion, the *stazzo* sits 3km south of Arzachena (follow the signs on the SP427).

North Coast

Santa Teresa di Gallura

Camping La Liccia CAMPGROUND €
(☑0789 75 51 90; www.campinglaliccia.com; SP90 km 59; camping 2 people, car & tent €24.50-31, 2-person bungalows €71-105; 🎿❋) 🏄 This eco-friendly campground, 5km west of town on the road towards Castelsardo, has fab facilities including a playground, pool and sports area.

B&B Domus de Janas B&B €€
(Map p160; ☑338 4990221; www.bbdomusde-janas.it; Via Carlo Felice 20a; s €50-100, d €70-130, tr €80-140, q €100-160; ❋🖥) Daria and Simon are your affable hosts at this sweet B&B in the centre of town. There are cracking sea views from the terrace and the rooms are cheery, scattered with art and knick-knacks.

Hotel Moderno HOTEL €€
(Map p160; ☑393 9177814, 0789 75 42 33; www.modernohotel.eu; Via Umberto 39; s €65-80, d €75-140, tr €105-180; ❋) This is a homey, family-run pick near the piazza. Rooms are bright and airy with little overt decor but traditional blue-and-white Gallurese bedspreads and tiny balconies.

Hotel Marinaro HOTEL €€
(Map p160; ☑0789 75 41 12; www.hotelmarinaro.com; Via Angioi 48; s €50-110, d €70-140; ❋@) Fresh, unfussy rooms, including connecting rooms for families, make this evergreen hotel a popular choice. Staff are friendly and the location, a quick hop from the main

square, makes it a good choice if you want to stay near the action.

Palau

L'Orso e Il Mare B&B €
(☑331 2222000; www.orsoeilmare.com; Vicolo Diaz 1, Palau; d €75-130, tr €95-140; ❋) Pietro gives his guests a genuinely warm welcome at this B&B, just steps from Piazza Fresi. The spacious rooms sport cool blue-and-white colour schemes. Breakfast is a fine spread of cakes, biscuits and fresh fruit salad.

Camping Baia Saraceno CAMPGROUND €
(☑0789 70 94 03; www.baiasaraceno.com; Punta Nera, Palau; camping 2 people, car & tent €30-36, 2-person bungalows €60-110) Beautifully located on Palau's beach and shaded by pine trees, this campground has an on-site pizzeria, playground and dive centre.

Hotel La Roccia HOTEL €€
(☑0789 70 95 28; www.hotellaroccia.com; Via dei Mille 15, Palau; s €50-90, d €80-150; P❋) A very friendly three-star hotel, La Roccia offers bright, spacious rooms and excellent value for money. The blue-and-white boating decor lends a Mediterranean feel and the balconies provide the bonus of some fantastic views.

Parco Nazionale Dell'arcipelago di La Maddalena

★B&B Petite Maison B&B €
(☑340 6463722, 0789 73 84 32; www.lapetitmaison.net; Via Livenza 7, La Maddalena; d €85-110) Liberally sprinkled with paintings and art deco furnishings, this B&B is a five-minute amble from the main square. Miriam's artistically presented breakfasts, with fresh homemade goodies, are served in a bougainvillea-draped garden. Credit cards (and kids) are not accepted.

B&B Mongiardino B&B €
(☑338 5034830; www.mongiardino.it; Località Mongiardino; d €60-100; P❋🖥) Set in lovingly tended gardens planted with olive and citrus trees, this sweet B&B is a terrific budget pick. It sits inland opposite the Museo Archaeologico Navale. The bright, comfortable rooms are kept spick and span. Breakfast is served on the terrace and there is a barbecue area for guest use.

The Interior

La Vignaredda
Residenza d'Epoca
HOTEL €

(☑ 347 1010198, 0796 2 08 18; www.lavignaredda.it; Via Gallura 14, Aggius; r €79-97, apt €97-157; P 🛜)
To really appreciate the silence that lies so heavily over this area, stay at this beautifully converted manor house in Aggius. Exposed granite, cosy nooks, traditional furnishings and family heirlooms lend character without spilling over into chintz. Everything is done with care and love – from the flowery gardens to the homemade cakes and freshly squeezed juice at breakfast.

B&B Domo De Resteblas
B&B €

(☑ 340 8208482; www.bbdomoderesteblas.it; Località Restelies C/o Via Dei Campi 6, Berchidda; s €35-50, d €54-70, tr €70-95; P 🛜 ♨) Tucked into the folds of vine- and olive-cloaked hills that sweep west of Berchidda, this B&B occupies a century-old farmhouse. The apartments have kitchens and balconies overlooking open countryside to the mountains beyond. There is a pool for cooling dips. Local cheeses and homemade cakes feature at breakfast. Ask your affable host Mauro if you can sample the home-produced Vermentino wine.

Il Gallo di Gallura
B&B €

(☑ 079 481 21 67; www.ilgallodigallura.com; Corso Matteotti 28, Tempio Pausania; d €60-80; P @) Sitting pretty in Tempio Pausania's historic centre is this family-run B&B housed in an early-19th-century *palazzo*. The rooms are sweet and sunny, done out in lemons and blues and typical Sardinian fabrics. Breakfast is an appealing spread of fresh juice, pastries and preserves. Look for the cockerel sign.

Agriturismo Muto Di Gallura
AGRITURISMO €€

(☑ 079 62 05 59; www.mutodigallura.com; Località Fraiga, Aggius; d €144-168, half board per person €84-94, menus €20-40; P ♨) ⚑ Free-roaming donkeys, cows, goats, sheep and hens, beautiful stone cottages nestled in cork oak woods, bucolic views, a quiet pool – what more could you want from an *agriturismo*? Nothing, except, perhaps, the delicious home-produced organic cheese, meat, vegies and wine that land on the dinner table. You can also organise horse riding, 4WD excursions and donkey trekking here.

NUORO & THE EAST

Nuoro & Around
★ Casa Solotti
B&B €

(☑ 0784 3 39 54, 328 6028975; www.casasolotti.it; Località Monte Ortobene; per person €26-35; P ✳🛜) This B&B reclines in a rambling garden amid woods and walking trails near the top of Monte Ortobene, 5km from central Nuoro. Decorated with stone and beams, the elegantly rustic rooms have tremendous views of the surrounding valley and the Golfo di Orosei in the distance. Staying here is a delight. Nothing is too much trouble for your hosts, Mario and Frédérique, who can arrange everything from horse riding to packed lunches and guided hikes in the Supramonte.

Silvia e Paolo
B&B €

(Map p174; ☑ 0784 3 12 80; www.silviaepaolo.it; Corso Garibaldi 58; s €33-40, d €55-65, tr €75; ✳🛜) Silvia and Paolo run this sweet B&B. Family treasures from dolls to old leather trunks make you feel right at home in the bright, spacious rooms. There's a roof terrace for observing the action on Corso Garibaldi by day and star-gazing by night, as well as a tasteful living room with films, books and maps of Sardinia.

Nuraghe Oro
B&B €

(Map p174; ☑ 0784 182 32 55; www.nugheoro.it; Via Matteotti 14; s €35-45, d €60-70, tr €85-95; ✳🛜) On the 6th floor of an elegant townhouse, this B&B has light, spacious and well-kept rooms, as well as fine city views from the verandah. Your friendly hosts, Max and Clara, put on a good spread at breakfast, with local fruit, cakes and dairy products. Free cots are available, as are cheaper rooms with shared bathrooms.

Agriturismo Testone
AGRITURISMO €

(☑ 0784 23 05 39; www.agriturismotestone.com; Via Giuseppe Verdi; r €76-90, half board per person €55-65; P) About 20km from Nuoro, deep in a cork oak forest, is this rustic farmstay, with exposed walls, heavy wooden furniture and hanging pots and pans. To get here from Nuoro, take the SS389 exit towards Orune-Bitti and follow for about 10km until the fork for Benetutti; turn left and after a further 3km turn right and follow the signs.

Supramonte

Oliena & Around

★ **Agriturismo Guthiddai** AGRITURISMO €
(☑ 0784 28 60 17; www.agriturismoguthiddai.com; Nuoro-Dorgali bivio Su Gologone; d €76-110, half board per person €64-80; ❋ 📶) On the road to Su Gologone, this bucolic, whitewashed farmstead sits at the foot of rugged mountains, surrounded by fig, olive and fruit trees. Olive oil, Cannonau wine and fruit and veg are all home produced. Rooms are exquisitely tiled in pale greens and cobalt blues. From Oliena, head to Dorgali, taking the turn-off right towards Valle di Lanaittu.

Bed & Breakfast Oliena B&B €
(☑ 0784 28 50 75; www.bed-and-breakfast-oliena. it; Via Alghero 10-12; ❋ 📶 🖨) Rimedia is the heart and soul of this cheery, lemon-fronted B&B in Oliena. She keeps the brightly hued, mountain-view rooms immaculately clean. The generous breakfasts with pastries, eggs, fruit and juice fire you up for a day hiking or biking in the Supramonte.

Hotel Monte Maccione HOTEL, CAMPGROUND €
(☑ 0784 28 83 63; www.coopenis.it; Località Monte Maccione; s/d/tr/q €49/80/114/144, camping 2 people & tent €18; 🅿 📶) Run by the Cooperativa Enis, this place offers simple, rustic rooms and astonishingly lovely views from its hilltop location, 4km south of Oliena on the SP22. This back-to-nature retreat is a great choice if you want to strike out into the mountains on foot.

★ **Su Gologone** HOTEL €€€
(☑ 0784 28 75 12; www.sugologone.it; Località Su Gologone; s incl half board €205-220, d €320-350, ste €420-550; 🅿 ❋ 📶 🖨) Treat yourself to a spot of rural luxury at Su Gologone, nestled in glorious countryside 7km east of Oliena. Rooms are decorated with original artworks and handicrafts, and the facilities are top notch – there's a pool, a spa, a wine cellar and a restaurant (meals around €55), which is considered one of Sardinia's best.

Barbagia

Barbagia Ollolai

Hotel Sa Orte HOTEL €
(☑ 0784 5 80 20; www.hotelsaorte.it; Via Roma 14, Fonni; s €35-40, d €60-80, tr €85-110; ❋) Housed in an attractively restored palazzo in the historic centre, this is one of Fonni's best hotels. The granite facade opens onto a vibrant modern interior decorated with tangerine walls, parquet floors and timber furniture.

Albergo Gusana HOTEL €
(☑ 0784 5 30 00; www.albergogusana.it; Località Lago di Gusana; s/d €50/70; 📶 🖨) A slice of civilization in the wild, forest-cloaked mountains of Barbagia, this bright, well-kept hotel rests in its own lakeside grounds. The surrounding silence ensure a good night's sleep, and it's a great base for families with a swimming pool, horse stables and playground.

Barbagia di Belvi

Sa Muvara HOTEL €€
(☑ 0784 62 93 36; www.samuvarahotel.com; Via Kennedy 33, Aritzo; s/d/q €95/140/220, half board per person €95-115; 🅿 ❋ 🖨) Tucked away in the mountains, this is the perfect getaway for hikers and cyclists, with large, airy rooms dressed with carved wood furniture. The spring-water pool, lush gardens and mini spa invite relaxation, and the restaurant serves up a feast of local fare (meals around €40).

Sarcidano

Antico Borgo B&B €
(☑ 0782 86 90 47; www.anticoborgoweb.it; Via Sant'Ambrogio 5, Laconi; s/d €45/70; ❋) You'll receive a heartfelt welcome from Peppe and Tomasina at this B&B, housed in a restored 18th-century *palazzo* opposite the parish church. The place oozes warmth and character, with an open fire, period furnishings and cosy rooms. Breakfast is a treat, with fresh fruit, juice, bread and homemade sweets.

Golfo di Orosei

Orosei & Around

B&B Marzellinu B&B €
(☑ 339 6000590; http://marzellinu.wordpress. com; Via Sas Linnas Siccas 96, Cala Liberotto; d €60-100; 🅿 📶) Reclining among pines and lawns, this B&B close to Cala Liberotto is a delight. The bright, cheerful rooms are kept immaculate – ask for La Peonia for a sea view. A footpath threads down to a secluded bay with crystal-clear water, perfect for snorkelling. Kids will love the kittens prowling around the grounds. There is a three-night minimum stay.

★**Albergo Diffuso Mannois**   B&B €€
(✆ 0784 99 10 40; www.mannois.it; Via G Angioy 32; s €40-85, d €70-140; ❄ ☎) Spread across three lovingly restored buildings in the medieval centre of Orosei, Albergo Diffuso Mannois is very special. Each of the light-filled, pastel-hued rooms is individually decorated, with lovely touches such as exposed stone, Sardinian fabrics and juniper-wood beams. Various excursions, including horse riding and diving, can be arranged here.

Anticos Palathos   HOTEL €€
(✆ 0784 9 86 04; www.anticospalathos.com; Via Nazionale 51; s €85-135, d €120-180; P ❄) Centred on a beautiful courtyard, this stone townhouse keeps it rustic with a vaulted breakfast room and characterful rooms featuring wrought-iron bedsteads and ornamental fireplaces. Freshly baked bread and pastries are served at breakfast.

Dorgali

To find a place to stay in Dorgali, try contacting **Cala 'e Luna Bookings** (✆ 0784 92 80 87; www.calaeluna.com; Via Lamarmora 4), a local accommodation booking service.

Sa Corte Antica   B&B €
(✆ 347 6473773; www.sacorteantica.it; Via Mannu 17; d €50-60, tr €65-75; ❄ ☎) Gathered around an old stone courtyard, this B&B housed in an 18th-century townhouse oozes charm from every brick and beam. The rooms are traditional and peaceful, with reed ceilings and wrought-iron bedsteads. Enjoy home-made bread and biscotti at breakfast.

Hotel Il Querceto   HOTEL €€
(✆ 0784 9 65 09; www.ilquerceto.com; Via Lamarmora 4; s €40-120, d €55-180, ste €300-350; P ❄ ☾) ✒ An ecofriendly hotel using solar and geothermal energy, Il Querceto boasts nicely low-key rooms with lashings of cream linen and honey-coloured tiles. The pools and oak-shaded garden invite relaxation, while the restaurant emphasises seasonal cuisine. It's just southwest of town.

Hotel S'Adde   HOTEL €€
(✆ 0784 9 44 12; http://hotelsadde.it; Via Concordia 38; s €40-70, d €70-110, half board per person €60-80; P ❄ ☎) Only a short, signposted walk up from the main thoroughfare, this welcoming chalet has pine-clad rooms with terraces and green views. The restaurant-pizzeria (meals €25 to €30) opens onto a 1st-floor terrace. Breakfast costs an extra €5.

Cala Gonone

★**Hotel L'Oasi**   B&B €
(✆ 0784 9 31 11; www.loasihotel.it; Via Garcia Lorca 13; s €69-83, d €86-139; P ❄ ☎) Perched on the cliffs above Cala Gonone and nestling in flowery gardens, this B&B offers enticing sea views from many of its breezy rooms. It's worth paying an extra €15 or so for half board, as the three-course dinners are prepared with fresh local produce. The friendly Carlesso family can advise on activities from climbing to diving. L'Oasi is a 700m uphill walk from the harbour.

Agriturismo
Nuraghe Mannu   AGRITURISMO, CAMPGROUND €
(✆ 393 288685824, 0784 9 32 64; www.agriturismonuraghemannu.com; Località Pranos; d €64-68, half board per person €50-52, camping 2 people, car & tent €18-24) ✒ Immersed in greenery and with blissful sea views, this is an authentic, ecofriendly working farm with four simple rooms, a restaurant open to all, and home-produced bread, milk, ricotta and sweets at breakfast. For campers, there are also five tent pitches available.

Hotel Villa Gustui Maris   HOTEL €€
(✆ 0784 92 00 76; www.villagustuimaris.it; Via Marco Polo 57; d €152-210, tr €220-276; ❄ @ ☾) Wake up to sweeping views of the Golfo di Orosei at this Mediterranean villa-style hotel, a stiff 800m uphill walk from the resort centre. Rooms are bright and spacious, with tiled floors, lashings of cream and terracotta, and balconies or terraces. The pool is great for a scenic swim.

Hotel Nuraghe Arvu   HOTEL €€
(✆ 0784 92 00 75; www.hotelnuraghearvu.com; Viale Bue Marino; d €140-230, tr €180-280; P ❄ ☎ ☾) A terrific pick for families, Nuraghe Arvu has neat white bungalows, which are decorated in natural materials and open onto verandahs. These are gathered around an attractive pool, with massage jets to pummel you into relaxation. The friendly staff can help arrange excursions and wine-tasting tours.

Hotel Nettuno   B&B €€
(✆ 0784 9 33 10; www.nettuno-hotel.it; Via Vasco de Gama 26; d €80-135, tr €110-160, q €120-185; ❄ ☎) This family-run B&B is a supercentral choice, a minute's walk from the beach. The simple tiled rooms are kept spick and span; a balcony will set you back an extra €10 per night. There's a garden for relaxing over a cool drink.

Hotel Costa Dorada
HOTEL €€

(📞 0784 9 33 32; www.hotelcostadorada.it; Lungomare Palmasera 45; s €93-115, d €146-190, half board per person €95-117; ❄️ 🛜) The vine-clad Costa Dorada offers dreamy sea views and tasteful rooms decorated with pastel colours, painted wood furnishings and local handicrafts. It's at the southern end of the *lungomare,* just across the road from the beach. The flowery garden is full of twittering birds and turtles.

Hotel Miramare
HOTEL €€

(📞 0784 931 40; www.htlmiramare.it; Piazza Giardini 12; s €50-102, d €84-155; ❄️ 🛜) This spruce white hotel near the harbour is Cala Gonone's oldest (it opened in 1955). Sea breezes cool the simple, tiled-floor rooms; the best have terraces overlooking the Med, while cheaper rooms face the church and mountains. Snag a lounger on the rooftop terrace to kick back and enjoy the view.

Ogliastra

Tortolì & Arbatax

For beachside, resort-style hotels, head for Porto Frailis, near Arbatax.

Camping La Pineta
CAMPGROUND €

(📞 0782 2 93 72; www.campingbungalowlapineta.it; Località Planargia, Barisardo; camping 2 people, car & tent €13-30.50, bungalows €40-115; 🅿️ 🛜) Hidden among the pine trees, a 400m walk from a fabulous beach, this family-run campground is a real find, though you will need your own wheels to find it. Pitches have plenty of tree shade and there are also well-equipped bungalows, a little bar-restaurant and a playground. It is situated near the town of Barisardo, 12km south of Tortolì.

La Vecchia Marina
HOTEL €€

(📞 0782 66 70 20; www.hotelvecchiamarina.it; Via Praga 1, Arbatax; d €80-140; 🅿️ ❄️ 🛜) Beams, terracotta floors and palm-dotted gardens give this low-rise, whitewashed hotel an almost colonial feel. The big, light rooms sport handcrafted furnishings. It's in a quiet area five minutes' stroll from the beach.

La Bitta
HOTEL €€€

(📞 0782 66 70 80; www.hotellabitta.it; Località Porto Frailis; d €192-234, half board per person €116-152; 🅿️ ❄️ 🛜 🏊) Right on the beach in Porto Frailis, this is a luxurious affair with palatial, vaulted rooms (sea views cost extra), a seafront pool and beauty treatments ranging from shiatsu to lymph drainage. Have a drink at the swish new lounge bar while admiring close-ups of local marine life splashing around in an enormous aquarium.

Lotzorai & Santa Maria Navarrese

★ The Lemon House
B&B €

(📞 0782 66 95 07; www.peteranne.it; Via Dante 10, Lotzorai; per person €30-42; 🛜) Peter and Anne run this lime-hued B&B, a terrific base for outdoor escapades, with a bouldering wall for limbering up and a relaxing roof terrace for winding down. The sports-loving duo can arrange bike hire and pick-ups, lend you a GPS and give you invaluable tips on hiking, climbing, mountain biking and kayaking. Be sure to try the homemade lemon marmalade at breakfast.

Ostello Bellavista
GUESTHOUSE €

(📞 0782 61 40 39; www.ostelloinogliastra.com; Via Pedra Longa, Santa Maria Navarrese; s €40-65, d €60-100; ❄️ 🛜) More a hotel than a hostel, this cheery hilltop place has a 'beautiful view', just as its name promises. Its plainly decorated rooms, some with balconies (bank on paying an extra €6 to €12 for these rooms), are in a series of buildings rising up the hill, so the higher you go the better the view you will get.

Albergo Santa Maria
HOTEL €€

(📞 0782 61 53 15; www.albergosantamaria.it; Via Plammas 30, Santa Maria Navarrese; s €65-85, d €115-155, half board per person €76-95; 🅿️ ❄️ 🛜) It's just a short amble from the beach to this low-rise, whitewashed hotel, where a warm welcome extends to all. The colourful rooms open onto balconies overlooking the courtyard or flower-dotted gardens. Substantial breakfasts and a gym (to work them off) are other pluses.

Ulassai

★ Hotel Su Marmuri
HOTEL €

(📞 0782 7 90 03; www.hotelsumarmuri.com; Corso Vittorio Emanuele 20; s €30-40, d €60-80, tr €75-90, q €90-120) Accommodation in Ulassai is provided by the irrepressible Tonino Lai and his wife at this well-known village institution. It offers simple, neat rooms and stupendous views. Tonino can offer you all the advice you need about the surrounding area, and delights in showing visitors its hidden corners – from nearby caves to scenic picnic spots.

Understand Sardinia

Sardinia Today

High unemployment, coal miner protests and a devastating cyclone have dented Sardinia's confidence and budget in recent times. In spite of the hardships it has faced, however, things are slowly looking up for the island, with a new ferry service providing much needed competition, tourist numbers climbing steadily, and Francesco Pigliaru bringing a breath of fresh air to Sardinian politics.

Best on Film

Padre Padrone (Father and Master; 1977) The true story of Gavino Ledda's harsh life as a shepherd.

Ballu a Tre Passi (Three-Step Dance; 2003) Four snapshots of life in Sardinia, with some beautiful shots of the Costa del Sud.

La Destinazione (The Destination; 2003) The story of a young Italian carabinieri (police officer) sent to a remote Sardinian village in Barbagia to investigate the murder of a shepherd.

Etiquette

Hospitality Accept offers of a glass of wine, beer or *mirto* when offered.

Culture Win the affection of locals by finding out about Sardinia, for instance that Grazia Deledda was a Nobel Prize winner and that ex-Chelsea-manager Gianfranco Zola is Sard.

Dress Don't go around dressed scantily for the beach in mountain areas where people can be quite conservative.

Language Remember that Sardo is not a dialect of Italian; it's a separate language.

Greetings Shake hands and say *buongiorno* (good day) or *buona sera* (good evening) to strangers; kiss both cheeks and say *come stai* (how are you) to friends.

Economic Woes & Natural Disasters

Sardinia felt the brunt of the Italian economic crisis in 2011 and 2012. Heavy industry such as the Alcoa aluminium smelter in Sulcis and many small businesses closed. The number of Italian tourists fell 20% to 30% year-on-year in 2011 and 2012 due to the combination of ferry price rises and the economic crises.

Unemployment remains incredibly high in Sardinia. Recent statistics show unemployment on the island hovering at 17.5%, which is considerably higher than the national rate of 12.6%. Particularly worrying, however, is youth unemployment (15- to 24-year-olds) at 42.4%, with prospects for young people entering the labour market looking dismal.

In August 2012, 100 miners barricaded themselves in the Carbosulcis coal mine in Iglesias to protest its closure, making headlines when 49-year-old Stefano Meletti slashed his wrists on live television, saying: 'If someone here has decided to the kill miners' families, ladies and gentlemen, we'll cut ourselves, we'll cut ourselves.' Despite the protests, closure of the loss-making mine remains imminent.

In a bid to boost flagging public morale, a hard-hat wearing Pope Francis paid a visit to Cagliari in September 2013, denouncing the idolatry of money, speaking of the devastation caused by unemployment and imploring the jobless to have hope for the future.

But further strains were put on the island when it was severely hit by Cyclone Cleopatra in November of the same year. Described by the BBC as 'apocalyptic', the cyclone's high winds and torrential rain left 18 dead and hundreds homeless. A swift clean-up operation, however, has left almost no visible traces of the cyclone and resorts have been completely rebuilt.

Political Change

The centre-left Partito Democratico candidate Francesco Pigliaru (42.45%) won Sardinia's regional elections in February 2014, defeating outgoing governor Ugo Cappellacci (39.65% of votes) of Berlusconi's centre-right Forza Italia party. Riding the tides of Prime Minister Matteo Renzi's popularity and Berlusconi's disgrace, Pigliaru was seen as a 'clean' candidate and not a career politician, with sound policies and an honest background as a Professor of Economics at the University of Cagliari.

In spring 2014, the European elections ushered in a new political era for Sardinia, which with only 1.6 million people is under-represented in the 'Italia Insulare' constituency consisting of Sardinia and the much-larger Sicily. In past years Sardinia had only managed to send MEPs to Brussels when Sicilian MEPs stepped down; a Sardinian MEP had not been directly elected since 1989. This time, however, Sardinia contributed three of the constituency's eight MEPs – the former governor Renato Soru (PD) was the most-voted candidate overall – reflecting how well-known the candidates were and how strongly the parties had performed on a national level.

Brighter Horizons

Despite the storm clouds still darkening Sardinia's economy, there are brighter horizons on the tourism industry front. The number of tourists started to creep up again in 2013, with a 13% year-on-year increase. The number of non-Italian tourists increased 20%. Non-Italians now make up half of all visitors, a trend that is set to continue as the island gradually starts to wake up to the fact that sustainable, year-round tourism is the way forward, and that it can't merely rely on Italian beach tourists in July and August.

As a response to the oligopolistic ferry price rises, a low-cost alternative, Go in Sardinia, was funded by hoteliers and launched in 2013; its summer service started in June 2014. It will operate between Livorno and the ports of Olbia and Arbatax, but whether it will be able to successfully compete against the bigger ferry companies remains to be seen.

In March 2014, the unveiling of the Giants of Monte Prama made headline news. Following years of renovation, the larger-than-life sandstone statues, shaped like boxers, wrestlers and archers, finally saw the light of day in stunning new exhibitions at the Museo Archeologico Nazionale in Cagliari and the Museo Civico in Cabras. Dating to the 8th and 9th centuries BC, the statues are among the most important examples of nuraghic statuary ever discovered and serve as remarkable reminders of a lost civilisation.

POPULATION: **1.67 MILLION**

AREA: **24,090 SQ KM**

GDP PER CAPITA: **€17,162**

GDP GROWTH: **-0.5%**

INFLATION: **0.8%**

UNEMPLOYMENT: **17.5%**

languages spoken
(% of population)

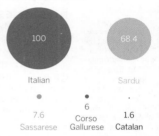

Italian	Sardu
100	68.4

Sassarese	Corso Gallurese	Catalan
7.6	6	1.6

the land
(%)

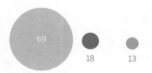

Highlands	Lowlands	Mountains
69	18	13

population per sq km

SARDINIA   ITALY   ROME

 ≈ 70 people

History

Sitting between Europe and Africa, Sardinia's strategic position and rich mineral reserves have brought tidal waves of power-hungry invaders to its shores; while its rugged, impenetrable mountains have attracted everyone from Stone Age men to 19th-century bandits in hiding. Thanks to a certain inward-looking pride and nostalgic spirit, the Sards have not allowed time and the elements to erase their story. Travellers can easily dip into the chapters of the island's past by exploring tombs, towers, forts and churches.

In his book *Le Colonne d'Ercole: Un' inchiesta* (The Pillars of Hercules: An investigation), Sergio Frau stakes a claim for Sardinia as the lost civilisation of Atlantis. The debate is reflective of an island whose origins lie beyond the reach of traditional history.

Mysteries of the Ancients

Palaeolithic & Neolithic Ages

When the first islanders arrived and where they came from are questions that have been puzzling researchers for centuries. The most likely hypothesis is that they landed on Sardinia's northern shores sometime during the lower Palaeolithic period (Old Stone Age). When flint tools were found at Perfugas in 1979, archaeologists muttered excitedly about primitive humans crossing from mainland Italy as far back as 350,000 BC. It's thought they came from Tuscany, although it's possible that other waves arrived from North Africa and the Iberian Peninsula via the Balearic Islands. Geneticists have attempted to solve the riddle by researching the island's curious genetic make-up – in certain parts of the interior a particular gene mutation is found in concentrations only otherwise present in Scandinavia, Bosnia & Hercegovina and Croatia. However, in spite of this research, the geneticists seem just as puzzled as the rest of us.

Wherever the early settlers came from, they were apparently happy with what they found, because by the neolithic period (8000 BC to 3000 BC), Sardinia was home to several thriving tribal communities. The island would have been a perfect home for the average neolithic family – it was covered with dense forests that were full of animals, there were caves for shelter, and land suitable for grazing and cultivation. Underlying everything were rich veins of obsidian, a volcanic black stone that was used for making tools and arrow tips. This black gold

TIMELINE	350,000 BC	4000–2700 BC	1800–1500 BC
	Fragments of basic flint tools indicate the first traces of human culture on the island.	Thriving Copper Age communities form around the town of Ozieri. Copper is smelted into ingots and traded, and the first *domus de janas* (rock tombs) appear.	The nuraghic period: most of the stone ruins that litter Sardinia date back to this time. Some 30,000 fortified stone towers are built.

became the Mediterranean's most coveted commodity, and was traded across the area – shards of Sardinian obsidian have been found as far away as France.

Most of what we know of this period, known as the Ozieri (or San Michele) culture, comes from findings unearthed in caves around Ozieri and in the Valle Lanaittu. Fragments of ceramics, tools and copper ingots attest to knowledge of smelting techniques and artistic awareness, while early *domus de janas* (literally 'fairy houses'; tombs cut into rock) tell of complex funerary rituals. Their menhirs and ancient rock tombs still stand today.

The funerary site of Pranu Muttedu on the central Sarcidano plain offers a deeper insight into Sardinia's neolithic Ozieri culture, strewn with *domus de janas* and around 50 menhirs. Another megalithic wonder is Biru 'e Concas in the Mandrolisai, one of Sardinia's largest collections of menhirs, with some 200 standing stones in situ. Around 30 of them are lined up east to west, presumably as a symbolic representation of the sun's trajectory.

Nuraghic Civilisation

A millennia or so after the Ozieri culture came the nuraghic people, whose 7000 *nuraghi* (Bronze Age towers and fortified settlements) scatter the island like pieces of a hard-to-solve puzzle. But according to archaeologists this is just tip of the iceberg stuff, with at least the same number of *nuraghi* estimated to lie beneath the ground, yet to be discovered. Most of these *nuraghi* were built between 1800 and 500 BC. These Bronze Age fortified settlements were used as watchtowers, sacred areas for religious rites and meeting places, and provide some of the few insights into nuraghic civilisation.

The discovery of Mycenaean ceramics in Sardinia and nuraghic pottery in Crete suggest an early trade in tableware and contact with other cultures. Evidence of pagan religious practices are provided by *pozzi sacri* (well temples). Built from around 1000 BC, these were often constructed so as to capture light at the yearly equinoxes, hinting at a naturalistic religion. The well temple at Santa Cristina is a prime example.

But perhaps the most revealing insights into nuraghic culture come from the *bronzetti* (bronze figurines) that populate many of Sardinia's archaeological museums, most notably those in Cagliari and Sassari. Scholars reckon that these primitive depictions of shepherd kings, warriors, farmers and sailors were used as decorative offerings in nuraghic temples.

One thing is certain: Sardinia's mysterious, unfathomable *nuraghi* reveal a highly cultured civilisation. The nuraghic people were sophisticated builders, constructing their temples with precisely cut stones and

Five Neolithic Wonders

Pranu Muttedu (p187), Goni

Museo delle Statue Menhir (p185), Laconi

Caves in the Valle di Lanaittu, Nuoro province

Museo Archeologico (p141), Ozieri

Dolmen Sa Coveccada (p143), Mores

Best Nuraghic Sites

Nuraghe Su Nuraxi (p79)

Tiscali (p191)

Nuraghe Losa (p107)

Santuario Santa Vittoria (p186)

Nuraghe di Palmavera (p127)

S'Ena 'e Thomes (p190) and Serra Orrios (p190)

1500 BC	1100 BC	1000 BC	650 BC
Sardinia's most important *nuraghe*, Nuraghe Su Nuraxi, is built near Barumini.	The Phoenicians establish the town of Nora on the southwest coast, one of a series of important trading posts along with Karalis (Cagliari) and Tharros.	The nuraghic people begin to build elaborate *pozzi sacri* (sacred wells).	Phoenicians build their first inland fortress on Monte Sirai following clashes with Sardinians.

no mortar; they travelled and exchanged (as revealed by the discovery of seal remains and mussel shells inland); and they had the time, skills and resources to stop and build villages, and to dedicate to arts such as ceramics and jewellery.

Masters of the Mediterranean

The Phoenicians

Some historians argue that the nuraghic populace of Sardinia were the Shardana, a piratical seafaring people who appear in early Egyptian inscriptions.

Sardinia's strategic position and its rich natural resources (silver and lead reserves) and fertile arable land have long made the island a target of the Mediterranean's big powers.

The first foreigners on the scene were the enterprising, sea-faring Phoenicians (from modern-day Lebanon). The master mariners of their day, they were primarily interested in Sardinia as a staging post – they had colonies on Sicily, Malta, Cyprus and Corsica – so Sardinia was an obvious addition. The exact date of their arrival is unclear, although Semitic inscriptions suggest that Spain-based Phoenicians may have set up at Nora, on the south coast of Sardinia, as early as 1100 BC.

In the early days the Phoenicians lived in relative harmony with the local nuraghic people, who seemed happy enough to leave the newcomers to their coastal settlements – Karalis (Cagliari), Bithia (near modern Chia), Sulci (modern Sant'Antioco), Tharros and Bosa. However, when the outsiders ventured inland and took over the lucrative silver and lead mines in the southwest, the locals took umbrage. Clashes ensued and the Phoenicians built their first inland fortress on Monte Sirai in 650 BC. This proved wise, as disgruntled Sardinians attacked several Phoenician bases in 509 BC.

Phoenician & Roman Must-Sees

Tharros (p99), Sinis Peninsula
....
Nora (p75), Pula
....
Villa di Tigellio (p44), Cagliari
....
Sant'Antioco, Isola di Sant'Antioco
....
Monte Sirai (p67), Carbonia
....
Anfiteatro Romano (p43), Cagliari

Against the ropes, the Phoenicians appealed to Carthage for aid. The Carthaginians were happy to oblige and joined Phoenician forces in conquering most of the island. Most, though, not all. As the Carthaginians found out to their cost, and the Romans would discover to theirs, the tough, mountainous area now known as the Barbagia didn't take kindly to foreign intrusion.

Set against the backdrop of the glittering Mediterranean, the archaeological remains of the mighty Phoenician port Tharros, founded in 730 BC, are one of Sardinia's most stunning sights. More tangible vestiges of the Phoenicians are visible in Sant'Antioco's historic centre, littered with necropolises and with an intact *tophet,* a sanctuary where the Phoenicians and Carthaginians buried their stillborn babies. Monti Sirai near Carbonia also offers a glimpse into the island's past with its ruined Phoenician fort, built in 650 BC.

550 BC	227 BC	216 BC	177 BC
The Carthaginians take control of this neck of the Mediterranean. Their influence extends to the island's west and south coast.	More than a decade after victory in the First Punic War (264–241 BC), Sardinia becomes a Roman province.	The Carthaginians are defeated. The Romans build roads and develop centres at Karalis (Cagliari), Nora, Sulcis, Tharros, Olbia and Turris Libisonis (Porto Torres).	Some 12,000 Sardinians die under Roman rule, and some 50,000 are sent to Rome as slaves.

Carthaginians & Romans

It was the Carthaginians, rather than the Phoenicians, who first dragged Sardinia into the Mediterranean's territorial disputes. By the 6th century BC, Greek dominion over the Mediterranean was being challenged by the North African Carthaginians. So when the Greeks established a base on Corsica, the Carthaginians were happy to accept Phoenician invitations to help them subdue the by-now rebellious Sardinians. It was the foot in the door that the Carthaginians needed to take control of the island and boost their defences against the growing threat from Rome.

The ambitious Roman Republic faced two main challenges to its desire to control the southern Mediterranean: the Greeks and the Carthaginians. The Romans saw off the Greeks first, and then, in 241 BC, turned their attention to Carthaginian-controlled Sardinia.

The Romans arrived in Sardinia buoyed by victory over Carthage in the First Punic War (264–241 BC). But if the legionnaires thought they were in for an easy ride, they were in for a shock. The new team of the Sards and their former enemies, the Carthaginians, were in no mood for warm welcomes. The Romans found themselves frequently battling insurgents, especially in the mountainous Gennargentu area, which they

A group of colossal nuraghic figures, the Giants of Monte Prama saw the light of day for the first time in almost 3000 years when they went on display in March 2014 at the Museo Civico in Cabras.

SARDONIC: THE LAST LAUGH

When Homer wrote about hero Odysseus smiling 'sardonically' when being attacked by one of his wife's former suitors, he was surely alluding to a grin in the face of danger. Yet the word sardonic, from the Greek root *sardánios,* has come to mean simply 'scornful' or 'grimly mocking' in today's usage.

If recent scientific findings are anything to go by, Homer may have been on the right track with his hint at danger. Studies carried out by scientists at the University of Eastern Piedmont in 2009 identified hemlock water dropwort *(Oenanthe crocata)* as being responsible for the sardonic smile from, of course, Sardinia. It seems that in pre-Roman times, ritual killings were carried out using the toxic perennial (known locally as 'water celery'). The elderly, infirm and indeed anyone who had become a burden to society were intoxicated with the poisonous brew, which made their facial muscles contract into a maniacal sardonic grin, before being finished off by being pushed from a steep rock or savagely beaten.

Regardless of whether the word sardonic refers to this sinister prehistoric malpractice, it seems that the findings could have positive implications in the field of medicine. The head of Cagliari University Botany Department, Mauro Ballero, believes that the molecule in hemlock water dropwort could be modified by pharmaceutical companies to have the opposite effect, working as a muscle relaxant to help people to recover from facial paralysis.

AD 456	456–534	600	705
In the wake of the fall of the Roman Empire, the Vandals land on Sardinia.	Byzantine chroniclers, not the most objective, record the almost 80 years of Vandal rule as a time of misery for islanders.	Christianity is finally imposed on the Barbagia region, the last to succumb to Byzantine proselytising.	Saracens begin a spate of attacks on the island's coastal cities. Sardinia is subjected to raids for several centuries.

dubbed Barbaria in reluctant homage to the sheer bloody-minded courage of the region's shepherd inhabitants.

In 215 BC Sardinian tribesmen, under their chieftain Ampsicora, joined the Carthaginians in the Second Punic War and revolted against their Roman masters. But it was a short-lived rebellion, and the following year the rebels were crushed at the second battle of Cornus.

Once they had Sardinia in their hands, the Romans set about shaping it to suit their own needs. Despite endemic malaria and frequent harassment from locals, they expanded the Carthaginian cities, built a road network to facilitate communications and organised a hugely efficient agricultural system. The Romans also severely decreased the island's population – in 177 BC around 12,000 Sardinians died and as many as 50,000 were sent to Rome as slaves. Many noble families managed to survive and gain Roman-citizen status and learned to speak Latin, but, on the whole, the island remained an underdeveloped and overexploited subject territory.

Raids & Resistance: Medieval Sardinia

Pisa vs Genoa

By the 9th century, the Arabs had emerged as a major force in the Mediterranean. They had conquered much of Spain, North Africa and Sicily, and were intent on further expansion. Sardinia, with its rich natural resources and absentee Byzantine rulers, made for an invit-

MALARIA

Sardinia has endured millennia of invasion and foreign control, but until 1946 the island's single-most dangerous enemy was malaria.

Although scientists reckon that the disease was probably present in prehistoric times – some maintain that *nuraghi* were built as defence against weak-flying mosquitoes – it became a serious problem with the arrival of the Carthaginians in the 5th century BC. Keen to exploit the island's agricultural potential, the colonists cut down swathes of lowland forest to free land for wheat cultivation. One of the effects of this was to increase flooding and create areas of free-standing water, perfect mosquito breeding grounds. The problem was exacerbated by the arrival of imported soldiers from North Africa, many of whom were infected.

By the time the Romans took control of the island in the 3rd century BC, Sardinia was a malarial hothouse, its *mal aria* (bad air) thought to bring certain death. Despite this, the Romans followed the Carthaginian lead and continued to exploit the island's fertile terrain. The Campidano plain became, along with Sicily and occupied North Africa, the granary of the entire Roman Empire.

1000–1400	1015	1297	1323
Sardinia is divided into four *giudicati* (provinces), the most famous being the Giudicato d'Arborea, centred on Oristano. The *giudicati* are eventually incorporated into Pisan and Genoese spheres.	Pisa and Genoa begin their long struggle for control of the island. By the late 13th century, the mainlanders control three-quarters of the island.	In the face of Catalan pressure, Pope Boniface VIII creates the Regnum Sardiniae et Corsicae (Kingdom of Sardinia and Corsica) and declares Jaume II of Aragon its king.	The Aragonese invade the southwest coast and take actual possession of the island.

ing target and the island was repeatedly raided in the 9th and 10th centuries. But as Arab power began to wane in the early 11th century, so Christian ambition flourished, and in 1015 Pope Benedict VIII asked the republics of Pisa and Genoa to lend Sardinia a hand against the common Islamic enemy. The ambitious princes of Pisa and Genoa were quick to sniff an opportunity and gladly acquiesced to the pope's requests.

At the time Sardinia was split into four self-governing *giudicati* (provinces), but for much of the 300-year period between the 11th and 14th centuries, the island was fought over by the rival mainlanders. Initially the Pisans had the upper hand in the north of the island, while the Genoese carried favour in the south, particularly around Cagliari. But Genoese influence was also strong in Porto Torres, and the *giudicati* swapped allegiances at the drop of a hat. Against this background of intrigue and rivalry, the period was strangely prosperous. The island absorbed the cultural mores of medieval Europe, and powerful monasteries ensured that islanders received the message of Roman Christianity loud and clear. The Pisan-Romanesque basalt churches of the Logudoro in the northwest remain a striking legacy of the period.

Fighting Spirit & Spanish Conquerors

Described as Sardinia's Boudicca or Joan of Arc, Eleonora d'Arborea (1340–1404) was the talismanic figure of Sardinia's medieval history and embodies the islanders' deep-rooted fighting soul. As the island's most inspirational ruler, she is remembered for her wisdom, moderation and enlightened humanity.

Queen of the Giudicato d'Arborea, one of four *giudicati* – the others were Cagliari, Logudoro (or Torres) in the northwest and Gallura in the northeast – into which the island had been divided, she became a symbol of Sardinian resistance for her unyielding opposition to the Pisans, Genoese and Catalan-Aragonese.

By the end of the 13th century, Arborea was the only *giudicato* not in the hands of the Pisans and Genoese. The Arboreans, however, toughed it out and actually increased their sphere of influence. At its height under King Marianus IV (1329–76) and Eleonora, the kingdom encompassed all of the modern-day provinces of Oristano and Medio Campidano, as well as much of the Barbagia mountain country.

Initially Arborea had supported the Catalan-Aragonese in their conquering of Cagliari and Iglesias, but when they realised that their allies were bent on controlling the whole island, their support for the foreigners quickly dried up. Eleonora became Giudicessa of Arborea in 1383, when her venal brother, Hugo III, was murdered along with his daughter. Surrounded by enemies within and without (her husband was

Medieval Marvels

Torre dell'Elefante (p39), Cagliari

Basilica della Santissima Trinità di Saccargia (p142), Logudoro

Chiesa di San Simplicio (p146), Olbia

Castello Malaspina (p103), Bosa

Centro Storico (p57), Iglesias

Torre Porta a Terra (p115), Alghero

1392	1400–1500	1478	1700
Sardinia's great heroine and ruler of the Giudicato d'Arborea, Eleonora d'Arborea, publishes the Carta de Logu, the island's first code of common law.	Under Catalan-Aragonese control, absentee landlords impose devastating taxes and leave the rural population to struggle against famine and plagues, which claim 50% of the island's population.	On 19 May Sardinian resistance to Aragonese control is crushed at the Battle of Macomer. Led by the Marquis of Oristano, Leonardo de Alagon, Sard forces prove no match for the Iberian army.	The death of the heirless Habsburg ruler Carlos II puts Sardinia up for grabs once again.

ELEONORA'S CARTA DE LOGU

Eleonora d'Arborea's greatest legacy was the Carta de Logu, which she published in 1392. This progressive code, based on Roman law, was far ahead of the social legislation of the period. The code was drafted by her father, Mariano, but Eleonora revised and completed it. To the delight of the islanders, it was published in Sardinian, thus forming the cornerstone of a nascent national consciousness. For the first time the big issues of land use and the right to appeal were codified, and women were granted a whole raft of rights, including the right to refuse marriage and – significantly in a rural society – property rights. Alfonso V was so impressed that he extended its laws throughout the island in 1421, and this remained so until 1871.

Eleonora never saw how influential her Carta de Logu became. She died of the plague in 1404, and the Aragonese took control of Arborea only 16 years after her death. Eleonora remains the most respected historical figure on the island.

imprisoned in Aragon), she silenced the rebels and for the next 20 years worked to maintain Arborea's independence in an uncertain world.

From 1383 to 1404, Eleonora bitterly opposed the Catalan-Aragonese. But Eleonora couldn't live forever and her death in 1404 paved the way for defeat. In 1409 the Sardinians were defeated at the Battle of Sanluri, in 1410 Oristano fell, and in 1420 the *giudicato's* exhausted Arborean rulers finally gave in to the inevitable and sold their provinces to the Catalans.

Spain & the Savoys
Aragonese Invaders

Log onto www.sardegna-turismo.it for historic itineraries of the island, taking you in the footsteps of the nuraghic people, Phoenicians, Romans and the *giudicati*.

Sardinia's Spanish chapter makes for some grim reading. Spanish involvement in Sardinia dates back as far as the early 14th century. In 1297 Pope Boniface VIII created the Regnum Sardiniae e Corsicae (Kingdom of Sardinia and Corsica) and granted it to the Catalan-Aragonese as an inducement to the Spaniards to relinquish their claims on Sicily. Unfortunately, however, the kingdom only existed on paper and the Aragonese were forced to wrench control of Sardinia from the hands of its stubborn islanders. In 1323 the Aragonese invaded the southwest coast, the first act in a chapter that was to last some 400 years.

Under the Catalan-Aragonese and the Spanish, the desperately poor Sardinian population was largely abandoned to itself – albeit on the crippling condition that it pay its taxes – and the island remained underdeveloped. But Spanish power faded in the latter half of the 17th century and the death of the heirless Habsburg ruler Carlos II in 1700 once again put Sardinia up for grabs.

1708	1720	1795–99	1823
English and Austrian forces seize Sardinia from King Felipe V of Spain during the War of the Spanish Succession, a European-wide scramble for the spoils of the rudderless Habsburg Empire.	Duke Vittorio Amedeo II of Savoy becomes King of Piedmont and Sardinia after the island is yo-yoed between competing powers: Austria, then Spain, Austria again, Spain for a second time and finally the Savoys.	After Piedmontese authorities deny requests for greater self-rule, angry mobs take to the streets of Cagliari, killing senior Savoy administrators. By 1799 the revolutionary flame has burnt itself out.	Intended to promote land ownership among the rural poor, the Enclosures Act sees the sale of centuries-old communal land and the abolition of communal rights. It's not popular and riots result.

Habsburgs & Piedmontese

The death of Carlos II triggered the War of the Spanish Succession, which set pro-Habsburg Austrian forces against pro-Bourbon French factions in a battle for the spoils of the Habsburg empire. In 1708 Austrian forces backed by English warships occupied Sardinia. There followed a period of intense politicking as the island was repeatedly passed back and forth between the Austrians and the Spanish, before ending up in the hands of the Duchy of Savoy.

Piedmontese rule (from 1720, until Italian unification in 1861) was no bed of roses, either, but in contrast to their Spanish predecessors the Savoy authorities did actually visit the areas they were governing. The island was ruled by a viceroy who, by and large, managed to maintain control.

In 1847 the island's status as a separate entity ruled through a viceroy came to an end. Tempted by reforms that had been introduced in the Savoys' mainland territories, a delegation requested the 'perfect union' of the Kingdom of Sardinia with Piedmont, in the hope of acquiring more equitable rule. The request was granted. At the same time, events were moving quickly elsewhere on the Italian peninsula. In a series of daring military campaigns that were led by Giuseppe Garibaldi and encouraged by King Carlo Emanuele, Sardinia managed to annexe the Italian mainland to create the united Kingdom of Italy in 1861.

Nowhere is the Spanish influence more palpable than in Alghero, which fell to Spanish invaders in 1353 after 30 years of resistance. Even today Catalan is still spoken, and street signs and menus are often in both languages.

Buried Treasures
Boom Years

Although all but extinct, Sardinia's mining industry has played a significant role in the island's history. Southwest Sardinia is riddled with empty mine shafts and abandoned mine works, hollow reminders of a once-booming sector.

Sardinia's rich mineral reserves were being tapped as far back as the 6th millennium BC. Obsidian was a major earner for early Ozieri communities and a much sought-after commodity. Later, the Romans and Pisans tapped into rich veins of lead and silver in the Iglesias and Sarrabus areas.

The history of Sardinian mining really took off in the mid-19th century. In 1840 legislation was introduced that gave the state (the ruling Savoys) control of underground resources, while allowing surface land to remain in private hands. This, combined with an increased demand

Italy's revolutionary hero, Giuseppe Garibaldi, died on 2 June 1882 on the Isola Caprera, his private island in the Arcipelago di La Maddalena. Today you can visit his home, the Compendio Garibaldino, for an insight into the man who succeeded in uniting Italy.

1840	1847	1861	1915
Legislation is introduced giving the state (the ruling Savoys) control of underground resources, which starts a mining boom.	Requests for the Kingdom of Sardinia, up to this point a separate entity ruled by a viceroy, to be merged with the Kingdom of Piedmont are granted. From this point on, Sardinia is governed from Turin.	In a series of military campaigns led by Giuseppe Garibaldi, King Carlo Emanuele annexes the Italian mainland to create the united Kingdom of Italy.	The Brigata Sassari (Sassari Brigade) is founded and sent into WWI action in the northeastern Alps. Its Sardinian soldiers earn a reputation for valour and suffer heavy losses – 2164 deaths, 12,858 wounded or lost.

for raw materials fuelled by European industrial expansion, started a mining boom on the island.

By the late 1860s there were 467 lead, iron and zinc mines in Sardinia, and at its peak the island was producing up to 10% of the world's zinc.

Inward investment had spillover effects. The birth of new towns, the introduction of electricity, construction of schools and hospitals – these were all made possible thanks to mining money.

But however much material conditions improved, the life of a miner was still desperately hard, and labour unrest was not uncommon – strikes were recorded in southwest Sardinia at Montevecchio in 1903, and a year later at Buggerru. The burgeoning post-WWI socialist movement attempted to further politicise Sardinia's mine workers, but without any great success.

> Iglesiente miners only went on strike in September, when the wild prickly pear came into fruit. This meant their families would have something to eat while the miners weren't earning a wage.

Fascism & Failure

Following the worldwide recession sparked off by the 1929 Wall Street Crash, the Sardinian mining industry enjoyed something of a boom under the Fascists. Production was increased at Montevecchio, and the Sulcis coal mines were set to maximum output. In 1938 the town of Carbonia in southwest Sardinia was built to house workers from the Sirai-Serbariu coalfield.

Mining output remained high throughout Italy's post-WWII boom years, but demand started to decline rapidly in the years that followed. Regular injections of public money couldn't stop the rot, which was further exacerbated by high production costs, the poor quality of the minerals and falling metal prices. One by one the mines were closed and, as of 2008, Sardinia's only operative mine is Nuraxi Figus, near Carbonia.

Bravery, Banditry & Identity

WWI Heroes

> Vittorio de Seta's 1961 classic film, Banditi a Orgosolo (Bandits of Orgosolo), brilliantly captures the harsh realities of rural life in mid-20th-century Sardinia.

Sardinia's martial spirit found recognition on a wider stage in the early 20th century. The island's contributions to Italy's campaigns in WWI are legendary. In 1915 the Brigata Sassari was formed and immediately dispatched to the northeastern Alps. The regiment was manned entirely by Sards, who quickly distinguished themselves in the merciless slaughter of the trenches. It is reckoned that Sardinia lost more young men per capita on the front than any other Italian region, and the regiment was decorated with four gold medals.

Kidnap Country

A less salubrious chapter is the island's tradition of banditry, which had reached epidemic proportions by the late 19th and early 20th centuries. In May 1899 the New York Times reported: 'The Italian Government is

1921	1926	1928–38	1943
The Partito Sardo d'Azione (PSd'Az; Sardinian Action Party) is formed by veterans of the Brigata Sassari. It aims to pursue regional autonomy and politicise the Sardinian public.	Sardinian writer Grazia Deledda wins the Nobel Prize for Literature.	As part of Mussolini's plans to make Italy economically self-sufficient, Sardinia is given a makeover. Large-scale irrigation, infrastructure and land-reclamation projects begin and new towns are established.	Allied bombing raids destroy three-quarters of Cagliari.

at last realizing that the increase of brigandage in certain parts of Sardinia, and especially in the Province of Sassari, is becoming serious, and steps are being taken by the authorities to bring the bandits to justice.' It was a crusade the government was destined to lose as poverty and an inhospitable environment fuelled banditry throughout the 20th century.

The town of Orgosolo, deep in Barbagia hill country, earned a reputation as a hotbed of lawlessness, and as recently as the 1990s gangs of kidnappers were still operating in its impenetrable countryside. Between 1960 and 1992, 621 people were kidnapped in Italy, 178 of them in Sardinia. Though Orgosolo has left this dark chapter of its past behind it, the town is now a canvas for vibrant, politically charged murals.

A Political Awakening

WWI was a watershed for Sardinia. Not only in terms of lives lost and horrors endured, but also as a political awakening. When Sardinian soldiers returned from the fighting in 1918, they were changed men. They had departed as illiterate farmers and returned as a politically conscious force. Many joined the new Partito Sardo d'Azione (PSd'Az; Sardinian Action Party), founded in Oristano in 1921 by Emilio Lussu and fellow veterans of the Brigata Sassari (the Sardinian regiment that served in WWI).

The party's central policy was administrative autonomy, embracing the burgeoning sense of regional identity that was spreading throughout the island. This led many to start viewing Sardinia as a region with its own distinct culture, aspirations and identity.

But a call for autonomy was just one of the cornerstones of the party's political manifesto. Combining socialist themes (a call for social justice and development of agricultural cooperatives) with free-market ideology (the need for economic liberalism and the removal of state protectionism), it created a distinct brand of Sardinian social-democratic thought.

More than 90 years on, the party is still active. It stood independently in the 2009 regional election, winning 4.3% of the Sardinian vote.

In 2013, the PSd'Az broke away from Ugo Cappellacci of Silvio Berlusconi's centre-right Forza Italia (FI) party. It rejoined the coalition,

In 1921 DH Lawrence spent six days travelling from Cagliari to Olbia. The result was *Sea and Sardinia,* his celebrated travelogue full of amusing and grumpy musings.

HISTORY BRAVERY, BANDITRY & IDENTITY

ISOLATION TO INDEPENDENCE

WWII left Sardinia shattered. The island was never actually invaded, but Allied bombing raids in 1943 destroyed three-quarters of Cagliari. Worse still, war isolated the island. The ferry between the mainland and Olbia was knocked out of action and did not return to daily operation until 1947. As a result of the political upheavals that rocked Italy in the aftermath of the war – in a 1946 referendum the nation voted to dump the monarchy and create a parliamentary republic – Sardinia was granted autonomy in 1948.

1948	1946–51	1950–70	1962
Sardinia becomes a semiautonomous region with a regional assembly, the Giunta Consultativa Sarda, that has control over agriculture, forestry, town planning, tourism and the police.	The sinister-sounding Sardinia Project finally rids the island of malaria. The US Army sprays 10,000 tonnes of DDT over the countryside. The effects are still being researched.	Sardinia benefits from the Cassa per il Mezzogiorno, a development fund for southern Italy. But improvements in agriculture, education, industry, transport and banking cannot prevent widespread emigration.	The Aga Khan forms the Consorzio della Costa Smeralda to develop a short stretch of northeastern coast. The resulting Emerald Coast kick-starts tourism on the island.

THE RISE AND RISE OF SORU

Dubbed the Sardinian Bill Gates, self-made billionaire Renato Soru has been central to tourism in the island's recent past. He founded the internet company Tiscali in 1998, was listed as one of the world's richest people by Forbes in 2001, entered politics in 2003 and was voted regional president a year later, a position he held until February 2009. But away from the controversial 'luxury tax' and *salvacoste* (save the coast) ban on coastal development, Soru's lasting achievements include overseeing the withdrawal of US atomic naval forces from the environmentally sensitive Arcipelago di La Maddalena after 35 years. This divided local opinion, with environmentalists and Soru fans applauding the move, and business owners mourning the loss of free-spending American sailors.

In the European elections in spring 2014, Renato Soru of the centre-left Partito Democratico (PD) staged a comeback when he was elected as an MEP. He was the most-voted candidate overall.

however, in time for the regional elections in 2014, which saw Francesco Pigliaru of the centre-left Partito Democratico (PD) beat Cappellacci. The PSd'Az won 4.7% of the vote.

Sun, Sex Scandals & Switzerland
The Rise of Tourism

Until malaria was eradicated in the mid-20th century, visitors (at least those with peaceful intent) were few and far between. DH Lawrence famously grumped his way round the island in 1921, and his words paint a fairly depressing picture of poverty and isolation. Were he to return today, he'd find a very different island. Poverty still exists, particularly in the rural interior, and unemployment remains a serious issue (in 2014 it stood at 18.6%), but despite that the island has changed almost beyond recognition.

Most of Nora's Punic-Roman ruins are submerged in the sea. For total historic immersion, hook up with a local diving company to explore them.

Before the Aga Khan 'discovered' the Costa Smeralda (Emerald Coast) in the late 1950s and developed it together with a consortium of international high rollers in the 1960s, Gallura's northeastern coast was a rocky backwater, barely capable of supporting the few shepherds who lived there. Now the Costa Smeralda is one of the world's glitziest destinations; its beaches are a playground for Russian oligarchs, celebrities, supermodels and VIPs, including former Formula One racing manager Flavio Briatore.

Berlusconi's Former Island Idyll

Sardinia became caught up in the scandal surrounding Italian Prime Minister Silvio Berlusconi thanks to the location on the Cos-

1985	1999	2004	2008
Sassari-born Francesco Cossiga is elected President of the Republic of Italy. He was Minister of the Interior when the Red Brigade (extreme-left terrorists) kidnapped and killed ex-PM Aldo Moro in 1978.	The EU identifies Sardinia as one of a handful of places in Europe in dire need of investment for 'development and structural upgrading'.	Self-made billionaire Renato Soru is elected president of Sardinia. He sets the cat among the pigeons by banning building within 2km of the coast and taxing holiday homes and mega-yachts.	After 36 years, the US Navy withdraws from the Arcipelago di La Maddalena. It had long divided opinion: friends pointed to the money it brought; critics highlighted the risks of hosting atomic submarines.

ta Smeralda of Villa Certosa, Berlusconi's extravagant €450 million holiday home – identified in November 2010 by 28-year-old escort Nadia Macri as one of the locations of the prime minister's alleged 'bunga bunga' sex parties. Much covered in the media, these parties were a major focus of the trial in which Berlusconi faced charges of under-age prostitution and abuse of power in relation to Karima el-Mahroug – a belly dancer more widely known by her stage name, Ruby Rubacuori, or Heart Stealer. Villa Certosa was put on the market in August 2011.

In 2013 the 'Rubygate' case came to a head when Berlusconi was found guilty of paying for sex with an under-age prostitute and using his power to cover it up. He was sentenced to seven years in prison and banned from public office for life. Berlusconi maintains his innocence and lodged an appeal against the conviction in January 2014, claiming that the accusations were unfounded.

Berlusconi was, however, definitively convicted for tax evasion and expelled from the Senate at the end of 2013. In May 2014, Berlusconi started a one-year community service sentence at a Catholic care home near Milan, having being found guilty of purchasing TV and film rights at inflated prices via offshore companies to evade paying taxes in Italy.

A SWISS SARDINIA

One is landlocked and famous for its mountains, the other is an island and renowned for its coastline. Apart from both being small and beautiful, Switzerland and Sardinia, some 1000km apart, appear to have little in common on the face of things. But that hasn't stopped Andrea Caruso, the co-founder of the Canton Marittimo (Maritime Canton) movement, from garnering support from independence seekers who would like the island to become the 27th Swiss canton.

Disillusioned with the island's future in the face of high unemployment, bureaucracy and a system that they claim has 'squandered economic potential and disenfranchised the ordinary citizen', the movement says that Sardinia becoming part of Switzerland would be 'common sense'. They believe that Switzerland would bring the island the efficiency, economic wealth and direct democracy it needs.

Dismissed by some as bonkers and hailed by others as a brainwave, the plea for Rome to sell the island to Switzerland has certainly caught the attention of the public and the press – both The Guardian and the BBC reported about it in early 2014 and, at the time of writing, the Canton Marittimo Facebook page had 5440 'likes' and counting. But though an online poll of 4000 German-speaking Swiss found that 93% would be in favour of Sardinia becoming the 27th canton, the Costa del Alps is, in real terms, still a distant dream.

2009	2011	2013	2014
Renato Soru is defeated in the February regional election by centre-right candidate Ugo Cappellacci.	In a May referendum, 98% of Sardinians vote against nuclear power. Enel gets the green light to build a 90 megawatt wind farm at Portoscuso.	Cyclone Cleopatra tears across the island, bringing apocalyptic flash floods and storms that kill 18 people and leave thousands homeless. Olbia is the worse affected area.	Fabrizio Aru comes third in the Giro d'Italia in May 2014 – the first time a Sard has ever been on the podium.

The Sardinian Way of Life

When DH Lawrence described Sardinia as 'lost between Europe and Africa, and belonging to nowhere' he was missing the point. Sardinia belongs to the Sardinians. History might suggest otherwise, but centuries of colonial oppression have done little to dent the islanders' fierce local pride and their patient, melancholic resolve. A strong sense of fraternity, respect for tradition and passion for a good *festa* – these are what unite Sardinians. But to speak of a regional identity is to overlook the island's geography.

Sardinia is an island of shepherds, home to around four million sheep (around 2.5 per capita).

SHEEP

Isolation & Introspection

'We never knew the sea, even if it was only about 150km away by the roads of those days,' says Maria Antonietta Goddi, a Cagliaritana by adoption who spent her early childhood in Bitti, a dusty inland town north of Nuoro. By modern roads, Bitti is only about 50km from the sea, but until relatively recently it was a world unto itself, cut off from the rest of the island by inhospitable mountains and a lack of infrastructure.

The same could be said of any one of hundreds of inland communities, left to fend for themselves by island authorities unable or unwilling to reach them. Such isolation nurtured introspection and a diffidence towards outsiders, while also preserving local traditions – many towns speak their own dialects, cook their own recipes and celebrate their own festivals that have been developed without any outside interference. It also exacerbated the ever-increasing divide between coast and interior. The advent of tourism and industrial development has had a far greater impact on coastal towns than on the island's hinterland, and there's still a world of difference between the modern-minded cities of Alghero, Sassari, Olbia and Cagliari and the traditional lifestyles of inland villages.

Yet for all the hardship isolation has inflicted on the islanders, it has left Sardinia with some unique qualities. In recent years researchers have been falling over themselves to study the island's uncontaminated gene pool, and musicologists have long appreciated the island's strange and unique musical traditions.

On the surface, Sardinians display none of the exuberance usually associated with mainland Italians, nor their malleability or lightness of heart. They come across as friendly and hospitable, but modest and quietly reserved. Unlike other islanders, they don't look outwards, longing for escape and opportunity; instead they appear becalmed in the past, gripped by an inward-looking intensity.

Life in the Slow Lane

Perhaps a reason for the Sardinians' celebrated longevity is the island's laid-back, unhurried approach to life. After all, who cares if you are a little late in the grand scheme of things? There are far more important matters in life, such as friends and family, enjoying your free time, and stopping to chat with the baker, the newsagent, the neighbour and his dog, and just about anyone else who crosses your path. Friendliness is paramount.

This go-slow approach comes naturally to Sardinians. Never mind if Massimo is waffling on about the economy for the umpteenth time that day, while the queue snakes to the back of his grocery store – you know he always has a big smile for you. Or that Silvia is deeply embroiled in conversation at the post-office counter – everyone knows that she could talk the hind leg off a donkey. Or that the tourist in front of you on the SS125 is driving at only 30km/h, braking on every bend and has now – *incredibile!* – stopped to take photos of a passing shepherd and his flock; this is frustrating, but you won't beep your horn, only an Italian would do that. And besides, patience is a Sardinian virtue.

La Famiglia

'My 32-year-old son is too fat. Should I put him on a diet?' It's the typical agony-aunt conundrum in the problem pages of Sardinia's magazines and newspapers. Paolo may be 32, but he will always be a boy in the eyes of his doting *mamma*. Like Italy, Sardinia can come across as something of a matriarchal society at times, with around 25% of men staying at home well into their 30s, and a smaller percentage of women following suit. While their decision to fly the nest late, typically not until they marry, is the subject of much ridicule, it is often an economic decision – many young people, particularly with unemployment at around 13.6%, simply can't afford to leave home.

Whichever way you look at it, the family is central to life in Sardinia, and so it comes as something of a surprise that the average rate of fertility is an incredibly low 1.1% (the EU average is 1.6%). The latest figures show that Sardinians are also waiting longer to have a family, with 32.5 being the average age for a woman to have her first baby.

La Donna

Il Corpo Delle Donne is on TV and barely dressed women are cavorting on the stage as the crowd cheers, lights flash and the music throbs; outside, a woman wearing traditional black vestments walks up the hill. Two

In 2007 Italy's oldest woman, Rafaella Monni, died in Arzana in the province of Ogliastra, at 109. Five years earlier the then oldest man in the world, 112-year-old Antonio Todde, had died in Tiana, province of Nuoro.

GENE GENIES

A kent'annos (may you live to be 100). This traditional greeting may sound like wishful thinking but, then again, maybe not – the odds are good in Sardinia. Forget super foods, macrobiotic diets and 10-years-younger supplements, this island holds the secret to longevity, apparently, with some 150 centenarians out of a population of 1.67 million, about twice the normal level. Of these, five live in the tiny village of Ovodda (population 1700). Ask Sardinians why and you'll get a different answer every time – the air, the outdoor living, eating and drinking well, God.

Previous studies have highlighted environmental and lifestyle factors (local Cannonau wines are rich in procyanidins, chemicals that contribute to red wine's heart-protecting qualities) as the main reasons for this longevity, but researchers from the University of Sassari remain convinced that there's a fundamental genetic element. The inhabitants of the mountainous province of Ogliastra have long been undisturbed by the outside world. As a result intermarriage has produced a remarkably pure gene pool, a veritable goldmine of genetic raw material.

A research team, led by Professor Luca Deiana, spoke on the findings of the AKent'Annos (AKeA) study at a conference in Pavia and Bareggio in May 2011. As well as revealing that some (but not all) of Sardinia's centenarians share genetic characteristics, Deiana brought to light other similarities: most 100 year olds are well-balanced optimists with good social and family networks and a strong sense of identity, and nearly all appear to have a diet rich in antioxidants.

MOTHER TONGUE

Sardo (or Sardu), Sardinia's first language, is the largest minority language in Italy. Originally derived from the Latin brought over by the Romans in the 3rd century BC, it has four main dialects: Logudorese (from the northwest), Campidanese (from the south), Gallurese (from the northeast) and Sassarese (from the Sassari area). These dialects are further complicated by the incorporation of distinct local influences, so in Alghero residents speak a variation of Catalan, and on the Isola di San Pietro locals converse in a 16th-century version of Genoese. The Gallura and Sassari dialects also reflect the proximity of Corsica.

Recent studies on the usage of Sardo brought to light some humorous facts: apparently 60.2% use the mother tongue when they're angry and 64% when they want to be funny, but only 26.5% to discuss politics and a mere 16.5% to speak about the kids.

women – one *molto sexy,* the other the respect-demanding mother, wife, nurturer. Of course, these are both extremes and to a degree stereotypes, but they nevertheless embody the dual attitude of men towards women in Sardinia, which largely resembles that of their Italian neighbours.

Attitudes are changing, but many families still live according to the classic model, with women staying at home and men going out to earn. These gender roles were originally dictated by the practical division of labour: with the men away from home pasturing their flocks, women were left running the house and raising the children; although nowadays they're as much about tradition and convention as practical necessity.

'It's nothing like in the past when girls weren't allowed to be out on the street past 8pm,' says Maria Angela Tosciri from Baunei. 'Today men and women are in many respects equal, as Sardinia opens up to tourism and new media.' According to Maria Antoinetta Goddi, in the interior there's a lot less chauvinism than in the rest of Sardinia; inland women impose themselves and make other people value them.

Faith & La Festa

The Island of the Ancients, by Ben Hills, features interviews with Sardinia's most extraordinary centenarians and reveals their life elixir.

Conservative and for much of the year politely reserved, Sardinians let go with a bang during their great festivals. These boisterous and spectacular occasions reveal much about the islanders' long-held beliefs, mixing myth with faith and folklore.

Religious belief has deep roots in Sardinia. The presence of *sacri pozzi* (well temples) in nuraghic settlements attests to naturalistic religious practices dating to the 2nd millennium BC. Christianity arrived in the 6th century and quickly established itself. Today Sardinian faith finds form in street parties as much as church services, and many of the island's biggest festivities are dedicated to much-loved saints. The greatest of them all, St Ephisius, an early Christian martyr and Sardinia's patron saint, is the star of Cagliari's huge May Day carnival.

Elsewhere on the island, you'll find a number of *chiese novenari* – small countryside chapels that are only opened for several days of the year to host saints' day celebrations. These churches are often surrounded by *cumbessias* (also known as *muristenes*), simple lodgings to house the pilgrims who come to venerate the saint honoured in the church.

Easter is an important event in Sardinia, marked by islandwide celebrations, many of which reflect Spanish influence. Castelsardo, Iglesias and Tempio Pausania all put on night processions featuring hooded members of religious brotherhoods more readily associated with Spain.

The Arts

Sardinia's arts have been tempered by the island's rich culture and rugged topography. Shielded from outside influences, Sardinian musical traditions are like nothing else on the planet and they fuel a contemporary fusion scene. Literary legends like Nobel Prize–winning Grazia Deledda reel you into the intrigues of small-town life in the wilds of mountainous Barbagia. Up and down the island you will encounter festivals where folk dancing, hand-carved masks and flamboyant costumes keep Sardinia's one-of-a-kind heritage very much alive.

Music

Canto a Tenore

If ever music could encapsulate the spirit of Sardinia's rugged mountains and pastoral landscapes, it is *canto a tenore*. This traditional male harmony singing is one of the oldest-known forms of vocal polyphony. It is performed by a four-part male choir, the *tenores,* made up of *sa oghe* (the soloist and lead voice), *su bassu* (bass), *sa contra* (contralto) and *sa mesu oghe* (countertenor). Little is known of the *canto's* origins but it's thought that the voices were originally inspired by the sounds of nature – the *contra* based on a sheep's bleat, the *bassu* on a cow's moo and the *mesu oghe* on the sound of the wind. The *canto* is performed in a tight circle, with the soloist singing a poem, often with a pastoral theme, to choral accompaniment.

Canto a tenore is most popular in the centre and north of the island, with the best-known groups coming from the Barbagia region. The most famous is the Tenores di Bitti, which has recorded on Peter Gabriel's Real World record label and performed at Womad festivals. Other well-known choirs hail from Oniferi, Orune and Orgosolo. In 2008 the *canto a tenore* was inscribed on the Unesco Representative List of the Intangible Cultural Heritage of Humanity.

A similar style, although more liturgical in nature, is the *canto a cuncordu,* again performed by four-part male groups. To hear this head for Castelsardo, Orosei and Santu Lussurgiu.

Launeddas

The *launeddas* is Sardinia's trademark musical instrument. A rudimentary wind instrument made of three reed canes and played using circular breathing, it is particularly popular at village festivals in the south. If you can't attend a festival, buy the legendary recordings *Launeddas,* by Efisio Melis and Antonio Lara. Other names to look out for on the *launeddas* circuit are Franco Melis, Luigi Lai, Andria Pisu and Franco Orlando Mascia.

For an interesting insight into Sardinian music, visit the Sardegna Cultura website, www.sardegnacultura.it (in Italian), which has recordings of traditional island music.

Read up about Sardinia's best-known traditional group and listen to them in action at www.tenores-dibitti.com.

Sardinia has produced some fine female vocalists, most notably Maria Carta, a 20th-century island legend. The folksy tunes of Elena Ledda are also widely known.

SEA & SARDINIA

Sardinia's wild, untamed landscapes, sense of space and age-old traditions sparked the fervent imagination of 20th-century literary giant DH Lawrence. The nine days he spent travelling the island with his wife Frieda inspired one of his most impassioned travel books, *Sea and Sardinia,* which Lawrence himself hailed a 'marvel of veracity'.

Travelling on the *trenino verde,* the Lawrences visited Cagliari, Mandas, Sorgono and Nuoro before taking a boat back to Sicily, where DH Lawrence dashed off the book entirely from memory in just six weeks. His rapturous prose beautifully captures the spirit of the island he described as 'left outside time and history; a place that is like "freedom itself"'. If you're planning a slow journey through Sardinia by narrow-gauge train, the book is the perfect travel companion. To follow in the Lawrences' footsteps, visit the itineraries page of www.sardegnaturismo.it.

Poetry

Like many of the island's art forms, Sardinian poetry is not, and never has been, the preserve of the chattering classes. It is a much-felt part of local culture, which in the 19th century gave rise to an early form of rap duelling, the so-called *gare poetiche* (poetry duels). At village festivals, villagers would gather to watch two verbal adversaries improvise rhyming repartee that was sarcastic, ironic or simply insulting. The audience loved it and would chime in with their own improvised shots! Little of this was ever written down, but you can find CDs featuring a classic duo from the mid-20th century, Remundo Piras and Peppe Sozu.

In the 1930s the Fascists banned the Sardinian *cantadores* (poets), whose attacks on church and state they deemed dangerous and subversive.

Bardic contests still take place in the mountain villages and there are two important poetry competitions, Ozieri's Premio di Ozieri and the Settembre dei Poeti in Seneghe.

Sardinia's most famous poet is Sebastiano Satta (1867–1914), who celebrated the wild beauty of the island in his poetry *Versi Ribelli* and *Canti Barbaricini.*

Dance & Festivals

Ballo Sardo

No Sardinian festival or celebration would be complete without folk dancing, referred to as *ballo sardo* (Sardinian dance) or *su ballu tundu* (dancing in the round), which is interpreted slightly differently from region to region. It generally involves a group of dancers or couples in a line or open circle, who hold hands or link arms and move gracefully across the floor with agile steps, twists and turns. Their movements often become sprightlier as the music quickens.

The Art-Culture section of www.marenostrum.it details up-and-coming cultural events and festivals, including art retrospectives and cinema events.

The *Launeddas* is often played during the dance, while a *canto a tenore* might accompany slower pieces. Like the *launeddas,* it is thought that *ballo sardo* dates back to nuraghic times. There has been much speculation on the connections between *ballo sardo* and the similar *sardana* (circular folk dance) of Catalonia in northeastern Spain.

The Art of Celebration

Sardinians find expression for their heritage, history, faith and identity through folk music, dance and intricately embroidered costumes at their rich and varied festivals. Many festivals have a religious origin, such as the numerous holy or feast days, the solemn Easter processions, and pilgrimages like the Festa di Sant'Efisio in Cagliari and the Festa del Redentore in Nuoro. As an agricultural island, seasonal products from cherries to asparagus, chestnuts, wine and tuna are another cause for celebration (and indulgence).

In the west, horse races and parades bring historic triumphs to life, from Sassari's spirited Cavalcata Sarda marking victory over the Saracens in AD 1000 to the fiery S'Ardia horse race in Sedilo trumpeting the victory of Roman Emperor Constantine over Maxentius in AD 312.

Literature

Sardinia's rural society had no great literary tradition, but the early 20th century marked a watershed. Grazia Deledda (1871–1936) won the 1926 Nobel Prize and a series of talented scribes began to emerge from the shadows. Their work provides an unsentimental picture of island life, as well as a fascinating insight into how the islanders see themselves.

Taking inspiration from the petty jealousies and harsh realities of the Nuoro society in which she grew up, Grazia Deledda towers above the world of Sardinian literature. Her best-known novel is *Canne al vento* (Reeds in the Wind), which recounts the slide into poverty of the aristocratic Pintor family, but all her works share a strong local flavour.

Also Nuoro born, Salvatore Satta (1902–75) is best known for *Il giorno del giudizio* (The Day of Judgement), a biting portrayal of small-town life, which is often compared to Giuseppe di Lampedusa's Sicilian classic *Il gattopardo* (The Leopard).

A contemporary of Satta, Giuseppe Dessì (1909–77) found fame with *Il disertore,* the story of a shepherd who deserts his WWI army unit and returns to his native Sardinia where he finds himself caught between a sense of duty and his own moral code.

One of the most famous works to have emerged from postwar Sardinia is *Padre Padrone,* Gavino Ledda's bleak autobiographical depiction of his early life as a shepherd. Later made into a critically acclaimed but little-known film by the Taviani brothers, it paints a harrowing picture of the relentlessness of poverty and the hardships it provokes.

The intractability of political and social life in postwar Italy is the central theme of *Il figlio di Bakunin* (Bakunin's Son), the one translated work of Sergio Atzeni (1952–95). One of the giants of Sardinia's

> Get the low-down on Sardinia's top literary event, Gavoi's Festa Letterario di Sardegna, at www.isoladelle-storie.it.

> Six Sardinian authors contributed to the book *Sei per la Sardegna* (Six for Sardinia; Marcello Fois). The anthology was written to raise money for victims of the 2013 floods.

SARDINIAN HANDICRAFTS

Filigree jewellery Cagliari, Alghero and Dorgali are the best places to purchase exquisitely crafted gold and silver *filigrana* (filigree work).

Red coral Top-quality coral is harvested off Alghero's Riviera del Corallo (Coral Riviera). In many cases coral is combined with filigree work.

Ceramics Oristano, Sassari and Assemini (north of Cagliari) are famous for their ceramics, glazed in blue or white or yellow and green, and embellished with naturalistic motifs such as birds and flowers.

Wool carpets Aggius and Tempio Pausania have a strong cottage industry in wool carpets, decorated with traditional geometric designs.

Basketry In the north, around Castelsardo and in Oristano, women still make traditional baskets from asphodel, rush, willow and dwarf palm leaves.

Festival masks The festival masks handcrafted in the Nuoro region are real works of art. Look out for Mamoiada's *mamuthones* and Ottana's *boes* and *merdules* masks.

Textiles Traditional hand-looming techniques are used in Ulassai to make one-of-a-kind towels, curtains and bedspreads.

Cork In Gallura, cork wood is used to make everything from decorative bowls to stools and chopping boards.

Pocket knives Handmade pocket knives with horn-carved handles are produced in Pattada and Arbus by a handful of remaining master craftsmen.

recent literary past, Atzeni, like Deledda before him, depicts a society that resists the simple reductions of comfortable moral and political assumptions.

In recent times Sardinia has produced a good crop of noir writers, including Flavio Soriga (b 1975), whose *Diavoli di Nuraio* (The Devil from Nuraio) won the Premio Italo Calvino prize in 2000.

Traditional Crafts

As befits an agricultural island, Sardinia has a long tradition of handicrafts, many of which make the most of local materials from cork wood to coral. But where objects were originally made for practical, everyday use, they are now largely made for decoration. Local ironworkers around Santu Lussurgiu, for example, have adapted to the modern market by replacing agricultural tools, the mainstay of their traditional income, with decorative lamps, gates and bedsteads.

Quality still remains high, however, and you can find some excellent deals. To be sure of reasonable prices and quality, head for the local Istituto Sardo Organizzazione Lavoro Artigiano (ISOLA) shop, which authenticates each piece it sells.

Each of the 370 villages and towns on the island has its own traditional costume.

The Sardinian Kitchen

Olives and lemons ripening in the sun, wild thyme, rosemary, juniper and myrtle perfuming coastal breezes, shepherds guiding their flocks home from the pastures to make ricotta, fishermen reeling in mullet and lobster from the Med at daybreak... this isn't romance, it's reality. Nowhere does slow food like Sardinia. Throw in views of mountains and sea, some fine home-produced Vermentino or Cannonau wine and stunningly fresh farm produce and you are looking at a great culinary experience – simple but great.

A Day at Sardinia's Table

Like most Italians, Sardinians rarely eat a sit-down *colazione* (breakfast), preferring a swift cappuccino and *cornetto* (croissant) standing at a bar. Out in the wilds, shepherds would start the day with a handful of bread and a slice of hard *pecorino* (sheep's milk) cheese.

Pranzo (lunch) remains a ritual observed by many Sardinians. Workers can't always get home, but across the island shops and businesses close for three to four hours to ensure lunch is properly taken and digested. A full meal will consist of an *antipasto* (starter) followed by a *primo* – usually a thick soup, pasta or risotto – and a *secondo* of meat or fish. Inlanders will invariably prefer meat, often served roasted or in thick stews. To finish *alla sarda* (in Sardinian style) go for cheese and a *digestivo,* perhaps a shot of grappa, although it is now usual to wind up with dessert and coffee.

Cena (the evening meal) was traditionally a simpler affair, but as work habits change and fewer people eat lunch at home, it increasingly becomes the main meal of the day.

Civraxiu takes its name from *cibaria,* the word for 'flour' during the Roman occupation when Sardinia was one of the major grain suppliers to the Empire.

WHEN IN...TRY...

➡ **Cagliari** *Burrida,* dogfish marinated in walnuts, garlic, vinegar and spices.

➡ **Gallura** *Zuppa cuata* or *zuppa gallurese,* a heart-warming casserole comprising layers of bread, cheese and *ragù* (meat and tomato sauce), drenched in broth and baked to a crispy crust.

➡ **Olbia** *Zuppa di cozze e vongole* (garlicky clam and mussel soup), *ricci* (sea urchins) and *ortidas* (fried sea anemones).

➡ **Barbagia** *Pecora in capoto,* a hearty, flavoursome ewe stew.

➡ **Alghero** *Aragosta alla catalana,* lobster with tomato and onion, and *ricci* when in season – March to April.

➡ **Cabras** *Muggini* (mullet) and *bottarga* (mullet roe).

➡ **Nuoro and Ogliastra** *Fioro sardo pecorino,* suckling lamb and pig, and wild boar.

Sardinian Cuisine
Daily Bread

Few experiences in Sardinia beat walking into a neighbourhood *panetteria* in the morning, breathing in the yeasty aromas and feasting your eyes on the loaves of freshly baked bread. The Sardinians hold the humble loaf in high esteem and have come up with literally hundreds of types of bread, each one particular to its region and town. Traditional bakeries pride themselves on using durum wheat of the best quality and age-old kneading techniques.

Originally from the Campidano region, the commonly seen *civraxiu* is a thick, circular loaf with a crispy crust and a soft white interior. Another common bread is the *spianata* or *spianada,* which is a little like Middle Eastern pitta. In Sassari snack bars you'll discover *fainè,* the chickpea-flour *farinata* flat bread imported centuries ago by Ligurians from northwestern Italy. The Spaniards contributed *panadas,* scrumptious little pies that can be filled with anything from minced lamb or pork to eel.

For special occasions such as weddings and religious feast days, bread is elevated to an art form called *su coccoi,* with intricate floral wreaths, hearts and animals that are impossibly delicate and almost too pretty to eat.

Music Paper

As crisp as a cracker, as light as a wafer and thin enough for the sun to shine through, *pane carasau,* also known as *carta da musica* (music paper), is the star of Sardinia's bread basket. It is most ubiquitous in the rural interior, particularly in the Gallura, Logudoro and Nuoro regions, where it is still made by hand using the simplest of ingredients – durum wheat, water and a pinch of salt – and then baked in a wood-fired oven to achieve its distinctive crispness. For centuries this long-lasting bread has been ideal for shepherds out in the pasture.

Brushed with olive oil and sprinkled with salt, *pane carasau* becomes a moreish snack known as *pane guttiau.* A fancier version often served as a first course is *pane frattau,* where *pane carasau* is topped with tomato sauce, grated *pecorino* and a soft-boiled egg.

Antipasti

A tasty Italian import, antipasti appear on almost every menu as a lead to *primi* (first courses). *Antipasti di terra* (of the land) is often a mouth-watering assortment of homemade bread, cured ham, tangy Sardinian salami, olives and a range of cooked, raw and marinated vegetables such as artichokes and eggplant. There is also *frittelle di zucchine,* an omelette stuffed with zucchini (courgettes), breadcrumbs and cheese. Along the coast you'll find *antipasti di mare* (of the sea), such as thinly sliced *bottarga* (mullet or tuna roe), the best of which comes from the lagoon town of Cabras. Cagliari is famous for its *burrida* (marinated dogfish).

Cheese, Glorious Cheese

Sardinia is an island of shepherds, so it's hardly surprising that cheesemaking is a fine art here. Cheese has been produced here for nearly 5000 years, and Sardinia makes about 80% of Italy's *pecorino.* Gourmands will delight in flavours and textures, from tangy *pecorino sardo* to smoked varieties, creamy goat's cheeses (such as *ircano* and *caprino*),

Top Sardinian Cookbooks

The Foods of Sicily & Sardinia, by Giuliano Bugialli

Sweet Myrtle & Bitter Honey: The Mediterranean Flavours of Sardinia, by Efisio Farris

Gastronomia in Sardegna, by Gian Paolo Caredda

A Sardinian Cookbook, by Giovanni Pilu and Roberta Muir

The Sardinian Cookbook: The Cooking and Culture of a Mediterranean Island, by Viktorija Todorovska

MAGGOTY CHEESE ANYONE?

Ask Sardinians about the island's infamous *casu marzu*, 'rotten cheese' alive with maggots, and watch them raise a knowing eyebrow, snigger at hilarious memories of trying to eat the stuff, or else swiftly change the subject. Everyone, it seems, has a story or an opinion about the *formaggio che salta* (cheese that jumps). It's creamier and tastier than anything you've ever tried, say some; it makes your skin crawl and festers in the gut, warn others.

If you were a horror-movie scriptwriter with a passion for *pecorino* you couldn't make it up: *pecorino* deliberately infested with the larvae of the *piophila casei* cheese fly, whose digestive acids break down the cheese fats, advancing fermentation and rapidly leading to decomposition. The pungent liquid that oozes out of the cheese is called the *lagrima* (tear). When eating the cheese, locals cover it with one hand to stop the sprightly little larvae from jumping into their face – they can leap up to 15cm, apparently. Others prefer to remove the maggots by placing the cheese into a paper bag and letting them starve of oxygen.

Tempted? Well, even if you are, you would have to be pretty determined to find the cheese. Though considered a 'traditional food' exempt from EU health regulations, it is still illegal to sell and serve *casu marzu*, and most is produced for private consumption. Its elusiveness adds to its mystery: ask those same Sardinians where to find *casu marzu* and they will probably make a wide, sweeping gesture and tell you in the mountains... maybe. Head to the lonesome Barbagia in summer and with a little luck and one very strong stomach, you might just find a farmer willing to reveal his secret stash.

ricottas and speciality cheeses like *canestrati*, with peppercorns and herbs.

Fiore sardo, a centuries-old cheese recipe, is eaten fresh, smoked or roasted and packs a fair punch. It is traditionally made from ewe's milk, but varieties such as *fresa* and *peretta* are made from cow's milk. The most popular goat's cheese is *caprino*, and the soft *crema del Gerrei* is a combination of goat's milk and ricotta.

Only the bravest connoisseurs will want to sample *formaggio marcio* or *casu marzu*, quite literally a 'rotten cheese' alive with maggots!

Sardinian Pasta

Sardinia generally has an individual way of doing things, and the island's pasta is no different.

Malloreddus, dense shell-shaped pasta made of semolina and flavoured with saffron, is usually served with *salsa alla campidanese* (sausage and tomato sauce) and is sometimes called *gnocchetti sardi*. Another uniquely Sardinian creation is *fregola*, a granular pasta similar to couscous, which is often served in soups and broths.

Culurgiones (spelt in various ways) is a ravioli-like pasta that appears on many menus. Typically it has a ricotta or *pecorino* filling and is coated in a tomato and herb sauce. *Culurgiones de l'Ogliastra*, made in Nuoro province, is stuffed with potato purée and sometimes meat and onions. A little *pecorino*, olive oil, garlic and mint are added, and a tomato sauce is the usual accompaniment.

Maccarones furriaos are strips of pasta folded and topped with a sauce (often tomato based) and melted cheese. *Maccarones de busa*, or just plain *busa*, is shaped by wrapping the pasta around knitting needles.

Other pastas you may come across are *pillus*, a small ribbon pasta, and *filindeu*, a threadlike noodle usually served in soups.

On the Spit

Sardinia's carnivorous heart beats to its own unique drum. Three specialities stand out: *porceddu* (suckling pig), *agnello* (lamb) and *capretto* (kid). These dishes are flavoured with Mediterranean herbs and spit-roasted.

The most famous of this culinary triumvirate is the *porceddu* (also spelt *porcheddu*), which is slow roasted until the skin crackles and the meat is meltingly tender, then left to stand on a bed of myrtle leaves.

Agnello is particularly popular around December, although it's served year-round. *Capretto* is harder to find on menus, but it gets more common up in the mountains, where it is flavoured with thyme.

A country classic – and a rarity – is *su carraxiu* (literally 'of the buried'): the meat is compressed between two layers of hot stones, covered in myrtle and left to cook slowly in a hole dug in the ground.

Sards also have a penchant for game birds, rabbit and wild boar. A wonderful local sauce for any meat dish is *al mirto* – made with red myrtle, it is a tangy addition.

> To hide evidence of their crime, bandits would slow roast stolen pigs in underground holes under bonfires. The technique is known as *su carraxiu*.

Fish & Seafood

Sardinians point out that they are by tradition *pastori, non pescatori* (shepherds, not fishermen). There is some tradition of seafood in Cagliari, Alghero, Cabras and other coastal towns, but elsewhere the phenomenon has arrived from beyond Sardinia.

At the top end of the scale, lobster (legally in season from March to August) is *the* local speciality, particularly in Alghero, where it's served as *aragosta alla catalana* with tomato and onion. *Muggine* (mullet) is popular on the Oristano coast, and *tonno* (tuna) dishes abound around the Isola di San Pietro. *Cassola* is a tasty fish soup, while *zuppa alla castellanese,* a Castelsardo speciality, is similar but with a distinct tomato edge.

Cagliari also has a long tradition of seafood recipes that run the gamut from sea bream to bass, although the most famous is based on the local *gattucio di mare* (dogfish). Clams, cockles, octopus and crab also feature, as do eels around the marshes of Cabras. For something more adventurous, try *orziadas* (deep-fried sea anemones) and *ricci* (sea urchins).

Room for Dessert

Sardinia's sweet trolley has always been constrained by the natural flavours of the island. Take the recipe for *amarettes* (almond biscuits): there are just three ingredients – almonds, sugar and eggs – but the biscuits are delightfully fluffy and moist.

WE DARE YOU TO TRY...

➡ *Casu marzu* – Rotten *pecorino* alive with maggots, if you can find it.

➡ *Cordula* – Lamb tripe grilled, fried or stewed with peas.

➡ *Granelle* – Calf's testicles sliced, covered in batter and lightly fried.

➡ *Salsiccia* or *salame di cavallo/d'asino* – Horsemeat or donkey sausages.

➡ *Tataliu* or *trattalia* – A mix of kidney, liver and intestines stewed or grilled on skewers. The dish is made with veal, lamb, kid or suckling pig.

➡ *Zimino russo* – A selection of roasted offal, usually from a calf, including the heart, diaphragm, liver, kidney and other red innards.

➡ *Zurrette* – A black pudding made of sheep's blood cooked, like haggis, in a sheep's stomach with herbs and fennel.

CHEAP TREATS

Hungry? These are our favourite snacks to nibble in Sardinia – yours for a fistful of change.

➡ **Fainè** Chickpea-flour flat bread with pizzalike toppings. Particularly popular in Alghero and the island's northwest.

➡ **Gelato** Ice cream for a piazza-side slurp.

➡ **Pane carasau** Crisp, crackerlike flat bread. The perfect picnic companion.

➡ **Pizza al taglio** Pizza by the slice.

➡ **Pecorino** Hard, nutty sheep's milk cheese. Goes well with fresh, crunchy bread.

Though traditionally an Easter recipe, you might spot *pardulas* (also known as *casadinas* and *formagelle*) in cake shops at other times of the year. These delectable mini cheesecakes are made from ricotta or *pecorino*, flavoured with saffron and baked in a crisp shell.

Other sweets and biscuits are strictly seasonal. *Ossus de mortu* (dead men's bones) biscuits, infused with cinnamon and studded with almonds, are served on All Saints' Day in November. After the grape harvest you'll start to see *papassinos de Vitzi* (almond and sultana biscuits) and *pabassinas cun saba,* mixed with almonds, honey, candied fruit and grape must. At festivities you may well come across *sospiri di Ozieri,* rich patties of minced almonds, sugar, honey and lemon glazed with icing, and *coffettura,* tiny baskets of finely shaved orange peel and almonds drenched in honey.

The island's most famous dessert, however, is the *seadas* (or *sebadas*), a deliciously light pastry (vaguely like a turnover) stuffed with bran, orange peel and ricotta or sour cheese and then drenched in *miele amaro* (bitter honey).

A Sweet for Every Town

Sweets, tarts, cakes and biscuits – Sardinia's dessert menu is rich and varied. Alongside the island staples, there's a never-ending list of local specialities.

'Every town has its own recipes,' explains Maria Antonietta Goddi, one of four sisters who along with their mother, the formidable Signora Maurizia, run Durke, a traditional sweet shop in Cagliari's Marina district.

'For example, there's a *dolce* (sweet) called *papassino* (from *papassa*, which means 'raisin') that's made all over Sardinia, but there are lots of local variations. So you have variations from Torralba, Benetutti, Bitti and Selargius in the province of Cagliari. The version from Selargius uses cinnamon and *vino cotto* (mulled wine).'

Such variations often reflect an area's history, incorporating foreign influences into traditional recipes. 'In the centre and the south of Sardinia, the Arab influence is very strong – orange blossom, cinnamon and vanilla are used a lot. In the north they use a lot of *vino cotto* and *vino selvatico* (wine from wild plants). In the centre they also use *pecorino* to make *casatinas,* which have a much stronger taste. Here in Cagliari we use a lot of ricotta, often with saffron.

'Then there's *torrone* (nougat), a *dolce* that is made in Sicily as well, but is made in Sardinia without the addition of sugar, so with honey, egg whites, almonds and walnuts.'

Sardinian Drinks

Coffee

The espresso is the standard coffee drink in Sardinia and is what you get if you ask for *un caffè*. *Doppio espresso* is a double shot and a *caffè americano* is a watered-down version. If you prefer your coffee with milk, there are various options. A *caffè latte,* regarded by locals as a breakfast drink, is coffee with a reasonable amount of milk. A *caffè macchiato* is an espresso with a dash of hot milk, and a *latte macchiato* is a glass of hot milk with a dash of coffee. The cappuccino is a frothy version of the *caffè latte.*

Dry and authoritative, www.winecountry.it provides technical details for all of Sardinia's major wines.

Wine

Sardinian wines might not be as venerated as those from Italy, but times are changing, as vintners push for a higher profile and quality gets better and better. Contemporary producers have started taming the mighty alcoholic content of their traditional blends and are now producing some light, dry whites and more sophisticated reds.

The best winegrowing regions for visitors are the Gallura for Vermentino whites, the Ogliastra, Baronia, Barbagia and Mandrolisai for Cannonau reds, and Sulcis in southwest Sardinia for Carignano reds and rosés.

WINE TASTING

You can buy and drink Sardinian wines at any *enoteca* (wine bar), but you'll get far more out of a proper tasting. Here is our pick of the best wineries and cellars that open their doors for tastings.

➡ **Sella e Mosca** (p126) Sardinia's top wine producer has free guided tours of its museum. Sample wines such as pale, crisp Vermentinos and ruby red Cannonaus with a hint of oak.

➡ **Cantine Surrau** (p155) A strikingly contemporary winery near Arzachena, with guided tours, art exhibitions and tastings. Be sure to try the intense, fruity Cannonau reds and the mineral-rich Vermentino whites.

➡ **Cantina del Vermentino** (p169) Pass through the arch to descend to this winery, where you can taste and buy some of the finest Vermentino whites to be found in the Gallura.

➡ **Antichi Poderi di Jerzu** (p198) Sip beefy Cannonau red wines in the town nicknamed the Citta del Vino (Wine Town), surrounded by fabulous scenery.

➡ **Cantina del Mandrolisai** (p185) In the heart of the hilly Mandrolisa, this *cantina* is famous for its beefy reds.

➡ **Cantine Argiolas** (p50) Just a short detour north from Cagliari brings you to this award-winning winery in vine-strewn Serdiana. Stop by for a guided tour and tasting.

➡ **Cantina Santadi** (p68) The biggest winery in the southwest, its reds include the highly rated Roccia Rubia and Grotta Rossa. Note that booking a visit can be done online.

➡ **Cantina Sociale di Santa Maria la Palma** (p129) South of Lago Baratz, Santa Maria la Palma is home to this winery. Stock up on fine wines at the enoteca or take a guided tour.

➡ **Tenute Olbios** (p149) A wine estate on the fringes of Olbia, producing excellent Vermentino whites. Go for tastings and guided vineyard tours.

TABLE MANNERS

➡ The person who invites usually pays, though splitting *il conto* (the bill) is becoming more common.

➡ Drinking cappuccino after a meal is a no-no for locals; after noon it's espresso only.

➡ Sardinians don't generally eat on the hoof (unless it's gelato).

➡ Eat spaghetti with a fork, not a spoon.

➡ Locals never season their food without trying it first.

➡ Don't finish the bread before the food arrives; it's for mopping up delicious sauces.

➡ Make eye contact when toasting.

➡ If you are invited to someone's home for a meal, always take wine, chocolates or flowers.

On the whole Sardinian wine is very reasonably priced, with quality labels often available from around €10 to €15 per bottle. You can buy wine directly from the producer or from a *cantina sociale* (wine-producers' cooperative). Lots of these organisations offer a *degustazione* (tasting). Many *agriturismi* (farm-stay accommodation) also produce their own wine, much of which is surprisingly good value.

Vermentino Whites

Introduced to Sardinia in the 18th century, the Vermentino grape flourishes on the sandy granite-based soil in the northeast. The area's best wine is the Vermentino di Gallura, Sardinia's only DOCG. A crisp aromatic white with a slightly bitter almond aftertaste, it's best drunk young as an aperitif or with fish. But Vermentino is not confined to the Gallura DOCG area, although the Vermentino di Sardegna produced elsewhere only carries the DOC rating.

Cannonau Reds

The island's best-known red wines are made from the Cannonau vine. This is cultivated across the island, although it's particularly widespread on the mountains around Oliena and Jerzu. Especially good paired with roasted meats, Cannonau reds are a rich, heavy drop that have been sustaining locals for centuries. Research has revealed that Cannonau wines are particularly rich in procyanidins, one of the chemicals that is reputed to give red wine its heart-protecting qualities, which may go some way to explaining the exceptional longevity of people in the Nuoro province.

Italian Wines, published by Gambero Rosso and Slow Food Editore, is the definitive annual guide to Italian wines. Producers and their labels are reviewed in encyclopaedic detail.

Vernaccia & Malvasia

Produced since Roman times on the alluvial plains around Oristano, Vernaccia is one of Sardinia's most famous wines. It's best known as an amber sherrylike drop usually taken as an aperitif or to accompany pastries like *mustazzolus*. However, there are nine Vernaccia wines, ranging from dry still whites to aged fortified wines.

Another excellent tipple, Malvasia (Malmsey) is produced in the Planaragia hills near Bosa, but it's also made around Cagliari (Malvasia di Cagliari). The Malvasia di Bosa, a delicious honey-coloured dessert wine, is widely available in the Bosa area.

TOP FIVE DINING EXPERIENCES

➡ **Trattoria Lo Romani** (p121) Great island food, friendly service and an elegant setting in Alghero's vibrant *centro storico* (historic centre).

➡ **Pintadera** (p61) Enjoy succulent chargrilled steaks, filling pastas and a laid-back trattoria vibe at this welcoming restaurant in Iglesias.

➡ **Sa Peschiera 'e Mar 'e Pontis** (p97) Savour locally caught fish at this seafood hot spot in Cabras on the Sinis Peninsula.

➡ **Su Gologone** (p180) Rural romance close to Oliena in the mountains of the Supramonte. Local and homegrown produce stars on the menu, and the *porceddu* (suckling pig) spit-roasted on an open fire is outstanding.

➡ **Frati Rossi** (p154) High-on-a-hill restaurant on the Costa Smeralda with dreamy sea views, stylish dining spaces and stunningly fresh seafood.

Spirits

Mirto is Sardinia's national drink, a smooth, powerful liqueur distilled from the fragrant purple fruit of the myrtle bush. In its most common form it's a purplish berry red, although a less common white version is also made.

But *mirto* is just the tip of the iceberg for Sardinian spirits. Islanders have developed a range of local firewaters made using easily found ingredients, such as *corbezzolo* (an autumnal plant that is similar to wild strawberry), prickly pears and basil. There's even a local form of *limoncello,* a sweet lemon-based tipple, similar to the better-known Amalfi Coast drink.

The strangely named *filu e ferru* (the iron wire) provides quite a kick. Similar to grappa, it is made from a distillate of grape skins and positively roars down the throat – the alcohol content hovers around 40%, with some home brews reaching an eye-watering 60%.

Zedda Piras is a reliable brand of *mirto* and *filu e ferru*.

To avoid taxes Sardinians hid their homemade *acquavita*. They'd mark the hideout with an iron wire (the *filu e ferru*), from which the drink derives its name.

Eating Out in Sardinia

The most basic sit-down eatery in Sardinia is called a *tavola calda* (literally 'hot table'), which generally offers canteen-style food. For a full meal you'll want to go to a trattoria or a *ristorante*. Traditionally, trattorias were family-run places that served a basic menu of local dishes at affordable prices and, thankfully, a few still do this. *Ristoranti* offer more choice, often with a more extensive wine list and smarter service. House wine is nearly always available and is the most inexpensive choice at between €5 and €10 for a litre. It generally comes in quarter-, half- and full-litre carafes. Some, but not all, restaurants will provide *acqua di rubinetto* (tap water) if you ask for it, but locals tend to order a bottle of *acqua frizzante* (sparkling mineral water) to drink with their meal. All eating establishments in Sardinia are officially nonsmoking.

On a restaurant/trattoria bill you can expect to be charged for *pane e coperto* (bread and a cover charge). This is standard and is added even if you don't ask for or eat the bread. Typically it ranges from €1 to €4. A S*ervizio* (service charge) of 10% to 15% may or may not be included in the bill; if it's not, tourists are expected to round up the bill or leave a 10% tip.

Vegetarians & Vegans

Vegetarians will have a tough time of it in Sardinia, a robustly meat-eating island. The good news is that vegetables are of a universally high standard and appear in many antipasti and *contorni* (side dishes). However, note that even apparently meat-free food such as risotto or soup is often prepared with meat stock. Vegans will find it even harder as so many dishes feature some sort of animal product, be it dairy, eggs or animal stock.

Cookery Classes

Sardinia is not as well served with cooking schools as many Italian regions, but there are a handful of places where you can get behind the stove. These include the Cooperativa Gorropu, based in the highlands around Dorgali; Hotel Gabbiano Azzurro, a seafront resort hotel in Golfo Aranci; and Hotel Lucrezia, in the flatlands north of Oristano. At Cantine Argiolas you can learn to cook Sardinian specialities like *fregola* and enjoy them with Argiolas wines.

There are a number of specialist operators selling cooking holidays to Sardinia. One such is Ciao Laura (www.ciaolaura.com), an American outfit that arranges culinary stays in Orosei, on the east coast. A four-day course costs €625, including accommodation.

To discover the nuances of Sardinian cuisine, consult www.sarnow.com and www.sardegnaturismo.it, which give a great overview of the specialities of each region.

Seasonal Food & Wine Festivals

A history of rural isolation has led to a fierce pride in local traditions, many of which find form in extravagant celebrations and food-based *sagre* (festivals dedicated to a particular food). Traditionally these were based on the farming calendar and provided a rare occasion for villagers to meet up, show off their most splendid costumes and prepare their finest recipes. Here's our pick of the best:

➡ **Sagra del Bogamarì** (p120) In Alghero, an ode to the humble *ricci*, held on several weekends in March.

➡ **Sagra degli Agrumi** Muravera's folksy Citrus Fair, held on the second or third weekend in April.

➡ **Sagra del Torrone** Located in Tonara in the Barbagia di Belvi, a sweet tribute to nougat; held on Easter Monday.

➡ **Girotonno** (p70) In Carloforte, this is a four-day festival celebrating the island's famous *mattanza* (tuna catch) in early June.

➡ **Sagra delle Castagne** An autumnal feast of chestnuts in the mountain town of the Aritzo, held on the last Sunday of October.

➡ **Rassegna del Vino Novello** (p100) In Milis, one of Sardinia's top wine festivals, where new wine is sniffed, tasted and sold; held in mid-November.

FOOD & DRINK MENU DECODER

aragosta	lobster
bottarga	mullet roe
burrida	dogfish with pine nuts, parsley and garlic
capretto	kid (goat)
carciofi	artichokes
cozze	mussels
culurgiones	ravioli filled with cheese and/or potato
fregola	semolina pasta (similar in texture to couscous), used in soups, stews and salads
malloreddus	literally 'fat little calves'; gnocchi-like semolina dough dumplings, often served with tomato sauce
mirto	myrtle berries; also a liqueur distilled from myrtle berries
pane carasau	unleavened, twice-baked flat bread
pecorino	hard ewe's milk cheese, also called *fiore sardo*
porceddu	suckling pig, often spit-roasted and served on a bed of myrtle leaves
ricci	sea urchins
sagra	culinary festival
seadas	light pastry turnovers filled with ricotta or *pecorino* cheese and lemon zest and drizzled with honey
tonno	tuna
vongole	clams
zuppa	soup or broth

Survival Guide

Directory A–Z

Customs Regulations

➡ Entering Italy from another EU country you can bring, duty-free: 10L spirits, 90L wine and 800 cigarettes.

➡ Arriving from a non-EU country, the limits are 1L spirits (or 2L fortified wine), 4L still wine, 60mL perfume, 16L beer, 200 cigarettes and other goods up to a value of €430; anything over this must be declared on arrival and duty paid.

➡ You can bring up to €10,000 cash into Italy.

➡ On leaving the EU, non-EU citizens can reclaim any value-added tax on expensive purchases made in shops offering tax-free shopping. For details, see www.globalrefund.com.

Discount Cards

➡ Those under 18 and over 65 are often entitled to free or discounted admission to state-run museums and cultural sights. Take proof of your age, ideally an ID card or passport.

➡ For students, an **International Student Identity Card** (ISIC; www.isic. org) entitles you to various shopping, accommodation and museum discounts. A similar card is available to teachers, the **International Teacher Identity Card** (ITIC;

Climate

Cagliari

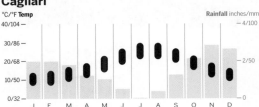

Olbia

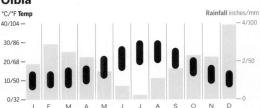

Oristano

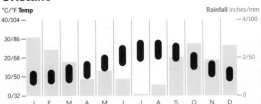

www.isic.org), and to non-students under 26 years, the **International Youth Travel Card** (IYTC; www.isic.org). The cost varies depending on where you get it, but reckon on about €15.

➡ There is also the **European Youth Card** (www.euro26. org), which offers a wide range of discounts across Europe. Card-holders do not need to be European citizens. It costs €11 if bought in Italy.

➡ Student cards are issued by student unions, hostelling organisations and some youth travel agencies. In Cagliari, Sassari and Nuoro, the **Centro Turistico Studentesco e Giovanile** (CTS; www.cts.it) youth travel agency can issue ISIC and ITIC cards and the European Youth Card.

Electricity

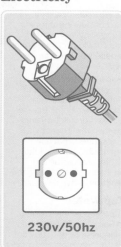

230v/50hz

230v/50hz

Embassies & Consulates

Most countries have an embassy in Rome, and several also maintain an honorary consulate in Cagliari. Passport inquiries should be addressed to the Rome-based offices.

Australian Embassy (✆emergencies 800 877790, tel, info 06 85 27 21; www.italy. embassy.gov.au; Via Antonio Bosio 5, Rome; ⌚9am-5pm Mon-Fri)

Canadian Embassy (✆06 854 44 29 11; www.canadaint-ernational.gc.ca/italy-italie; Via Zara 30, Rome)

Dutch Consulate (✆070 67 08 30; http://italie.nlam-bassade.org; Via Roma 101, Cagliari)

French Embassy (✆06 68 60 11; www.ambafrance-it.org; Piazza Farnese 67, Rome)

German Consulate (✆070 30 72 29; www.rom.diplo.de; Via Rafa Garzia 9, Cagliari)

Irish Embassy (✆06 585 23 81; www.ambasciata-irlanda. it; Villa Spada, Via Giacomo Medici 1, Rome)

New Zealand Embassy (✆06 853 75 01; www.nzem-bassy.com/italy; Via Clitunno 44, Rome)

Spanish Embassy (✆06 684 04 01; www. ambaspagna.191.it; Palazzo Borghese, Largo Fontanella Borghese 19, Rome)

UK Embassy (✆06 4220 0001; www.gov.uk/govern-ment/world/organisations/british-embassy-rome; Via XX Settembre 80a, Rome)

US Embassy (✆06 4 67 41; http://italy.usembassy.gov; Via Vittorio Veneto 119a, Rome)

Food

For detailed information on food and eating in Sardinia, see The Sardinian Kitchen (p239).

Gay & Lesbian Travellers

➡ Discretion is the key. Although homosexuality is legal, Sardinian attitudes remain largely conservative. There is practically no open gay scene on the island and overt displays of affection could attract unpleasant attention, especially in the rural interior.

➡ The most tolerant places are the island's two largest cities, Sassari and Cagliari.

➡ The island's most high-profile gay activist organisation is the Sassari-based **Movimento Omosessuale Sardo** (MOS; ✆079 21 90 24; www. movimentomosessualesardo. org; Via Rockfeller 16c, Sassari). Check out its website for listings and information on gay-friendly accommodation, clubs and beaches.

EATING PRICE RANGES

The following price ranges refer to a meal consisting of two courses, a glass of house wine and *coperto* (cover charge) for one person.

€ less than €25

€€ €25 to €45

€€€ more than €45

Note that most eating establishments add a *coperto* of around €1.50 to €2.50. Some also include *servizio* (a service charge) of 10% to 15%.

➡ Other points of reference include Cagliari's **Associazione Arc** (www.associazionearc.eu) which, together with MOS, organises **Sardegna Pride** (www.sardegnapride.org). First held in Cagliari in 2013, this colourful parade took to the seafront streets of Alghero in June 2014.

➡ Also useful is the national gay organisation **Arcigay** (www.arcigay.it/Sardegna).

➡ The English-language www.gayfriendlyitaly.com is an excellent resource with background information on gay life in Italy, links, and listings of gay-friendly B&Bs and beaches in Sardinia.

Health

Health Insurance

➡ The European Health Insurance Card (EHIC) entitles EU citizens and nationals of Switzerland, Iceland, Norway and Liechtenstein to free or reduced-cost state-provided health care for treatment that becomes necessary while in Sardinia or other parts of Italy.

➡ Each family member will need a separate card.

➡ The card is available from health centres and, in some countries, online. For more information see http://ec.europa.eu/social/main.jsp?catId=559. In the UK, get application forms from post offices, or download them from the Department of Health website (www.dh.gov.uk), which has comprehensive information about the card's coverage.

➡ The EHIC does not cover private health care, so make sure that you are treated by a state health-care provider. You will need to pay directly and fill in a treatment form; keep the form to claim any refunds. In general, you can claim back around 70% of the standard treatment cost.

➡ Citizens from other countries should check if there is a reciprocal arrangement for free medical care between their country and Italy. Australia, for instance, has such an agreement – carry your Medicare card.

➡ If you need health insurance, make sure you get a policy that covers you for the worst possible scenario, such as an accident requiring an emergency flight home.

➡ Find out in advance if your insurance plan will make payments directly to providers or reimburse you later for overseas health expenditures.

Availability & Cost of Health Care

Health care is readily available throughout Sardinia, but standards can vary.

➡ *Farmacie* (pharmacies), which are marked by a green cross, can give valuable medical advice and sell over-the-counter medication for minor illnesses. They can also advise when more specialised help is required and point you in the right direction.

➡ Pharmacies generally keep the same hours as shops, typically from around 9am to 1pm and 4.30pm to 8pm Monday to Friday and on Saturday mornings. Outside of these hours they open on a rotation basis for emergency purposes. Closed pharmacies display a list of the nearest ones open.

➡ For emergency treatment, go straight to the *pronto soccorso* (casualty) section of a public hospital, where you can also get emergency dental treatment.

➡ If you need an ambulance anywhere in Sardinia call ☑118.

➡ The Guardia Medica is an on-call medical service that offers assistance throughout the night (8pm to 8am) on weekends and on public holidays. It does not provide emergency care (for that go to the *pronto soccorso* department at the nearest hospital), although it will make home visits when absolutely necessary. The service is available in most major towns.

Bites & Stings

➡ Mosquitoes are a real nuisance around low-lying marshy areas such as Cabras and Olbia; you should be particularly wary if you are considering camping. If travelling in summer, you should pack mosquito repellent as a matter of course.

➡ Jellyfish are not uncommon in Sardinian waters. But while their stings are painful, they're not dangerous. Dousing in vinegar will deactivate any stingers that have not fired. Calamine lotion, antihistamines and analgesics may reduce the reaction and relieve pain.

Tap Water

Tap water is fine to drink in Sardinia, although many islanders prefer to buy bottled *acqua minerale* (mineral water), either *frizzante* (sparkling) or *naturale* (still).

Insurance

➡ Travel insurance to cover theft, loss and medical problems is highly recommended. It may also cover you for cancellation or delays to your travel arrangements.

➡ Paying for tickets with a credit card often provides limited travel accident insurance – ask your credit-card company what it will cover.

➡ Always check that your policy covers any activities you might be planning such as scuba diving, motorcycling, climbing, even trekking.

➡ Check that the policy covers ambulances or an emergency flight home.

➡ Find out in advance if your insurance plan will make payments directly to providers or reimburse you later for overseas health expenditures. If you have to claim later, make sure you keep all documentation.

➡ See the Health section for more on health insurance and the Transport chapter (p259) for more on car insurance.

➡ Worldwide travel insurance is available at www.lonelyplanet.com/travel-insurance. You can buy, extend and claim online anytime – even if you're already on the road.

Internet Access

➡ Wi-fi is available in most accommodation options, from hostels and B&Bs to luxury hotels. In most cases access is free but some (top-end) hotels charge a small fee.

➡ Due to the widespread availability of wi-fi there are far fewer internet cafes than there used to be, although in major centres such as

Cagliari and Alghero you can still find them. You certainly can't rely on finding an internet cafe in small towns and villages. Access typically costs up to €5 per hour.

➡ Note also that whenever you use an internet cafe you're legally obliged to show an ID card or passport.

➡ Some hotels provide a computer for guest use.

➡ In reviews, accommodation providers that have a computer for guest use are flagged with an internet icon (@); the wi-fi icon (📶) indicates anywhere with wi-fi access.

Legal Matters

You're unlikely to have anything to do with the police unless you have to report a theft or are stopped while driving for a random road check.

The police is divided into three main bodies: the *polizia,* who wear navy-blue jackets; the *carabinieri,* in a black uniform with a red stripe; and the grey-clad *guardia di finanza,* responsible for fighting tax evasion and drug smuggling.

If you run into trouble, you're most likely to end up dealing with the *polizia* or *carabinieri*. That is, unless you're on the receiving end of a parking ticket, in which case you'll be cursing the *vigili urbani,* the local traffic police.

➡ Under Italy's tough drug laws, possession of any controlled substance can get you into hot water. If caught with 5g of cannabis you can, in theory, be prosecuted as a trafficker. The same applies to tiny amounts of other drugs. Those caught with amounts below this threshold can be subject to minor penalties.

➡ The legal limit for a driver's blood-alcohol reading is 0.05% and random breath tests do occur.

➡ If you are detained for any alleged offence, you should be given verbal and written notice of the charges laid against you within 24 hours.

➡ You have no right to a phone call upon arrest, but you can choose not to respond to questions without the presence of a lawyer.

➡ The prosecutor must apply to a magistrate for you to be held in preventive custody

---

PRACTICALITIES

➡ **Weights & Measures** Metric.

➡ **Smoking** Banned in all enclosed public spaces.

➡ **Newspapers** The two main newspapers are Cagliari's *L'Unione Sarda* (www.unionesarda.it) and Sassari's *La Nuova Sardegna* (lanuovasardegna.gelocal.it). These papers tend to focus on island affairs and pay scant attention to national and international news. You can get English-language newspapers in most tourist centres, in summer only, and usually a day or two late.

➡ **Radio Radiolina** (www.radiolina.it) is a popular local radio station, broadcasting music, news and chat. National stations **RAI-1**, **RAI-2** and **RAI-3** (www.rai.it) play a mix of phone-ins, sport, news and music. Frequencies change depending on where you are.

➡ **TV** Local TV channels, such as **Videolina** (www.videolina.it) and **Sardegna 1** (www.sardegna1.tv), are usually pretty dire, pumping out news, football and traditional costumed dancing. National channels include the state-run **RAI-1**, **RAI-2** and **RAI-3** (www.rai.it) and the main commercial stations **Canale 5** (www.mediaset.it/canale5), **Italia 1** (www.mediaset.it/italia1), **Rete 4** (www.mediaset.it/rete4) run by Silvio Berlusconi's Mediaset company, as well as **La7** (www.la7.it).

awaiting trial (depending on the seriousness of the offence) within 48 hours of your arrest.

➡ If the magistrate orders preventive custody, you have the right to contest it within the following 10 days.

Maps

For travelling around the island, a good-quality map comes in very useful. The Touring Club Italiano's **Touring Editore** (www.touringclub.com) does an excellent island map at a scale of 1:200,000. Available online or at bookshops in Sardinia, it costs €7.90.

Money

➡ Sardinia's unit of currency is the euro (€), which is divided into 100 cents.

➡ Coin denominations are one, two, five, 10, 20 and 50 cents and €1 and €2. The seven euro notes come in denominations of €5, €10, €20, €50, €100, €200 and €500.

➡ Money can be exchanged in banks, post offices and exchange offices.

➡ Banks generally offer the best rates, but shop around, as rates tend to fluctuate considerably.

ATMs

➡ ATMs (known in Italian as *bancomat*) are widely available in Sardinia and are undoubtedly the simplest (and safest) way to access your money while travelling. Most accept cards tied into the Visa, MasterCard, Cirrus or Maestro systems. As a precaution, though, check that the appropriate logo is displayed on the ATM before inserting your card.

➡ The daily limit for cash withdrawal is €250.

➡ ATM withdrawals incur fees – check with your bank for precise details. Typically,

you'll be charged a per transaction withdrawal fee (usually around 1.5%) as well as a foreign currency conversion charge of around 2.5% to 3%. If you're using a credit card, you might also be hit by interest on the cash withdrawn.

Cash

➡ Cash is readily available from ATMs, so there's little point in bringing large quantities with you.

➡ When travelling around the island, you'll need cash for many day-to-day transactions, as credit cards are not always accepted, especially in many B&Bs and cheaper trattorias.

Credit Cards

➡ Credit cards are good for major purchases such as hotel stays and car hire, as well as for providing emergency cover. They also make life easier if you need to book accommodation while on the road – many places request a credit-card number when you reserve a room.

➡ Major cards such as Visa, MasterCard, Eurocard, Cirrus and Eurocheque are accepted in Sardinia.

➡ Check charges with your bank, but most banks now build a fee of around 2.5% to 3% into every foreign transaction.

➡ Note that not everywhere accepts payment by credit card. Some smaller B&Bs, *agriturismi* (farm-stays), pizzerias and trattorias only take cash. Check beforehand to avoid embarrassment.

➡ If your card is lost, stolen or swallowed by an ATM, telephone one of the following toll-free numbers to block it:

Amex (☎06 729 00 347)

MasterCard (☎800 870866)

Visa (☎800 819014)

Tipping

➡ You're not expected to tip on top of restaurant service charges, but if you think the service warrants it, feel free to round up the bill or leave a little extra – 10% is fine.

➡ In bars, Italians often leave small change (€0.10/0.20) as a tip.

➡ Tipping taxi drivers is not common practice, but you should tip the porter at top-end hotels.

WHERE	CUSTOMARY TIP
bar	round to nearest euro
hotel cleaning staff	€1 per day
hotel porter	€1 to €1.50 per bag
restaurant	if service isn't included, a euro or two in pizzerias, 10% in restaurants
taxi	optional, but most people round up to the nearest euro

Opening Hours

➡ Opening hours vary enormously depending on the season (summer/winter) and place (big towns/villages). In some smaller, more out-of-the-way places, business hours might simply depend on how long the owner decides to stay open for.

➡ In reviews, the hours listed are the most commonly applied ones. Where necessary seasonal variations are noted.

Post

➡ Italy's, and by association Sardinia's, postal system **Poste** (☎803160; www.poste.it) is reasonably reliable. Unfortunately, Sardinia's distance from the mainland doesn't help matters.

➡ Stamps *(francobolli)* are available at post offices and tobacconists *(tabacchi)* – look for the official sign, a big white 'T' against a blue-black background. Letters often need to be weighed, so what you get at the tobacconist's for international airmail will occasionally be an approximation of the proper rate.

Public Holidays

Most Italians take their annual holiday in August. As a consequence many city businesses and shops close for a couple of weeks around 15 August, a day known in Italy as Ferragosto. Settimana Santa (Easter Week) is another busy holiday period.

National public holidays include:

Capodanno (New Year's Day) 1 January

Epifania (Epiphany) 6 January

Pasqua (Easter Sunday) March/April

Pasquetta (Easter Monday) March/April

Giorno della Liberazione (Liberation Day) 25 April

Festa del Lavoro (Labour Day) 1 May

Festa della Repubblica (Republic Day) 2 June

Ferragosto (Feast of the Assumption) 15 August

Ognissanti (All Saints' Day) 1 November

Immacolata Concezione (Feast of the Immaculate Conception) 8 December

Natale (Christmas Day) 25 December

Festa di Santo Stefano (Boxing Day) 26 December

Safe Travel

Despite past notoriety as a centre of banditry and kidnapping, Sardinia is a peaceful island. Muggings, moped-assisted bag-snatching and overcharging in hotels are almost unheard of, and your stay should be trouble free.

Theft

Although theft is not a big problem in Sardinia, you should still use your common sense.

➡ A money belt with your essentials (passport, cash, credit cards) is a good idea. However, to avoid delving into it in public, carry a wallet with a day's cash.

➡ If you're carrying a bag or camera, wear the strap across your body and away from the road.

➡ Be careful when you sit down at a street-side table – never drape your bag over an empty chair by the road or put it where you can't see it.

➡ Don't leave valuables lying around your hotel room.

➡ Never leave valuables visible in your car – in fact, try not to leave anything in the car and certainly not overnight.

➡ In case of theft or loss, always report the incident at the *questura* (municipal police station) within 24 hours and ask for a

STANDARD OPENING HOURS

BUSINESS TYPE	STANDARD OPENING HOURS	NOTES
Banks	8.30am-1.30pm & 2.45-4.30pm Mon-Fri	Exchange offices usually keep longer hours.
Bars	7pm-1am Mon-Sat	Bars and cafes with live music or DJs often open till 1am weekdays, till 2am Fri and Sat.
Cafes	7am or 8am-8pm	
Clubs	10pm-3am, 4am or 5am Thu-Sat	
Pharmacies	9am-1pm & 4.30-8pm Mon-Fri, 9am-1pm Sat	When closed, pharmacies post a list of places open in the vicinity.
Post Offices	8.20am-7pm Mon-Fri, 8am-12.35pm Sat	Smaller branch offices often close at 2pm weekdays.
Restaurants	lunch noon-2.30pm or 3pm, dinner 7-10pm or 11pm	In summer (Jun-Sep) most open 7 days for lunch and dinner. In coastal resorts over winter (Nov-Mar) most close; those that stay open usually shut 1 day a week.
Shops	9am-1pm & 4-8pm Mon-Sat	In touristy areas, shops stay open later in summer, sometimes till 11pm. In big towns, some department stores and supermarkets open to 7.30pm Mon-Sat; some supermarkets open Sun morning. Food shops often close Thu afternoons; some shops shut Mon mornings.

statement, otherwise your travel-insurance company won't pay out.

Telephone
Mobile Phones

➡ Phones operate on the GSM 900/1800 network, which is compatible with the rest of Europe and Australia but not with the North American GSM 1900 or the Japanese system (although some GSM 1900/900 phones do work in Italy).

➡ Most modern smartphones are multiband, meaning they are compatible with a variety of international networks – check with your service provider. But beware of calls being routed internationally (very expensive for a local call).

➡ If you can unlock your phone (check with your service provider), your best bet is to activate a temporary or prepaid account at an Italian phone company store.

➡ To activate a prepaid Italian SIM card can cost as little as €10 (sometimes with €10 of calls already on the card). Pay-as-you-go SIM cards are readily available at phone and electronic stores in Sardinia.

➡ To recharge a card, simply pop into the nearest outlet or buy a *ricarica* (charge card) from a *tabacchi* (tobacconist).

➡ **TIM** (www.tim.it), **Wind** (www.wind.it) and **Vodafone** (www.vodafone.it) all offer SIM cards and all have retail outlets across the island.

➡ When you buy a card, make sure you have your ID card or passport with you.

Phone Codes

Sardinian area codes These all begin with a 0 and consist of up to four digits. The area code is an integral part of the telephone number and must always be dialled, even when calling locally.

Mobile phone numbers These begin with a three-figure prefix, typically 330, 331 etc.

Toll-free (free-phone) numbers Known as *numeri verdi*, these usually start with 800.

Non-geographical numbers These typically start with 840, 848 or 199.

Six-digit national-rate numbers You might come across some six-digit numbers. Well-known examples include the numbers for Alitalia and Trenitalia train information.

Directory enquiries Dial 1254.

Calling Sardinia from abroad Call your international access number, then Italy's country code (39) and then the local number (including the area code with the leading 0).

Calling abroad from Sardinia Dial 00 to get out of Italy, then the relevant country and area codes, followed by the telephone number.

The cheapest options for calling internationally Free or low-cost computer programs or smartphone apps such as Skype or Viber.

Time

➡ Sardinian time is one hour ahead of GMT/UTC.

➡ Daylight-saving time, when clocks are moved forward one hour, commences on the last Sunday in March. Clocks are put back an hour on the last Sunday in October.

➡ Italy operates on a 24-hour clock, so 6pm is written as 18.00.

Toilets

➡ Most toilets in Sardinia are of the Western-style sit-down variety.

➡ Public toilets are not widespread. If you're caught short, the best thing to do is to nip into a cafe or bar, all of which are required by law to have a toilet.

Tourist Information

➡ Tourist information is widely available in Sardinia, although the quality varies enormously. On the whole, offices in important tourist centres such as Alghero, Cala Gonone, Santa Teresa di Gallura and Villasimius are efficient and helpful with English-speaking staff.

➡ Alongside the 'official' tourist offices there are a plethora of private agencies advertising tourist information, plus tours and accommodation. In some cases, these places are more useful than the official sources.

➡ Tourist offices can usually provide a city/town map, accommodation lists and

GOVERNMENT TRAVEL ADVICE

The following government websites offer up-to-date travel advisories:

Australian Department of Foreign Affairs (www.smarttraveller.gov.au)

British Foreign Office (www.gov.uk/foreign-travel-advice)

Canadian Department of Foreign Affairs (http://travel.gc.ca/travelling/health-safety)

New Zealand Ministry of Foreign Affairs & Trade (www.safetravel.govt.nz)

US State Department (http://travel.state.gov)

information on the major sights. They can also help with public-transport information.

➡ Offices are generally open 9am to 1pm and then from 4pm to 6pm Monday to Friday. However, hours are usually extended in summer, when some offices also open on Saturday and Sunday.

➡ Most offices will respond to written and telephone requests for information. Useful websites include:

Sardegna Turismo (www. sardegnaturismo.it) The official website of Sardinia's regional tourist authority. It's an excellent source of up-to-date information, covering things to see and do, events, accommodation, transport and much more.

Italia (www.italia.it) Multilingual site of the Italian National Tourist Office. Click on the Discover Italy link and then Sardinia for an introduction to the island. Practical information is available for Italy in general but the Sardinia section is more inspirational than practical.

Travellers with Disabilities

Sardinia has little infrastructure to ease the way for disabled travellers, and few museums and monuments have wheelchair access. A notable exception is Cagliari's Museo Archeologico Nazionale.

Under European law, airports are obliged to provide assistance to passengers with disabilities, so if you need help en route to Sardinia, or on arrival, tell your airline when you book your ticket and they should inform the airport. Information on services available at Rome's two airports is available online at www.adrassistance.it.

If you need assistance travelling by train, contact the **Rete Ferroviaria Italiana** (RFI; ☑800 90 60 60, 199 30 30 60; www.rfi.it), which has two dedicated telephone

lines, active daily between 6.45am and 9.30pm.

The Italian State Tourist Office in your country may be able to provide advice on Italian associations for the disabled and information on what help is available in the country.

Some useful sources of information:

Accessible Italy (☑378 941111; www.accessibleitaly. com) A San Marino–based company that specialises in holiday services for travellers with disabilities, including tours and the hiring of adapted transport.

Associazione Italiana Assistenza Spastici (☑070 37 91 01; www.aiasnazionale.it; Viale Poetto 312, Cagliari) The Italian Spastics Assistance Association has a branch in Cagliari.

Lonely Planet (www.lonelyplanet.com) Check out the Travel for All community on Google+, with posts, tips and shared experiences.

Sardinia For All (www. sardiniaforall.it) Run by a Sassari-based cooperative, La Luna, this website has lists of accessible hotels, *agriturismi* (farm stays) and B&Bs in Sardinia's northwest, around Alghero, Stintino, Porto Torres and Sassari.

Visas

Visa Requirements

➡ Italy is one of the 26 European countries to make up the Schengen area. There are no customs controls when travelling between Schengen countries, so the visa rules that apply to Italy apply to all Schengen countries.

➡ The standard tourist visa for a Schengen country is valid for 90 days and allows unlimited travel within the entire Schengen zone. You must apply for it in the country of your residence and you cannot apply for more than two in any 12-month period. They are not renewable within Italy.

➡ EU citizens do not need a visa to enter Italy. A valid ID card or passport is sufficient.

➡ Nationals of some other countries, including Australia, Canada, Israel, Japan, New Zealand, Norway, Switzerland and the US do not need a visa for stays of up to 90 days.

➡ All non-EU and non-Schengen nationals entering Italy for more than 90 days or for any reason other than tourism (such as study or work) may need a specific visa. Check www.esteri. it/visti/home_eng.asp or contact an Italian consulate for details. If necessary start your application well in advance as it can take months.

➡ Technically all foreign visitors to Sardinia are supposed to register with the local police within eight days of their arrival. However, if you are staying in a hotel, you don't need to bother, as the hotel does this for you – this is the reason why they always take your passport details.

➡ Up-to-date visa information is available on www.lonelyplanet.com – follow links through to the Italy destination guide and then practical information.

Permesso di Soggiorno

➡ A *permesso di soggiorno* (permit to stay, also referred to as a residence permit) is required by all non-EU nationals who stay in Sardinia longer than three months. In theory, you should apply for one within eight days of arriving in Italy.

➡ EU citizens do not require a *permesso di soggiorno* but are required to register with the local registry office (*ufficio anagrafe*) if they stay for more than three months.

➡ To get one you'll need an application form; a valid passport, containing a stamp with your date of entry into Italy (ask for this as it's not automatic); a photocopy of your passport with visa, if required; four passport-style photographs; proof of your ability to support yourself financially (ideally a letter from an employer or school/university); and a €16 official stamp (known as a *marca da bollo*). You'll also need to pay a fee of between €80 and €200 depending on the type of *permesso di soggiorno* you're applying for.

➜ Up-to-date information is available on the website of the **Polizia di Stato** (www.poliziadistato.it).

Study Visas

➜ Non-EU citizens who want to study in Sardinia must have a study visa. These must be obtained before you arrive in Italy from your nearest Italian embassy or consulate.

➜ When you apply you will normally require confirmation of your enrolment, proof of payment of fees, proof that you can support yourself financially, and proof of valid health-insurance cover.

➜ The visa covers only the period of the enrolment.

➜ This type of visa is renewable in Italy but, again, only with confirmation of ongoing enrolment and proof that you are able to support yourself financially.

➜ For more information refer to the website of the Italian Foreign Ministry (www.esteri.it/visti/index_eng.asp).

Work Visas

➜ To work in Italy all non-EU nationals require a work visa. Apply to your nearest Italian embassy or consulate.

➜ You'll need a valid passport, proof of health insurance and a *permesso di lavoro* (work permit).

➜ The work permit is obtained in Italy by your employer and then forwarded to you prior to your visa application.

➜ Citizens of Australia, New Zealand and Canada aged between 18 and 30 (35 for Canadians) can apply for a Working Holiday Visa. This allows you to stay in Italy for a year and work for up to six months. Check with your nearest Italian consulate for details.

Volunteering

Volunteering opportunities are fairly limited in Sardinia. Websites like www.volunteerabroad.com and www.transitionsabroad.com have links to organisations offering volunteering positions in Italy and Sardinia. A common request is for mother-tongue English speakers to work at summer schools/camps.

Other organisations and resources that might be of use:

Workaway (www.workaway.info) A British outfit that organises placements with host families/organisations. In return for work on anything from babysitting to building, gardening or restoration projects, you get board and lodging.

World Wide Opportunities On Organic Farms (WWOOF; www.wwoof.it) An international outfit that can put you in touch with organic farms or ventures offering unpaid work (harvesting olives, helping with beehives, tending vegetable patches, help with milking and cheese making etc.).

Volunteers For Peace (www.vfp.org) A US-based nonprofit organisation. Can link you up with a voluntary service project dealing with social work, the environment, education or the arts.

Women Travellers

➜ Sardinians are almost universally polite to women, and it is unlikely that you will suffer the sort of harassment that you might in parts of mainland Italy.

➜ If you do find yourself the recipient of unwanted male attention, it's best to ignore it. If that doesn't work, politely tell your would-be companion that you are waiting for your *marito* (husband) or *fidanzato* (boyfriend) and, if necessary, walk away.

➜ Avoid becoming aggressive as this may result in a confrontation. If all else fails, approach the nearest member of the police.

➜ It is wise – and polite – to dress modestly in inland Sardinia. Communities here are very conservative, and you will still see older women wearing the traditional long, pleated skirts and shawls. Take your cue from the local women.

Work

High unemployment in Sardinia, particularly among young people, means job opportunities are scarce on the island.

➜ EU nationals have an automatic right to work in Italy. Non-EU nationals require a work visa.

➜ Working 'on the black' (that is, without documents) is risky. The only instance in which the authorities regularly turn a blind eye is during fruit harvests.

Finding Work

Seasonal work in resorts, bars, restaurants and hotels does exist but most jobs are snapped up by young Sardinians or Italians coming over from the mainland.

Other possibilities include English-language teaching – in a company, language school or through private lessons – and au pairing.

A useful online resource:

Season Workers (www.seasonworkers.com) Lists seasonal job opportunities on summer resorts.

Transport

GETTING THERE & AWAY

The easiest and fastest way to get to Sardinia is by air. A number of international airlines serve the island and if you are coming from elsewhere in Europe you should have no problem finding a direct flight.

If you're travelling from outside Europe, you will have to fly to Italy and pick up a connecting flight from the mainland. There are flights to Sardinia from most Italian airports but most frequently from Rome and Milan.

Note that some low-cost European carriers only operate seasonal flights, typically between May and October.

As a slower but cheaper alternative to flying, ferries serve Sardinia from Genoa, Livorno, Civitavecchia and Naples.

Flights, cars and tours can be booked online at lonelyplanet.com/bookings.

Entering the Region

➜ EU and Swiss citizens can travel to Italy with their national ID card alone. People from countries that do not issue ID cards must carry a valid passport. All other nationalities must have a full valid passport and may be required to fill out a landing card on arrival in Italy.

➜ If you are flying to Sardinia via the Italian mainland, all customs and immigration formalities will take place at the mainland airport. The Sardinian leg of your journey will be considered an internal flight.

➜ You should carry your ID card or passport when travelling on internal flights or ferry crossings.

Air

High season in Sardinia is June to September. Holidays such as Easter also see a huge jump in prices.

Airports & Airlines

Flights from Italian and European cities serve Sardinia's three main airports. Flight schedules are available on the websites of all three airports.

Elmas (☑070 21 12 11; www.sogaer.it) Sardinia's main airport is about 7km northwest of Cagliari, on the island's southern coast.

Fertilia (www.aeroportodialghero.it) Situated about 10km from Alghero, in the northwest.

Aeroporto Olbia Costa Smeralda (www.geasar.it) This is the main gateway for the northeast, some 5km south of Olbia.

International airlines operate year-round flights from cities across Europe including Barcelona, Brussels, Dortmund, Dublin, Düsseldorf, Eindhoven, Frankfurt, London, Madrid, Munich, Oslo, Paris and Stockholm.

Domestic flights connect with mainland Italian airports including Rome, Milan, Naples, Bari, Bologna, Turin, Venice and Verona.

Note that there's a marked increase in flights to and from Sardinia in summer, with many seasonal flights operating between June and September.

Italian airlines serving Sardinia:

Air Dolomiti (www.airdolomiti.it)

Air One (www.flyairone.it)

Alitalia (www.alitalia.it) Italy's national carrier.

Meridiana (www.meridiana.it)

Land

Sardinia is the most isolated island in the Mediterranean, some 200km from the nearest land mass, so any overland trip will include a ferry leg.

➜ The shortest ferry crossing from the Italian mainland is from Civitavecchia to Olbia on Sardinia's northeast coast, though there are various alternatives.

➜ If you are travelling by bus, train or car to Italy, check whether you require visas for the countries you intend to pass through.

Border Crossings

Aside from the coast roads linking Italy with France and Slovenia, border crossings into Italy mostly involve tunnels through the Alps or mountain passes. The major points of entry:

Austria From Innsbruck to Bolzano via A22/E45 (Brenner Pass); Villach to Tarvisio via A23/E55.

France From Nice to Ventimiglia via A10/E80; Modane to Turin via A32/E70 (Fréjus Tunnel); Chamonix to Courmayeur via A5/E25 (Mont Blanc Tunnel).

Slovenia From Sežana to Trieste via SS58/E70.

Switzerland From Martigny to Aosta via SS27/E27 (Grand St Bernard Tunnel); Lugano to Como via A9/E35.

➜ The tunnels listed above are all open year-round.

➜ Mountain passes are often closed in winter and sometimes even in autumn and spring, making the tunnels a less scenic but more reliable option.

➜ When driving on certain high roads in winter, you're legally obliged to carry snow chains in your car.

➜ For more details on getting to Italy overland, see www.lonelyplanet.com/italy/transport/getting-there-away.

Bus

Buses are the cheapest overland option to Italy, but services are less frequent, less comfortable and significantly slower than trains.

➜ **Eurolines** (www.eurolines.com) is a consortium of 29 European coach companies operating across Europe with offices in all major European cities.

➜ Italy-bound buses head to a number of cities, including Genoa and Naples, and Rome where you can catch a train up to Civitavecchia for the onward ferry journey.

Car & Motorcycle

➜ As Italy and its neighbours France, Switzerland, Austria and Slovenia are all members of the Schengen area – meaning they have abolished controls at common borders – you should have no problems driving into Italy. Authorities do however retain the right to check you and your vehicle.

➜ It's unlikely but at the border crossing you might be asked to show your vehicle's registration papers and proof of third-party insurance.

➜ For many drivers the most convenient Italian port to sail from will be Genoa, from where year-round ferries connect with Sardinia. You could, however, continue 190km southeast to Livorno, from where the sea crossing is shorter.

➜ Drivers coming from the UK, Spain or France may prefer to connect with ferries sailing from Marseille.

➜ Useful online resources include:

Ideamerge (www.ideamerge.com) Click on the Moto Europa Guide to Driving in Europe.

Michelin (www.viamichelin.com) A good route planner with printable maps and driving directions.

Train

Italy's main ports are all accessible by train:

Genoa via Paris and Milan or Turin

Livorno via Paris and Milan

Civitavecchia via Paris, Milan and Rome

Naples via Paris and Milan

➜ If travelling through France by train, you can pick up a summer ferry from Marseille to Porto Torres.

➜ If you want to transport your car by rail, the Dutch Motorail service operates a weekly passenger and car train (between April and October) from s'Hertogenbosch in the Netherlands to Livorno. Check details at www.autoslaaptrein.nl.

➜ For the latest fare information on journeys to Italy, including Eurostar, contact **International Rail** (☎ 0871 231 0790; www.internationalrail.com) or **Voyages-sncf** (www.voyages-sncf.com).

➜ For advice, information and handy rail tips check out the encyclopaedic website **The Man in Seat Sixty-One** (www.seat61.com). There is almost nothing this website can't tell you about travelling in Europe, or indeed anywhere in the world, by train.

Sea

Sardinia is accessible by ferry from ports in Spain, France and Italy.

➜ The arrival points in Sardinia are Olbia, Golfo Aranci, Santa Teresa di Gallura and Porto Torres in the north; Arbatax on the east coast; and Cagliari in the south.

➜ Services are most frequent between mid-June and mid-September, when it is advisable to book well ahead.

➜ You can book tickets at travel agents throughout Italy or directly online. Useful ferry websites:

Traghetti Web (www.traghettiweb.it) Comprehensive site listing major routes and ferry companies. Also has online booking.

AFerry (www.aferry.co.uk) Information on routes, ferry operators and online booking.

From Corsica

The main crossing from Corsica to Sardinia is between Bonifacio and Santa Teresa di Gallura on the northern coast, though ferries also depart from Bastia, Ajaccio and Propriano.

Saremar (☎199 118877; www.saremar.it)

Operates up to three daily departures between Bonifacio and Santa Teresa di Gallura. Reckon on about €16 per adult, €21 per car plus taxes. The trip takes one hour.

Moby Lines (☎199 30 30 40; www.mobylines.it)

Operates four daily crossings from Bonifacio to Santa Teresa

di Gallura between mid-April and late September. High-season tickets cost from about €22 per person or €30 with a small car.

SNCM (☎in France 3260; www.sncm.fr)

Ferries to Porto Torres from Marseille via Propriano or, less frequently, Ajaccio. From Propriano to Porto Torres, bank on about €26 per person or €38 with a car.

From Mainland France

Both **SNCM** (☎in France 3260; www.sncm.fr) and **La Méridionale** (☎in France 491 994 509; www.lameridionale.fr) operate ferries from Marseille to Porto Torres (via Corsica). Crossing time is 15 to 17 hours. Tickets for a reclinable seat cost €78 and for a small car €141.

FERRIES TO SARDINIA

The following is a rundown of the main ferry routes to Sardinia, the companies that operate them and the route details. Prices quoted are intended as a rough guide only; fares are for a 2nd-class *poltrona* (reclinable seat) in high season. Children aged four to 12 generally pay around half-price; children under four go free. Unless otherwise stated port taxes, which can add up to more than €50 per crossing, are not included in the fares listed here.

FROM	TO	COMPANY	FARE	CAR	DURATION (HR)	FREQUENCY
Civitavecchia	Arbatax	Tirrenia	€23	€45	10½	2 weekly
Civitavecchia	Cagliari	Tirrenia	€56	€116	13-16	daily
Civitavecchia	Olbia	Moby	€65	€90	5	daily mid-Apr–Sep
Civitavecchia	Olbia	Tirrenia	€32	€70	5-8	daily
Genoa	Arbatax	Tirrenia	€91	€149	15-18	2 weekly
Genoa	Olbia	Moby	€73	€104	10½	daily end-May–mid-Oct
Genoa	Olbia	Tirrenia	€41	€142	10-12	up to 5 weekly
Genoa	Porto Torres	GNV	€74+	€194+	11	up to 4 weekly end-May–mid-Sep
Genoa	Porto Torres	Tirrenia	€60	€80	11	daily
Livorno	Arbatax	Go in Sardinia	€70+	€122+	11½	1 weekly Jun-Sep
Livorno	Golfo Aranci	Sardinia Ferries	€80	€98	10	daily
Livorno	Olbia	Go in Sardinia	€70+	€122+	9	up to 6 weekly Jun-Sep
Livorno	Olbia	Moby	€60	€106	6½-8	daily
Naples	Cagliari	Tirrenia	€46	€105	13½	2 weekly
Palermo	Cagliari	Tirrenia	€40	€100	12	1 weekly
Piombino	Olbia	Moby	€60	€93	5-8½	daily end-May–Sep

+ Includes all taxes.

Ferry Operators

Go in Sardinia (☎0789 75 41 30; www.goinsardinia.it) To Olbia and Arbatax from Livorno.

Grandi Navi Veloci (☎010 209 45 91; www.gnv.it) To Porto Torres from Genoa.

Moby Lines (☎199 303040; www.moby.it) To Olbia from Civitavecchia, Genoa, Livorno and Piombino.

Sardinia Ferries (☎199 400500; www.sardiniaferries.com) To Golfo Aranci from Livorno.

Tirrenia (☎892123; www.tirrenia.it) To Cagliari from Civitavecchia, Naples, Palermo and Trapani; to Olbia from Civitavecchia and Genoa; to Arbatax from Civitavecchia and Genoa; to Porto Torres from Genoa.

For tickets and information in Porto Torres, contact **Agenzia Paglietti** (☑079 51 41 42; Corso Vittorio Emanuele 19, Porto Torres).

From Spain

Grimaldi Lines (☑081 496444; www.grimaldi-lines. com) operates ferries from Barcelona to Porto Torres. Tickets for a reclinable seat cost €20 to €35 per person (plus €25 tax) and €50 to €90 for a car. Journey time is 11¾ hours. Services run from mid-April to October with up to five weekly sailings between mid-June and early September.

From Mainland Italy & Sicily

Year-round ferries sail from Genoa, Livorno, Civitavecchia, Naples and Palermo. Seasonal services run from Piombino in Tuscany.

➡ Seasonal crossings generally operate from mid-April to the end of September.

➡ As well as reclinable seats, most ferries also offer cabins with en-suite bathrooms. Prices vary according to the number of occupants (generally one to four) and position (with or without window). Note that cabins don't always cost a lot more than a reclinable seat, particularly in the low season – it's always worth checking.

➡ Most companies offer discounts on return trips and other deals – check the website or ask your travel agent.

GETTING AROUND

If at all possible it is preferable to have your own car in Sardinia. Getting around the island on public transport is difficult and time-consuming but not impossible. In most cases buses are preferable to trains, which are nearly

always slower and often involve slow changes.

Bicycle

Sardinia lends itself well to cycling – the roads are rarely busy outside of high summer, the scenery is magnificent and it doesn't rain much. But bear in mind that the going can be tough and that the hilly (sometimes mountainous) terrain will take it out of you and your bike.

➡ Bikes are available for hire in most major towns and resorts, including Alghero, Santa Teresa di Gallura, La Maddalena, Palau and Olbia.

➡ Rates range from around €10 per day to as much as €25 for mountain bikes.

➡ You cannot cycle on the SS131, Sardinia's principal road, which runs from Cagliari in the south to the northern port of Porto Torres.

➡ If cycling in summer, make sure you have plenty of water and sunblock as the heat can be exhausting.

➡ Bikes can be taken on regional trains but you'll need to buy a separate bike ticket (€3.50).

➡ In the UK, **Cyclists' Touring Club** (☑0844 736 84 50; www.ctc.org.uk) can help you plan your own bike trip or organise guided tours. Membership costs £41.

Bringing Your Own Bicycle

➡ Transporting your bike to Sardinia poses no special problems.

➡ You can transport your bike by plane. Different airlines apply different rules, but most will require that your bike is packed in a bike bag or box, that the pedals and handlebars are turned flush with the frame, and that tyres are deflated.

➡ Some airlines charge a fee for transporting a bike, typically €30 to €60. Others

include it in your baggage allowance. In this case charges only apply if you exceed your baggage weight allowance.

➡ You can carry bikes with you on ferries to Sardinia for a small fee, usually €3 to €10.

➡ Be sure to bring tools, spare parts, a helmet, lights and a secure bike lock.

Boat

Boat tours are a popular way of exploring Sardinia's coastline, particularly in summer. You'll also need to take a ferry to reach the Isola di San Pietro, off Sardinia's southwestern coast, and the Isola di La Maddalena in the north.

Note that services are cut back considerably over the winter months, so always check ahead. If taking a car in summer, try to arrive in good time as boats fill up quickly.

➡ Boat tours generally run from late March or early April to October. They are an excellent way to see Sardinia's more inaccessible coastal highlights.

➡ The most popular tours include trips out of Cala Gonone and Santa Maria Navarrese along the majestic Golfo di Orosei. Also highly recommended is a cruise from Palau around the islands of the Maddalena archipelago.

➡ Boats frequently head out of Porto San Paolo, south of Olbia, for trips around Isola Tavolara and the nearby coast. From Alghero you can take boat trips up to Capo Caccia and the Grotta di Nettuno; from the Sinis Peninsula boat tours head over to Isola di Mal di Ventre.

➡ Most trips are by motorboats or small ferries, but a handful of sailing vessels are also on hand.

➡ **Enermar** (☑0789 70 84 84; www.enermar.it), **Saremar** (☑199 118877;

www.saremar.it) and **Delcomar** (📞0781 85 71 23; www.delcomar.it) connect Palau with the Isola di La Maddalena. In summer services run every 30 minutes and cost €6.80 for the 15-minute crossing or €16.50 with a small car.

➡ Saremar has up to 15 sailings daily from Portovesme to Carloforte on the Isola di San Pietro. Saremar also links Carloforte with Calasetta on the neighbouring Isola di Sant'Antioco.

➡ Delcomar operates nightly crossings from Portovesme to Carloforte, as well as between Carloforte and Calasetta.

Bus

Bus services within Sardinia are provided by the **Azienda Regionale Sarda Trasporti** (ARST; 📞800 865042; www. arst.sardegna.it), which runs the majority of local and long-distance buses. ARST also operates a limited network of private narrow-gauge railways, most notably the Trenino Verde.

➡ All of the island's principal towns have an ARST bus terminus, usually centrally located.

➡ In smaller towns and villages there will simply be a *fermata* (stop) for intercity buses, not always in an immediately apparent location.

➡ Tickets must usually be bought prior to boarding at stations or designated bars, *tabacchi* (tobacconists) or newsstands near the bus stop. On some services you can buy tickets on board but they'll cost slightly extra.

➡ Timetables are sometimes posted next to the bus stop, but don't hold your breath.

➡ Tourist offices in bigger towns can usually provide timetables for their area. Alternatively ask at the bar/ newsstand where you buy your ticket.

➡ In smaller locations you may need to ask where you can buy tickets.

➡ Note that while services might be frequent on weekdays they are cut back drastically on Sundays and holidays – runs between smaller towns often fall to one or none. Keep this in mind if you depend on buses, as it is easy to get stranded in smaller places, especially on weekends.

Car & Motorcycle

Driving in Sardinia is reasonably stress free. Traffic is only really a concern in the main towns (Cagliari, Sassari and Olbia) and in high summer, and local drivers are fairly courteous. The main hazards you're likely to face are flocks of sheep and the stunning scenery.

➡ Main roads are generally in reasonable condition although to really explore the island you'll need to use the system of smaller provincial roads *(strade provinciali)*, marked as P or SP on maps. These are sometimes little more than country lanes, but they provide access to some of the more beautiful scenery and the many small towns and villages.

➡ Many spectacular beaches and rural *agriturismi* (farm stays) are only accessible by dirt tracks.

➡ Sardinia is very popular with German and Austrian motorcyclists who enjoy racing around the island's scenic roads and hairpin bends.

➡ Unless you're touring it's probably easier to rent a motorbike once you're in Sardinia.

Automobile Associations

Italy's motoring organisation is the **Automobile Club d'Italia** (ACI; 📞roadside assistance with a non-Italian phone 800 116800, roadside assistance with an Italian phone 803116; www.aci.it). Foreigners do not have to join but instead pay a fee in case of breakdown assistance (€115 to €138, 20% more on weekends and holidays). Further charges will also apply if your car needs to be towed away. Check the website for details.

The UK's **AA** (📞0800 085 2721; www.theaa.co.uk) and the **RAC** (📞0800 015 6000; www. rac.co.uk) both offer European breakdown cover.

Bringing Your Own Vehicle

When driving in Italy you'll need to have the following documents with you:

➡ your vehicle-registration certificate

➡ a valid driving licence

➡ proof of 3rd party liability insurance cover.

You'll also need a warning triangle to use in case of an accident, and a fluorescent safety vest to be worn if you have to get out of your car in the event of a breakdown.

A first-aid kit, a spare-bulb kit and a fire extinguisher are also recommended.

Driving Licence

➡ All EU driving licences are recognised in Sardinia.

➡ Holders of non-EU licences must get an International Driving Permit (IDP) to accompany their national licence. Your national automobile association can issue this. It is valid for 12 months.

Fuel

➡ There are plenty of filling stations in and around towns and on main roads. Smaller stations tend to close between about 1pm and 3.30pm and on Sunday afternoons.

➡ Many stations have self-service *(fai da te)* pumps that you can use 24 hours a day. To use one insert a bank note into the payment machine and press the number of the pump you want.

→ Unleaded petrol is marked as *benzina senza piombo*, diesel as *gasolio*.

→ Fuel is pretty expensive in Sardinia. Prices vary from one filling station to another but reckon on around €1.70 per litre for unleaded petrol and €1.60 per litre for diesel.

Hire

→ It is *always* cheaper to arrange car hire before you arrive in Sardinia.

→ All the major international car-hire outlets have offices at the airports, where you usually pick up your car and deposit it at the end of your stay. You'll also find rental agencies in some of the main cities and in most coastal resorts.

→ Age restrictions vary from agency to agency but generally you'll need to be 21 or over.

→ If you're under 25, you'll probably have to pay a young-driver's supplement on top of the usual rates.

→ To hire, you'll need a credit card and a valid driving licence.

→ In tourist hot spots like Santa Teresa di Gallura and Alghero you'll find rental outlets offering motorcycles and scooters.

→ Most agencies will not hire out motorcycles to people under 18.

→ Note that many places require a sizeable deposit and that you could be responsible for reimbursing part of the cost of the bike if it is stolen.

The main national and international agencies:

Avis (☑199 100133; www. avisautonoleggio.it)

Budget (☑199 307373; www. budgetautonoleggio.it)

Europcar (☑199 307030; www.europcar.it)

Hertz (☑199 112211; www. hertz.it)

Italy By Car (☑334 6481920; www.italybycar.it)

Maggiore (☑199 151120; www.maggiore.it)

Insurance

→ Third-party motor insurance is a minimum requirement in Italy.

→ Residents of non-EU countries should check with their car insurer whether they need an International Insurance Certificate, known as a *Carta Verde* (Green Card).

→ It's not obligatory but you could ask your insurer for a European Accident Statement form, which can simplify matters in the event of an accident.

→ Similarly, a European breakdown-assistance policy will make life easier in the event of a breakdown.

Road Conditions

Sardinia's road network is dictated by its geography. Much of the mountainous interior is untarnished by tarmac, and it's generally easier to travel north–south (or vice versa) than east–west.

→ The island's principal artery, the mostly dual-carriageway SS131 (known as the Carlo Felice), runs from Cagliari to Porto Torres via Oristano, Macomer and Sassari. Branching off it at Abbasanta, the SS131DCN runs up to Nuoro and Olbia.

→ Another principal road, the SS130, runs west from Cagliari to Iglesias.

→ You'll find dual-carriageways between Sassari and Alghero, and between Porto Torres and the SS291 Sassari–Alghero road.

→ Along the north coast, the SS200 bypasses Castelsardo en route from Porto Torres to Santa Teresa di Gallura. From nearby Palau, the SS125, or Orientale Sarda, is another

key artery, running down the east side of the island to Cagliari in the south.

→ These and many roads in the more touristy coastal areas are reasonably well maintained but can be narrow and curvy.

→ In summer, when the island fills with visitors, it is virtually impossible not to get caught in traffic jams along many roads. The area between Olbia and Santa Teresa di Gallura is particularly bad.

→ Inland, the quality of roads is uneven. Main roads are mostly good but narrow and winding, while many secondary routes are in poor shape, particularly after bad weather when heavy rain can open axle-busting potholes in the road surfaces.

→ Getting in and out of the cities, notably Cagliari and Sassari, can be a test of nerves as traffic chokes approach-roads and exits.

→ You will also be surprised by the number of unpaved roads on the island – a worry if in an expensive rental car. Many *agriturismi* (farmstays), prehistoric sites and beaches are only accessible by dirt tracks.

Road Rules

→ In Sardinia, as in the rest of continental Europe, drive on the right-hand side of the road and overtake on the left.

→ Unless otherwise indicated, you must always give way to cars entering an intersection from the right.

→ It is compulsory to wear front and rear seatbelts. If you are caught not wearing a seatbelt, you could be required to pay an on-the-spot fine.

→ Helmets are compulsory on all two-wheeled vehicles.

→ Random breath tests take place. If you're involved in an accident while under the influence of alcohol, the penalties can be severe. The blood-alcohol limit is 0.05%.

→ Speed limits on main highways (there are no *autostrade* in Sardinia) are 110km/h, on secondary highways 90km/h, and in built-up areas 50km/h.

→ Speeding fines follow EU standards and are proportionate to the number of kilometres you are driving over the limit, reaching a maximum of €3280 and the possible suspension of your licence.

→ Drivers are obliged to keep headlights switched on day and night on all dual carriageways.

→ No licence is required to ride a scooter under 50cc, but you must be 14 or over and you can't carry passengers. To ride a scooter up to 125cc, you must be 16 or over and have a licence (a car driving licence will do). For motorcycles over 125cc you must be 18 or over and have a motorcycle licence.

→ There is no daytime lights-on requirement for motorcycles.

→ On a motorcycle you can enter restricted traffic areas in cities and towns without any problems. Also traffic police generally turn a blind eye to motorcycles or scooters parked on footpaths.

Hitching

→ Hitching is never entirely safe in any country, and we don't recommend it. Travellers who decide to hitch should understand that they are taking a small but potentially serious risk.

→ Hitching is extremely uncommon in Sardinia. Sardinians can be wary of picking up strangers, which makes travelling this way a frustrating business.

→ Never hitch where drivers can't stop in good time or without causing an obstruction.

→ Look presentable, carry as little luggage as possible, and hold a sign in Italian indicating your destination.

→ Do not use the normal thumbs-up signal, as this can offend (in these parts it means 'up yours'!).

→ Women travelling on their own would be extremely ill-advised to hitch.

Local Transport

Buses and trains are the main options for getting around in Sardinia.

→ All the major towns have a reasonable local bus service.

→ Generally, you won't need buses to get around town centres, which tend to be fairly compact. In most places, the sights, hotels, and bus/train stations are all within walking distance of each other.

→ Bus tickets (around €1.20) must be purchased from newspaper stands or *tabacchi* and stamped on the bus.

→ All three airports are linked by local bus services to their respective town centres.

Tours

Throughout the island local operators offer all manner of guided excursions and tours. You'll also find hundreds of

PARKING & TRAFFIC RESTRICTIONS

Parking in Sardinian cities and at popular beaches can be a headache.

→ Blue lines denote pay-and-display parking – buy tickets at the coin-operated meters, from tobacconists or from parking assistants. Rates vary but reckon on about €1 per hour. Typically charges are applied between 8am and 1pm and then from 4pm to 8pm. Outside of these hours you can park your car for free. Note, however, that in some places charges are applied from 8am to 8pm.

→ White lines denote free parking and yellow lines indicate spaces reserved for drivers with specific passes.

→ As a general rule, the easiest time to find street parking is the early afternoon between 2pm and 4pm.

→ When driving in city centres watch out for traffic restrictions. Areas in the historic centres of Cagliari, Alghero, Sassari, Oristano and Nuoro are off limits to unauthorised traffic during certain hours.

→ If you slip into a **ZTL** (*zona a traffico limitato* or limited traffic zone) you risk being caught on camera and fined. And being in a hire car won't save you. The rental agency will simply pass on your details to the authorities and you'll receive a fine at your home address, possibly months later. Adding insult to injury, the hire-car company might also charge you an administration fee for passing on your contact details.

CLIMATE CHANGE & TRAVEL

Every form of transport that relies on carbon-based fuel generates CO_2, the main cause of human-induced climate change. Modern travel is dependent on aeroplanes, which might use less fuel per kilometre per person than most cars but travel much greater distances. The altitude at which aircraft emit gases (including CO_2) and particles also contributes to their climate change impact. Many websites offer 'carbon calculators' that allow people to estimate the carbon emissions generated by their journey and, for those who wish to do so, to offset the impact of the greenhouse gases emitted with contributions to portfolios of climate-friendly initiatives throughout the world. Lonely Planet offsets the carbon footprint of all staff and author travel.

outfits running boat trips along Sardinia's coastal waters. Popular spots include Alghero, Cala Gonone, Stintino, Santa Maria Navarrese and Porto San Paolo.

Specialist tour agencies:

Agenzia La Nassa (☎079 52 00 60; www.escursioniasinara.it; Via Sassari 39, Stintino) For guided tours of the Parco Nazionale dell'Asinara.

Barbagia No Limits (☎347 1736345, 0784 182 03 73; www.barbagianolimits.it; Via Cagliari 186, Gavoi) This adventure-sports outfit organises all sorts of outdoor activities in the Barbagia area of eastern Sardinia, including caving trips, jeep tours and survival courses.

Esedra Sardegna (☎0785 37 42 58; www.esedrasardegna.it; Corso Vittorio Emanuele 64, Bosa) Runs excursions in and around Bosa. Packages range from river cruises and boat tours to guided birdwatching trips.

Jara Escursioni (☎348 2924983, 070 936 42 77; www.parcodellagiara.it; Via Tuveri, Tuili) Operating out of the tiny village of Tuili, this small local group leads guided tours of the Giara di Gesturi.

Linea del Parco (☎079 52 31 18; www.lineadelparco.it; Porto Mannu, Stintino) Linea del Parco offers a number of tours by bus or Land Rover, horse rides and boat excursions to the Parco Nazionale dell'Asinara.

Mare e Natura (☎339 9850435, 079 52 00 97; www.marenatura.it; Via Sassari 77,

Stintino) One of several companies that organises land and boat tours of the Parco Nazionale dell'Asinara.

Train

➜ Sardinia's rail network is limited and on many routes a bus is quicker. That said, travelling by train is straightforward and cheap.

➜ You will find train *orari* (timetables) posted on station noticeboards. *Partenze* (departures) and *arrivi* (arrivals) are clearly indicated.

➜ Note that there are all sorts of permutations on schedules, with services much reduced on Sundays. Handy indicators to look out for are *feriale* (Monday to Saturday) and *festivo* (Sunday and holidays only).

➜ Only one type of train runs in Sardinia – the basic *regionale*. These tend to be chuggers that stop at every village on the way, so you won't get anywhere fast by train.

➜ Some trains offer 1st and 2nd class, but you won't find there's a big difference between them, other than few people opt to pay extra for 1st class.

➜ It is not worth buying a Eurail or InterRail pass if you are only travelling in Sardinia. The following train services operate within Sardinia:

Trenitalia (☎892021; www.trenitalia.com) Italy's state-run train company runs the bulk of Sardinia's limited network. The main Trenitalia line runs from Cagliari to Oristano and on to Chilivano-Ozieri, where it divides into two branch lines: one heads northwest to Sassari and Porto Torres; the other goes northeast to Olbia and Golfo Aranci.

Macomer is another important hub with connections to Nuoro.

Azienda Regionale Sarda Trasporti (ARST; ☎800 865042; www.arst.sardegna.it) ARST operates a limited network of private narrow-gauge railways *(servizi ferroviari)*, and the Trenino Verde.

Trenino Verde (☎070 58 02 46; www.treninoverde.com) A tourist train that runs through some of the island's most dramatic and inaccessible countryside. As a means of public transport, it's of limited use – it's extremely slow and covers few likely destinations – but it's an excellent way of experiencing parts of the island that you otherwise probably wouldn't see.

Between mid-June and early September, the Trenino Verde operates four lines: Arbatax to Mandas (which connects with the Mandas–Cagliari rail/metro service); Isili to Sorgono; Bosa Marina to Macomer (which links with the Macomer–Nuoro line); and Palau to Nulvi (where you can connect with a regular service to Sassari) via Tempio Pausania.

Of the four routes, the Mandas–Arbatax line is the most impressive.

Language

In Italy, regional dialects are an important part of identity in many parts of the country, but you'll have no trouble being understood anywhere if you stick to standard Italian and this also holds true for Sardinia. Many Sardinians are bilingual, switching from Sardinian, the island tongue, to Italian with equal ease. Their pronunciation of Italian is refreshingly clear and easy to understand, even if you have only a limited command of the language.

The sounds used in spoken Italian can all be found in English. If you read our coloured pronunciation guides as if they were English, you'll be understood. The stressed syllables are indicated with italics. Note that ai is pronounced as in 'aisle', ay as in 'say', ow as in 'how', dz as the 'ds' in 'lids', and that r is a strong and rolled sound. Keep in mind that Italian consonants can have a stronger, emphatic pronunciation – if the consonant is written as a double letter, it should be pronounced a little stronger, eg *sonno son*·no (sleep) versus *sono so*·no (I am).

BASICS

Italian has two words for 'you' – use the polite form *Lei* lay if you're talking to strangers, officials or people older than you. With people familiar to you or younger than you, you can use the informal form *tu* too.

In Italian, all nouns and adjectives are either masculine or feminine, and so are the articles *il/la* eel/la (the) and *un/una* oon/*oo*·na (a) that go with the nouns.

WANT MORE?

For in-depth language information and handy phrases, check out Lonely Planet's *Italian Phrasebook*. You'll find it at **shop.lonelyplanet.com**, or you can buy Lonely Planet's iPhone phrasebooks at the Apple App Store.

In this chapter the polite/informal and masculine/feminine options are included where necessary, separated with a slash and indicated with 'pol/inf' and 'm/f'.

Hello.	*Buongiorno.*	bwon·*jor*·no
Goodbye.	*Arrivederci.*	a·ree·ve·*der*·chee
Yes./No.	*Sì./No.*	see/no
Excuse me.	*Mi scusi.* (pol)	mee *skoo*·zee
	Scusami. (inf)	*skoo*·za·mee
Sorry.	*Mi dispiace.*	mee dees·*pya*·che
Please.	*Per favore.*	per fa·*vo*·re
Thank you.	*Grazie.*	*gra*·tsye
You're welcome.	*Prego.*	*pre*·go

How are you?
Come sta/stai? (pol/inf)　　*ko*·me sta/stai

Fine. And you?
Bene. E Lei/tu? (pol/inf)　　*be*·ne e lay/too

What's your name?
Come si chiama? pol　　*ko*·me see *kya*·ma

My name is ...
Mi chiamo ...　　mee *kya*·mo ...

Do you speak English?
Parla/Parli　　*par*·la/*par*·lee
inglese? (pol/inf)　　een·*gle*·ze

I don't understand.
Non capisco.　　non ka·*pee*·sko

ACCOMMODATION

Do you have a ... room?	*Avete una camera ...?*	a·*ve*·te *oo*·na *ka*·me·ra ...
double	*doppia con letto matrimoniale*	*do*·pya kon *le*·to ma·tree·mo·*nya*·le
single	*singola*	*seen*·go·la
How much is it per ...?	*Quanto costa per ...?*	*kwan*·to *kos*·ta per ...
night	*una notte*	*oo*·na *no*·te
person	*persona*	per·*so*·na

Is breakfast included?
La colazione è compresa? — la ko·la·tsyo·ne e kom·pre·sa

air-con	*aria condizionata*	a·rya kon·dee·tsyo·na·ta
bathroom	*bagno*	ba·nyo
campsite	*campeggio*	kam·pe·jo
guesthouse	*pensione*	pen·syo·ne
hotel	*albergo*	al·ber·go
youth hostel	*ostello della gioventù*	os·te·lo de·la jo·ven·too
window	*finestra*	fee·nes·tra

DIRECTIONS

Where's ...?
Dov'è ...? — do·ve ...

What's the address?
Qual è l'indirizzo? — kwa·le leen·dee·ree·tso

Could you please write it down?
Può scriverlo, per favore? — pwo skree·ver·lo per fa·vo·re

KEY PATTERNS

To get by in Italian, mix and match these simple patterns with words of your choice:

When's (the next flight)?
A che ora è (il prossimo volo)? — a ke o·ra e (eel pro·see·mo vo·lo)

Where's (the station)?
Dov'è (la stazione)? — do·ve (la sta·tsyo·ne)

I'm looking for (a hotel).
Sto cercando (un albergo). — sto cher·kan·do (oon al·ber·go)

Do you have (a map)?
Ha (una pianta)? — a (oo·na pyan·ta)

Is there (a toilet)?
C'è (un gabinetto)? — che (oon ga·bee·ne·to)

I'd like (a coffee).
Vorrei (un caffè). — vo·ray (oon ka·fe)

I'd like to (hire a car).
Vorrei (noleggiare una macchina). — vo·ray (no·le·ja·re oo·na ma·kee·na)

Can I (enter)?
Posso (entrare)? — po·so (en·tra·re)

Could you please (help me)?
Può (aiutarmi), per favore? — pwo (a·yoo·tar·mee) per fa·vo·re

Do I have to (book a seat)?
Devo (prenotare un posto)? — de·vo (pre·no·ta·re oon po·sto)

Can you show me (on the map)?
Può mostrarmi (sulla pianta)? — pwo mos·trar·mee (soo·la pyan·ta)

at the corner	*all'angolo*	a·lan·go·lo
at the traffic lights	*al semaforo*	al se·ma·fo·ro
behind	*dietro*	dye·tro
far	*lontano*	lon·ta·no
in front of	*davanti a*	da·van·tee a
left	*a sinistra*	a see·nee·stra
near	*vicino*	vee·chee·no
next to	*accanto a*	a·kan·to a
opposite	*di fronte a*	dee fron·te a
right	*a destra*	a de·stra
straight ahead	*sempre diritto*	sem·pre dee·ree·to

EATING & DRINKING

What would you recommend?
Cosa mi consiglia? — ko·za mee kon·see·lya

What's in that dish?
Quali ingredienti ci sono in questo piatto? — kwa·li een·gre·dyen·tee chee so·no een kwe·sto pya·to

What's the local speciality?
Qual è la specialità di questa regione? — kwa·le la spe·cha·lee·ta dee kwe·sta re·jo·ne

That was delicious!
Era squisito! — e·ra skwee·zee·to

Cheers!
Salute! — sa·loo·te

Please bring the bill.
Mi porta il conto, per favore? — mee por·ta eel kon·to per fa·vo·re

I'd like to reserve a table for ...	*Vorrei prenotare un tavolo per ...*	vo·ray pre·no·ta·re oon ta·vo·lo per ...
(two) people	*(due) persone*	(doo·e) per·so·ne
(eight) o'clock	*le (otto)*	le (o·to)

I don't eat ...	*Non mangio ...*	non man·jo ...
eggs	*uova*	wo·va
fish	*pesce*	pe·she
nuts	*noci*	no·chee
(red) meat	*carne (rossa)*	kar·ne (ro·sa)

Key Words

bar	locale	lo·ka·le
bottle	bottiglia	bo·tee·lya
breakfast	prima colazione	pree·ma ko·la·tsyo·ne
cafe	bar	bar
cold	freddo	fre·do
dinner	cena	che·na
drink list	lista delle bevande	lee·sta de·le be·van·de
fork	forchetta	for·ke·ta
glass	bicchiere	bee·kye·re
grocery store	alimentari	a·lee·men·ta·ree
hot	caldo	kal·do
knife	coltello	kol·te·lo
lunch	pranzo	pran·dzo
market	mercato	mer·ka·to
menu	menù	me·noo
plate	piatto	pya·to
restaurant	ristorante	ree·sto·ran·te
spicy	piccante	pee·kan·te
spoon	cucchiaio	koo·kya·yo
vegetarian (food)	vegetariano	ve·je·ta·rya·no
with	con	kon
without	senza	sen·tsa

Meat & Fish

beef	manzo	man·dzo
chicken	pollo	po·lo
duck	anatra	a·na·tra
fish	pesce	pe·she
herring	aringa	a·reen·ga
lamb	agnello	a·nye·lo
lobster	aragosta	a·ra·gos·ta
meat	carne	kar·ne
mussels	cozze	ko·tse
oysters	ostriche	o·stree·ke
pork	maiale	ma·ya·le
prawn	gambero	gam·be·ro
salmon	salmone	sal·mo·ne
scallops	capasante	ka·pa·san·te
seafood	frutti di mare	froo·tee dee ma·re
shrimp	gambero	gam·be·ro
squid	calamari	ka·la·ma·ree
trout	trota	tro·ta
tuna	tonno	to·no
turkey	tacchino	ta·kee·no
veal	vitello	vee·te·lo

Signs	
Entrata/Ingresso	Entrance
Uscita	Exit
Aperto	Open
Chiuso	Closed
Informazioni	Information
Proibito/Vietato	Prohibited
Gabinetti/Servizi	Toilets
Uomini	Men
Donne	Women

Fruit & Vegetables

apple	mela	me·la
beans	fagioli	fa·jo·lee
cabbage	cavolo	ka·vo·lo
capsicum	peperone	pe·pe·ro·ne
carrot	carota	ka·ro·ta
cauliflower	cavolfiore	ka·vol·fyo·re
cucumber	cetriolo	che·tree·o·lo
fruit	frutta	froo·ta
grapes	uva	oo·va
lemon	limone	lee·mo·ne
lentils	lenticchie	len·tee·kye
mushroom	funghi	foon·gee
nuts	noci	no·chee
onions	cipolle	chee·po·le
orange	arancia	a·ran·cha
peach	pesca	pe·ska
peas	piselli	pee·ze·lee
pineapple	ananas	a·na·nas
plum	prugna	proo·nya
potatoes	patate	pa·ta·te
spinach	spinaci	spee·na·chee
tomatoes	pomodori	po·mo·do·ree
vegetables	verdura	ver·doo·ra

Other

bread	pane	pa·ne
butter	burro	boo·ro
cheese	formaggio	for·ma·jo
eggs	uova	wo·va
honey	miele	mye·le

ice	ghiaccio	gya·cho
jam	marmellata	mar·me·la·ta
noodles	pasta	pas·ta
oil	olio	o·lyo
pepper	pepe	pe·pe
rice	riso	ree·zo
salt	sale	sa·le
soup	minestra	mee·nes·tra
soy sauce	salsa di soia	sal·sa dee so·ya
sugar	zucchero	tsoo·ke·ro
vinegar	aceto	a·che·to

Drinks

beer	birra	bee·ra
coffee	caffè	ka·fe
(orange) juice	succo (d'arancia)	soo·ko (da·ran·cha)
milk	latte	la·te
red wine	vino rosso	vee·no ro·so
soft drink	bibita	bee·bee·ta
tea	tè	te
(mineral) water	acqua (minerale)	a·kwa (mee·ne·ra·le)
white wine	vino bianco	vee·no byan·ko

Numbers

1	uno	oo·no
2	due	doo·e
3	tre	tre
4	quattro	kwa·tro
5	cinque	cheen·kwe
6	sei	say
7	sette	se·te
8	otto	o·to
9	nove	no·ve
10	dieci	dye·chee
20	venti	ven·tee
30	trenta	tren·ta
40	quaranta	kwa·ran·ta
50	cinquanta	cheen·kwan·ta
60	sessanta	se·san·ta
70	settanta	se·tan·ta
80	ottanta	o·tan·ta
90	novanta	no·van·ta
100	cento	chen·to
1000	mille	mee·le

EMERGENCIES

Help!
Aiuto! — a·yoo·to

Leave me alone!
Lasciami in pace! — la·sha·mee een pa·che

I'm lost.
Mi sono perso/a. (m/f) — mee so·no per·so/a

There's been an accident.
C'è stato un incidente. — che sta·to oon een·chee·den·te

Call the police!
Chiami la polizia! — kya·mee la po·lee·tsee·a

Call a doctor!
Chiami un medico! — kya·mee oon me·dee·ko

Where are the toilets?
Dove sono i gabinetti? — do·ve so·no ee ga·bee·ne·tee

I'm sick.
Mi sento male. — mee sen·to ma·le

It hurts here.
Mi fa male qui. — mee fa ma·le kwee

I'm allergic to ...
Sono allergico/a a ... (m/f) — so·no a·ler·jee·ko/a a ...

SHOPPING & SERVICES

I'd like to buy ...
Vorrei comprare ... — vo·ray kom·pra·re ...

I'm just looking.
Sto solo guardando. — sto so·lo gwar·dan·do

Can I look at it?
Posso dare un'occhiata? — po·so da·re oo·no·kya·ta

How much is this?
Quanto costa questo? — kwan·to kos·ta kwe·sto

It's too expensive.
È troppo caro/a. (m/f) — e tro·po ka·ro/a

Can you lower the price?
Può farmi lo sconto? — pwo far·mee lo skon·to

There's a mistake in the bill.
C'è un errore nel conto. — che oo·ne·ro·re nel kon·to

ATM	Bancomat	ban·ko·mat
post office	ufficio postale	oo·fee·cho pos·ta·le
tourist office	ufficio del turismo	oo·fee·cho del too·reez·mo

TIME & DATES

What time is it? Che ora è? — ke o·ra e

It's one o'clock. È l'una. — e loo·na

It's (two) o'clock. Sono le (due). — so·no le (doo·e)

Half past (one). (L'una) e mezza. — (loo·na) e me·dza

in the morning	*di mattina*	dee ma·*tee*·na
in the afternoon	*di pomeriggio*	dee po·me·ree·jo
in the evening	*di sera*	dee se·ra
yesterday	*ieri*	ye·ree
today	*oggi*	o·jee
tomorrow	*domani*	do·ma·nee
Monday	*lunedì*	loo·ne·dee
Tuesday	*martedì*	mar·te·dee
Wednesday	*mercoledì*	mer·ko·le·dee
Thursday	*giovedì*	jo·ve·dee
Friday	*venerdì*	ve·ner·dee
Saturday	*sabato*	sa·ba·to
Sunday	*domenica*	do·me·nee·ka
January	*gennaio*	je·na·yo
February	*febbraio*	fe·bra·yo
March	*marzo*	mar·tso
April	*aprile*	a·pree·le
May	*maggio*	ma·jo
June	*giugno*	joo·nyo
July	*luglio*	loo·lyo
August	*agosto*	a·gos·to
September	*settembre*	se·tem·bre
October	*ottobre*	o·to·bre
November	*novembre*	no·vem·bre
December	*dicembre*	dee·chem·bre

TRANSPORT

Public Transport

At what time does the ... leave/arrive?	*A che ora parte/ arriva ...?*	a ke o·ra par·te/ a·ree·va ...
boat	*la nave*	la na·ve
bus	*l'autobus*	low·to·boos
ferry	*il traghetto*	eel tra·ge·to
metro	*la metro-politana*	la me·tro·po·lee·ta·na
plane	*l'aereo*	la·e·re·o
train	*il treno*	eel tre·no
... ticket	*un biglietto ...*	oon bee·lye·to
one-way	*di sola andata*	dee so·la an·da·ta
return	*di andata e ritorno*	dee an·da·ta e ree·tor·no

bus stop	*fermata dell'autobus*	fer·ma·ta del ow·to·boos
platform	*binario*	bee·na·ryo
ticket office	*biglietteria*	bee·lye·te·ree·a
timetable	*orario*	o·ra·ryo
train station	*stazione ferroviaria*	sta·tsyo·ne fe·ro·vyar·ya

Does it stop at ...?
Si ferma a ...? see fer·ma a ...

Please tell me when we get to ...
Mi dica per favore mee dee·ka per fa·vo·re
quando arriviamo a ... kwan·do a·ree·vya·mo a ...

I want to get off here.
Voglio scendere qui. vo·lyo shen·de·re kwee

Driving and Cycling

I'd like to hire a/an ...	*Vorrei noleggiare un/una ... (m/f)*	vo·ray no·le·ja·re oon/oo·na ...
4WD	*fuoristrada (m)*	fwo·ree·stra·da
bicycle	*bicicletta (f)*	bee·chee·kle·ta
car	*macchina (f)*	ma·kee·na
motorbike	*moto (f)*	mo·to
bicycle pump	*pompa della bicicletta*	pom·pa de·la bee·chee·kle·ta
child seat	*seggiolino*	se·jo·lee·no
helmet	*casco*	kas·ko
mechanic	*meccanico*	me·ka·nee·ko
petrol/gas	*benzina*	ben·dzee·na
service station	*stazione di servizio*	sta·tsyo·ne dee ser·vee·tsyo

Is this the road to ...?
Questa strada porta a ...? kwe·sta stra·da por·ta a ...

(How long) Can I park here?
(Per quanto tempo) (per kwan·to tem·po)
Posso parcheggiare qui? po·so par·ke·ja·re kwee

The car/motorbike has broken down (at ...).
La macchina/moto si è la ma·kee·na/mo·to see e
guastata (a ...). gwas·ta·ta (a ...)

I have a flat tyre.
Ho una gomma bucata. o oo·na go·ma boo·ka·ta

I've run out of petrol.
Ho esaurito la o e·zow·ree·to la
benzina. ben·dzee·na

GLOSSARY

AAST – Azienda Autonoma di Soggiorno e Turismo (tourist office)
ACI – Automobile Club d'Italia (Italian automobile club)
acqua – water
agnello – lamb
agriturismo – farm-stay accommodation
albergo – hotel (up to five stars)
albergo diffuso – hotel spread over more than one site, typically in the historic centre of a town
alimentari – food shops
alto – high
anfiteatro – amphitheatre
aperitivo – aperitif
aragosta – lobster
ARST – Azienda Regionale Sarda Trasporti (state bus company)

bancomat – ATM
benzina – petrol
benzina senza piombo – unleaded petrol
borgo – ancient town or village
bottarga – mullet roe
burrida – dogfish with pine nuts, parsley and garlic

calamari – squid
camera – room
campanile – bell tower
cappella – chapel
capretto – kid (goat)
carabinieri – military police (see *polizia*)
carciofi – artichokes
Carnevale – carnival period between Epiphany and Lent
castello – castle
cattedrale – cathedral
cena – evening meal
centro – centre
centro storico – literally 'historical centre'; old town
chiesa – church
colazione – breakfast
comune – equivalent to a municipality or county; town or city council
coperto – cover charge
cornetto – croissant
corso – main street, avenue

cortile – courtyard
cotto/a – cooked
cozze – mussels
CTS – Centro Turistico Studentesco e Giovanile (student/youth travel agency)
culurgiones – ravioli filled with cheese and/or potato
cumbessias – pilgrims' lodgings found in courtyards around churches, traditionally the scene of religious festivities (of up to nine days' duration) in honour of a particular saint
cupola – dome

digestivo – after-dinner liqueur
dolci – sweets
domus de janas – literally 'fairy house'; ancient tomb cut into rock
duomo – cathedral

ENIT – Ente Nazionale Italiano per il Turismo (Italian state tourist office)
enoteca – wine bar or wine shop

farmacia – pharmacy
festa – festival
fiume – (main) river
fontana – fountain
formaggio – cheese
fregola – a large couscouslike grain
fritto/a – fried
frutti di mare – seafood
funghi – mushrooms

gasolio – diesel
gelateria – ice-cream shop
giudicato – province; in medieval times Sardinia was divided into the Giudicato of Cagliari, Giudicato of Logudoro, Giudicato of Gallura and Giudicato of Arborea
golfo – gulf
grotta – cave
guardia medica – emergency call-out doctor service

insalata – salad
isola – island

lago – lake
largo – (small) square
latte – milk
libreria – bookshop
lido – managed section of beach
lungomare – seafront road; promenade

macchia – Mediterranean scrub
malloreddus – semolina dumplings
mare – sea
mattanza – literally 'slaughter'; the annual tuna catch in southwest Sardinia
miele – honey
mirto – myrtle berries; also a liqueur distilled from myrtle berries
monte – mountain, mount
muggine – mullet
municipio – town hall
muristenes – see *cumbessias*

Natale – Christmas
nuraghe – Bronze Age stone towers and fortified settlements

oratorio – oratory
ospedale – hospital

palazzo – palace; a large building of any type, including an apartment block
panadas – savoury pie
pane – bread
panino – bread roll
parco – park
Pasqua – Easter
passeggiata – traditional evening stroll
pasticceria – pastry shop
pensione – small hotel, often with board
piazza – square
pietà – literally 'pity or compassion'; sculpture, drawing or painting of the dead Christ supported by the Madonna
pinacoteca – art gallery
polizia – police
polpo – octopus
poltrona – literally 'armchair'; airline-type chair on a ferry

ponte – bridge
porceddu – suckling pig
porto – port
pronto soccorso – first aid, casualty ward
prosciutto – cured ham

questura – police station

rio – secondary river
riserva naturale – nature reserve
ristorante – restaurant

sagra – festival, usually dedicated to one culinary item, such as funghi (mushrooms), wine etc
saline – saltpans
santuario – sanctuary, often with a country chapel

scalette – 'little stairs' (as in Scalette di Santa Chiara, a steep stairway up into Cagliari's Il Castello district)
sebadas – fried pastry with ricotta
seppia – cuttlefish
servizio – service fee
spiaggia – beach
stagno – lagoon
stazione marittima – ferry terminal
stazzo/u – farmstead in the Gallura region
strada – street, road

tavola calda – canteen-style eatery
teatro – theatre
tempio – temple
terme – thermal baths

tholos – name used to describe the conical tower of a *nuraghe*
tomba di gigante – literally 'giant's tomb'; ancient mass grave
tonnara – tuna-processing plant
tonno – tuna
tophet – sacred Phoenician or Carthaginian burial ground for children and babies
torre – tower
trippa – tripe

via – street, road
viale – avenue
vicolo – alley, alleyway
vino (rosso/bianco) – wine (red/white)
vongole – clams

zucchero – sugar
zuppa – soup or broth

Behind the Scenes

SEND US YOUR FEEDBACK

We love to hear from travellers – your comments keep us on our toes and help make our books better. Our well-travelled team reads every word on what you loved or loathed about this book. Although we cannot reply individually to your submissions, we always guarantee that your feedback goes straight to the appropriate authors, in time for the next edition. Each person who sends us information is thanked in the next edition – the most useful submissions are rewarded with a selection of digital PDF chapters.

Visit **lonelyplanet.com/contact** to submit your updates and suggestions or to ask for help. Our award-winning website also features inspirational travel stories, news and discussions.

Note: We may edit, reproduce and incorporate your comments in Lonely Planet products such as guidebooks, websites and digital products, so let us know if you don't want your comments reproduced or your name acknowledged. For a copy of our privacy policy visit lonelyplanet.com/privacy.

OUR READERS

Many thanks to the travellers who used the last edition and wrote to us with helpful hints, useful advice and interesting anecdotes:

Bill Howard, Daphne Howarth, Els Kleinherenbrink, James Lu, Jane Johnson, Jasmes Jeannette, Joana Baptista, Kathryn Hooper, Val Macready, Valerie Mitchell, Veronica Martin.

AUTHOR THANKS
Kerry Christiani

Mille grazie to the people of Sardinia for their ever-warm welcome and invaluable tips. In particular, a big thank you to outdoor pros Peter and Anne at the Lemon House in Lotzorai, Corrado Conca for his arrampicata tips, and to Maria Antonietta Goddi at Durke, Cagliari, for sweet inspiration. Special thanks, too, to Fabrizio Vella at Gola Su Gorropu and Francesco Muntoni of Cardedu Kayak. Last but not least, thanks to my husband Andy Christiani for being a brilliant travel companion.

Duncan Garwood

Thanks to fellow author Kerry Christiani, and to Jo Cooke and Anna Tyler at LP. In Sardinia, *grazie* to everyone who helped and offered advice, in particular Laura Zicchi, Valeria Spada, the helpful ladies at Archeotur in Sant'Antioco, Leandro Medda, Francesco Melis, Monica Ledda, Fabrizio Busia, the ladies at the Museo Casa Deriu in Bosa, and Marija in Alghero. As always, *grazie di cuore* to Lidia and the boys, Ben and Nick.

ACKNOWLEDGEMENTS

Climate map data adapted from Peel MC, Finlayson BL & McMahon TA (2007) 'Updated World Map of the Köppen-Geiger Climate Classification', Hydrology and Earth System Sciences, 11, 163344.

Cover photograph: Cala Goloritzè on the Golfo di Orosei, Roetting/Pollex/Getty.

THIS BOOK

This 5th edition of Lonely Planet's *Sardinia* guidebook was researched and written by Kerry Christiani and Duncan Garwood. The previous edition was written by Kerry Christiani and Vesna Maric, and earlier editions were written by Duncan Garwood, Paula Hardy and Damien Simonis. This guidebook was commissioned in Lonely Planet's London office, and produced by the following:

Commissioning Editor Jo Cooke

Destination Editor Anna Tyler

Product Editor Briohny Hooper

Senior Cartographer Anthony Phelan

Book Designer Katherine Marsh

Assisting Editors Rosie Nicholson, Samantha Forge, Carly Hall, Anne Mulvaney, Charlotte Orr

Assisting Cartographer Mark Griffiths

Cover Researcher Naomi Parker

Thanks to Helvi Cranfield, Ryan Evans, Larissa Frost, Anna Harris, Jouve India, Elizabeth Jones, Claire Murphy, Claire Naylor, Karyn Noble, Ellie Simpson, Lauren Wellicome, Juan Winata

Index

NOTES

Map Legend

Sights

- Beach
- Bird Sanctuary
- Buddhist
- Castle/Palace
- Christian
- Confucian
- Hindu
- Islamic
- Jain
- Jewish
- Monument
- Museum/Gallery/Historic Building
- Ruin
- Sento Hot Baths/Onsen
- Shinto
- Sikh
- Taoist
- Winery/Vineyard
- Zoo/Wildlife Sanctuary
- Other Sight

Activities, Courses & Tours

- Bodysurfing
- Diving
- Canoeing/Kayaking
- Course/Tour
- Skiing
- Snorkelling
- Surfing
- Swimming/Pool
- Walking
- Windsurfing
- Other Activity

Sleeping

- Sleeping
- Camping

Eating

- Eating

Drinking & Nightlife

- Drinking & Nightlife
- Cafe

Entertainment

- Entertainment

Shopping

- Shopping

Information

- Bank
- Embassy/Consulate
- Hospital/Medical
- Internet
- Police
- Post Office
- Telephone
- Toilet
- Tourist Information
- Other Information

Geographic

- Beach
- Hut/Shelter
- Lighthouse
- Lookout
- Mountain/Volcano
- Oasis
- Park
- Pass
- Picnic Area
- Waterfall

Population

- Capital (National)
- Capital (State/Province)
- City/Large Town
- Town/Village

Transport

- Airport
- Border crossing
- Bus
- Cable car/Funicular
- Cycling
- Ferry
- Metro station
- Monorail
- Parking
- Petrol station
- S-Bahn/S-train/Subway station
- Taxi
- T-bane/Tunnelbana station
- Train station/Railway
- Tram
- Tube station
- U-Bahn/Underground station
- Other Transport

Note: Not all symbols displayed above appear on the maps in this book

Routes

- Tollway
- Freeway
- Primary
- Secondary
- Tertiary
- Lane
- Unsealed road
- Road under construction
- Plaza/Mall
- Steps
- Tunnel
- Pedestrian overpass
- Walking Tour
- Walking Tour detour
- Path/Walking Trail

Boundaries

- International
- State/Province
- Disputed
- Regional/Suburb
- Marine Park
- Cliff
- Wall

Hydrography

- River, Creek
- Intermittent River
- Canal
- Water
- Dry/Salt/Intermittent Lake
- Reef

Areas

- Airport/Runway
- Beach/Desert
- Cemetery (Christian)
- Cemetery (Other)
- Glacier
- Mudflat
- Park/Forest
- Sight (Building)
- Sportsground
- Swamp/Mangrove

OUR STORY

A beat-up old car, a few dollars in the pocket and a sense of adventure. In 1972 that's all Tony and Maureen Wheeler needed for the trip of a lifetime – across Europe and Asia overland to Australia. It took several months, and at the end – broke but inspired – they sat at their kitchen table writing and stapling together their first travel guide, *Across Asia on the Cheap*. Within a week they'd sold 1500 copies. Lonely Planet was born.

Today, Lonely Planet has offices in Franklin, London, Melbourne, Oakland, Beijing and Delhi, with more than 600 staff and writers. We share Tony's belief that 'a great guidebook should do three things: inform, educate and amuse'.

OUR WRITERS

Kerry Christiani

Coordinating Author, Cagliari & the Sarrabus, Olbia, the Costa Smeralda & the Gallura, Nuoro & the East Kerry's relationship with Sardinia began one post-graduation summer when, craving a little dolce vita, she embarked on a grand tour of Italy in a 1960s bubble caravan. She's been coming back ever since. Witnessing the springtime eruption of wildflowers in the Supramonte, watching sombre Easter parades stream through Cagliari's Il Castelo district, hiking to remote bays in the Golfo di Orosei and exploring the wave-lashed, red granite coastline of Cardedu were among her memorable moments researching this guide. An award-winning travel writer, Kerry has authored and coauthored some 20 guidebooks, including Lonely Planet's *Italy*. She lists her latest work at www.kerrychristiani.com. Kerry also wrote the Plan Your Trip and Understand sections.

Duncan Garwood

Iglesias & the Southwest, Oristano & the West, Alghero & the Northwest, The Coast Since first visiting Sardinia in 2008, Duncan has taken every opportunity to return to the island. He has covered it for several Lonely Planet guides, including the third edition of this book, and loves to explore its wild, untamed countryside and hidden nooks. An Italian-speaker, Duncan has worked on more than 25 Lonely Planet guidebooks and regularly writes on Italy for newspapers and websites. Duncan also wrote the Sardinia Outdoors chapter and the Survival Guide section.

Published by Lonely Planet Publications Pty Ltd
ABN 36 005 607 983
5th edition – Jan 2015
ISBN 978 1 74220 735 3
© Lonely Planet 2015   Photographs © as indicated 2015
10 9 8 7 6 5 4 3 2 1
Printed in Singapore